THE AFTERLIVES OF WALTER SCOTT

D1743986

Sir Walter Scott (1771–1832) was once a household name, but is now largely forgotten. This book explores how Scott's work became an all-pervasive point of reference for cultural memory and collective identity in the nineteenth century, and why it no longer has this role.

Ann Rigney breaks new ground in memory studies and the study of literary reception by examining the dynamics of cultural memory and the 'social life' of literary texts across several generations and multiple media. She pays attention to the remediation of the Waverley novels as they travelled into painting, the theatre, and material culture, as well as to the role of 'Scott' as a memory site in the public sphere for a century after his death. Using a wide range of examples and supported by many illustrations, Rigney demonstrates how remembering Scott's work helped shape national and transnational identities up to World War I, and contributed to the emergence of the idea of an English-speaking world encompassing Scotland, the British Empire, and the United States.

Scott's work forged a potent alliance between memory, literature, and identity that was eminently suited to modernization. His legacy continues in the widespread belief that engaging with the past is a condition for transcending it.

To Alistair
Happy Birthday
love
Isabel

The Afterlives of
Walter Scott

Memory on the Move

ANN RIGNEY

OXFORD
UNIVERSITY PRESS

OXFORD

UNIVERSITY PRESS

Great Clarendon Street, Oxford, OX2 6DP,
United Kingdom

Oxford University Press is a department of the University of Oxford.
It furthers the University's objective of excellence in research, scholarship,
and education by publishing worldwide. Oxford is a registered trade mark of
Oxford University Press in the UK and in certain other countries

© Ann Rigney 2012

The moral rights of the author have been asserted

First published 2012
First published in paperback 2017

Impression: 1

Published in the United States of America by Oxford University Press
198 Madison Avenue, New York, NY 10016, United States of America

British Library Cataloguing in Publication Data
Data available

Library of Congress Cataloging in Publication Data
Data available

ISBN 978–0–19–964401–8 (Hbk.)
ISBN 978–0–19–880640–0 (Pbk.)

Printed and bound by
CPI Group (UK) Ltd, Croydon, CR0 4YY

Links to third party websites are provided by Oxford in good faith and
for information only. Oxford disclaims any responsibility for the materials
contained in any third party website referenced in this work.

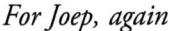

For Joep, again

Acknowledgements

The multiple afterlives of Walter Scott have taken me into the most unexpected of intellectual places and lured me into odd corners of multiple libraries and odd regions of the Internet. In the process I have incurred debts to many individuals and several institutions. I was fortunate that my project struck a chord with many of the people I encountered over the past ten years, leading to new suggestions for reading, new images, or tips for where I might also look for traces of Sir Walter and all his works. I cannot mention everyone who contributed generously in this way, often on the most unlikely of occasions, so must be content with expressing my general gratitude to all those willing to engage with what at times did seem like a very quirky pursuit. Nevertheless, some individuals deserve especial mention for what turned out to be particularly valuable leads: Els Andringa, Mary Ellen Brown, Harald Hendrix, Brian Lambkin, Liedeke Plate, Ann Rowland, Marco de Waard, and William Uricchio. To a passing comment of Ann Dooley I owe the idea of devoting an entire book to the afterlives of Scott.

For vital help and material assistance in tracking down texts and images, I am particularly grateful to Barnita Bagchi, Frank Brandsma, Leith Davis, Patrick Geary, Yoriko Koyabashi Sato, Alison Lumsden, Yuko Matsui, Pamela Pattynama, Murray Pittock, Maarten Prak, Ilona Scharree, Wim van Anrooij, and Simon Waegemakers. Special mention needs to be made in this regard of Helen Solterer, who carried books and ideas across the Atlantic, and Rolf Loeber, whose regular truffle-hunting in second-hand bookshops yielded some great surprises. The assistance of Paul Barnaby, curator of the Corson Collection at the Edinburgh University Library, was invaluable in making available to me often uncatalogued materials in the extraordinary collection left behind by James Corson. Indeed, my analysis would have been much poorer if Corson had not been so fanatical about collecting all mentions of Scott and anything remotely associated with him in the press, and I am all the happier to acknowledge his work here since I suspect that this particular part of his devotion to Scott has had few appreciators until now. At the Netherlands Institute for Advanced Studies (NIAS), Eline de Ploeg made a great job of tracking down illustrations for me, while also offering expert support, together with Petry Kievit-Tyson, in my constant struggle against the dictatorship of Word.

Throughout this project, I have been fortunate to work in collegial environments. In Utrecht the members of our research group 'The

Dynamics of Cultural Remembrance'—Laura Basu, Jesseka Batteau, Paulus Bijl, Chiara de Cesari, Alana Gillespie, Nicole Immler, David Wertheim—have provided me in the past four years with regular injections of intellectual energy, many heady discussions about cultural memory, and a constant challenge to revise my ideas. I carried out the basic research for this book in the Widener Library during an intense period as an associate of the Celtic Studies Department at Harvard University in 2003. I am very grateful to Patrick Ford and the other members of the department for facilitating my stay and to Margaret Higonnet for providing such a warm welcome to Cambridge. In 2009–10 I had the privilege of being a fellow at the NIAS and the ten months spent at that gracious institution allowed me finally to turn earlier versions of chapters into a completed manuscript. I am grateful to all my fellow fellows at the NIAS for their stimulating company as well as to the friendly and efficient staff both in the library and on the workfloor. The spontaneously formed 'memory group' at the NIAS—Anna-Maria Brandstetter, Astrid Erll, Pamela Pattynama, and Julia Noordegraaf—were a constant source of inspiration as well as of bibliographical references: our weekly seminars will remain in my memory as academic highpoints. Astrid Erll deserves additional mention as a fellow-traveller: she has been a wonderful colleague and collaborator for several years now and I have benefited hugely from her unparalleled knowledge of the field of memory studies and her analytic insight.

This book has benefited from the critical feedback of a number of readers to whose generosity and sharpness I am equally endebted. Chief among them is Ian Duncan, who combines a deep knowledge of Scott studies with an intellectual generosity that is unsurpassed: like many authors before me, I have benefited from his rigorous reading of the complete first draft of my book. Turning the first draft into the present book has also meant profiting from the comments of an anonymous reader from Oxford University Press who helped me to rethink some aspects of my argument. Other colleagues have offered valuable feedback on separate chapters at various stages in their genesis and I gratefully acknowledge it here: Babs Boter, Marshall Brown, Leith Davis, Ina Ferris, Meir Sternberg, Helen Solterer, Jay Winter, and Christopher Whatley.

An early version of Chapter 1 appeared as 'Portable Monuments: Literature, Cultural Memory and the Case of Jeanie Deans', in *Poetics Today* 25.2 (2004): 361–96; an early version of Chapter 4 appeared as 'The Many Afterlives of Ivanhoe' in Karin Tilmans, Frank van Vree, and Jay Winter (eds), *Performing the Past: Memory, History, and Identity in Modern Europe* (Amsterdam University Press, 2010), 207–34; an early version of Chapter 5 appeared as 'Abbotsford: Dislocation and Cultural

Remembrance' in Harald Hendrix (ed.), *Writers' Houses and the Making of Memory* (New York: Routledge, 2008), 75–91. All original essays have been substantially revised and expanded. I am very grateful to Helena Buescu for having invited me to participate in a conference on *Philology, Memory, Forgetting* at the University of Lisbon, where I presented the first version of the epilogue in November 2008. It has been a pleasure to work with the editorial team at Oxford University Press, with particular thanks owing to Jacqueline Baker, Ariane Petit, Jane Olin-Ammentorp, Charles Lauder, Jr., and Kathie Gill.

This book was made possible by the financial assistance of the Netherlands Organisation for Scientific Research (NWO) as well as by the NIAS and the Research Institute for History and Culture, Utrecht University (OGC).

The input of Joep Leerssen is in a league of its own: not only an endless source of reading tips and materials, he has also engaged critically with the manuscript in all its stages and, partner *extraordinaire*, has provided moral support and inspiration along the way. To him, once again, this book is dedicated.

A Note on the Cover

As I was settling into the final stages of research for this study, artist Mike Bouchet was preparing an exhibit for the Venice Biennale in 2009. It took the form of a prefabricated house that was to float in the waters of the historic lagoon as an example of American suburban life and its portability. The exhibit turned into an unplanned artistic happening, however, when the house keeled over and sank. Having later retrieved the remains of the house, Bouchet turned its wreckage into a new installation and called this new work *Sir Walter Scott* in reference to the design type of the modular suburban home whose name in a contemporary catalogue forms a distant echo of Scott's widespread influence on architectural styles and on the street-scape of English-speaking suburbs in the nineteenth century.

Interestingly, Bouchet's original exhibit was simply called *Watershed 2009*. It was only after the house sank and was dismembered that he changed its title to *Sir Walter Scott*, the implication being that the latter name was more appropriate for a shipwreck. For me this brought another piece of cultural memory into play: the shipwrecked paddle-steamer *Walter Scott* that figures in Chapter 13 of *Huckleberry Finn*. It seems that Scott continuously returns both as a shipwreck and as an inspiration for new work. I am very grateful to Mike Bouchet for allowing me to use an image of his installation, as it figured at the Cobra Museum in Amsterdam in 2010, for the cover of *Afterlives*.

Contents

List of Illustrations

Introduction

There are towns called Waverley spread across the globe: in Victoria, Australia; in Nova Scotia; near the border of South Africa with Swaziland, and in no less than twenty-two states in the USA.[1] There are districts called Waverley in Dunedin, Melbourne, Johannesburg, Pretoria, Bloemfontein, Cape Town, Belmont (Massachusetts), and Baltimore (Maryland). There are streets called Waverley in Auckland, Winnipeg, Ottawa, Palo Alto, Dublin, Glasgow, Southport, and Nottingham; and although Calcutta/Kolkota has been re-named, it still has its 'Waverley Lane' in the downtown area dating back to pre-independence times. Finally, there are countless hotels, guesthouses, schools, and other public venues, including the main railway station in Edinburgh and the well-known movie theatre in Manhattan, that are all called Waverley or Waverly. Dispersed though they are across the globe, the common name serves as a reminder of the time when these disparate places were all joined together by two things: the fact of being (former) British colonies and the fact of their ostensible admiration for Walter Scott, the author of the first modern bestseller and the first historical novel: *Waverley: or 'Tis Sixty Years Since* (1814).

It is unlikely that the present-day residents of Scott Road/Scott Weg in Cape Town or Waverley Gardens in Melbourne will be aware of the literary origins of their street; even less likely that they will have read the book in question. Fans are thinner on the ground nowadays. For those who know its meaning, however, the name 'Waverley' in these far-flung urban spaces evokes different temporal layers: the English-speaking world at the end of the nineteenth century when most of these towns, districts, and streets originated; the first decades of the nineteenth century when Walter Scott produced his enormously popular *oeuvre*; finally, at the deepest level, the historical worlds of Scotland, Great Britain, and medieval Europe that Scott had evoked in his novels and poems. Choosing the name Waverley (and related names like Abbotsford, Kenilworth, and Ivanhoe) was a way of implanting a sense of history in new urban environments and of nostalgically flagging a collective affiliation to an imagined history in newly settled territories. Loyalty to the memory of Scott's work, along with a more general trust in literature as a way of

Figure Intro.1: Waverley Ave., Newton, MA.

eliciting recognition and enthusiasm, presumably also fed the decision of many hotel-owners to inscribe the name of the novel on their gates and doors. Enthusiasm and loyalty certainly lay behind the erection of the colossal 200-ft-high monument to Walter Scott in the centre of Edinburgh in 1840 and, several decades later, of its partial copy in Central Park, New York.

The Afterlives of Walter Scott explains how Scott's *oeuvre* became such an all-pervasive point of reference, and how it ceased to be one. It shows how Waverley and everything associated with it was picked up in different cultural domains and transmitted across generations and cultural groups for more than a century. It covers some of the same ground as Stuart Kelly's recently published essay *Scott-land*, in that it too is concerned with the ways in which everyday life became saturated by echoes of Scott.[2] But the scope of *Afterlives* is more comprehensive, and its analysis more far-reaching: it extends to Scott's afterlife in multiple areas of cultural production across the English-speaking world, and explains how the memory of Waverley helped articulate national and transnational identities in the latter half of the nineteenth century.

The Afterlives of Walter Scott thus offers in the first instance a close study of a particular case. But it examines that case in order to give a keyhole

Figure Intro.2: Scott Rd., Cape Town, South Africa.

perspective on a set of larger issues. What does the remembering and forgetting of Scott tell us about the relationship between literature, modernization, and nation-building since the early nineteenth century? What did it mean for literature to play such a central role in collective remembrance and as a marker of identity? And what does the transience of his canonicity tell us about the prospects for long-term cultural memory in a world of rapid turnovers?

I will argue that Scott provided a blueprint for imagining a relationship to the past that was eminently suitable to conditions of life in the nineteenth century, characterized as it was by increasing mobility, the growing power of the media, urbanization, and mass migration. Against the background of rapid change, Scott opened up the past as an imaginative resource, inspiring a fashion for history as a key to collective identity that continues down to the present day.[3] At the same time, and this is one of the paradoxes that I explore, this imaginative engagement with a fabricated memory was as much about learning to live with change as it was about honouring tradition, as much about looking to the future as about dwelling on the past. For this reason, I argue, Scott's entire *oeuvre* can be seen at one and the same time as a major contributor to the cult of memory in modern societies and as a huge investment in making that past irrelevant as an active force in the present. He showcased the past, but only in order to provide the imaginative conditions for taking leave of it: he defused its capacity to disrupt the present by turning it into an object of display. Since Scott thus incorporated transience into the very principle of historicization, his own obsolescence was part and parcel of his continuing legacy. His being so quickly forgotten was paradoxically a sign of his influence. Such dualities make Scott a figure of continuing relevance for our ongoing attempts to articulate a workable relationship between memory and modernization, between the legacy of the past and the potential for societies to become different.

THE WAVERLEY PHENOMENON

Between 1814 and 1826, Scott published a total of twenty-six novels, all of them anonymously. In the opening lines of the first one, he explained the significance of its title by the fact that it marked a new departure: 'I have . . . assumed for my hero, WAVERLEY, an uncontaminated name, bearing with its sound little of good or evil, excepting what the reader shall hereafter be pleased to affix to it.'[4] An 'uncontaminated name': since Scott was starting out on an experiment in prose fiction at a time when novels had rather a bad name, this was a canny move. It was a gesture designed to clear an imaginative space for an experiment in memory-making beyond existing generic categories and traditions, and out of reach of the possible prejudices of his readers. This 'uncontaminated' book was putatively without any precedent in literary history and without any precedent in the work of the well-known writer.[5] Although Scott had already made a huge name for himself as a highly successful and critically acclaimed poet, he chose to publish his first novel anonymously. This decision may have been a potentially face-saving device, a way of safeguarding his reputation in the event the experiment should fail, or it may have been a commercial tactic designed to pique curiosity, or both. But either way it ended up becoming a long-term strategy in which one book after another was published 'by the author of Waverley'. Commercial genius that he was as well as being an immensely gifted storyteller, Scott maintained this branding of his novels long after his actual identity had become an open secret.[6] The name Waverley soon became 'contaminated' with meaning, as we have seen, synonymous with a brand of historical fiction that crossed the boundaries between high literature and popular entertainment, between commerce and culture, and that offered, in a hitherto unprecedented way, an imaginative engagement with the past in the form of colourful stories. Until the supply ran out with the death of Scott in 1832, it whetted readers' appetites with an apparently unlimited promise of more.

Waverley turned out then to be a prelude to a staggeringly successful series. William St. Clair's magisterial study of reading practices in the nineteenth century shows that the rate of dissemination of the Waverley novels, as these were collectively known, was truly extraordinary, with Scott's work continuously breaking publishing records and setting new trends.[7] The publication of each of the novels met with such excitement that reviewers complained that their own role as cultural gatekeepers was being made redundant by the speed with which readers were rushing out to buy each new novel as it appeared.[8] The popularity of the Waverley novels and the rapidity with which they were produced and disseminated did much to create a unified public imagination based on the sense that everyone was simultaneously reading the same book about a common past—or rather, about a past that was *becoming* collective through the mediation of the novel. With the appearance of relatively inexpensive collected editions of the Waverley novels as of 1829 (another publishing innovation), they also reached new reading publics, performing the 'literary equivalent of the extension of suffrage', as Ian Duncan has called it.[9] This would enable householders of respectable but moderate means to acquire for their own possession literary works that were both entertaining and, as time went on, part of a national cultural heritage that was deeply embedded in the educational system.[10] So influential were the Waverley novels that St. Clair goes so far as to claim that they shaped the chivalric mind-set of the generation who signed up for the trenches in World War I, echoing Mark Twain's more famous assertion, to which I will later return, that Scott was responsible for the American Civil War.[11] At the very least, such claims are a measure of the cultural power attributed to Scott and of his role as a cultural icon. As one critic described this influence: 'To have been alive and literate in the nineteenth century was to have been affected in some way by the Waverley novels.'[12] The inscription of Scott-related names into the urban landscape represents simply the most visible evidence of the percolation of his work into everyday lives.

MODERNIZATION AND MEMORY-MAKING

The question how societies remember and how that remembrance is related to the shaping of collective identities has been central to inquiries in a wide range of disciplines for at least twenty years. This has led to a growing body of insight into how stories are produced and shared with the help of media, with the term 'cultural memory' being used to indicate the symbolic, mediated, and performative character of collective remembering. In Chapter 1, I will elaborate on these discussions and describe in more detail the role played by the arts, literature in particular, in creating shared narratives and hence in collectivizing memory. Central to the role of literature as a medium of collective memory-making, I shall argue, is its ability to cross existing cultural borders and to provide an imaginative template for articulating values and defining identities.

One of the recurrent themes in recent discussions calling for elaboration from the outset is the idea that the active cultivation of memory is a by-product of modernization. The story runs more or less as follows. Memory only became an issue, whether as something to be cultivated or as a source of anxiety, when people started to see the present and future as systemically different from the past. This idea did not originate in the nineteenth century, of course. But there is a general agreement that the age of Revolutions had intensified the belief that the present was at a crossroads between a distant past and an uncertain future; that there was a radical disjunction between the ever-changing present in which people shared an identity as contemporaries and a past that was now viewed as a foreign country.[13] A new sense of being 'stranded in the present', as Peter Fritzsche has called it, was compounded in the nineteenth century by the increasing rate of migration, in the first instance from the country to the city, which led to a widespread sense of dislocation and up-rootedness. The rate and scale of such changes led to a massive investment in new practices and institutions of memory—in the arts, in museums and archives, in the academy—that subsequently became the cornerstones of nineteenth-century historicism and nation-building. In one of the most influential contributions to this general narrative, Pierre Nora claimed almost a quarter of a century ago that synthetic 'sites of memory' (*lieux de mémoire*) became important in the modern period because a decline in traditional 'environments of memory' (*milieux de mémoire*) had created a new need for points of collective reference and symbolic stability in the midst of dramatic change.[14] He argued that people only began to cultivate particular 'sites' as repositories of memory, which they did on an unprecedented scale in the nineteenth century, when the sense of being continuously connected to a common past had been eroded by political upheavals, urbanization, and the extension of the scale in which communities had to be imagined.

In studies of public remembrance in contemporary culture, this basic narrative about modernization and memory has been reiterated in a new guise, with the events of the twentieth century replacing the age of Revolutions as a catalyst of change. The massive ruptures caused by the two World Wars, it is believed, have renewed the self-reflexive cultivation of memory and brought it to a new level of intensity.[15] As Andreas Huyssen in particular has argued, the desire to-remember-lest-we-forget in our world of rapid change is itself leading to such a rapid turnover of stories with the help of new media that there is no time to cherish any story in particular before the next wave occurs. In this way, anxiety about amnesia is leading to a hyper-production of memory and this, in turn, leads paradoxically to ever more rapid obsolescence. This means, according to Huyssen, that it is becoming ever more difficult to establish temporal horizons beyond the continuously changing present, and all the more difficult to create either durable memories or a view of the future.

These general discussions about the relation between modernization and memory-making form the background to the present study of Scott. Several recent publications have highlighted Scott's modernity: the fact that the Author of Waverley engaged with the most burning issues of his own age, and that his work makes most sense when read against the background of the upheavals wrought by the Napoleonic wars, incipient industrialization, and colonial expansion.[16] His association with historicism has long been established: the fact that he contributed, as a collector, historian, and editor, as well as a poet and novelist, to the cultivation of historical knowledge in various fields and to the shaping of historicist practices in the aftermath of Revolution. Drawing these two strands of analysis together—Scott the modernist, Scott the historicist—I will argue that the key to his huge success was his forging of a potent alliance between fiction, memory, and identity that was well-adapted to the modernizing conditions of his age. A manufacturer of collective memory par excellence, his novels inaugurated with the help of innovative narrative techniques a tradition of imaginatively engaging with the past that was at once highly personal, historically informed, and thoroughly synthetic. The success of his novels marked the beginning of a mass-media era in which collective memory was based on imagined experience reaching across enormous territories, rather than on lived experience and the sharing of stories in face-to-face contexts.

As part of this process, Scott's fiction helped specifically in stimulating identification across existing social and ethnic borders, in a way that was well matched to an age where people were migrating, mixing, and ever-more connected through media. As the spread of the name Waverley already suggested, Scott's writings about Scottish, British, and European history moved across the globe and managed to appeal to a vast reading public dispersed throughout the Anglophone world (and with the help of translations, beyond it). It offered a common point of reference in defining affiliations both within the national framework of Scotland and within the multinational and transnational framework of Great Britain and the Empire. In this regard, Scott's imaginative engagement with the past was a major generator of what Alison Landsberg has called, with reference to early cinema in the United States, 'prosthetic memory'. By this she meant the power of fiction to provoke empathy with actors belonging to another group and to imaginatively adopt those actors as part of one's collective past. Because of its ability to generate prosthetic memory, fiction has had an important role to play in acculturating new immigrants to the USA, providing the imaginative conditions for affiliations to a new national narrative.[17] As we shall see later, Scott's work too had an important role to play in generating prosthetic memory, albeit with the technologies of his time. Exploiting the power of fiction to cross borders, he created novels and poems that generated a secular pantheon of imaginary and historical figures—Ivanhoe, for example, but also Flora McIvor, the Lady of the Lake, and Rob Roy—that provided a collective point of reference for a multinational readership across and beyond the British Isles. That it was artificially produced did not detract from its effect; on the contrary.

The case of Scott offers in this way new perspectives on the interplay between modernization, memory-making, and the role of literature that I will be exploring in greater detail later. It also offers more: a unique opportunity to trace continuities and changes over a span of what is by now almost seven generations. From the publication of his *Minstrelsy of the Scottish Border* (1802) and *The Lay of the Last Minstrel* (1805) onwards, Scott's writings were immensely successful both at home and abroad, as shown by the publication sales, the number of theatrical adaptations and collected editions, and the speed and intensity with which his work was translated. The database at the National Library of Scotland lists some three thousand versions in other languages. Despite its initial success, his poetry fell rather quickly off the radar screen of literary taste (though traces of its popularity remain, most notably in 'Hail to the Chief', the anthem of the US presidents that derives from a musical version of *The Lady of the Lake*, 1810). In contrast, most of the novels have been continuously in print for the best part of two hundred years, and continue to be reprinted. This well-documented case—involving the reproduction of his works, their adaptations to other media, and the recollection of the figure of the author himself—will allow us to study the vicissitudes of remembrance over a longer period. Tracing the case of Scott helps give a history to modern memory.

It is especially in this regard that the present study breaks new ground. Writers like Nora and Huyssen have arguably themselves been replicating the discourse of modernization in emphasizing radical new departures and imminent crises. Whether the reference is to the early nineteenth century or to the late twentieth century there has been a tendency to see the relation between modernization and memory practices in terms of a radical new departure into an uncertain future. A long-term perspective on cultural memory in the period since 1800 has been lacking and temporal foreshortening the order of the day. The dynamics of collective remembrance over a longer period has not yet received the sustained attention it deserves, whether in theoretical reflection or in the form of empirical studies demonstrating the extent to which modern societies are capable, or not, of transmitting memories over a longer period.[18] The present study makes up for this lack by adopting a radically dynamic approach to cultural memory (seeing it as always in motion) and by analysing, with reference to the case of Scott, the persistence and mutation of collective remembrance over several generations. Written at a time when the pace of cultural change seems more rapid than ever, this book provides a unique observation point on the long-term dynamics of cultural memory.

'Once the memory boom is history, as no doubt it will be, will anyone have remembered anything at all?' Andreas Huyssen has asked this question of the contemporary period, implicitly suggesting that present memories may not have a future.[19] I ask the same sort of question here, but retrospectively and non-rhetorically: what did happen over time to the stories produced by Scott as part of the memory boom to which he contributed at the beginning of the nineteenth century? What did their future bring?

TRANSIENT MONUMENTALITY

It is not easy to pinpoint an exact turning point in Scott's fame. But no one will dispute the fact that he and his works are less well-known nowadays than at his death in 1832, when newspapers in Great Britain, the USA, and France appeared with black edgings as a sign of mourning and when a committee was immediately formed to put up the colossal monument to his memory that now dominates the centre of Edinburgh. Once the Great Unknown, Scott has largely become the Great Forgotten. The most striking thing about Scott's cultural afterlife is the contrast between, on the one hand, the extraordinary impact of his work and its ubiquity for almost a century after his death; on the other hand, the speed with which 'Scott and all his works' went out of favour. Between the heights of his fame and his relative obscurity nowadays lies an as-yet untold story about the dynamics both of remembrance and of forgetting.

An anxiety about amnesia, as I will show, accompanied his memory from an early stage. There are few historical figures whose meteoric rise to fame was followed so quickly by the aura of being old-fashioned. Despite his phenomenal popularity (or because of it?), Scott is often remembered nowadays for the speed with which he fell out of favour. His reputation itself reflects the long tail of his work as an iconic has-been. This is borne out in Virginia Woolf's *To the Lighthouse* (1927), where she depicts the philosopher Mr Ramsay, worried that his own work will also be ignored after his death, sitting down to read some novel by Scott whom one of the other characters had dismissed as a forgotten author: 'No-one reads Scott anymore.' In depicting Mr Ramsay's kinship with Scott-the-forgotten, Woolf underscores the fact that the Author of Waverley is beyond his sell-by date, but nevertheless allows her character to thoroughly enjoy his read as if to acknowledge that her predecessor has his attractions, but only for an older, and soon-to-be-forgotten generation.[20]

Scott's works, or at least some of them, are regularly studied as part of university courses and, judging by the number of novels in print, they are still read by many amateurs for interest and pleasure. The enormous monument to his memory still stands in the centre of Edinburgh. But there is no doubt that Scott is less of a communal point of reference than he was even at the time when Woolf was writing and when Bertrand Russell could illustrate his argument about the truth of propositions by invoking as self-explanatory the statement 'The Author of Waverley was Scotch.'[21] Among the many symptoms of Scott's changing status was the headline that appeared in the *Border Telegraph* on 14 August 1956, on the anniversary of his birth: 'Immortal Memory? Is Sir Walter Scott forgotten?' As I shall show, similar concerns were already being voiced in the 1840s by commentators who felt that Scott could not sustain the fame to which he had so phenomenally risen in his lifetime. The relative speed with which he became both 'immortal' and a 'has been' indicates that an accelerated dynamic of cultural change and obsolescence was already experienced at this earlier period and that Scott, the fabricator of memories on a large scale and the figurehead of modern memory, may himself have been the victim of the culture of rapid turnovers he himself helped inaugurate with one bestseller after the next. Should one be surprised at his relatively short afterlife or amazed at the fact that it has lasted, albeit in a diminished and mutated form, all of six generations? I opt for the latter.

THE SOCIAL LIFE OF LITERARY WORKS

Not unexpectedly there is a substantial body of critical writing on Scott and the literary and social context in which he worked, with valuable new insights into the complexities of particular novels continuing to be generated. In line with the traditions of literary scholarship, however, most criticism is aimed at producing new readings of individual works. It was surprising in view of Scott's immense stature to find just how little scholarly attention has been paid to the analysis of his cultural afterlife, with one notable exception being the major survey of Scott's European reception edited by Murray Pittock and published in 2007. *The Reception of Sir Walter Scott in Europe* tracks Scott's popularity across the countries of Europe and his role as a model for a whole generation of historical novelists from Catalonia to Slovenia and from Spain to Russia (it also includes some brief overviews of his impact on painting, opera, and tourism).[22] Where Pittock's collection is focused on the European reception, the present-study concentrates instead on the English-speaking world. Crucially, it also approaches the question of reception from a much broader perspective and from the theoretical framework offered by recent discussions in cultural memory studies. Indeed, as my use of the term 'social life' indicates, what is at stake here is something that is linked to, but nevertheless distinct from, 'reception' in the usual sense of critical status or impact on other writers. The very nature of Scott's influence, penetrating as it did into both intellectual life and material culture, demands a different approach from that offered by traditional literary criticism, making of public monuments and street signs as legitimate an object of investigation as novels and poems. In many ways, this approach is dictated by the very nature of Scott's creativity and the example he himself set. Through his writings, but also through his work as designer of Abbotsford, he played an important role in inaugurating a holistic approach to the past in which the historical imagination spilled over into material culture and everyday behaviour, exemplifying what Arjun Appadurai has described as a key feature of modernity: the extension of the life of the imagination into everyday life.[23]

In his famous *Cours de linguistique générale* (1916), Ferdinand de Saussure advocated a new science that would take as its object 'the life of signs in society'.[24] What I propose is a variation on Saussure's project: 'the life of texts in society'. This calls for a study of reception that goes beyond the matter of literary value and beyond the medium of writing in order to show the multiple appropriations of Scott's work in a whole range of cultural practices. Above all, it means going beyond the analysis of discrete cultural products to the examination of the migration of stories across cultural spheres, media, and constituencies and its effect on social relations.[25] As the idea of a 'life' suggests, what is at issue here is not only the stories as such, but the underlying portability that enables them to move into different media and social contexts. Against the tradition of methodological textualism that has long dominated literary studies, it takes as its object of study the long-term trajectories of stories. Against the methodological nationalism that has also traditionally marked literary scholarship, it considers the places where texts end up to be as legitimate an object of study as the places where they originated.[26] Accordingly, the cultural memory of Scott's work will be located here, not only in the persistence of his texts across time, but above all in their reappearance in new guises in different places and media; in their capacity to move, mobilize, and generate new cultural activities.[27] A central theoretical assumption is that a memory is alive only as long as it generates new versions of itself.

Two factors provide the key to understanding the movements of Scott's work, a push one and a pull one. On the one hand, there is the push factor of what I shall call 'procreativity' or productive remembrance: the capacity of Scott's work to generate new versions in the form of other texts and other media. On the other hand, there is the pull factor of appropriation: the desire of different groups and later generations to adapt Scott's work to meet their own ideological, aesthetic, and creative needs. As the term 'appropriation' suggests, reading and adapting are viewed here as ways of actively engaging with Scott's work and not merely as a mirror of its magic.[28] How the push and the pull factors relate to each other and how latter-day appropriations reflect the original work even as they depart in new directions are key issues to be addressed, along with the even more fundamental question why Scott's work in particular should have had such a proliferating afterlife.

This book charts the long 'Scott century', running roughly from the first appearance of *Waverley* in 1814 to the centenary of the writer's death in 1932 with occasional excursions into more contemporary appropriations in cinema and literature. It tracks the multifarious afterlife of Scott's writing across several generations, not just in critical responses, but in new cultural products, in material culture, and in public expressions of allegiance to Scott on the part of different constituencies. Commenting on a novel like *Rob Roy*, adapting it to the stage, putting up a monument to Scott, buying a Wedgwood plate depicting Ivanhoe, or visiting Scott's famous neo-Gothic mansion at Abbotsford are all taken here to be versions of the Waverley story and part of its ever-mutating cultural afterlife as it moved to other stories, to paintings, to film, to material culture, and to what Michel de Certeau has termed, the 'practices of everyday life'.[29] As I shall show in detail in Chapters 2, 3, and 4, Scott's work generated multiple adaptations within new media and new sensibilities. Although it was played out using the newest media, this combination of remembrance and continuous updating was more characteristic of oral cultures than of the systemic innovation usually associated with consumerist modes of cultural production. Its study reveals unexpected continuities against a background of continuous novelty. The Waverley phenomenon thus cuts across the opposition discerned by Nora between traditional memory (based on continuity between past and present) and modern, historicizing memory (based on a perceived gap between past and present). One of the challenges of this study will be to analyse and conceptualize productive remembrance as a key feature of culture in what, within the technical limits of the pre-digital age, was already a time of intermedial sampling and recycling.

Integrating more general discussions on the workings of cultural memory, the book proposes a dynamic and multilayered approach to literature, based on the interlinked concepts of 'mobility' (literary works migrate across media and reading constituencies) and 'monumentality' (literary compositions provide stable points of reference in calibrating collectively held values). Concretely, this means two intersecting lines of inquiry. These follow, on the one hand, the movements and transformations of Scott's stories; on the other hand, the recurrence of the Waverley novels and the Author of Waverley as monumental, canonical, points of reference in public commemorations, expressions of loyalty, and critical commentaries. Combining these two strands of analysis, the book demonstrates how the appropriations of Waverley became linked to discourses about collective identities in the second half of the nineteenth century, and argues that Scott's particular strength as a memory-maker was that his work, as literature, was not tied down to any one place or community, but could operate in both national and transnational frameworks. While it was active in the shaping of Scottishness, it also played a key role, together with the work of Burns and Shakespeare, in the emergence at the end of the nineteenth century of the idea of an Anglophone cultural sphere with its special relationship between the British Empire and the United States.

Intersecting with the history of its multiple adaptations, then, Scott and his works became an object of historicizing recollection. Functioning as what Jan Assmann has called a 'figure of memory' (*Erinnerungsfigur*), the name Walter Scott and other names associated with him became short-hand for a whole package of experiences and values. Not just in the streets and monuments mentioned earlier, but also in the many critical assessments of his work, and in the rituals and festivities surrounding the centenaries of his birth and death.[30] As I shall show in detail in Chapter 6, the celebration of the writer's memory provides a key to understanding the role that literature played, alongside military and political events, as a focus for public remembrance prior to World War I. For this was above all the age of Literature when figures of Great Writers were the key to a collective identity based on a trust in shared cultural values and pride in an individual's achievements. This celebratory mode of remembrance sits uneasily with the traumatic paradigm that has become dominant since World War II, in both cultural practice and academic analysis, and that locates collective remembrance in the binding force of pain rather than of pleasure. Analysing the case of Scott inevitably forces one to think beyond contemporary horizons about the transience of memory cultures and, linked to this, the role of pleasure in creating communality.

PREVIEW

Given the size of Scott's *oeuvre* and its immense impact, exhaustiveness was not an option. I have chosen instead a cross-sectional approach centred on key texts and their appropriation in particular media or by particular groups. I refer regularly to Scott's poetry and discuss *The Lady of the Lake* (1810) in Chapter 5, but my primary focus is nevertheless on his novels, considered as new variations on the poems, since this was the Scott genre with the most profound and lasting impact. Here too selection was necessary, of course, but I nevertheless hope to offer enough points of access to the Waverley phenomenon to give a sense of the interplay between its different aspects. With this aim in mind, each chapter examines a particular aspect of Scott's afterlife and takes a different point of departure in his *oeuvre*.

Chapter 1 concentrates on the case of *The Heart of Mid-Lothian* (1818) in order to reflect on the multiple roles that a nineteenth-century novel could play as a medium of cultural memory. The main concern is with explaining the qualities that made Scott's fiction memorable and describing its multifaceted afterlife both as a monumental object of reference and as a story to be re-written and appropriated in new contexts. Chapter 2 focuses on Scott's procreativity in other media in order to explain the apparent paradox that novelistic adaptation was linked both to the desire for new forms of immediacy and to the pleasure of reiteration. In particular I focus on the repeated productions of *Rob Roy* (1817) and explain its popularity on stage as a way of performing Scottishness 'live'. Chapter 3 examines procreativity in the case of *Ivanhoe* (1819), the Scott novel that has generated the greatest number of versions of itself on page, stage, and screen: why was this novel so procreative and, relative to other works by Scott, over such a long period? I argue that people have felt continuously called upon to re-write Scott's story of medieval England because of a structural ambivalence that resonated with contemporary identity formations in several countries. Chapter 4 pursues this discussion with reference to *Ivanhoe*'s afterlife in the USA, critically revisiting Mark Twain's claim that Scott somehow 'caused' the Civil War. I argue that Scott did not cause it, but that he did help shape its imaginary and, as an icon known both north and south, its subsequent remembrance. Chapter 5 turns to spatial practices and to Scott's role in the emergence of synthetic 'sites of memory' that provided memory-laden destinations at a time of increased mobility and intensified tourism. Focusing on Abbotsford as a prefabricated memory site, it shows how Scott's work shaped transnational, and specifically transatlantic identities among migrants and offered destinations for those who returned to the British Isles as tourists. Chapter 6 concentrates on the recollections of Scott himself, especially his funeral and the setting up of the enormous monument in 1840 and the lavish centenary celebrations of 1871: what do these public displays tell us about literary canonicity in the age of empire? My claim is that Scott provided a consensual point of reference that different parties could then use to stake out their position within the imagined confederation of the English-speaking world. Chapter 7 examines the discourse of generationality that emerged around the figure of Scott in the twentieth century, and argues that he had himself prepared for his own becoming a 'lost cause' by promoting a discourse of progress in the guise of historicism. Finally, the Epilogue considers what is at stake almost two hundred years after *Waverley*, in either remembering or in forgetting the works of Scott: the ability to think of transience as a constitutive part of collective memory.

Scott and Waverley may now have an out-of-date ring to them—this was confirmed recently when I bought a copy of *The Lady of the Lake* and of *The Talisman* (1825), both published by the significantly named Dodo Press.[31] But Scott, I argue, should nevertheless be seen as a figure of modernity. Exemplary in this regard is the fact that he installed the latest hi-tech pneumatic bells in his Gothic dream house at Abbotsford, even as he shaped these bells to resemble medieval gargoyles. He was a man of his own time as much as a conjurer of memories, and it was because he was so modern in the 1810s and 1820s that he has now become out-of-date, part of another age: a resonant figure of monumental transience. Scott's cultural power lasted at most until World War I when, as if symbolically to mark the end of an era, some of the fonts for his collected works were melted down for munitions.[32] By that point, the consensus surrounding Scott had turned into general indifference and left him sidelined as an overly familiar icon of a history that was 'wrapped up' and could no longer mobilize; as an echo of a more innocent age when the world was younger, our parents read historical romances, and the world had not yet been hit by the trauma of modern warfare. In the long term, the case suggests, controversy may be more important than consensus in mobilizing remembrance. But even if the figure of Scott himself is no longer very visible in contemporary culture, I argue that his long-term legacy continues to be felt not just in the historical epics of Hollywood but also, and more profoundly, in the widely expressed belief that representing the past is a condition for transcending it on behalf of a new future.

1
Portable Monuments

A four-masted sailing ship that arrived in Québec in 1843; a hybrid rose with a crimson colour; an Australian class of potato; a lounge bar; the steam locomotive that pulled the daily express train from London to Edinburgh in 1900; a paddle steamer plying the Clyde in the 1930s; the geriatric unit in Helensburgh Victoria Infirmary, Dunbartonshire. Listing all these items side by side may read like a bizarre exercise worthy of a Borgesian encyclopedia: what can possibly connect these plants, purveyors, and places? The answer is fiction. For these things do have something in common, and that is the fact that they have all been called 'Jeanie Deans', after the heroine of Walter Scott's novel *The Heart of Mid-Lothian* (1818): Jeanie Deans the four-master; Jeanie Deans the rose, Jeanie Deans the tuber (aka Abundance); Jeanie Deans the lounge bar; Jeanie Deans the locomotive of the Teutonic class; the PS-Jeanie Deans; Jeanie Deans the hospital ward.[1] This proliferation of Jeanie Deans in so many domains of everyday life bears quiet testimony to the popularity and recognition value that Scott once enjoyed and to the role his work played in providing a secular pantheon of literary characters.[2] What does it now tell us about the role of Scott's work, in particular *The Heart of Mid-Lothian*, as a medium of collective memory? Why did the story of Jeanie Deans come to 'stick' in this way and have such a long afterlife? And what did it mean for Jeanie to migrate from a book to material culture?[3]

THE DYNAMICS OF CULTURAL MEMORY

The concept of 'cultural memory' has emerged in the past decade as a heuristic tool with which to describe how stories about the past emerge as common points of reference and, in the process, help to define collective identities.[4] It draws attention to the historically variable mnemonic practices through which stories about the past are shaped and shared;[5] to those 'acts of transfer that make remembering in common possible', to use a phrase from Paul Connerton.[6] As this emphasis on 'remembering' suggests, cultural memory can best be seen in performative terms, as a way of recollecting the past and shaping its image using a whole range of media, rather than merely in preservative terms, as a way of transmitting unchanged something inherited from an earlier age.

The concept of cultural memory as defined here is closely linked to that of collective memory. Where the former concept highlights the role of mediation and performance in producing a shared relationship to the past, the term 'collective memory', first developed by Maurice Halbwachs in the 1920s, emphasizes instead the social dimensions of memory-sharing and hence highlights the actors and organizations involved.[7] The difference is one of perspective rather than of principle, however. So while the focus in this study is on 'cultural' memory (or 'remembrance', when the performative dimensions are being emphasized) I shall use the alternative term 'collective memory' on those occasions when I need to highlight actors rather than storytelling practices. I do so on the understanding, of course, that 'collective' does not imply the existence of a single super-entity but rather the continuous emergence of mnemonic communities, both embodied and imagined, through face-to-face communication as well as long-distance media.[8] Oral testimony, printed stories, images, paintings, theatre, memorials, commemorations: as this diverse list indicates, shared stories about the past are produced in the interplay between multiple cultural forms, each with its own technical possibilities and limitations.

With a growing body of literature on the subject, it is by now generally accepted that selectivity and recursivity are key factors in cultural remembrance since they help bring into existence a limited number of memory sites. Following Pierre Nora, 'memory sites' can be defined as actual locations or symbolic points of reference that serve as dense repositories of historical meaning (a 'minimum of signs with a maximum amount of meaning', as Nora put it) and hence as communal orientation points in negotiations about collective self-definitions.[9] Approaching a similar conclusion from a broader understanding of canonicity, Jan Assmann has described cultural memory in terms of the 'reusable texts, images, and rituals specific to each society in each epoch, whose "cultivation" serves to stabilize and convey that society's self-image.'[10]

This book will provide lots of evidence to support the idea that remembrance crystallizes into a limited number of sites of collective significance (particular novels, characters, the figure of 'Scott' himself) and that they do so by being repeated over again, in different media and different forums which maximize their public presence.[11] However, while recognizing the importance of common memory sites, I will nevertheless take the discussion in a new direction by highlighting the dynamic aspects of cultural remembrance alongside its points of stability. After all, it is presumably only because collective identity is not fixed in a definitive way that it needs periodically to be renegotiated or, in Assmann's terms, cultivated, stabilized, and 'conveyed' to the group. Seen from the dynamic perspective proposed here, then, cultural memory is always emergent, dependent on being periodically reiterated and adapted to new circumstances through an interplay between particular memory sites ('reusable texts and images'), acts of remembrance, and shifting social frameworks.[12] These memory sites are not fixed entities or finished products, moreover, but rather imaginative resources for generating new meanings and contesting old ones. They are points of relative stability within a dynamic system in which both consensus and contestation are vital ingredients and in which both forgetting and remembering come into play.[13]

This dynamic approach offers among other things a new perspective on literature as a medium of collective memory. Not surprisingly, a lot has already been written on the role of creative writers in shaping views of the past, including the many contemporary writers who have been practicing variations on the historical novel.[14] It is generally assumed that novelists have something distinctive to contribute to the making of collective memory, both by telling stories in a complex and imaginative way and by critically reflecting on other mnemonic practices, including historiography. In keeping with critical traditions, literary scholars have been particularly predisposed to see literary texts as agents of 'counter-memory': memories sidelined in dominant narratives for ideological reasons or because they involve otherwise inexpressible traumatic experiences.[15] Literature and the other arts have thus been attributed a structural role in providing an alternative to official forms of remembrance and in giving expression to the otherwise inexpressible. I shall get back to this point later. Suffice it here to point out that literary scholars, despite their claims that creative writing opens up new sites of memory, have rarely extended their analysis to the broader cultural field in which memories circulate and are contested. On the contrary: in keeping with critical traditions, the unit of analysis has been the discrete text seen as the *terminus ad quem* of everything that came before with claims being made about the role of literature on the basis of readings of single works independent of their afterlife.

As indicated earlier, the present study goes beyond methodological textualism by focusing on the social life of texts and their shifting role in the dynamics of cultural memory. The 'social life of texts' supposes that literary texts have multiple afterlives in different material manifestations and social contexts. They partake both of 'monumentality' (as valued display texts they persist across time) and of 'mobility' (in being appropriated in new editions, readings, adaptations, and contexts they are continuously subject to change, just as they themselves often rework earlier stories).[16] A text that initially works as an agent of counter-memory in foregrounding hitherto marginalized stories and opening up critical perspectives on dominant narratives can later become an agent of consensus memory if it becomes canonized as an object of recollection in its own right.

The aim of the present chapter is to provide an initial map of this complexity. As the many Jeanie Deans invoked earlier indicate, this first chapter focuses on *The Heart of Mid-Lothian* (1818) so as to offer a fresh perspective on the Waverley novels as active agents in the shaping of cultural memory. Since one of my assumptions is that a text plays multiple roles over a longer period, the spotlight will turn in sequence on several facets of this one novel: a public forum relaying and showcasing earlier stories, an artistic composition, an object of critical appropriation and transmedial adaptation, and an icon of memory. In bringing these dimensions together, the analysis will show how the novel offered a point of relative stability at the same time as it was continuously adapted so that its material manifestations, its content, and its meaning morphed along the way. A portable monument, it moved across time, space, media, and imaginations even as the original text remained unchanged.

Where stone monuments are fixed in particular locations, stories travel. Thus the missionary Reginald Heber described in his *Narrative of a Journey through the Upper Provinces of India* (1828) how, when making his way through the Indian plains en route to Bhangalpoor, he found himself recalling Jeanie Deans and her homesickness as she made her way—also on a mission—through the flatness of England.[17] His evocation of the novel suggests that literature too can become a 'portable Fatherland' ('portatives Vaterland'), as Heinrich Heine once described language.[18] This mobility was more than just a matter of actual books carried in luggage, although pocket-sized editions suitable for travellers were indeed a feature of the publication history of Scott's novels.[19] Nor was it merely a matter of individuals like Heber travelling with the memory of particular stories. Crucially for the analysis here, Scott's work travelled across materials (in the form of new editions), languages (in the form of translations), interpretive frames (in the form of critical commentaries), and media (in the form of adaptations) in which the original novel was both recollected and transformed. How did these various morphings of the Waverley novels play into social identities? Did Scott, himself a memory-maker par excellence, prefigure this afterlife? How did the 'pull' of readers relate to the 'push' of the text? As the analysis advances, it will become apparent that the afterlife of Waverley included appropriations both by those defending the status quo and those seeking to imagine a different future.

RELAYING STORIES:
HELEN WALKER TO JEANIE DEANS

The Heart of Mid-Lothian appeared as part of the Second Series of the 'Tales of my Landlord' purportedly collected and reported by Jedediah Cleishbotham, one of Scott's many avatars. Within the series of the Waverley novels, it immediately followed *Rob Roy* (1817) and was itself followed by *The Bride of Lammermoor* (1819). As he was writing it, Scott also apparently considered it to be his real masterpiece.[20] More recently, Ian Duncan has described it as the author's 'most ambitious and complex fiction', while it also became one of Scott's most enduringly popular novels—a position between 'high' and popular culture that is typical of Scott's work.[21] While unique in its setting and its characters, however, it also displays many of the features characterizing the Waverley novels. From the point of view of both its composition and its long-term reception, it is as exemplary as any one text might ever be of Scott's *oeuvre*.

Like the other Waverley novels set in Scotland, *The Heart of Mid-Lothian* explored the border between living memory and mediated narratives; or, to use the distinction introduced by Jan Assmann, between 'communicative memory' based on the first-hand recall of experience on the part of participants and witnesses and cultural memory proper where recollection has become entirely dependent on mediated accounts.[22] The subtitle to *Waverley*, the first novel—''tis sixty years since'—had already indicated Scott's preoccupation with generational change, and with the fascinating transition from first-hand testimony to mediated memory. If at one level the novels were autonomous literary compositions, at another level they were just one of the many forms of memorializing in which Scott was self-consciously involved. Besides being a poet and novelist, he was also an editor and an avid collector of relics and manuscripts, who moved freely between the material and the textual in his engagement with the past (I will discuss his role as collector in more detail in Chapter 5). In a study entitled *Literary Memory* (2003), Catherine Jones has shown convincingly that Scott's work was itself shot through by multiple discourses on memory that were circulating at the close of the eighteenth century.[23]

That Scott's writings were bound up with his other mnemonic practices and that his stories were on the move between different materializations was borne out by his erection of a gravestone in 1830 to the memory of Helen Walker, the woman who had provided the prototype for the heroine of his *Heart of Mid-Lothian*. The monument, which Scott paid for and for which he wrote the inscription, read as follows:

THIS STONE WAS ERECTED | BY THE AUTHOR OF WAVERLEY | TO THE MEMORY | OF | HELEN WALKER | WHO DIED IN THE YEAR OF GOD 1791 | THIS HUMBLE INDIVID-UAL | PRACTISED IN REAL LIFE | THE VIRTUES | WITH WHICH FICTION HAS INVESTED | THE IMAGINARY CHARACTER OF | JEANIE DEANS: | REFUSING THE SLIGHTEST DEPARTURE | FROM VERACITY, | EVEN TO SAVE THE LIFE OF A SISTER, | SHE NEVERTHE-LESS SHOWED HER | KINDNESS AND FORTITUDE, | IN RESCUING HER | FROM THE SEVERITY OF THE LAW, | AT THE EXPENSE OF PERSONAL EXERTIONS | WHICH THE TIME RENDERED AS DIFFICULT | AS THE MOTIVE WAS LAUDABLE. | RESPECT THE GRAVE OF POVERTY | WHEN COMBINED WITH LOVE OF TRUTH | AND DEAR AFFECTION[24]

Helen Walker, whose bones lie under this rather prolix stone, was the pious daughter of a strict Presbyterian in southern Scotland. Her younger sister, Isobel Walker, was put on trial in 1737 for infanticide, having concealed a pregnancy out of wedlock and probably having killed her child. When Helen refused on principle to perjure herself to save Isobel, the latter was condemned to death according to the harsh laws of the time. Helen then took it upon herself to walk the whole way to London in search of a royal pardon for her sister, which she did actually succeed in getting. Isobel was saved, and went on to marry her original lover, while Helen went back to her old life and remained single.

Or so the story goes. Such was the outline of Helen Walker's life that had been narrated to Scott by an anonymous correspondent (later named as a Mrs Goldie). In a nice illustration of the workings of communicative memory based on face-to-face contact, Mrs Goldie had run into Helen Walker as an old lady and, impressed by her demeanor, had inquired about her from neighbours and heard her story from them. When Helen Walker died shortly afterwards, Mrs Goldie initially planned to erect a gravestone to her, but instead sent the story off to Scott on the grounds that he might be interested in using it for a novel 'so as to perpetuate her memory in a more durable manner'.[25] Scott took up the invitation and based his novel on the Helen Walker story, nevertheless also erecting the gravestone towards the end of his life in 1830 as a material complement to the new magnum opus edition of the novel that appeared in the same year. The introduction to that edition also included verbatim Mrs Goldie's original narrative, thereby clinching the key position of the novel in the circulation of stories.[26]

The existence of Helen Walker has been confirmed by several people who claim to have met her, and there is also evidence corroborating the fact that her sister was accused of infanticide and subsequently pardoned (Scott does not seem to have actually consulted the official sources relating to these legal proceedings, which confirm that Isobel was indeed pardoned, but imply that the pardon could not have been issued directly to her sister).[27] In fact, Helen Walker does not seem to have made it at all into any of the official archives from the eighteenth century. The only source for the story of her refusal to commit perjury and of her walking the whole way to London to obtain a pardon was in effect Mrs Goldie and the local gossip that she had picked up. In a later account provided by John McDiarmid (a journalist at the *Scotsman* and an acquaintance of Mrs Goldie), who had interviewed different neighbours, it is, ironically, the novel that is invoked as a source for the story about the trip to London...In a postscript to his introduction to the magnum opus 1830 edition, Scott in turn quotes John McDiarmid as a source for supplementary details of Helen Walker's life.[28] The search for the original source thus turns into a sort of textual Moebius strip whereby life and literature are inextricably mixed up with each other, with one source leading into another, and being in turn supported by it. A recent study by Peter Garside has suggested, moreover, that the topos of a 'heroic walk in the cause of virtue' originated in a popular novel from 1807. This does not mean that Helen's walk was necessarily invented, but that the existence of a novel on such a subject might have attracted Mrs Goldie and, later, Scott to the story of Helen Walker.[29] Its memorability could have been 'premediated', to use Astrid Erll's term, meaning that an earlier story provided a model for recognizing the tell-worthiness of later events.[30] At the very least, this suggests the interpenetration at this time of local oral traditions and an international media-based repertoire of stories, with written texts becoming at times 're-oralized'.[31] This interpenetration between the written and the oral, which we will also encounter in discussing *Ivanhoe* in Chapter 4, belies the idea proposed by Pierre Nora that a clear-cut distinction can be drawn between traditional 'memory environments' (based on face-to-face contact) and the mediated construction of memory sites in the modern period.[32]

Whatever the actual facts of the matter were, and they are by now probably impossible to trace, we can note that Scott treated Mrs Goldie's information as a piece of oral testimony and turned the story of the two sisters into the centrepiece of a five-hundred-page novel. As we shall see later on, he also reworked and expanded the story in ways that resonated with some of the central themes of his *oeuvre*—most notably the theme of cultural differences and how to live with them. But as the Introduction to the most recent edition suggests, he was also specifically responding to criticism levelled at one of his earlier novels. By making a devout Presbyterian the heroine of his story, Scott provided some symbolic reparation for the offence his earlier novel *Old Mortality* (1816) had caused to fellow-Scots who identified with the Covenanting tradition and who considered that he had unjustly portrayed them as mere fanatics in his novel about their struggles in the late seventeenth century.[33] In this way, the novel was not only caught up on the wider circulation of stories at this time, but also represented a reprise of Scott's own work.

Before examining in more detail how Scott recalled and transformed earlier narratives in producing this work of fiction, more needs to be said about the public status of novels at this time. For why did Mrs Goldie send the story to Scott in the first place?

PROVIDING A FORUM

Mrs Goldie's initiative in sending the Walker story to Scott seems to have originated in a belief that certain life histories were worthy of public remembrance; her initial impulse to put up a gravestone seems to have arisen from the same source. But why choose a novel rather than a funerary monument as the means to make that story public? To a certain extent the answer to this question must be speculative since not much can be reconstructed about Mrs Goldie herself. Did her confidence that a text might somehow be 'more durable' than a stone monument reflect, consciously or unconsciously, the Horatian *aere perennius*? I shall come back to this principle later. But in order to explain why she chose a *novel* rather than any other sort of text—a play, for example, or a biography—we must consider the public role of that medium at the beginning of the nineteenth century.

That Mrs Goldie should have written to Scott and not to some other writer is indicative of his status—or rather the status of the Author of Waverley (his identity was not yet firmly established)—as the channel through which a deserving story might be circulated more widely. The success of *Waverley* in 1814 and of his subsequent novels was due, it is now widely believed, not just to Scott's literary skills but also to his canny combination of 'respectable' historical themes with elements from the popular, but hitherto relatively low-prestige novelistic tradition.[34] Nor was Mrs Goldie being idiosyncratic in looking to Scott as a public figure: from the publication of *Waverley* onwards, the Author of Waverley was at the receiving end of a lively correspondence with readers all over Scotland, particularly from interested parties who thought he might have use for certain details of family or local history. These reactions show that Scott's work provided a virtual public sphere where private persons, through family or local connections, sought and found representation in the collective history of Scotland.[35] Those who assumed the role of Scott's informants were also ensuring their own place in future memory, whether they intended this or not. Through his public role as Author of Waverley, then, Scott's work became a relay station for local memories, both living and inherited, whereby various accounts of the past converged on a central cultural field of force and became a common point of reference. This convergence of stories within the cultural framework of the novel adds another dimension to the by-now familiar thesis that the modern media played a role in the formation of imagined communities. Whereas Benedict Anderson and, more recently, Jonathan Culler have pointed out the ways in which the very form of fictional narrative meant that novels could create the sense of a shared social space and a shared historical time, Scott's novels also played a more specific role as a public medium for channelling and framing disparate local memories. It was a mass-medium successor to the parish pump, and one with a global reach.[36] In Chapter 6 I will come back to this relation between literature and imagined communities when discussing the commemorations of Scott.

But the *public* character of the novelistic medium is not itself sufficient to explain why a novel like *The Heart of Mid-Lothian* became a vehicle for certain types of memories rather than for others. In this case, for the story of an obscure Presbyterian woman called Helen Walker whose actions were never recorded in any official archive. Without the intervention of the novel, her life would almost certainly have disappeared into oblivion along with the passing of those who personally remembered her and could talk about her. Nor is Scott's interest in unsung female figures unique: since the emergence of the genre at the beginning of the nineteenth century there has been a significant connection between historical novels and actors who did not make it into the archives, because they were socially too insignificant or because they were the victims of events and hence not in a position to tell their own story. In introducing an obscure woman into public memory, someone who was neither politically nor socially important, Scott took over themes that had been emerging in women's writing at this time and spearheaded a whole novelistic tradition of counter-history, which is perhaps best summed up by Victor Hugo's claim in *Les misérables* to be writing the 'internal' history that had been missed by historians concentrating on the political and the public: 'the history of the inside, of ordinary people as they work, suffer and wait, of downtrodden women, of the dying child'.[37] Geoffrey Hartman has more recently echoed Hugo's sentiments in claiming that literature provides a forum for human complexities left out of both official accounts of the past and the inauthentic versions of the past circulating through the mass media:

When art remains accessible, it provides a counterforce to manufactured and monolithic memory . . . Scientific historical research, however essential it is for its negative virtues of rectifying error and denouncing falsification, has no positive resources to lessen grief, endow calamity with meaning, foster a new vision of the world, or legitimate new groups.[38]

The imaginative power brought into play by creative writers has certainly been a vital ingredient of their ability to open up the past and generate empathy for obscure lives. But in trying to explain a novelist's concern with the experiences of marginal themes and actors, it is also necessary to compare fictional representations with the alternatives. If we accept that culture is always affected by what Michel Foucault has called 'the principle of scarcity', then it follows that there is only a limited number of imaginative resources and cultural forms available at any given moment.[39] Given the limits set by historians at the time Scott began writing, the novel offered an alternative forum for narrating stories that could not be easily accommodated within the generic conventions of historiography proper—that 'real solemn history' with wars and pestilences and hardly any women, which Jane Austen's character had complained of a decade before in *Northanger Abbey* (written 1803; published 1818).[40] Since the novel was still a relatively *parvenu* genre in 1818, Scott could use it as an experimental space for including cases that might otherwise have been forgotten and for weaving multiple discourses and discursive forms into his literary narrative—all of this against the background of the alternative forms of history, from antiquarian collecting to historiography and philology, that he was exploring elsewhere.[41]

Helen Walker paid a price for representation in the public sphere and, more specifically, in the framework of a novel. To be sure, she was commemorated in public, in an extensive narrative that holds the reader's attention for hours. But, as her very gravestone indicates, she was transformed in the process into the first of many a Jeanie Deans. She goes down in history, but only under another name; she gains a place in the public memory, but at the cost of losing her identity. Her life is literally transformed into literature while she herself is, at least temporarily, forgotten. The irony of this public transformation becomes complete when we consider the title of McDiarmid's supplementary account of her life, mentioned earlier. When McDiarmid brought out his expanded account of the life of Helen Walker in 1830, he called it 'The Real History of Jeanie Deans', a title that highlights the fact that, from the publication of the novel onwards, all 'real' histories of Helen Walker can only be reconstructed through her better known novelistic counterpart Jeanie Deans. It was she and not Helen who accordingly appeared on the north-east buttress of the enormous Scott monument erected in Edinburgh between 1840 and 1844.[42]

This brings me from the role of *The Heart of Mid-Lothian* in transmitting stories to its character as a literary composition with its own relative autonomy and monumentality.

COMPOSING MEMORY

The Heart of Mid-Lothian carries Scott's trademark integration of individual and collective stories and reiterates some of the central concerns informing his work: civil conflict and its resolution, the relations between Scotland and England within the framework of the Union, the ideological, moral, and geographical differences within Scotland itself. In many ways, the travels of Jeanie Deans recollect and invert those of Edward Waverley: where he travelled from England to the Highlands and ended up in the Lowlands, Jeanie goes from the Lowlands to England and then ends in the Highlands. As a number of commentators have pointed out, the movements of Scott's characters help trace out geopolitical maps through which Great Britain is being re-imagined (more on this in Chapter 5).[43]

In fleshing out the character and life of Helen Walker, Scott had recourse to his rich imagination for the details—after all, his source was no more than a hundred lines long. Since he was working within the conventions of the novel, he was free to invent within the (sometimes disputed) borders of what was historically plausible, while also calling upon his huge store of knowledge concerning the history and mores of Scotland in the eighteenth century.[44] In the process he dovetailed the story of Helen Walker with another historical episode from the same period in Scottish history: the Porteous affair. The result is an orchestrated mixture, a composite. As I shall argue, the novel survived in the long term not because it offered a singular, coherent view on Scottish history, but because its different parts never quite matched up even as they were poetically juxtaposed in a distinctly literary configuration.

The Porteous affair, as it was called, had taken place in Scotland in 1737, more or less concurrently with the Walker Trial, though in Edinburgh rather than Roxburgh. In contrast to the story of Walker, which was known only in a restricted circle, this affair was already well known at the time Scott wrote his novel. As one reviewer put it, it was a 'traditional fact' and 'a story deeply registered in the Memory of many now living'.[45]

Figure 1.1: *The Death of Porteous.* Drawing T. M. Richardson; engraving J. Tingle. From *Landscape-Historical Illustrations of Scotland and the Waverley Novels* (London, 1836–8).

The rather complicated facts run more or less as follows: a captain of the Edinburgh city guard, a man called Porteous, was put on trial for having been instrumental in the cold-blooded killing of a number of demonstrators in the city; although he was found guilty and condemned to death, an unexpected royal pardon saved him from execution; this angered the citizens of Edinburgh so much that a group of them, disguised as women, broke into the prison in the middle of the night where Porteous was being held and carried out their own ceremonious execution of the oppressor; London reacted with punitive measures against the city, but those responsible for the midnight execution were never brought to trial. The whole episode remained in cultural memory as an example of the power of Scottish tenacity and native sense of justice to overcome the arbitrariness of English rule. We need to realize that the story was situated just a few decades after the parliamentary union between Scotland and England, which had taken place in 1707, and that Scott himself was writing just a generation after the Jacobite defeat at Culloden, the subject of *Waverley*.[46] The fact that he was also writing in 1818 against the background of imminent social unrest and the spectre of the violent demonstrations that had marked the French Revolution adds an extra force to his depiction of the Porteous Riot.[47]

The Heart of Mid-Lothian begins with a lurid, almost phantasmagoric, account of the dramatic lynching of Porteous in nocturnal Edinburgh, deviating little from the very extensive documentation of that event published in 1737, though making the proceedings more orderly than they had been in reality.[48] In order to whet the appetites of readers, Scott's publishers had also planted an article on the Porteous riots in the *Edinburgh Magazine* in June 1818, a month in advance of the novel.[49] The page opposite the title page of the first edition in turn carried an advertisement for a reprint of *Criminal Trials, Illustrative of the Tale Entitled 'The Heart of Mid-Lothian,' published from the original record.* Thanks to the novel, then, the memory of the case and the original records of the case were re-circulated and brought back into the culture. But they appeared now as illustrations of the fiction derived from them. Just as the publication of the novel meant that Helen Walker took on a new identity as 'the real Jeanie Deans', so too did the original record of the Porteous case become an illustration to the novel (a reprint from 1909 again appeals to the reader's familiarity with the episode, suggesting this 'memorable and striking chapter in the history of Scotland' had been retrieved from oblivion through the good offices of Scott).[50]

In reality the two historical cases—the Porteous affair and the affair of Helen Walker and her sister—had nothing to do with each other except the fact that they roughly coincided in time and roughly coincided in place (taking 'Scotland' to be a single location, that is). Scott brings them together by treating them within the framework of the same book. Seen in this light, the novel resembles less historiography and the other narrative forms with which it is usually compared, than a museum: like a collection, the novel is based on re-locating items and reassembling them in new configurations for the purposes of display.[51] In being brought side by side, the symmetries and differences between the Porteous and the Walker case become foregrounded: both are about legal processes in Scotland, the granting of pardons by London, and the intervention by Scottish citizens. The two episodes are historical in the sense that they are documented, but it is the novel that brings them together for the first time as part of Scottish history and allows them to play off each other like objects displayed side by side in a museum. Or, to use a more literary model, they resonate with each other in the manner of what Roman Jakobson famously defined as the 'poetic' function of language: the introduction of repetition in information flows.[52] In the case of *The Heart of Mid-Lothian* the juxtaposition of comparable events in the unfolding story (the Porteous affair; the Deans affair) endows these tangentially related events with a connection and hence with a mutually reinforcing meaning. Placed side by side, the equivalences and the differences between them become highlighted. Scott's novelistic synthesis of cultural memory from disparate sources was not just a matter of creating a story along chronological lines, then, but of organizing events into poetic patterns.

None of which takes from the fact that Scott did go to some lengths to weave these episodes into a single story and that narrativity, in the sense used by Hayden White, also has an important role to play in its effect. Scott not only brought the two episodes together within the same novelistic frame, but also used his poetic licence to flesh them out in a way that increases their mutual resonance. A detailed discussion of the very incident-rich plot would lead too far; suffice it to point out three crucial deviations from the historical record that heightened the drama and provided a point of intersection between the private and the public. To begin with, the imprisonment of Effie/Isobel is re-located to the 'Heart of Mid-Lothian', as the Edinburgh prison was then called, so as to be there at the same time as Porteous. It is worth noting in passing that the actual prison had been demolished the year before Scott wrote his novel and that *The Heart of Mid-Lothian*, therefore, is among other things a memorial to a lost building (parts of which Scott also recycled in the building of Abbotsford; more on this in Chapter 5).[53] Secondly, the leader of the nocturnal lynching party who assassinated Porteous is turned into the father of the dead baby, a double involvement that suggests an intimate, personal connection between the two affairs. Finally, where the historical

Isobel Walker went on to marry the man who had made her pregnant and presumably lived 'happily ever after' (at least nothing more is known of her since her pardon), her fictional counterpart Effie Deans marries the nocturnal rioter and becomes Lady Staunton in the process (the original child whose alleged murder was behind the whole Walker drama turns out to be alive after all and has matured into a good-for-nothing criminal who ends up murdering his own father). The thrust of the plot becomes all the clearer when the fate of the unfortunate Effie is compared with that of her virtuous sister Jeanie: whereas the historical Helen Walker remained unmarried, Scott deviates wildly from his sources by allowing her fictional counterpart Jeanie Deans to inherit the land, rewarding her with a husband, multiple children, prosperity, and a new home in the Highlands, thanks to the paternalistic intervention of the Duke of Argyll. Her sister Effie, in contrast, fails in the novel to have any children within wedlock, is made a widow by her illegitimate child, and ends up going into exile in a French convent while her good-for-nothing son is packed off to the wilds of North America. The future is clearly with those who respect the law while being ready to defend their rights if necessary, using eloquence and force of character rather than violence. Operating a bit like an immigration officer of the symbolic realm, Scott allowed the virtuous to stay in Scotland while removing undesirables to the next world or to foreign fields. If the novel begins in documented history it ends clearly in the realm of wish-fulfilment. The final volume, as we shall see later on, has also attracted the most criticism and puzzlement.

The many twists of the plot are highly contrived and a number of early reviewers found them implausible.[54] But its basic significance would seem to run more or less as follows: although those who break the law come to a sorry end, there is nevertheless a problem with the current rule of law since justice in Scotland has become dependent on decisions taken far away in London; hence the need for greater self-regulation on the part of the Scots (spearheaded in the novel by the Duke of Argyll and embodied in the Highland arcadia where Jeanie ends up).[55] In this way, the novel seems at one and the same time to accept the legitimacy of the union and to assert the moral and jurisprudential autonomy of Scotland. This was a logically problematic position, but nevertheless consonant with the generic logic of the romance as well as with the discourse about multinational Britishness that was emerging at this time, and to which I will return in Chapter 6.

Fictionality and moralizing always go together; Oscar Wilde famously quipped in *The Importance of Being Earnest* (1895): 'The good end happily, and the bad unhappily. That is what fiction means.'[56] Hayden White too has argued that there is a structural affinity between 'narra-tivizing' events (turning them into a story, with or without the use of invention) and moralizing them (re-constructing events as a struggle between individual desire and the law).[57] White's basic point also applies to *The Heart of Mid-Lothian*, with one crucial difference: Scott narrativized events while using the generic filter of romance and hence at the cost of losing part of his purchase on history. If his composite story ends happily with the good rewarded and the bad deported, then this is in part thanks to the self-consciously imaginary and wish-fulfilling character of the narrative, and not because of its truthfulness. Ian Duncan has located the fascination of the Waverley novels, and of *The Heart of Mid-Lothian* in particular, precisely in this ambivalence: they both represent history and continuously flag their own character as romance. His conclusion is worth quoting in full:

> The romance estate is a result not of a historical process but of its interruption. Its occupants are not accommodated within a logic of history but delivered from it, by a miraculous grace that translates history into private terms of its own. The solution is a fiction-within-history that invokes and scatters its claims upon truth.[58]

CREATING MEMORABILITY

More could be said about *The Heart of Mid-Lothian* as a piece of narrative art, especially about its playful use of multiple narrators in the story frame. My particular concern here, however, is with the link between narrativization and memorability: the qualities that invited other people to recall, reproduce, or otherwise re-appropriate it at a later point in time. What made Scott's work procreative in this sense?

Patricia Meyer Spacks has described Jeanie Deans as a 'memorable heroine of fiction' who after almost two centuries 'remains a splendid imaginative creation'.[59] Thanks to his literary skills and powerful imagination, Scott had narrativized the life of Helen Walker, transforming her into a character in whose struggles readers become imaginatively involved. Without the benefit of this narrative artistry, there would have been little to remember about her life and, like so many other violets, she would have been born to blush unseen. While this basic point might be made of any well-written biography, the case of Helen Walker/Jeanie Deans is notable because the memorability of the story became divorced from the matter of historical accuracy. As such it provides support for Alison Landsberg's claims about the power of fiction to generate 'prosthetic memories'— stories that are gripping and affecting, without necessarily being based in truth or on a previously shared identity.[60]

Jeanie's memorability was not only a function of the storytelling as such, however, but also of the values her character embodied, the link between moralization and narrativity posited by White proving useful again here. Lady Louisa Stewart praised Scott for having succeeded where everyone else had failed, namely in making a 'good' character the most interesting one.[61] Indeed the moral economy of the plot privileges the upright woman who trusted to English justice and walked to London to get a pardon for her sister above the rioters who took the law into their own hands. In this way, Scott had made Jeanie/Helen doubly memorable: she is the beneficiary of intense and empathetic attention, and her achievements are celebrated and symbolically rewarded in the development of the plot. This suggests that exemplariness and the capacity to provide a moral compass may be as important as authenticity and truth in the production of collective figures of memory, to recall Assmann's *Erinnerungsfiguren*. Even after the identity of Jeanie's prototype was disclosed in the years immediately following the publication of the novel, the historical origins of her figure has been less an issue than the moral significance of her character seen as representative of a certain age in Scottish history and a certain class in Scottish society, and hence as an icon to be cherished in the future. Although the protagonists of Scott's other novels are not all as virtuous as Jeanie or as firmly endowed with agency, the basic connection between individual characters, value, and memorability holds true in other cases as well (most notably in the case of Rebecca; see Chapter 3).

As theorists of cultural memory have argued with increasing frequency in recent years, however, remembering is inseparable from forgetting. Ernest Renan was already aware of this in his classic essay 'Qu'est-ce qu'une nation?' (1882) when he claimed that nation-building is based on collectively remembering certain things and on being able to forget other, more divisive events.[62] 'Forgetting' in this paradoxically active sense is not just a matter of simply ignoring events, but of *being able* to ignore them despite their potentially troubling character. This dialectic between memory and forgetting sheds new light on Scott's combination of the Porteous and Walker affairs within the framework of the novel: although the narrative begins with the detailed recollection of the carnivalesque execution of Porteous it then goes on effectively to occlude the memory of that event by the story of Jeanie Deans and, in the final volume, her happy-ever-after existence in the Highlands. Recalling a disquieting memory while simultaneously tempering its affective power was typical for Scott, as I have shown elsewhere.[63] *Old Mortality* (1816), for example, portrays the bitter religious conflict of the seventeenth century, but in such a way that it also attempts to resolve the bitterness by acknowledging the conflictual experiences of both parties so that bygones may be bygones. In the case of *The Heart of Mid-Lothian*, the logic of the narrative tends towards overwriting the memory of Porteous with the alternative story of Jeanie Deans. But ironically, the very power of Scott's own description of the midnight execution means that the depiction of the darkened city in the grip of violence is not so easily forgotten by the reader for whom it has been re-created. In Scott's work every 'act of interment', as Murray Pittock has noted in another context, tends towards becoming an act of revivification.[64] Certainly, in this case, the overtly romantic and idyllic ending—acknowledged as such by many commentators—is not convincing enough to erase the imaginative impact of the Porteous riots whose memory shadows the outcome. Although the general thrust is clear, the book nevertheless remains fraught by a certain tension between 'moving on' and 'going back' or, as Duncan has put it, between 'fatal historical fact' and 'extravagant spiritual impossibility'.[65]

Until now, narrativity has been seen as the key to stabilization in cultural memory since it makes the past imaginable in an orderly, memorable, and hence reproducible way.[66] *The Heart of Mid-Lothian* bears this out, but only up to a point. Although the novel provides strong and memorable scenes and characters, the composition as a whole is nevertheless fraught with a destabilizing sense of being out of joint: vacillating between history and romance, between recalling and overwriting, between coherence and contradiction. Such ambivalence provides another key to understanding the long-term fascination of Scott's work and its specifically aesthetic value. The cultural longevity of *The Heart of Mid-Lothian* and the other Waverley novels, I shall argue, had as much to do with the perennial sense that they were out of joint and therefore needed to be retro-fitted as it had to do with their imaginative powers in stabilizing memory through narrativization.[67] Ambivalence helped make them pro-creative by inviting new attempts to pin them down.

THE NOVEL RECOLLECTED: CRITICAL APPROPRIATIONS

Since the appearance of *The Heart of Mid-Lothian* almost two hundred years ago, the novel has never been out of print. Like other Waverley works, it was reprinted in at least five different English editions in Scott's own lifetime, and was subsequently reproduced with some variations as part of the collected, often illustrated editions of Waverley novels that were such a feature of Victorian literary culture.[68] The National Union Catalogue lists no fewer than 87 editions between 1818 and 1900. In the twentieth century it has been reprinted in various standalone editions and, most recently, as part of the Edinburgh Edition of the Waverley Novels (where the editors have been at pains to replicate Scott's original manuscript version of 1818 rather than the revised edition that Scott himself had brought out in 1830). It has also appeared in abridged form and been translated more than fifty times, into at least twenty languages, from the first French translation in 1818 to the more recent versions in Czech and Chinese (the number of translations is quite surprising for a work that is so specific in its use of locality and dialect but all the more proof of Scott's ability to cross the borders of existing communities).[69] Every new edition in English and every new translation constitutes a public act of recollection that allows the novel to start circulating again within the English-speaking world or to cross over into new cultural areas. This capacity of the novel to reproduce itself gives it a unique relationship to time as well as the aura of being both fixed and infinitely reproducible: whereas historical events like the Porteous Riot happened once and for all, the story of Jeanie Deans and Scott's depiction of those riots have repeatedly been revived at later periods as well as in places outside of Scotland.

In later editions of *The Heart of Mid-Lothian*, its monumentality as a canonical work was often enhanced by a sumptuous and solemn materiality, including lavish illustrations that made the book an object to be cherished in its own right. Throughout the nineteenth century it appeared in collected editions, designed with varying degrees of luxury to be stored on middle-class shelves as a source for family reading, but also as a sign of membership in the imagined community of those who appreciated good literature and had a vested interest in the preservation of the national canon—be this defined as Scottish, British, or Anglophone (all of these terms apply at some point, as we shall see later).[70] The publication of a collected edition during Scott's lifetime, the so-called magnum opus edition of 1829–33, and the centenary edition of 1871 were also bound up with the public memorialization of Scott the author, which I discuss in greater detail in Chapter 6.

The reproduction of the novel in the form of new editions or translations is just one part of its literary afterlife, however. As Judith Wilt in particular has shown, Scott was an all-pervasive source of inspiration for Victorian novelists who appropriated some of his themes and techniques even as they dismissed his work as out-dated.[71] More importantly for the analysis here, *The Heart of Mid-Lothian* generated critical commentary, beginning with the earliest reviews. Despite some complaints about the implausibilities of the last volume and accusations that it was merely a way for Scott to meet his contractual obligations, the earliest reviewers were generally positive, praising the combination of subject matter and narra-tivizing style: the fact that it offered a colourful but generally plausible image of eighteenth-century life in a highly readable form.[72] The earliest critics were above all concerned in their accounts of the novel with its accuracy as a portrayal of Scottish manners and with the moral character-istics of Jeanie (with some discussion of the extent to which it was an improvement or not on previous Waverley novels).[73] Thus where *Old Mortality* (1816), which dealt with a well-known and traumatic civil conflict, had led to extended discussions on the validity of Scott's repre-sentation of history and in particular of the character of the Covenanters, readers of *The Heart of Mid-Lothian* do not seem to have been overly concerned with the historical basis of the plot—or indeed with the plot as such since the focus was on character. Most critical discussions of *The Heart of Mid-Lothian* in the nineteenth century, after the first wave of reviewing had passed, were part of more general assessments of the Waverley novels and reflect the vicissitudes of Scott's critical fortunes.[74]

I shall be discussing those critical fortunes in more detail in Chapter 7, showing how Scott's fame was both enhanced and undermined by his popularity and commercial success. Suffice it here to point out the relative marginalization of Scott's work among critics in the first half of the twentieth century: neither E. M. Forster nor F. R. Leavis had much time for *The Heart of Mid-Lothian* or indeed for any other works by Scott in their seminal works on the English novel, *Aspects of the Novel* (1927) and *The Great Tradition* (1948), instead favouring fiction in which the moral and psychological complexity of individual characters prevailed over social developments. It took the Marxist (and notoriously anti-modernist) framework offered by the Hungarian György Lukács to first open up fruitful new perspectives on *The Heart of Mid-Lothian* in partic-ular. In his path-breaking study of the historical novel, originally pub-lished in Russian in 1937 and translated into English in 1962, Lukács argued that Scott's historical fiction was not just about local colour and antiquated notions of chivalry, as the novelist's eroded reputation in the twentieth century might suggest, but about historicity itself. He claimed that although Scott's overt politics were conservative, his creative work demonstrated a keen awareness of the capacity of people to shape the worlds they inhabit and the futures towards which they are heading. In making this point, Lukács highlighted the figure of Jeanie Deans as a historically and morally significant character, welcoming (and appropriat-ing) her story as an example of how ordinary individuals could rise to the occasion and become actors on the world-historical stage—a reading that once again subordinated the historicity of Jeanie Deans to her exemplary function as a guide to the future. In Lukács' particular version, which has nothing to say on the subject of Porteous and is dismissive of the final volume, this novel from the post-Waterloo period is still relevant today because of the insight it gives into the potential role of ordinary citizens in making history:

The story of these inner battles and of this struggle to save her sister show the rich humanity and simple heroism of a really great human being. Yet Scott's picture of his heroine never for a moment obscures her narrow Puritan and Scottish peasant traits, indeed it is they which again and again form the specific character of the naïve and grand heroism of this popular figure.[75]

Although the status of the Waverley novels within the broader field of literary criticism has fluctuated in the twentieth century, *The Heart of Mid-Lothian* has maintained its place, alongside the other 'Scottish' works written between 1814 and 1819, in the core canon of the Waverley novels. A poll among Scott scholars in 1999 identified it as the then current favourite.[76] Not surprisingly, however, interpretations of the story of Jeanie and Effie Deans have shifted with the times and refracted broader cultural changes. Several critics have produced gendered renditions highlighting the primacy of women in the novel and focusing on the relations between the two sisters or on the question of infanticide. (It is indicative of changing interpretive frames and cultural norms that Effie nowadays tends to eclipse the more virtuous Jeanie, where Lady Louisa Stewart had seen the latter as the indisputed centre of attention.[77]) Other critics have produced postcolonial readings focused on the background of the novel in the Highland clearances and the fact that Jeanie is awarded land from which other people had probably been forced to emigrate: so many readings producing so many new versions of the novel and, in the process, revealing both the complexity of the original text and the priorities of those appropriating it in new terms.

It is worth noting the vested interest on the part of all of us engaged in criticism to reveal the contemporary resonances of the texts we are studying, appropriating them in light of our current values and aspirations so that, freshly interpreted, they can start doing new cultural work. After all, 'cultivating' canonical texts and images in the form of new interpretations is an important tool for calibrating and stabilizing collective identity, to recall Jan Assmann. Thus when Andrew Lincoln expressed a desire to 'recover a sense of Scott's relevance today' in his *Walter Scott and Modernity* (2007), he was making explicit something that underpins most literary criticism as such: the need to find that the book you admire also addresses contemporary issues.[78] Noting the existence of such an appropriative desire, however, should not be taken to imply that meaning is only in the eye of the interpreter, since all effective readings depend on the characteristics of the original and its ability to generate new interpretations. In this respect it is worth noting, as evidence of the agency of Scott's original work, the amount of attention paid by recent critics to the last volume of *The Heart of Mid-Lothian*—the part that, from the first days on, has been felt to mark a stylistic and generic break with the rest. These new readings of the novel (by Judith Wilt, Ian Duncan, James Kerr, and Charlotte Sussman among others) suggest once again that it is the structural tensions and contradictions within *The Heart of Mid-Lothian*, rather than the things it immediately gets right, which feed its cultural longevity and prevent its reduction to a simple set of (forgettable) characters and themes. Philology is the art of generating complexity, as Hans Ulrich Gumbrecht has put it, by articulating and resolving contradictions that were always already there.[79] The present analysis of *The Heart of Mid-Lothian* should be seen as both an observer and participant in this endeavour.

THE NOVEL RECOLLECTED: ADAPTATIONS

Scott was not only himself prolific, but his work was also extremely procreative: it inspired a huge number of other writers, artists, playwrights, and even manufacturers of textiles or makers of ceramics.[80] Where critical commentaries have respected in principle the integrity of Scott's text (indeed their hermeneutic creativity is based on the inalterable 'thereness' of the original), the re-workings in other media span the distance between the respect for the bard's work that befits canonicity and the free appropriations of his stories that are more characteristic of popular culture. Since I will be analysing the multiple adaptations of the Waverley novels to other media in later chapters, suffice it here to indicate the range and significance of such remediations with reference to *The Heart of Mid-Lothian*.

Like other Waverley works, the novel was repeatedly illustrated in the form of engravings, sold separately or used in illustrated editions, as well as of standalone paintings.[81] In the process, the narrative was transformed into a canon of dramatic moments. While the most famous individual painting of *The Heart of Mid-Lothian* was arguably James Drummond's *The Porteous Mob* (1855), the most popular scene among the fifty or so canvases devoted to the novel was the moment full of drama and pathos when Jeanie visits her sister in prison and then decides to go on her mission, which was depicted over and again and used to illustrate new editions. Remarkably, the emphasis of several artists, most notably John Millais (1877) and James McNeill Whistler (1876–8), anticipated the recent critical interest in Effie Deans by focusing on the younger 'fallen'

FROM C. R. LESLIE, R.A.

MEETING OF THE SISTERS.

Figure 1.2: *The Meeting of the Sisters.* Drawing C. R. Leslie; engraving C. Rolls (1823). Reproduced from Sir Walter Scott, Bart., *The Heart of Mid-Lothian* (Edinburgh, 1886).

Figure 1.3: James McNeill Whistler, *Arrangement in Yellow and Grey: Effie Deans* (1876–8).

sister at the cost of her more virtuous sibling. As this visual shift from Jeanie to Effie illustrates, the story not only travelled to another medium, but its emphasis was modified in the process.[82]

The same can be said of the many re-workings of *The Heart of Mid-Lothian* for the stage and screen, beginning almost immediately after the publication of the novel. All the Waverley novels were adapted to the stage and *The Heart of Mid-Lothian* was one of the most popular, as H. Philip Bolton has shown in his invaluable survey. There were at least three hundred and fifty recorded productions in the British Isles and the United

States and at least twenty-one published versions of the relevant scripts. With the exception of Lacy's rather unsuccessful *The Heart of Mid-Lothian; or, the Sisters of St. Leonard's* (1863), most other versions followed the mould established in Thomas Dibdin's *The Heart of Mid-Lothian: or, the Lily of St. Leonard's: A Melodramatic Romance* (1819) and concentrated on the trial/pardon story, overlooking both the Porteous affair and the events of the final volume. Interestingly in view of what was said earlier about the dynamics of forgetting and remembering in Scott's narration, the riots in Edinburgh were almost totally absent from the many versions on the stage—although the affair itself had enjoyed a modest revival thanks to Scott's fiction and Drummond's painting, this did not carry over in a significant way into the theatrical afterlife of the novel. Nevertheless, adaptations of the novel generally made much of the setting in Edinburgh and often used elaborate painted scenery and lighting to set off the different locales.[83]

Dramatizations of the novel covered the broad spectrum of nineteenth-century theatrical genres, including melodrama (Daniel Terry, *The Heart of Mid-Lothian: A Musical Drama in Three Acts* [1819], for example, or Gaetano Rossi, *La Prigione di Edimburgo* [1838]), burlesque (William Brough, *The Great Sensation Trial, or, Circumstantial Effie-Deans: a Burlesque Extravaganza*, 1863), and high opera (Hamish MacCunn, *Jeanie Deans: A Grand Opera in Four Acts*, 1894).[84] Although this reiterated interest in the novel fed into an early film version called *A Woman's Triumph* (USA, 1914), directed by J. Searle Dawley, theatrical remediations seem to have almost completely dried up in the twentieth century, with the exception of a new version called *The Journey of Jeannie Deans* that was produced at the Edinburgh Festival Fringe in 2008.[85] One commentator has suggested that William Brough's burlesque in 1863 had pulled so powerful a punch that it was difficult to take the story of the sisters seriously again.[86] The BBC did produce a radio version (1953) and a two-part television play (1966), which can be taken as signs of a continued cultural life, albeit one that was considerably diminished compared to the summer of 1819 when Dibdin's version was performed at the Surrey Theatre in London, the Theatre Royal, York, and the Theatre Royal, Liverpool, running, in the case of the Surrey, to at least seventy-two performances.[87] As these examples indicate, the social life of *The Heart of Mid-Lothian* is inseparable from its later manifestations on the stage and in visualizations. These dramatic and pictorial versions were radically selective with respect to the novel, but they were nonetheless vital in helping transmit and shape the memory of Jeanie Deans/Helen Walker over at least two generations.

THE MORPHINGS OF JEANIE

One of the effects of the many reprints and remediations of the novel is that 'Jeanie Deans' became something of a household word in the nineteenth century, especially in Scotland. From the revised and annotated edition of 1830 onwards, most reprints of the novel have included an introduction by Scott in which he narrates the story of Helen Walker and reproduces his correspondence with Mrs Goldie. In principle, therefore, the story of Helen Walker has long been available for those willing to look it up, together with that of her fictional successor Jeanie Deans. The result has been a certain amount of fame, a persistent if minor afterlife for the prototype Scott had overwritten: Helen Walker was the subject of John McDiarmid's 'The Real Life of Jeanie Deans', mentioned earlier, and she figured *in propria persona* in Charlotte Yonge's *Book of Golden Deeds* (1864) as she did in the anonymous 'Jennie Deans [*sic*] and Helen Walker' published in *Godey's Lady's Book and Magazine* (1855)—basically a retelling of the Walker story through the prism of the novel. More recently, Helen Walker has figured in an Internet heritage site devoted to celebrating women's role in Scottish history, a modest renewal of interest in Helen in the post-feminist era, which suggests that cultural memory loss is *reversible* as long as the relevant information has been stored somewhere as an inert part of what Aleida Assmann calls 'archival memory' (in contrast to the working memory of society that plays into its current identity).[88] And of course, Helen has also received some attention in scholarly discussions of the novel—including the present one.[89]

These various recollections of Helen Walker remain nevertheless fairly marginal phenomena and it is above all the memory of the fictitious Jeanie Deans that has enjoyed a widespread cultural life.[90] The existence of a broadsheet ballad called 'Jeanie Deans' (published in Glasgow sometime between 1880 and 1900) suggests that she had gained the status of a folk heroine even as the role of Scott in bringing her to public attention was acknowledged. In a fascinating combination of folk culture and printed media, the last lines invoke the memory of Scott alongside the memory of the 'gallant' and 'Scottish' Jeanie:

> 'Jeanie woman,' though departed,
> We will keep the honoured name
> Of one so true and loyal-hearted,
> Written on the scroll of fame.
> Sir Walter Scott immortalised you—

'Thou wer't one of nature's queens'—
And in our hearts we'll ever praise you,
Gallant, Scottish, Jeanie Deans.[91]

The afterlife of Jeanie Deans, as the examples adduced so far suggest, took the form of multiple versions in theatrical, pictorial, and written form (including chapbooks), in which the basic story was recalled in more or less detail.[92] It is symptomatic of the enormous impact of Scott's work, however, that his characters also became so well known that they could enjoy a new life as cultural icons independent of any direct knowledge of Scott's writings. This meant that Jeanie became part of a creative commons *avant la lettre* or part of what Erll calls a 'collective text' that was no longer owned or controlled by Scott but open to new uses on the part of fans and admirers.[93] As David Brewer has argued, the tendency of readers to imaginatively expand on the lives of novelistic characters often clashed at this period with the desire of authors to impose their authorial control (a control all the more fraught by the decision to publish anonymously).[94] In the case of Scott, this tension was arguably compounded by the fact that his fictions drew on pre-existing narratives that were already part of cultural memory.

One way or another, the figure of Jeanie Deans ended up circulating independently of any particular narrative or drama. Indeed, Jeanie Deans operated in cultural spheres that had nothing to do with literature as such. As I indicated at the outset of this chapter, the name Jeanie Deans travelled from the domain of literature and became inscribed as a marker of cultural memory in material objects that were at the heart of modern economic life: from horticulture and transportation systems to hotels and hostelries. In this way she became what can best be described as a 'portable' memory site that could be carried over into new locations.

The prominence of Jeanie Deans, along with other Scott characters, is particularly noteworthy in the naming of ships and locomotives since it literally augments their mobility. The Mississippi was plied by a paddle steamer called *Jeanie Deans*, weighing 503 tonnes (built 1860) and another one weighing 485 tonnes (1852), both operating from St. Louis.[95] Several decades later, a fleet of steamers on the river Clyde, beginning in the 1880s, was called after various characters in Scott's *oeuvre,* and included the famous paddle-steamer *Jeanie Deans* built in 1931 (as if to drive the point home, the first-class lounge was furnished in light oak and with etchings from *The Heart of Mid-Lothian*). The same fleet also included a ship called *Waverley* that had a 'Jeanie Deans' lounge—this mixing up of different stories illustrates once more the way in which memories are dislocated from their original context and then collected

Figure 1.4: *PS-Jeanie Deans* (*c*.1931).

again to form composite and symbolically laden memory sites.[96] A similar pattern emerges in the development of the Scottish railway network: this included the famous railway station in Edinburgh (known as 'Waverley' since 1854); at least one train called after Scott himself, a type of locomotive called the 'Scott class', a 'Waverley route', and various generations of engines called after his characters including the ubiquitous Jeanie.[97] Going by the fact that new locomotives were given the names of secondary characters from Scott's work (Madge Wildfire, Vich Ian Vohr) as late as 1909, detailed knowledge of the novels could apparently be presumed right up to World War I.[98]

As I shall show in Chapter 5, Scott's work became caught up in complex ways with a new culture of mobility based on tourism and migration, a fact reflected in the use of his names on various forms of transport. But the literal ubiquity of Jeanie Deans was in the first place part and parcel of a more general invocation of Scott and his *oeuvre* as symbol of Scottish heritage or, perhaps even more generally, of heritage as such. Names like Jeanie Deans helped recall particular narratives in everyday spaces and material objects, and its recurrence can be construed

as a manifestation of 'banal canonicity' (by analogy with 'banal nationalism') as distinct from official commemorations.[99] For those who only had
a second-hand knowledge of the novels—through the theatre or popular
images, for example—the names of Jeanie Deans and company invoked a
generalized acquaintance with Scott's *oeuvre* or the idea of a common
(Scottish or literary) heritage. In this sense they are what Juri Lotman calls
'mnemonic symbols': symbols that do not so much recall the past as that
they remind us of a memory.[100] So long as its meaning was not entirely
eroded, Jeanie Deans helped to stamp the contemporary world with the
mark of the old and to 'plant' a synthetic memory in new suburban and
colonial spaces and on new economic endeavours.

Were an epidemiological study of the viral spread of Jeanie Deans
and similar Scott names across the English-speaking world ever possible,
it would provide insight into the spread of literature and its particular
role in the long nineteenth century as a common point of reference and,
linked to this, as a framework for the acculturation of new technologies
and new locations.[101] With the help of such markers, modernization
and urban renewal were connected up to cultural heritage and rooted in
existing traditions. In being carried over into new cultural situations and
linked with other aspects of Scottish life, the memory of Jeanie Deans
was perpetuated at the same time as it helped generate new forms of
heritage. The fact that Edinburgh's most famous football club should
carry the name Heart of Midlothian can be ascribed to a similar process
of mnemonic transfer even if present-day football fans no longer make the
connection in constructing the history of the club.[102] Both locomotive-
Jeanie and steamship-Jeanie have become established parts of the engineering heritage of Scotland and this, as an Internet search confirms, is
the object of much devoted study and remembrance on the part of
professional and amateur devotees. In this memorial layering, shared
points of reference both accrete and erode: where Jeanie Deans replaced
Helen Walker in 1818, the memory of a steam engine c.q. steamship
c.q. football club has subsequently overwritten Scott's character. The
affectionately written *Jeanie Deans 1931–1967: An Illustrated Biography*
refers to the steamship, not to the (imagined) woman who walked to
London.[103]

In all of these morphings, Jeanie Deans takes on a life as a cultural icon
that is rooted in *The Heart of Mid-Lothian* but takes place independently
of it. As a cultural icon her story is circulated in an ever reduced form,
however, and this means that, although her name is inscribed in various
cultural spheres, there is no guarantee that the original story of Jeanie
Deans, not to mention Helen Walker, will also be remembered. There is

evidence that the general public today is no longer as familiar with some of the more obscure characters from Scott as were those generations who travelled by steam train and to whom those Scott locomotives were addressed. Forgetting and memory loss are part of the evolution of cultural memory and at a certain point, some people will presumably know Jeanie Deans more as a lounge bar than as a Presbyterian. The fact that some memories are lost and others gained is not to suggest, however, that memorial dynamics are either linear or irrevocable. After all, Helen Walker has made a modest comeback even if she will be forever upstaged by her fictional counterpart—or rather upstaged as long as the name Jeanie Deans continues to ring a collective bell.

CONCLUSION

Jeanie's role as a communal point of reference is certainly diminished nowadays as compared to the first half of the nineteenth century. Scott's *oeuvre* no longer has the same social status it once had, when the Waverley novels connected people through their shared enthusiasm and helped define a public imagination based on a common repertoire of stories and characters. But *The Heart of Mid-Lothian* as such still remains a highly readable text for a contemporary audience—at least if you are not put off by the lengthy passages of dialect which even Scott's earliest readers found a bit difficult.[104] To be sure, the book has become dated in many ways, and Scott's apparent confidence in the existence of a natural justice whereby the good are rewarded and the bad dismissed seems naïve from the perspective of the twenty-first century. Nevertheless, my own reading has shown that the book, through its powers of description, dramatization, and characterization, can still engage a contemporary reader and interest her in the fate of eighteenth-century characters struggling to understand the nature of justice and rewards in a world as unsettled as our own. Furthermore, it arouses interest in the nineteenth-century world of Scott and in *his* agenda in 1818 as he struggled and ultimately failed to resolve in poetic form the tensions immanent in the history of Scotland.

Not everyone will share this appreciation of *The Heart of Mid-Lothian*, but the basic point remains: that Scott's works—by virtue of their poetical and fictional properties—have the potential to re-activate eroded memories in later generations and to implant new ones. Linked to this, they have the power to arouse interest in histories that are *not* one's own, in the history of groups with which one has not identified until now. As their early reception demonstrated, the Waverley novels were relayers of traditions, but also the source of new traditions and of a prosthetic memory that helped broaden the horizon of what people believed to be their heritage.

It was paradoxically because of its thoroughly *inauthentic* character that Scott's work had such a role to play in identity-building in the nineteenth century. Symptomatic of the latter was the term 'national drama' or 'Scotch drama' that figured on the playbills for *The Heart of Mid-Lothian*, especially in productions in Edinburgh and Glasgow.[105] This labelling of the dramatic versions of the novel indicates that they were playing a role in the articulation of collective identities through performances on the British stage, to which I will return in greater detail in Chapter 2. This particular labelling was largely absent from productions outside of Scotland—although it did occur occasionally at other locations (in Liverpool, for example).[106] It would appear that *The Heart of Mid-Lothian*, because of the use of dialect and highly localized settings, was somewhat less popular abroad than some of Scott's other works.[107] But the fact that there were productions at all outside of Scotland, along with many translations, indicates that there was nevertheless a widespread interest in the story, along with all of Scott's other works, on the part of people for whom this was not directly a 'national' tale. Scottish emigrants to the New World formed in this regard a distinct group (more on this in Chapter 5).

The Heart of Mid-Lothian, like other Waverley novels as we shall see, mobilized loyalty within an insider 'national' framework at the same time as it operated transnationally. It provided the imaginative conditions for stepping outside of one's own social framework and geographic horizon. Indeed this capacity to cross the borders of existing mnemonic communities is characteristic of literature and other works of art and provides a key to understanding its role in the formation of collective memory both in the nineteenth century and in more recent times (the same point might be made, for example, about recent historical fiction on Balkan history by such writers as Ismail Kadare and Danilo Kiš, readily available in translation and hence presumably in touch with a 'foreign' readership). The way in which uninterested parties become vicariously involved in the experience of others is as crucial to the elaboration of shared views of the past as the putatively spontaneous identification with one's own ethnic group.

The case of Jeanie Deans/Helen Walker shows some of the complexity of Scott's role in the dynamics of cultural remembrance. His fiction created memorability by depicting characters within the framework of a crafted narrative that invited appropriation and recollection, and migrated across texts, different media, and different communities. The novel has persisted as a stable artefact in the petrified manner of a monument, and at the same time it has continuously morphed almost to a point of non-recognition and at a speed that reflects the culture of rapid turnovers that Scott himself helped inaugurate. The fact that Jeanie Deans has ended up upstaging Helen Walker, and migrated from a novel to a steam engine, means that artificial—even patently untrue—memories crafted by writers may prove more tenacious in practice than those based on documented facts. This is an uncomfortable idea for historians, perhaps, but opens fascinating perspectives for cultural analysis.

2

Procreativity: Remediation and *Rob Roy*

As with genes, immortality is more a matter of replication than of the
longevity of individual vehicles.

—Daniel C. Dennett, *Darwin's Dangerous Idea* (1995)

In April 1819, the Covent Garden theatre advertised a play called *Heart of
Midlothian: Musical Drama* that would meet with enough public enthusiasm to run for sixteen nights. The daily playbills did not mention the
name of the playwright, but they did identify the person responsible for
the musical arrangements—'The Overture and Musick, which are selec-
tions from the most approved Scotch Airs, arranged by Mr Bishop'. They
also identified the artist responsible for painting the scenery: 'from
Sketches made by Alex. Nasmith, Esq of Edinburgh'. Apparently the
scenery was one of the distinctive selling points of this particular production, since the bills also listed the many locations that would be on display:
'Salisbury Craigs and Arthur's Seat, with Deans's cottage in the distance;
Deans's cottage on St. Leonard's Craigs . . . Hall of Tolbooth; Muschat's
Cairn; and Holyrood House . . . The High Street, with the Tolbooth, St
Giles's Church', and so on.[1]

This was one of the many theatrical productions of *The Heart of Mid-
Lothian* mentioned earlier and as such just one of the many hundreds of
productions of Scott's work that filled the British stage from the mid-
1810s onwards. The Covent Garden production in April 1819 was an
ephemeral affair lasting just a couple of weeks. But it was part of a larger
series of Scott productions that continued for almost a century in which
the novels were recursively transposed to the stage. Just as the books had
provided a public forum for reworking other stories, the theatre in turn
provided a platform for recycling the novels and giving them new life. In
this case, Scott's story, traditional music, and landscape painting combined to generate an atmosphere of pure Scottishness for a London
audience. Indeed, the importance of the Scottish scenery to this particular
production suggests that the theatrical spectacle was a variation on yet

another cultural practice: tourism (which was itself in part inspired by Scott's work, as I shall show in Chapter 5). Whether tourism was shaped by theatre or the other way around, it is clear that this theatrical production was caught up in an intermedial dynamic in which Scott's stories were both objects of appropriation and cultural agents: reproduced and transformed on many platforms with the encouragement of Scott himself, they were also helping to shape other cultural practices and inspire new work.

The combination of painting, music, scriptwriting, and acting offered by the theatre serves as a reminder that multimediality (the simultaneous use of different media) and intermediality (the cross-fertilization between media) are not recent phenomena. Nor did the convergence of media on a common platform have to wait for the arrival of the Internet: the popular theatre brought together and recycled elements from other platforms, as did indeed Scott's novels themselves.[2] These were both autonomous works of art and cultural cogwheels, caught up in the ongoing transfer of stories across different media and different platforms, in which both repetition and transformation were at play, and many agents involved, including Scott himself and his publishers. This bears emphasizing in view of the tenacious assumption among literary critics, not only that the proper unit of cultural analysis is a discrete text, but also that adaptations, imitations, and tie-ins are merely derivative forms of culture. My concern with the social life of texts entails breaking with this tradition by following the morphings of individual works as they travel to other media and by considering these derivative forms of production as interesting in their own right. In order to grasp the combination of innovation and repetition at work in such derivative forms, I will refer to productive remembrance (acts of recall that also involve producing a new image or story) and link it with what I have been calling Scott's procreativity: the ability of his works to generate new versions of itself in other people's acts of productive remembrance. Procreativity, as we shall see, produces unexpected continuities within a culture of rapid turnovers and ephemeral sensations. Linked to this, I shall argue, it also plays a distinct role in shaping collective identities by appealing to the familiar and the traditional, but in a modern guise and in an immediate way. These identities are based on the common appreciation of earlier stories and on maximizing the pleasurable interaction with them, rather than on the solemn recollection of political and military events.

REMEDIATING AND REMEMBRANCE

The usual way of judging the cultural impact of writers is by counting the number of new editions and sales figures. An alternative is to examine the intensity with which their work was replicated in other cultural expressions. In this regard, the Waverley novels had an astoundingly fertile second-life. The intensity and range of their productive reception by other people is testimony to their mnemonic power: they invited recall and set creative energies in motion to produce new paintings and plays, and indeed versions in almost every conceivable medium. One of the paradoxes of the popularity of the Waverley novels, as already indicated in the case of Jeanie Deans, is that they became common property and left the authorial control of their maker (although Scott, as we shall see in Chapter 6, was also feted as a cultural icon in his own right). The value of his fiction was not linked to auratic scarcity, but rather to communality. It enjoyed 'social canonicity', the term David Brewer uses with reference to popular fiction at this period, in which value was expressed by collective appropriation and proliferation in a maximum number of media.[3]

The challenge is to analyse this particular interplay between remembrance and creativity, between repetition and novelty. A starting point is offered by John Ellis, who once wrote in a very brief but illuminating essay that adaptations 'trade on the memory of the original' and represent 'a massive investment (financial and psychic) in the desire to repeat particular acts of consumption within a form of representation that discourages such a repetition'.[4] In many ways, Scott himself had set the ball rolling by becoming his own replicator and creating a new pleasure in repetition within the framework of constantly renewed novelty. He did so by presenting the Waverley novels as part of a series (itself revolutionary and a foretaste of much culture to come), and by producing novels that, while projecting highly distinctive narrative worlds, also resonated with each other and, as we have seen, with other stories already in circulation in oral history as well as in print. For all that each novel brought into life a new range of remarkable characters and situations held together by a unique storyline, they also represented variations on the same Waverley model—to the delight of many of his readers, to the dismay of some critics.[5] What is more, Scott's writings also gave rise to new versions in the form of images, dramatizations, costumes, tourist itineraries, architecture, interior decorating, as well as the names of places, ships, and railways mentioned earlier. This everyday remembrance reflected the penetration of the Waverley model into both private and public spheres, and the ubiquitous presence of the past that Scott himself had helped to cultivate.

Because of the traditional predilection of twentieth-century criticism for innovation and defamiliarization, and for those exceptional individuals who staked out the future rather than recycled the past, this enormous body of diverse material has not been studied in any integrated and extensive way (though happily there are some specialist studies of Scott's impact on painting and drama upon which I can draw). This neglect can be linked to the derivative and sometimes trivial character of many of these spin-offs and tie-ins, whose aesthetic merit and historic interest is moot. But it has certainly also to do with a general lack of conceptual tools within traditional literary criticism to talk about reiterations, repetitions, and gradual transformations in culture.[6] Given the all-out prioritizing of 'the first' above 'the repeated' in twentieth-century aesthetics, it is only recently that repetition and repetition-with-a-difference has emerged as an active ingredient in the making of culture and hence as an issue in cultural analysis. Things changed with the emergence since the 1960s of an academic critique of originality and continue to change with the growing salience of intertextuality, 'sampling', and 'covering' as dominant modes of cultural production in the digital age.[7] As our appreciation of these derivative forms increases, so too does the retrospective perception that reworking, recycling, and tie-ins were also an important feature of nineteenth-century culture, sometimes driven by a commercial desire to maximize the number of products from any given original, but sometimes also by a desire to prolong and intensify the memory of stories that had already given pleasure, while yet offering something new.[8] The importance of sampling is brought out in the following title published by Thomas Hailes Lacy in the 1860s with its extraordinary sedimentation of versions and agents, of replication and novelty: *The Heart of Mid-Lothian; or, the Sisters of St. Leonard's: A Drama, (with unregistered effects) in Three Acts. Adapted from Sir Walter Scott's admired novel, with introductions from T. Dibdin's play, W. Murray's alteration of the same, Eugène Scribe's opera, and Dion Boucicault's amalgamation of the above; Colin Hazlewood's adjustment and re-adjustment, J.B. Johnstone's appropriation, and other equally original versions, together with a very small amount of new matter* (London, *c.*1863).

As Linda Hutcheon's *Theory of Adaptation* (2006) clearly shows, recent attempts to analyse derivative (palimpsestic, second-hand) forms of cultural production have yielded a variety of concepts (intertextuality, appropriation, transcoding…) and a range of insights into what is at stake intellectually, aesthetically, and even legally, when a new work reworks an old one.[9] By and large, however, studies of adaptation (to stick with this umbrella term for the moment) have taken what I call a bilateral approach: that is to say, they focus on the relations between two versions of a story and, taking the later version as the *terminus ad quem* of the exchange, they examine the difference between the earlier and the later versions, often to the advantage of the latter, which, following a modernist narrative of progress, is often construed as a critical subversion of the original. While I draw in what follows on some recent studies of adaptation, my approach will nevertheless be significantly different. Since the concern of this study is not so much with the aesthetic effects of particular versions, but with how reworking Scott was an agent of cultural memory, its focus inevitably extends beyond the bilateral relations between discrete texts to the broader cultural landscape and to the long-term framework in which particular adaptations had both a prehistory and an afterlife. The point is not just to reiterate the over-familiar argument that there are no absolute origins in culture and no places of absolute stability since culture is always on the move. Instead, it is to take this fact as a starting point for locating different sorts of repetitions within the dynamics of change or, more specifically, for locating remembrance in a mode of production that was based on novelty. How to conceptualize adaptations in such a way that they are neither reduced to mere repetitions nor automatically assumed to be critical subversions of the original?

There is certainly evidence that Scott's works were picked up and reworked in a whole range of cultural practices, from the evening dresses in 'La mode écossaise' that were popular fashion statements in 1820s Paris, to the Waverley textiles that were designed to fill the interiors of neo-gothic houses inspired by Abbotsford, to the *tableaux vivants* of Waverley characters performed in private homes, to the hundreds of paintings, the many films, and the thousands of theatrical productions inspired by his work.[10] Although architecture, fashion, and place-names do not tradition-ally fall within the purview of literary criticism, they are impossible to ignore in the case of Scott. One of the claims of this study is that an important part of Scott's legacy lies in his having extended the life of the historical imagination to the material world (especially the urban and domestic worlds of middle-class readers) and to his having integrated memory into everyday, embodied life—down to the clothes people wore, the upholstery they sat on, and the games they played.[11] What began as poetry and narrative thus ended up in the way in which people named their streets, decorated their houses, and, later in the century with the production by the Wedgwood Company of an Ivanhoe dinner service, ate their meals.[12] In this way, his work helped to re-introduce signs of collective memory into the everyday environment, creating the banal canonicity referred to earlier. In contrast to traditional *milieux de mémoire*

Figure 2.1: *The Lady of the Lake*, printed cotton (*c.*1830).

in Pierre Nora's sense, however, this everyday memory was a highly mediated one in which the imagination played a key role, thus exemplifying Appadurai's contention that one of the key features of modernity is the fact that imagination is no longer confined to the arts and ritual, but informs everyday life.

It would be going too far to claim that Scott consciously envisaged how his stories would be translated into other media and practices. But he certainly colluded with it. Although he worked within the confines of the printed book, his use of language and narrative design seem to be already on the verge of turning into a piece of theatre, a painting, or even tourist excursion (to which I will return in more detail in Chapter 5). Because his depictions of the past were highly visual, he can be said to have helped imagine the paintings and spectacles, including the cinematic ones, to which his own work later gave rise.[13] Indeed, the term cinematographic can be legitimately applied *avant la lettre* to his depiction of the Porteous riots in *The Heart of Mid-Lothian* or the siege of Torquilstone castle in *Ivanhoe*. One reviewer of *The Lady of the Lake* (1810) exclaimed that Scott 'sees everything with a painter's eye',[14] a point echoed in 1834 with reference to the novels by a French critic who praised Scott for having 'drawn' all his scenes: 'Every one of [his] pages is a painting which one only has to reproduce.'[15] Certainly a scene such as that in *Waverley* where the romantic hero has a vision of Flora McIvor within a natural amphitheatre lent itself easily to the word *tableau*; and indeed Scott invited this comparison by comparing his character to one 'of those lovely forms which decorate the landscapes of Poussin'.[16]

The invitation to visualize the novels was eagerly taken up. To begin with, Scott and his publishers included engravings, specially commissioned from a team of artists, in the magnum opus edition of the Waverley novels (1829–33) so that later editions were usually accompanied by actual and not just virtual images. As Richard Hill has shown, Scott valued antiquarian and topographical accuracy as a visual auxiliary to his own narrative rather than illustrations of high drama that would have been a distraction from it, and tried to control the selection of images with this in mind.[17] The symbiosis between the novels and illustrations was facilitated by the introduction of cheap steel-plate engraving and it culminated in the lavishly illustrated Abbotsford Edition of 1842–7 that set a new trend in Victorian publishing.[18] This tendency to translate the stories into pictures also led to the publication of stand-alone collections of engravings supplementing the texts in the form of virtual art galleries. These offered portraits of the main characters, as in *The Waverley Gallery of the Principal Female Characters in Sir Walter Scott's Romances; From Original Paintings by Eminent Artists* (1841), but more often, they consisted of depictions of the locations associated with particular scenes in the novels and seen through the lens of the story; these included *Landscape-Historical Illustrations of Scotland and the Waverley Novels; from Drawings by J. M. W. Turner, Professor R.A.* (1836–8) and *Landscape-Historical Illustrations of the Waverley Novels* (1840).[19]

Outside the field of book publications, Scott's writings also gave rise to countless stand-alone drawings, engravings, and paintings both in Great Britain and elsewhere, especially France.[20] His work, according to Richard Altick, almost singlehandedly touched off a century-long tradition of 'literary landscapes' inspired by poetry and novels.[21] Painters continued to produce Scott paintings until the 1880s, while shifting in the process along with the fashions of the time from the aesthetics of sublime landscapes to historical drama, to genre painting. Thus Turner's drawings for the magnum opus edition of the novels gave way to Daniel Maclise's enormous historical tableaux of the 1840s and to the intimate scenes of John Everett Millais's *The Bride of Lammermoor* (1878) and James McNeill Whistler's *Arrangement in Yellow and Grey: Effie Deans* (1876–8). Although it lasted into the final decades of the century, as these last examples show, Scott's power to generate images reached its highpoint in the period 1830 to 1850 when more than four hundred paintings illustrating his works were exhibited. In 1843, for example, no fewer than thirty of such paintings appeared at the annual exhibition of the Royal Academy, the Scottish Academy, and the British Institution. At the Paris salon of 1831, thirty items were inspired by Scott, which was more than the number inspired by biblical or mythological themes.[22] Where the earlier visualizations of his work had concentrated on locations, took the form of engravings, and were largely inspired by his poems, the many paintings produced from the 1830s onwards followed the model of historical genre paintings, concentrating in full colour on characters at a dramatic moment in the action.[23]

In all this painterly activity recalling Scott's novels, selective mechanisms were nevertheless at work and these take some unravelling. Given *Waverley*'s prominence as a flagship of the series, for example, it is surprising to note that it inspired virtually no painting at all (nor did it inspire much dramatization, as we will see below). In contrast, scenes from *The Bride of Lammermoor* and *The Heart of Mid-Lothian* gave rise to no fewer than eighty paintings each. Their popularity was only surpassed by that of *Ivanhoe*, which was painted more than one hundred times. Moreover, within that Ivanhoe corpus pride of place was given to the figure of Rebecca, to whom a third of these paintings was devoted.[24] As we shall see, the preference of painters for certain works coincided to a large extent, but not entirely, with the preferences of dramatists. *Ivanhoe* was notably prominent in both spheres, a point I will come back to in Chapter 3. Even within the treatment of particular stories, moreover, there was selection going on: *The Heart of Mid-Lothian* has already shown how some scenes, such as the meeting of the two sisters in prison, were depicted over and over again, becoming iconic for the story as a whole. In some cases, popular images fed into theatrical productions in the form of costumes, decors, and *tableaux vivants,* while theatrical productions in turn inspired some of the popular images in circulation.[25]

While the paintings and drawings often circulated independently of the novels, they nevertheless 'traded upon the memory' of the original, to recall John Ellis's phrase. James McNeill Whistler was asked by the buyer of his Effie Deans painting to add Scott's words to the canvas: 'she sunk her head upon her hand and remained seemingly unconscious as a statue'.[26] The painting (now with words added) was a trigger to recall Scott's work at the same time as it also offered the visual delights of a painting in the here and now. The addition of the words in the case of Whistler's painting made explicit a mechanism that was surely behind all of the other Scott paintings: these were both autonomous visual artefacts, interesting in their own right, and cues recalling a story that was told elsewhere and whose broad outlines were presumed familiar to the viewer even if they did not necessarily have direct knowledge of the text. As the painterly shift of focus to Effie indicates, 'trading on the memory' of the novel also involved modifying it to fit latter-day preoccupations: in remediating and recalling the story, people were also adapting it to current notions of what was memorable.

When Scott's contemporaries highlighted the visual qualities of his writings and claimed excitedly that they were suitable for reproduction as paintings, they were intuitively operating from an understanding of the relations between the different arts that resonates with more recent theories, which see media as interrelated rather than as discrete systems, and as continuously emergent rather than stable. The most thorough-going elaboration of this emergence view of mediation is offered in Jay Bolter and Richard Grusin's seminal *Remediation: Understanding New Media* (2000), which argues that every act of mediation (that is, every attempt to describe the world) is always already an act of remediation (that is, a re-working of an earlier attempt, not necessarily using the same technologies). Cultural dynamics are thus driven by the constantly renewed effort to create a greater sense of immediacy with the help of new techniques and representational technologies. In the process, media are continuously 'commenting on, reproducing, and replacing each other' since they 'need each other in order to function as media at all'.[27]

Up to a point the theory of remediation provides a model for the analysis of the productive remembrance of Scott's work and the complex interplay between word, image, material culture, and performative practices that it entailed. The history of his afterlife in other media runs parallel to the history of modern media technologies: steel engravings, dioramas, photography, magic lanterns, and, from the twentieth century on, film, radio, television, computer games.[28] The emergence of new technologies over the decades seems indeed to have continuously stimulated fresh adaptations by providing new possibilities for revivifying the story. Bolter and Grusin link remediation exclusively, however, to the desire to produce new sensations and they view cultural history as an asymptotic, ever-renewed gravitation towards the production of immediacy with the help of technology. The evidence collected here shows, however, that remediations of Scott were caught up in complex ways with remembering rather than overwriting earlier stories; while they fed into a desire for the sensation of immediacy (and this makes them highly modern), they did so while evoking the memory of a story told in another medium. Immediacy and recollection worked together or, to put this in media-theoretical terms, remediation worked together with premediation: the shaping force of an earlier narrative on new productions.[29] Productive remembrance needs to be seen as caught up between the old and the new, and bound up with the desire to appropriate the old in such a way as to make it fit into contemporary interests.

In what follows, I describe some of this complexity by examining adaptations of Scott's work in one particular medium: the theatre, where 'liveness' was bound up with the recycling of stories, paintings, and other expressions. It was also the most popular, if most ephemeral platform when it came to remediations of Scott's works in the nineteenth century. How did performance (the unique immediacy of things happening in the here and now) connect to the remembrance of things read or heard elsewhere? I argue that the liveness of theatre provided a platform for performing identity and memory in a non-historicizing mode.

STAGING SCOTT

As part of a general performative turn in the humanities, theatricality and the popular theatre have recently come into critical focus as key elements of nineteenth-century cultural life in Great Britain.[30] Within this framework, the afterlife of Scott's work must be sought not only in reading, but also on the stage where it had a salient role in the ninety-odd years between the publication of *Waverley* and the first feature films of the

1910s.[31] The theatre played an important role in disseminating novelistic works among urban groups who, because of limitations in education or income, would otherwise have had little access to them. In some cases the theatrical scripts were themselves the basis for new chapbook editions of the Waverley novels, which further extended their social reach.[32] The dramatizations also generated the publication of 'Musical illustrations' to the novels on a par with the compilations of landscape drawings.[33] For those theatre audiences who had not actually read the novels in question, but knew them by reputation as part of what Ellis calls 'general cultural memory',[34] watching the plays was a substitute for reading and, as the playbills often suggested, a way of putting a story in dramatic form to the name of a famous book. For those groups who had access both to the novels and to the theatre, the latter could serve to recall the original through the lenses of the drama, with all the sensual immediacy of a live performance, something that during the best part of the century was likely to be a fairly noisy and crowded affair.[35]

In view of the important role attributed to newspapers and novels in generating imagined communities in the nineteenth century, the fact that the theatre provided a continuing forum for face-to-face contacts within an urban setting is sometimes overlooked. David Worrall has shown with respect to the Georgian era that the theatres provided an important platform for sociability, giving rise to subcultural networks within the larger cities that, in some cases, worked as an alternative public sphere.[36] In an age when television had not yet been imagined and panoramas or dioramas were the best alternative, theatres also offered a platform for re-enacting events from recent history in the mode of grand spectacle: thus the coronation ceremony of George IV in Westminster Abbey in 1820 was re-enacted in tableau form every night on a weekly basis just as some of the sea battles against Napoleon's forces were replayed on stage 'with real Men of War and Floating Batteries'. Scott's own funeral would be transposed to the stage in the form of a funerary masque in 1832. The step from the theatrical stage to the staging of public life was a small one.

That being said, the value of theatrical versions of contemporary events seems to have lain not in their news value as such, but in their character as a spectacle to be enjoyed collectively as a sensual experience and, as one advertisement put it, to produce 'an unprecedented climax of astonishment and applause'.[37] In advance of the great spectacles of the Victorian Age (exemplified by the Great Exhibition of 1851 and the Crystal Palace), the theatre was the venue for collectively shared displays, with live performance in an impressive setting as important as the story being related.[38] So strong was the visual component in one Scott production that a critic complained in 1826 that in time, 'Old Drury will be called the Dramorama.'[39]

Scott was a very active supporter of the Theatre Royal in Edinburgh, even reputed to have aroused Scottish theatre 'from lethargy and stagnation'.[40] He also attended productions of the Waverley plays in various locations, and wrote about the theatre. It is all the more surprising, then, given his immense success in so many other fields from poetry to antiquarianism, and the presence of so many theatrical elements in his fiction, that he had little talent or inclination for play-writing.[41] His imagination was apparently more suited to the looser form of the romance than to the rigours imposed by a brief performance, and to writing rather than performance as such. The closest he came to theatrical success was his orchestration of George IV's spectacular visit to Edinburgh in 1822, which has been described as an adaptation to the theatre of public life of the story of Waverley. With lavish displays of tartan that extended even to the person of the king, the distinctiveness of Scottish culture was celebrated hyperbolically even as the political union with England was being acted out again.[42] As the Royal Visit illustrates, and as I shall show in more detail in Chapters 4 and 6, the theatre and public life were closely interlinked in a century when public processions and mass meetings were more regular occurrences than has been traditionally recognized.

If Scott himself was no playwright, his *oeuvre* triggered a staggering amount of theatrical productions, including the many versions of *The Heart of Mid-Lothian* mentioned earlier. From 1816 on, when Daniel Terry staged a version of *Guy Mannering*, almost all the Waverley novels were put on stage within months of being published. Whenever a new novel seemed imminent, dramatists jostled to get hold of the manuscript or advance copies of the book so as to score a première (indeed, Scott is known to have helped his friend Terry in this way).[43] While it became quite common to dramatize fiction in the nineteenth century (novels by Dickens and the Brontës, for example, also made it very quickly to the stage), the sheer number of theatrical productions inspired by Scott has been surpassed only by productions of Shakespeare.[44] In *Scott Dramatized* (1992), H. Philip Bolton provides evidence for more than four thousand theatrical productions derived from Scott's works in the course of the nineteenth century in Great Britain and North America, some of which have been mentioned in Chapter 1; Barbara Bell has analysed more than five thousand Scott playbills relating to productions in Scotland alone.[45] The crest of that theatrical tsunami followed on the initial publication of the novels and lasted throughout the 1820s and 1830s. But even with the ebbing of this tide, Scott plays continued to be performed for the best part of a hundred years, albeit more selectively: there were several new scripts and libretti produced up to the 1890s and a smaller peak in productions in the 1870s, presumably as part of the renewed attention to Scott as a cultural monument on the occasion of his centenary.[46] In the twentieth century, cinema and television (and to a lesser extent, radio) took over as a forum, though they did so, as we shall see later, with reference to an ever more reduced repertoire. This vast body of theatrical activity has been charted, but with a couple of exceptions, not yet studied in much depth.

The multimedial character of the stage performances is indicated by the ubiquitous use of 'melodrama', 'musical drama', 'musical play', 'romantic opera', and 'operatic romance' in the subtitles of the Scott adaptations. The proliferation of terms is also symptomatic of the diversity, both social and artistic, of the theatrical productions of the Waverley novels. When Scott's fiction first appeared in print, the only theatres licensed by law to put on serious drama, i.e. based on the spoken word, were the so-called legitimate or 'patent' theatres (including the Theatre Royals at Drury Lane and Covent Garden).[47] This left the many other theatres emerging throughout Great Britain to specialize in performances where the spoken word was subordinated to other forms of theatricality. In practice the divisions between the serious and the popular theatres were less strict than the law envisaged and than some more high-minded critics, regretting the absence of a thriving literary theatre, would have liked.[48] The corpus of Scott productions indicates that varying combinations of script, music, and spectacle occurred across the board, both in the popular and in the legitimate theatres (a legal distinction that was dropped in 1843).[49] The Scott dramatizations were so influential in the long term, according to Barbara Bell, because they helped give the non-patented theatres a 're-spectable, semi-legitimate' repertoire that was based in literature.[50] As we have already seen in the case of *The Heart of Mid-Lothian* the theatrical productions were often the occasion for tie-ins in the form of chapbook versions of the stories. Here too we see how the Waverley phenomenon operated in a translation zone at the interface between 'high' and 'low' culture.

With varying degrees of emphasis, music was a key component of theatrical productions in the 1820s as were the spectacular settings, the latter morphing into the sensationalist aesthetics of high Victorian melo-drama as well as into grand opera. In his classic study *The Melodramatic Imagination* (1985), Peter Brooks argued that a 'mode of excess', arising from the non-verbal aesthetics of the illegitimate theatres, penetrated all walks of theatrical and literary life throughout the nineteenth century, and cut across distinctions between the serious and the popular.[51] While the aesthetics described by Brooks defined the basic theatrical language of the Scott dramatizations, one should be wary of lumping all productions together since they served different groups of theatre-goers. There was also considerable generic range: 'international' opera in the Italian style, spectacular melodrama with huge production values, sensationalist melodrama in Victorian style, and circus-like acts with live animals (as in Astley's Amphitheatre, which was in operation from the late eighteenth century up to 1895). Symptomatic of their position between a literary culture increasingly protected by copyright and a popular culture serving a growing urban population was the fact that these various dramatic versions were regularly (re)composed on a cut-and-paste method from earlier plays, stories, and musical events, forming compositional medleys whose authorship was multiple and often anonymous.[52] There are some two hundred and fifty published Scott scripts extant, along with many songbooks derived from the theatrical productions.[53] There were probably other unpublished versions but these can no longer be traced since the records of performance do not always indicate the name of the playwright.

In tracking Scott's immense and long-lasting ripples into the world of theatre, I have been fortunate, as mentioned earlier, in being able to draw on the treasure-trove of information offered in Bolton's *Scott Dramatized*. I have also benefited from Jerome Mitchell's *Walter Scott Operas* (1977) and *More Walter Scott Operas* (1996), whose accumulative titles already speak volumes about the proliferation involved (arguably because of their association with classical music and high culture, the Scott operas have been studied in more detail than the plays).[54] Mitchell has identified no fewer than ninety operas inspired by Scott, some of which were key in circulating Scott's stories across Europe: *The Lady of the Lake* is by now best known internationally through the mediation of Rossini's *Donna del Lago* (1819), while *The Bride of Lammermoor* is remembered through Donizetti's *Lucia* (1835), a staple of the modern international operatic repertoire. Versions in which classical music was not the dominant mode (i.e. the vast majority of the Scott plays that are my focus here) would seem to have been largely confined to the English-speaking world.[55] Conversely, the operatic versions by Rossini, Donizetti, and other Europeans were less widespread in England than the other dramatic forms and, as Christina Fuhrman has shown in a recent article called 'Scott Repatriated', were greeted with some reticence in London as European appropriations of what had come to be seen as distinctly British heritage.[56]

Particularly in the 1820s and 1830s it was not uncommon for various Waverley plays to be offered in British theatres side by side as part of an evening programme; for example, patrons of the Theatre Royal in Glasgow were treated to both *The Heart of Mid-Lothian* and *Rob Roy* on 30 December 1826 while patrons of the Theatre Royal in Edinburgh were offered a double bill of *Waverley* and *The Heart of Mid-Lothian* on

23 February 1830.[57] Nor was it uncommon for two versions of the same play to run concurrently at different theatres—in March 1825 citizens in Edinburgh could choose between two versions of *Rob Roy*, one at the Theatre Royal, the other at the Caledonian; as late as February 1863, patrons in London could choose between two *Hearts of Mid-Lothian:* Dion Boucicault's *The Trial of Effie Deans; or, the Heart of Midlothian* at Astley's Theatre Royal and, across the river at the Surrey Theatre, an anonymous *Effie Deans: or, The Lily of St. Leonard's*.[58] Given all these different versions multiplied by the number of productions and performances at multiple locations, it is difficult to assess the scale of these activities and their social penetration. But even the most conservative estimates point to a major cultural phenomenon that, with only a couple of notable exceptions, has been allowed to pass under the radar screen of literary critics and even of theatre historians, its existence noted, if at all, as a curious form of cultural pathology.[59]

For some theatregoers the plays may have been the first or only encounter with the Waverley novels, though there is incidental evidence showing that some people attended more than one stage version of the same play or went back to see the same production twice. William Hazlitt, for example, attended the two versions of *Ivanhoe* running concurrently at Drury Lane and Covent Garden in 1820 and wrote up a comparative analysis for the *London Magazine* in which he intimated his desire to go back and see the Drury Lane production.[60] One enthusiast complained of a Glasgow production of *Rob Roy* in 1840 that 'although we have seen it [Rob Roy] played above two hundred times, including in its casts all sorts of persons, from Macready to Mumford, an [*sic*] in all sorts of places—theatre, barn, and booth, we never saw it more wretchedly performed.'[61] The wording suggests that this patron's disgruntlement was with the quality of the performance rather than with the fact it was the umpteenth production of *Rob Roy* that he had attended. After all, new productions and live performances meant that the play was continuously being renewed in contrast to the more fixed form of books and films.

The playbills advertising such productions regularly invoked Scott's reputation, with references to the 'celebrated' author or the 'celebrated' novel. It was quite common, however, for the performance to be presented without any explicit reference to Scott while assuming that the public knew they were dealing with a new version of an old story. Very quickly Scott's stories seem to have acquired the status of collective texts and were treated as common property, although in this case they also retained their association with the pseudo-anonymous 'author of Waverley'. As Isaac Pocock wrote in 1820 in the preface to the printed edition of his version of *Rob Roy*, his contemporaries expected fidelity to the novel and to the 'name of Walter Scott'—a direct, but not unique reference to Scott himself that is all the more striking in view of the fact that he had not officially declared his authorship:

the whole of the novel-reading world, in which is included nine tenths of the audience, come with the romance at their fingers' ends, and expect to find a literal transcript of it on the stage; the whole three volumes, the usual quantum in which these popular works are doled out, must be spoken and acted in three brief hours, or at least without any material deviations. Any aberration from the direct broad road of romance, is considered a high crime and misdemeanour against the name of Walter Scott.[62]

Playbills from the late 1810s on seemed also to suppose a rough knowledge of the main outlines of the story since they unhesitatingly revealed the outcome of the drama and regularly enumerated the various scenes that the public could look forward to enjoying along with the musical interludes. The pleasure on offer apparently lay, then, in the fresh re-enactment of something that was already known rather than in the unfolding of something unpredictable. This is borne out by the fact that critics—and judging by the passage just quoted above, the audiences— usually evaluated the success of the production in terms of its fidelity or lack of it with respect to the original novel and, as time passed, also with respect to earlier productions. Only on rare occasions did Waverley playwrights break so free from the memory of the original as to be evaluated on their own merits as autonomous dramas. This did happen a generation after the first adaptations in the case of Boucicault's *The Trial of Effie Deans* (1863), which reduced the whole of Scott's rambling novel to a courtroom drama.[63] The London *Times* praised the playwright for having 'endeavoured to construct a drama that will create an interest independent of its connexion with the novel' in contrast to the other version at the Surrey Theatre, running at the same time, which was both more faithful to the original and more spectacular in its appeal.[64] While the reviewer from the *Times,* perhaps suffering from a spot of Waverley fatigue, implicitly preferred Boucicault's innovations to his rival's fidelity to the memory of Scott, the crowd at the Surrey seems to have had no such desire to change a winning horse. Having been treated to a scaffold on stage along with 'a huge cataract of real water, which falls from nearly the top of the stage and really breaks against the craggy rocks at the bottom', the 'mass of humanity that crowded every part of the theatre burst out into an uproarious demonstration of satisfaction at the termination of the drama.'[65]

So far I've been referring to the Waverley novels as if they were uniformly procreative in the theatre. But there were important differences between them and these are worth considering as indications of the way in which the theatrical medium filtered, channelled, and promoted memories. Bolton shows that five novels in particular—*Rob Roy, Guy Mannering, The Bride of Lammermoor, The Heart of Mid-Lothian*, and *Ivanhoe*—inspired almost two-thirds of the Waverley productions, with more than half accounted for by *Rob Roy* and *Guy Mannering* alone. The popularity presumably also worked accumulatively, with success breeding success and later productions mixing and matching the successful features of earlier ones. For reasons that have yet to become clear some works fell out of the picture while others, like *Guy Mannering*, enjoyed an intense afterlife on the stage but not elsewhere. I shall come back to some possible explanations later. Suffice it here to recall that the first novel to fall by the theatrical wayside was *Waverley* itself. Despite the symbolic importance of the name, *Waverley* (1814) generated few paintings, as has been noted already, and it only gave rise to three dozen or so theatrical productions, beginning in 1822 (that is, after the other novels had been dramatized) and ending in the 1870s. It generated just one operatic version, Holstein's *Hochländer* (1876), which led a tenuous life until its last revival in 1900.[66] Unlike other works, moreover, *Waverley* did not even enjoy the honour of being parodied. Most surprising of all, there has never been a production of *Waverley* in film or television (nor, as far as I have been able to establish, on radio).[67] Despite the fact that it gave its name to streets across the globe, as mentioned earlier, and became the icon of Walter Scott and all his works, the story of Waverley never crossed over into drama. This may have been because the novel was the first one and difficult to adapt to the stage; but since the latter didn't stop playwrights in other cases, it seems more plausible to look to the fact that it arrived too soon to ride the dramatizing wave and was so quickly overtaken by *Guy Mannering* (1815) and *Rob Roy* (1817) that it was less subject to remembrance in its own right.[68] The afterlife of each work followed its own trajectory.

An analysis of all this material would take a lifetime. I have opted to concentrate instead in what follows on the dramatizations of the most popular of all the plays, *Rob Roy*. The intensity with which it was produced over and over again up to World War I, especially in the Scottish theatres, offers a unique perspective on the cultural resonance of Walter Scott and a key to 'live' theatre as a medium of cultural remembrance.

ROB ROY

On the last evening of his visit to Edinburgh, King George IV attended a performance at the Theatre Royal of *Rob Roy; or, Auld Langsyne; National*

Opera.[69] A wet night it was and a very crowded theatre, as James Dibdin recalled the occasion in his *Annals of the Edinburgh Stage*:

Inside the house the crush was intense, while matters were made infinitely worse by the cloud of steam that ascended from the saturated garments of those present. Good humour, however, prevailed, and Scotch songs were sung in chorus to pass the time away until the arrival, about 7.30 of the box occupants.[70]

When the king arrived and the curtain rose, the chorus of Scottish songs turned into an enthusiastic singing (*con amore*, as Dibdin put it) of 'God Save the King'. That it should have been *Rob Roy* above all that was used on such a politically sensitive occasion is indicative both of its popularity and of the status it had acquired as a specifically 'national' opera. This status would be maintained for a long time: a century later in 1962, when the King of Norway came on a state visit to Edinburgh in the company of the British Royal Family, it was again *Rob Roy* that was put on for their majestic benefit.[71] Although by that time neither the play nor the theatre enjoyed the same popularity as in 1822, it was apparently felt appropriate to perform *Rob Roy* once again, not as a matter of current fashion or taste, but rather as part of a self-reflexive tradition of performing Scottishness and 'conveying' it at home and to the outside world.[72]

Although there are relatively few visualizations of the novel *Rob Roy* extant, there is no doubt but that it dominated the stage, especially in Scotland.[73] Between its first stage appearance in early 1818 and the most recent one in 1990, the story of the eighteenth-century Scottish outlaw, whose career was embroiled in both modern economic life and Jacobite rebellion, has been produced almost one thousand times.[74] The hundreds of programme bills extant, advertising both new productions and revivals of old ones, often invoked the 'popular novel', the 'very popular novel', or the 'highly-admired novel' on which the play was based ('founded on the popular novel of Rob Roy'; 'founded on the highly esteemed work of the late Sir Walter Scott').[75] While the memory of the novel and its author was regularly invoked with various degrees of solemnity, the name of the dramatist was only seldom mentioned. But it seems probable that the vast majority of these anonymous versions were based on a single version: Isaac Pocock's *Rob Roy MacGregor; or, Auld Lang Syne! A musical drama, in three acts, founded on the popular novel of Rob Roy, first performed at the Theatre-Royal, Covent-Garden, Thursday, March 12, 1818* (London: John Miller, 1818).

In a rare appearance, Pocock turned up in an 1879 advertisement for a Rob Roy 'dramatized by Isaac Pocock with the consent and approval of SIR WALTER SCOTT'.[76] There is no evidence that this version had been officially endorsed by Scott, as the playbill claimed, but the invoca-

W. 16.   THEATRE-ROYAL, EDINBURGH.   N. 96.

FIFTH NIGHT THIS SEASON OF ROB ROY.

This present Evening, WEDNESDAY, March 7. 1821,   87a

Will be performed, for the 5th Time this Season, the National Opera of

ROB ROY MACGREGOR,
OR
AULD LANGSYNE.

WITH THE ORIGINAL MUSIC, SCENERY, MACHINERY, DRESSES, AND DECORATIONS.

The Opera written by J. Pocock, Esq. Author of The Miller and his Men, For England Ho, &c. &c.
The Vocal Music selected from the National Melodies of Scotland.—The Poetry partly Selected from the Works of Burns.
The Medley National Overture and Marches composed, selected, and arranged by Davy.
The Scenery designed by Mr Pyett, and by Mr Grieve, of the Theatre-Royal, Covent-Garden,
and Executed by them, Mr William Grieve, and numerous Assistants.
The Dresses and Decorations by Mr Marshall, Mrs Garbutt, and their Assistants.
The Machinery invented by, and under the entire Superintendance of Mr Ronaldson.
Sir Frederick Vernon by Mr ANDERSON—Rashleigh Osbaldiston by Mr ALEXANDER,
Francis Osbaldiston by Mr HUCKEL,
Mr Owen by Mr ROBERTS—Captain Thornton, Mr W. MURRAY—Major Galbraith by Mr WEEKES,
Rob Roy Macgregor Campbell by Mr CALCRAFT—Bailie Nicol Jarvie by Mr MACKAY,
MacStewart by Mr DENHAM—Jobson by Mr BELL—Dougal by Mr DUFF,
Willie by Master RONALDSON—Andrew by Mr AIKIN—Lancie by Mr DOUGLAS,
Sergeant by Mr STANLEY—Sanders Wylie by Mr LEE,
Highlanders by Messrs Lawson, Lorimer, Reinard, Charteris, Robb, Belsham, Orrock, Blenheim, Burgess, Stormont, Lennox, Cross
Grange, Simpson, Johnston, Waters, Thomson, Hastie, Laing, Williamson, Rogers, Barclay, Bremner, &c. &c.
Travellers by Messrs Gordon, Guise, Gairdner, Holmes, Harrison, Heavyside, Horton, Keswick, Kremlin, Kant, Lindsay, Sanderson,
Lennox Troopers by Messrs Broadhurst, Sandilands, Robertson, and Macnewson,
English Soldiers by Messrs Grant, Heath, Thomson, Donald, Meldrum, Marshall, Reid, Sandilands, and Robb Rutherford, Veitch, &c.
Helen Macgregor by Mrs RENAUD,
Martha by Miss M. NICOL—Mattie by Miss NICOL—Hostess by Mrs MACKAY—Jean M'Alpine by Mrs NICOL,
Diana Vernon by Miss ROCK.

In Act Second, Miss C. NICOL will perform a favourite PAS SEUL to the National Air of

THE BLUE BELLS OF SCOTLAND.

The Scenery will be exhibited in the following Succession:

ACT the FIRST.	ACT the SECOND.
1. INTERIOR of VILLAGE INN.	1. THE COLLEGE GARDENS of GLASGOW.
2. LIBRARY IN OSBALDISTON HALL.	AND VIEW of THE SPIRE of St MUNGO.
3. ROOM IN BAILIE NICOL JARVIE's.	2. LIBRARY IN OSBALDISTON HALL.
4. THE OLD BRIDGE of GLASGOW.	3. INTERIOR of JEAN M'ALPINE's CHANGE HOUSE.
5. HALL IN GLASGOW TOLBOOTH.	4. THE CLACHAN of ABERFOYLE.
6. CELL IN THE TOLBOOTH of GLASGOW.	AND DISTANT VIEW of THE HIGHLAND LOCH.

ACT the THIRD.

1. THE PASS of LOCHARD.	3. INTERIOR of JEAN M'ALPINE's CHANGEHOUSE.
2. ROMANTIC GLEN IN THE HIGHLANDS.	4. VIEW ON LOCH LOMOND, MOONLIGHT.

At the End of the Play, Miss M. NICOL will perform a Favourite PAS SEUL.

To which will be added, in consequence of its having been received with unbounded Applause on Saturday last,
the favourite Farce of

THE CRITIC,
OR A TRAGEDY REHEARSED.

Sir Fretful Plagiary by Mr TERRY—Puff by Mr JONES,
Dangle by Mr W. MURRAY—Sneer by Mr ROBERTS—Prompter by Mr BELL—Servant by Mr AIKIN,
Mrs Dangle by Mrs EYRE.
Characters in the Tragedy.—Lord Burleigh by Mr MACKAY—Earl of Leicester by Mr DENHAM,
Sir Walter Raleigh by Mr LEE—Sir C. Hatton by Mr DUFF—Don Ferola Whiskerandos by Mr ALEXANDER,
Governor of Tilbury Fort by Mr ANDERSON—Beefeater by Mr WEEKES—1st Centinel, Mr AIKIN—2d Centinel, Mr STANLEY,
Tilburina by Mrs NICOL—Confidant by Mrs MACKAY—1st Neice by Miss NICOL—2d Neice by Miss J. NICOL.

☞ From the Applause which last Night attended the Performance of

HENRI QUATRE,

As an Afterpiece, it will be repeated To-Morrow and Saturday Evenings.

To-Morrow Evening, The ANTIQUARY.
On Friday, a Variety of Entertainments.
On Saturday, will be revived Shakespeare's AS YOU LIKE IT.

Figure 2.2: Playbill *Rob Roy*, Theatre Royal (1821).

tion of the Great Man's authority implies that Pocock's version was seen as somehow the 'official' or canonical one. The fact that Pocock's script was often republished (there were eight editions up to 1864) is also indicative of its popularity as the basis for new productions.[77] There was no other obvious rival, the only other published versions being George Soane's *Rob*

Roy: A Drama in Three Acts (1818) and the burlesque *Robbing Roy; or, Scotched and Kilt* (1879), neither of which was produced very often. But the most important indication of Pocock's influence is in the titles given to the many productions which, by and large, carry a variation on his subtitle with the tell-tale inclusion of *Auld Lang Syne.*

What made Pocock's play stick in the public's mind? Scott had provided a portrait of commercial life in Glasgow that was recognizable to a middle-class public, while at the same time he tapped into a vibrant interest in Rob Roy among the public at large; his publishers had also whetted the appetites of the public by re-circulating some of the familiar legends in advance of the novel's appearance.[78] Rob Roy, before ever he became the figurehead of Scott's novel, was something of a celebrity and had, among other things, given his name to a play staged in Durham as recently as 1810.[79] This interest in Rob Roy was itself also part of a certain vogue for outlaw figures in the popular culture of the time; witness the renewed interest in the figure of Robin Hood, whose ubiquity in this period has been well mapped (indeed Stephen Knight has suggested that the appearance of Scott's *Rob Roy* may in turn have inspired another novel called *Robin Hood*, which appeared in 1819).[80] That the two outlaws were linked in the popular imagination—one working as an avatar for the other around a basic narrative of resistance—is borne out by William Wordsworth's poem 'Rob Roy's Grave' (1803), which predates Scott's novel by a decade and begins with a comparison between the two men: 'A famous man is Robin Hood | the English ballad-singer's joy! | And Scotland has a thief as good | An outlaw of as daring mood; | She has her brave ROB ROY!' Scott's novel had resonated with these deep-seated stories of banditry—what might be called the popular memory of bandits—while giving them a renewed and culturally legitimate impulse. Reflecting this interplay between literary culture and popular memory, the novel and its theatrical versions together generated new spin-offs in the form of chapbooks and ballads.[81]

Since Pocock stuck quite close to the novel (and relative to other Waverley dramatizations, he used extensive dialogue) his play drew its imaginative appeal from Scott's original exploration of the interface between the worlds of Glasgow, London, and the Highlands. Up to a point, then, his success was merely a matter of his riding on the crest of the novel's success, inheriting the imaginative power of the novel along with its deeper roots in popular memory. In adapting the novel, Pocock also demonstrated considerable skill as a playwright. He succeeded in transposing Scott's lengthy and unwieldy romance into the confines of a three-act drama without deviating on any major points from the original (this again in contrast to George Soane's version, which had appeared almost simultaneously in 1818 but was deemed to have so far deviated from the 'popular novel' as to have made the latter unrecognizable).[82] Pocock reduced the number of characters while giving a prominent place to the comic ones alongside Rob Roy; he condensed certain incidents in the plot, channelled the actors towards the same locations, and began *in medias res* when Rashleigh Osbaldistone had already engineered the downfall of the family firm. The broad lines of the plot are nevertheless maintained and indeed some of its inconsistencies are ironed out with only a few of Scott's many threads left dangling. Given the limitations of the dramatic medium this was itself something of an achievement, as was the colourful dialogue, which allowed room for some great character-acting, particularly in the role of the Bailie Nicol Jarvie. This was to become something of a famous set-piece for actor Charles Mackay (the origin of the 'Real McKay', according to Bolton) of whose performances it was said: 'it is not acting, it is reality.'[83]

Beyond its qualities as a play and the effective acting, what seems to have clinched the success of Pocock's version was its music. The history of the many stage productions of *Rob Roy* is above all a history of the songs that accompanied it. It was, as the subtitle put it, a 'musical drama'—literally, a melodrama. The melodramatic in this case, however, was less a matter of Brooks' 'aesthetics of excess' and the abundant use of pathetic tableaux, than it was a matter of embedding musical interludes in the narrative. In some later productions indeed the generic label shifted to 'operatic drama', 'musical play', and even 'opera'.[84] From the word go, songs were inserted into the script, many of which had been composed from well-known poems and set to traditional Scottish airs by John Davy and Henry Bishop. The lyrics were only tangentially connected to the narrative, but this was not a compositional problem within a theatrical framework that accommodated medleys and 'variety' more easily than a long and continuous script. The *Auld Lang Syne* that was such a fixed feature in the plays' titles referred of course to Burns' song, which already thematized the injunction to remember (and specifically to collectively remember this moment): 'Should auld acquaintance be forgot, and never brought to mind?' Repeated from one production to the next Burns' *Auld Lang Syne* became a signature song for the play itself—indeed, Bolton argues that the cultural longevity of the song that has since become a fixed feature of New Year's celebrations in the English-speaking world was generated by the success of the Rob Roy play.[85]

The various productions were built up around a fixed repertoire of songs that included, along with *Auld Lang Syne*, *My Love is like a Red, Red Rose* (also from Burns), and *A Famous Man was Robin Hood* (based on the poem by Wordsworth). These, together with the opening song *Soon the Sun will Gae to Rest* and the closing song *Pardon Now the Bold Outlaw* were regular features in productions—a degree of 'stickiness' that is surprising in view of the cut-and-paste aesthetics evidenced in many of the other Waverley plays where scripts tended to be continuously modified from one production to the next. In the case of *Rob Roy*, the fixed items on the musical menu were regularly supplemented by other songs, usually selected from a repertoire of traditional Scots airs or from other Waverley plays (though it is interesting to note the addition of a popular Irish air—Thomas Moore's *Minstrel Boy*—at a performance in Dublin in 1851).[86] As the programme bills indicate, each production sold itself in effect on the songs it had on offer: whereas in other plays, the tableaux were advertised, in the case of *Rob Roy* it was above all the musical interludes and, to a lesser extent, the dances and actors that were important.[87] The public was promised both a play and a medley of familiar songs that were almost invariably coded as Scottish. By all accounts, the performances had something of the character of a concert. The dramatization of the novel provided not just an occasion for revisiting a popular story, but also an occasion for activating other forms of cultural heritage in other media, though 'evergreens' or 'favourites' may be a more appropriate word here than heritage. Bolton has suggested, moreover, that the inclusion of traditional ballads and airs offered in particular a way for displaced Highlanders now working in the industrialized cities to enjoy familiar melodies, copies of which were sometimes sold in the lobbies.[88]

Surprisingly, relatively little attention has been paid in cultural memory studies to the mnemonic function of music and to aurality as a connector between past and present.[89] But the term 'evergreen' itself indicates that singing is an important medium of collective memory, one that provides a living and, indeed, embodied connection between the past and the present through the voices of the participants. The memorability of songs, like that of the poetry on which they are often based, is less based on narrative and the recollection of past events, than it is on the self-reflexive reiteration of sound and word patterns.[90] Remarkably, many of the songs that figured at the Rob Roy performances were based on poems by Burns, Moore, Wordsworth, and Scott himself. As if to doubly ensure their stickiness they were now combined with traditional melodies whose music resonated in the here and now with the deep aural memory of the listeners. (I have found no direct evidence of sing-alongs during the plays themselves, though enthusiastic fans are known to have left the theatre in Perth in 1818 roaring 'Rob Roy for ever' and the audience waiting for the royal performance in 1822, as we have seen, passed the time in collective singing.[91])

The case of *Rob Roy* suggests indeed that music in the nineteenth-century theatre provided what Pierre Nora has called a *milieu de mémoire* (memory environment): a relationship to the past based on the continuity of repetition rather than on the rupture implied in historicizing modes of remembrance that look back to the past from a distance. Repetition and re-citation would certainly seem to be key to the revivals of *Rob Roy* throughout the nineteenth century, where the charm of the songs lay in their familiarity rather than in their novelty, and in the (nostalgic) presence of the past in the musical performance.

In the case of *Rob Roy,* more so than in the case of *Guy Mannering,* which it resembles in many other respects, this pleasure of reiteration took on a distinctly national character. As such, it bears out the general point made by Michael Ragussis in his recent *Theatrical Nation* (2010), namely, that the theatre provided 'unusually vivid (visual and aural) representations of ethnic and national identities' and thereby constituted a live communal environment 'in which the community publicly inspected and responded to these representations and to one another.'[92] Ragussis does not explicitly refer to adaptations of *Rob Roy,* but his formulation is particularly apt to describe their character. The repeated invocation of the concept of the national (which we have already encountered in the case of *The Heart of Mid-Lothian*) indicates that performances of the play were also performances of what it meant to be Scottish. Indicative in this regard is the fact that Scott and Burns—the Siamese twins of Scottish literature—were sometimes mentioned side by side on the same programme, in a potent combination which we will be encountering again in Chapter 6.[93] While the title of the first known performance on 17 January 1818 simply referred to Rob Roy, the influence of Pocock's version ensured that it became more and more frequently subtitled *Or, Auld Lang Syne.* This memory cue for Scottishness later became written into the title of the play, to which was then added a further subtitle designating its national character. From August 1819, then, when *Rob Roy MacGregor; or, Auld Lang Syne* at the Theatre Royal in Edinburgh was announced as a 'national opera', it became common for the attribute 'national' to be applied in various combinations to subsequent productions, including the one attended by George IV. 'National drama', 'national play', 'national melodrama', 'national opera': these all featured at various points.[94] The term 'national' was also extended to particular features of the production: in 1849, for example, a programme bill referred to the 'national air' of Auld Lang Syne while another referred to the 'admired national pas seul of Miss Eyre', and yet another advertised a dance to the 'national air' of the 'The Blue Bells of Scotland'.[95] All this talk of 'national' suggests that productions of *Rob Roy* were both a way of reiterating narrative and songs and a way of performing a collective identity in a pleasurable and convivial form. As Barbara Bell has argued, they were also part of a new awareness of the distinctiveness of Scottish theatre, with its own key actors, decors, stories, that the Scott repertoire had helped generate as an object of pride and cultivation.[96]

All of these ingredients are present in the account given by the *Scotsman* on 20 February 1819 of the opening night of Pocock's play in Edinburgh (attended incidentally by Scott himself, again recognized as its progenitor):

He who is without affections does not deserve the name of man. But he who is at once a man and a *Scotsman,* must be delighted with 'Rob Roy MacGregor, of [*sic*] Auld Lang Syne.'...Why should not we be proud of our national genius, humour, music, kindness and fidelity? *Why not be national? We found ourselves pre-eminently so on Monday evening.* Our recollection of the novel of Rob Roy, and the almost universal genius of its author, with the perfect conviction that he is a Scotsman, and was then present in the theatre, gave sufficient interest to this musical drama at the commencement; and the manner in which the different parts were cast and supported, not only preserved it to the last, but made it grow upon us, so as to become absolutely intoxicating. So perfect was the illusion, from the admirable combination of scenery, costume, character, expression and *acting*, that, in a word, we were 'hurried off our feet.' [emphasis AR][97]

As this rave review suggests, 'being national' was not just a feature of the production as such. It was rather the capacity of all those present to be moved at the same time, indeed 'intoxicated' by the multimedial combination of spectacle, music, acting, the memory of the book, and in this case, the physical presence of the writer. 'National' was something one could 'pre-eminently be' of a Monday evening—in a theatre. In 1784, Friedrich Schiller had proposed the theatre was a platform for creating national solidarity through shared experience.[98] The case of Rob Roy suggests that the popular theatre did fulfil such a function in Scotland in the nineteenth century, albeit in a more demotic and less moralizing form than that envisaged by the German theorist of the public sphere. The theatre was a place where readers and non-readers alike came together as a public and 'conveyed' their self-image in the presence of each other.

It is no coincidence that the celebration of nationality quoted above should have appeared in the *Scotsman* since it would appear from the hundreds of productions listed by Bolton that the epithet 'national' was used almost exclusively with reference to productions in Scotland (and these account for a large proportion of the total number of *Rob Roys*) while it was absent at other venues, where the term 'Scotch' was often used instead to designate the distinctiveness of the heritage on display in a foreign setting.[99] This difference in designating what was essentially the same play is striking especially since Scott's works and their dramatizations were in circulation throughout the British Isles. But it is indicative of the relationality of national identities and of the play's capacity to articulate different positions on the two islands both from within a 'national' Scottish perspective and from an outsider one. A certain self-conscious memorialization of the play itself developed in the course of all these repetitions, with frequent reference made in the playbills to the 'original music' and to its status as part of the national canon. This status was clinched by its production for the benefit of the visiting monarch in 1822 (after which the subtitle 'national' became standard) and further reinforced by its revival on the occasion of the lavish commemorations of Scott's centenary in 1871, which I will be discussing at greater length in Chapter 6. On these later occasions, the play itself was not just performed in all its immediacy, but a piece of theatrico-national history was also literally re-enacted.

Reflecting the performative turn in the humanities referred to earlier, increasing attention has been paid in recent years to performative practices, alongside narratives, in the production of cultural memory. Reflecting this shift in perspective, commemorative ceremonies have come to be seen as performative in the sense that they involve music, spectacle, and so on, but also performative in the linguistic sense that they make things happen: in this case, they create communality through an embodied and self-reflexive act of remembrance that is shared at a particular time and place.[100] This change of perspective has highlighted the importance of commemorations in creating communities in the nineteenth century that were embodied (they involved people being together in the same place and time) rather than just 'imagined' in Benedict Anderson's sense (that is, connected through media).[101] In Chapter 6 I will discuss the commemorations of Scott himself in greater detail. Here my concern is rather with extending the idea of performative remembrance to the theatre and to the pleasures of reiterating *Rob Roy* as part of a self-reflexive cultivation of a collective text. Barbara Bell has described the impact in Scotland of the 'national dramas' based on Scott's work in terms of their offering a 'public arena' in which people could 'assert their shared cultural identity' by witnessing over and again their national heroes and heroines in national costume and with Scottish accents.[102] Whether or not the audience actually shared a common past, they did share the common experience of 'being national' thanks to the theatre, at least for the duration of the performance.

It would be pushing the argument too far to suggest that the theatrical versions of *Rob Roy* constituted some sort of commemorative ritual in any strict sense—though Royal presences on different occasions did give the performance of *Rob Roy* in Edinburgh official weight as a formal recognition of Scottish cultural identity within the political union. Even on less august occasions, however, performances of *Rob Roy* in Scotland appear to have had both a commemorative character (recalling the memory of Scott, Rob Roy, popular songs, Highlands) and a ritualistic one (based on reciting and repeating). The complaint voiced in *The Edinburgh Dramatic Review* in March 1825 about 'national dramas' to the effect that they were loose compilations dependent on the memory of the public unwittingly articulated the underlying principle at work:

These national dramas, however, are not to be judged by strict rules; the connection between the different scenes is extremely loose; and the memory of the audience is required as an adhesive plaister to bind them together.[103]

Within the pleasurable framework of an evening's theatre, the memory of outlaws and depopulated Highlands was invoked for the benefit of urban audiences, many of them recent emigrants to the burgeoning Scottish cities. The public's pleasure and, on occasion, their possibly nostalgic 'intoxication' with Scottishness, to recall the review in the *Scotsman*, was linked to their being able to participate in an event that was absolutely familiar and cherished (the play, the songs) and yet absolutely unique (the immediacy of the particular performance). Ernest Renan famously wrote that the memory of suffering can connect people more than the memory of joy, and a similar perspective has informed much recent reflection on collective memory and identity, with trauma and suffering being seen as the basis of solidarity.[104] Written and performed in a different age, the case of *Rob Roy* serves as a reminder that pleasure too can be binding and that repetition in the singular mode of a live performance can itself be a source of pleasure, albeit one that may be structurally tinged with nostalgia against the background of change.

ROB ROY, FOREVER?

Recent theories of remediation emphasize the drive towards new experiences and new sensations, John Ellis suggesting that adaptations aim to 'efface the memory' of the original text on which they are based. The theatrical productions of *Rob Roy* that I have been discussing here emerged against the background of an incipient consumerist culture, but nevertheless worked not by effacing the memory of the original, but by reiterating it within the immediacy of a singular performance. As such, the theatre supplemented other 'long-distance' forms of culture, by providing a forum alongside novels and newspapers in which experience was shared in an embodied way more characteristic of oral societies than of the media-saturated world of Scott.

Before rounding up this discussion of Scott in the theatre, it should be pointed out that theatrical productions of *Rob Roy* dried up abruptly in the first decades of the twentieth century, having gradually declined in the preceding decades. With the exception of incidental theatrical productions in Edinburgh in 1922, 1931, and 1962, the cultural afterlife of *Rob Roy* in the twentieth century has been on the screen rather than on the stage. Like many of Scott's other works, the novel was adapted at a very early stage to the movies with the appearance of films called *Rob Roy* in 1911 (dir. Arthur Vivian), 1913 (dir. Henry J. Vernot), 1922 (dir. W. P. Kellino), 1953 (dir. Michael French), and 1995 (dir. Michael Caton Jones), along with two BBC series for television in 1961 and 1971. This development answers to the classic model of remediation whereby each new technology leads to a transformation of old stories into new interfaces.[105] The (diminished) afterlife of *Rob Roy* in the twentieth century, like that of other Scott stories, was as much bound up with the screen as with print.

Apart from revivals of some of the Scott-based operas, the theatre did not figure much in this more recent afterlife. Certainly the song-filled and the *live* character of the evenings in the theatres of the 1800s was not carried over, could not be carried over, into the silent cinema. The cinema was international in its reach, rather than embodied locally, and this meant that the shift to film was not merely a change of medium, but also of social function. It is telling in this regard that none of the twentieth-century screen versions of *Rob Roy* have either *Auld Lang Syne* or 'national' in their subtitles. The new screen technologies offered new possibilities for bringing the eighteenth century to life, but they also diminished the ability to mobilize audiences around a live performance. Canonicity in this case had a shelf-life: dramatizations of *Rob Roy* (with the symbolic weight of Scott behind them) had a symbolic, social, and aesthetic value in the nineteenth century that they largely ceased to have in the twentieth.

There is another twist: while the shift to a new medium could have been taken as an opportunity to go back to Scott's original as a model, it is striking that the movies made in the twentieth century seem to have turned instead to the folk traditions concerning the historical Rob Roy. Although the 1911 and 1913 films are unfortunately no longer available for viewing, the list of dramatis personae indicates a fidelity to the Scott/Pocock script at least as far as the basic narrative is concerned.

W. P. Kellino's 1922 version is quite different: no Baillie, no Osbaldistone, no Diana Vernon, but instead the story of Rob Roy's fight at the head of his clan against injustice and the tyranny of the Marquis of Montrose. In a convoluted way, the first intertitle of the film, which has happily been preserved in the British Film Institute, both acknowledges and dismisses Scott's legacy: 'To Scotland, not to Scott, did we go for the facts on which our story of "Rob Roy" is built. There, amid the mountain lochs and glens, nature made peace and man made war.' Even as it piggybacked on Scott's reputation, the intertitle indicates a return to the folkloric representations of Rob Roy circulating prior to Scott's novel, and on which Scott himself had drawn.

Scott's novel together with its dramatizations and various other spinoffs helped ensure that the memory of Rob Roy remained alive throughout the nineteenth century. Even when it was no longer associated with the novel, this figure of memory circulated as part of a collective text that belonged to everyone who wanted to appropriate it rather than to a single author. Thus the blockbuster Hollywood version of *Rob Roy* (1995), starring Liam Neeson, was based more on the 1922 film version than on Scott's original, and hence indirectly reconnected with the folkloric tradition that Scott had helped revivify.[106] The 1995 film was a travesty of the memory of Scott's work, but also its legitimate offspring. On the one hand, Scott's novel was a unique work of literature that offered an imaginative and complex reconstruction of Scottish life in the eighteenth century, more complex than any dramatic or filmic version could ever be. On the other hand, it drew on folkloric traditions which it reworked and, in this light, the later popular versions of Rob Roy represent a fitting outcome of a *translatio* that began with the novelist's own sampling of folklore. Scott had chosen the name *Waverley*, it will be recalled, because it was 'uncontaminated' by any associations. For the same reason, he had hesitated in 1817 before conceding to his publisher's proposal that he use 'Rob Roy' for his latest novel because it was the name of a 'real hero': 'Nay', answered Scott, 'never let me have to write up to a name. You well know that I have generally adopted a title that told nothing.'[107] Scott's strategic instincts proved correct as far as the branding of his work was concerned: in the case of popular remembrance of Rob Roy, his own novel resonated so well with other versions that it was ultimately overwritten by them.

A parallel story could be told about the persistence of *Rob Roy* as a text and about the painstaking reconstruction of the 'original' edition in the Edinburgh Edition of the Waverley Novels (2008). But by looking only at the text at its moment of genesis, one misses out on its rich afterlife as an object of transformation in other media and its appropriation by various groups. It has by now become something of a commonplace that all traditions are constructed; that they are based on the representation of imagined genealogies. This case suggests the contrary: that the remediations of Scott's work over the course of what is now almost two centuries constitute a continuous tradition, one that is real and not just imagined although it is made up of new starts and new departures alongside reiterations. It represents a tradition of inventions rather than an invention of tradition. From the perspective of our understanding of cultural remembrance in the age of new media and fast turnovers, this tradition of inventions suggests an underlying connectedness between generations that needs to be seriously considered as part of the fabric of modern culture, despite our habitual reliance on a discourse of imminent obsolescence.

Cultural memory, to recall Jan Assmann's words, amounts to a collection of 'reusable texts, images, and rituals specific... whose "cultivation" serves to stabilize and convey that society's self-image.' In the case of *Rob Roy* collective identities were 'cultivated' through the reiteration of the same script in new performances. The next chapters will address the case of *Ivanhoe*, which followed a different trajectory: the script itself was continuously rewritten in an attempt to stabilize a society's inherently contested self-image.

3

Re-scripting *Ivanhoe*

The principal nations of Europe are all of mixed blood
—Ernest Renan, 'What is a Nation?' (1882)

One of the characters in Jonathan Franzen's *The Corrections* (2001) experiences a moment of panic in the run-up to Christmas when, having fallen out of favour with the world and his family, he has forgotten to buy presents and now looks in his panic to Walter Scott:

He'd solved the problem of family Christmas gifts on the last possible mailing day, when, in a great rush, he'd pulled old bargains and remainders off his bookshelves and wrapped them in aluminium foil and tied them up with red ribbon and refused to imagine how his nine-year-old nephew Caleb, for example, might react to an Oxford annotated edition of Ivanhoe whose main qualifications as a gift was that it was still in its original shrink-wrap.[1]

That Franzen should use an annotated edition of *Ivanhoe* to exemplify an inappropriate gift for a young nephew indicates a dramatic loss in status for a novel that had excited so many people in the 1820s. The amusing reference to a permanently shrink-wrapped edition fits in with a more widespread perception of Scott and all his works as an egregious 'has been' in the year 2000, as someone who used to be very popular, particularly among young people, but who is no longer read. He is at most preserved, but no longer actually unwrapped. Yet he is apparently not totally forgotten: the very fact that Franzen can enjoy this little dig at Scott in a popular novel presupposes that his readers will still recognize the name 'Ivanhoe' and remember more or less to what it refers. Almost two centuries after its initial publication *Ivanhoe* persists in the general cultural memory—although if we are to believe Franzen, only as an icon of a 'has been', a shrink-wrapped symbol of pastness itself.

A generation earlier, *Ivanhoe* also had a walk-on part in *Slaughterhouse-Five* (1969), Kurt Vonnegut's novel about the bombing of Dresden and its psychological impact. One of the characters is a novelist called Kilgore

Trout, who, when invited to a banal birthday party, finds himself a big hit since everybody was 'thrilled to have a real author at the party, even though they had never read his books'. Among those thrilled was 'a Maggie White, who had given up being a dental assistant to become a homemaker for an optometrist. She was very pretty. The last book she had read was Ivanhoe.'[2]

Since Ivanhoe, like Waverley (and unlike Rob Roy) is an exclusively Scott figure, its unglossed appearance in these recent novels, no matter how condescending the reference, is evidence of a direct link back to the publication of the novel in 1819. Moreover, Scott's continuing influence was not only palpably present in the name. It was also active in the fact that *Slaughterhouse-Five* is a modernist variation on the classical historical novel developed by Scott: while the style is quite different, it inherits from the author of Waverley the idea of putting an ingenuous witness to historical events at the centre of a narrative.[3] In the first instance, however, Vonnegut's throwaway reference to *Ivanhoe* was a way of recalling *Ivanhoe*'s status as a children's story, a position enhanced by its publication in the famous *Classics Illustrated* series, which for decades now has offered to generations of young readers classical novels in the abridged form of comics.[4] Whether Vonnegut's Maggie White had read *Ivanhoe* in the original or in the form of an abridgement or comic is not made clear, but the significance of the analogy is unambiguous: if someone has ever only read one book in his or her life, then that book was probably *Ivanhoe*. For Vonnegut, and presumably for many people now reaching middle age, Scott's story is as much an icon of youthful innocence as of literary history.

But the fact that the name 'Ivanhoe' is still recognizable at all to a contemporary public after almost two hundred years testifies to the immense popularity of Scott's story across several generations and across several continents. Indeed (as I myself have experienced time and again in talking about this project), Ivanhoe is the only name from the entire Scott repertoire that is still recognizable for many people nowadays. This novel of medieval England is arguably the best known, most widely disseminated, most internationally successful, and most enduring of all Scott's works, several of which were record-breaking best-sellers.[5] It was remediated more often, in more media, and for longer than any other work by Scott. Where *Rob Roy* enjoyed an extraordinarily rich afterlife in nineteenth-century theatres, but hardly figured at all in painting and place names, *Ivanhoe* was remediated time and again in the visual arts, in the theatre, in movies, in place names, on television, in computer gaming, and even in the material form of Wedgwood porcelain.[6] Indeed, the familiarity with the name that Franzen presupposed in 2000 is probably due not so much to direct familiarity with Scott's text itself as to the international dissemination of the story through television, where an *Ivanhoe* series (1958; dir. Arthur Crabtree et al.) starring Roger Moore made a big impact on the generation growing up in the 1960s across the Western world.[7] The many media that have carried stories of Ivanhoe thus worked in a mutually reinforcing way in turning the novel into a collective text in an international arena that people know in its broad outlines without necessarily knowing the original or its place in Scott's *oeuvre*.[8]

The reception of *Ivanhoe*, like so many of Scott's works but even more so, yields mind-boggling statistics. Besides countless editions in English, it has appeared in translation in at least thirty-six languages and it continues to generate new versions. The Library of Scotland has recorded more than six hundred translations, including recent ones in Turkish and Vietnamese, and several ones in Japanese, in which language a guide to 'The world of Ivanhoe' was also published as recently as 2009.[9] The novel has been abridged and illustrated for juveniles, as well as adapted to multiple media. It has influenced the perception of the Middle Ages among several generations of readers, including a number of historians who have admitted being so inspired or, alternatively, so goaded by its romantic fancies as to

Figure 3.1: *Friar Tuck meets the Black Knight,* Wedgwood plate (*c.*1880).

develop a vocation for historical research.[10] In short, 'Ivanhoe' (that is, the text and its reception) represents a media phenomenon that stretches from the early nineteenth century, when it became an international bestseller, to the early twenty-first century, where it persists on the outer reaches of the cultural margins, arguably in the process of disappearing from sight like a flare that is almost, but not quite, extinguished. Providing a direct link back to the world of 1819, the longevity of this particular story bears witness once again to the cultural continuities that persist in the age of mass media and modernization. Arguably because of its very popularity, *Ivanhoe* has not received the critical attention that one might have expected from such a modern classic. With a couple of notable exceptions, it has stayed on the margins of the Scott canon as somehow deserving of less attention and demanding less exegesis than his major novels dealing with Scotland; at worst merely proof that Scott had written a blockbuster. As was noted recently, it has the dubious honour of having been claimed as their favourite book both by the former British Prime Minister Tony Blair and by the Vietnamese Marxist leader Ho Chi Minh.[11]

But all of this begs the question: why was *Ivanhoe* in particular so popular? Of all the Scott novels, why did it survive longest in the culture at large? Part of the answer must be in the familiar fact, as true for memory as for other walks of life, that success breeds success. Memory sites emerge as such by being reiterated across different media and hence by becoming exposed to different groups and acquiring multiple layers of meaning.[12] Because the figure of Ivanhoe was repeatedly invoked in so many different spheres, then, his name became all the more usable by the next party as a recognizable icon and as such preferable to other (increasingly obscure) Scott figures. But since exposure in other media applied to so many of Scott's stories, it is not enough to explain Ivanhoe's particularly tenacious long-term procreativity.

The case of *Ivanhoe* thus offers a unique opportunity to examine the role of literature as a medium of cultural remembrance over a longer period of time. As we shall see in this chapter and the next, remembering Ivanhoe across almost two centuries says something both about those doing the remembering and about the text that continuously invited recall: in appropriating *Ivanhoe* within a new medium, people recalibrated it according to their own frame of reference with its shifting agendas and horizon of expectations.[13] In the present chapter, I shall examine more closely the interplay between the memorability of Scott's original story and its later appropriations to stage and screen, before going on in the next chapter to illustrate how *Ivanhoe* has been appropriated in the theatre of identity politics and used as a common currency in negotiating differences.

A NARRATIVE TEMPLATE

As readers of *Ivanhoe: A Romance* will know, Scott portrayed the world of medieval England in vivid scenes centred on a limited number of locations and a small cast of highly colourful and hence highly memorable figures. His narrative seems to premediate its own conversion into moving images and theatre. With an antiquarian's eye for the material, he depicted places, persons, and clothing in extraordinary detail, setting scenes so that they might be imagined in their three-dimensionality by a latter-day readership, literally in colour. Take the following introduction to the swineherd Gurth:

The man had no covering upon his head, which was only defended by his own thick hair, matted and twisted together, and scorched by the influence of the sun into a rusty dark-red colour, forming a contrast with the overgrown beard upon his cheeks, which was rather of a yellow or amber hue.[14]

Or his description of the banqueting hall at Rotherwood:

There was a huge fireplace at either end of the hall, but as the chimneys were constructed in a very clumsy manner, at least as much of the smoke found its way into the apartment as escaped by the proper vent. The constant vapour which this occasioned had polished the rafters and beams of the low-browed hall, by encrusting them with a black varnish of soot.[15]

In characteristic fashion, Scott's invocation of the blackness of the smoke-filled beams or of the dark-red colour of Gurth's weather-beaten face help to imagine the past as a material space where people lived and breathed. As Thomas Carlyle once put it in assessing Scott's achievements:

these Historical Novels have taught all men this truth ... that the bygone ages of the world were actually filled by living men, not by protocols, state papers, controversies and abstractions of men. Not abstractions were they, not diagrams and theorems; but men, in buff or other coats and breeches, with colour in their cheeks, with passions in their stomach, and the idioms, features and vitalities of very men.[16]

While these qualities were present in all of Scott's works, they were all the more striking in the case of *Ivanhoe* since, in contrast to the Scottish novels, it dealt with such a historically distant period about which relatively little was known.[17] By translating the Middle Ages into imaginable characters and situations, Scott provided figures of memory for the origins of modern Britain at a time when there were few contemporary representations of that period available, and certainly none which provided such telling details of everyday life within the framework of a story. Within the technological limits of his own age, then, Scott went far towards producing those 'prosthetic' effects usually associated with early cinema. That we should now have come to think of the Middle Ages as colourful (as opposed to the black-and-white of World War I) is arguably one of the many legacies of Scott. Given these qualities, it is not surprising that it generated so many pictorial remediations in the form both of popular engravings and of oil paintings by major artists, and that it inspired a new generation of historians to write in a more narrativized way.[18] The historian Macaulay once compared him admiringly to the maker of the stained-glass windows in Lincoln Cathedral: like him, Scott had succeeded in bringing the past to life in colour.[19]

It is above all its emplotment of history, however, and not just its vivid descriptions, that ensured *Ivanhoe*'s long-term impact. The action-packed plot depicts the emergence of a modern nation from the conflict between two ethnic groups, one the conqueror of the other, and it was this underlying design that ensured its long-term resonance. Designed around the basic opposition between the Normans and the Saxons, colonizers and aboriginals, modernizers and traditionalists, the action is propelled forward by the persecution of the local inhabitants (both Saxons and Jews) by a group of lawless Norman knights, and it works through various crises towards a closure in which conflicts are ostensibly resolved and a new England/Britain emerges under the leadership of King Richard and the rule of law. In figuring the Middle Ages around this central conflict, Scott re-worked existing narratives about the feudal 'Norman yoke' and its suppression of native liberties and fused these with his earlier novels, popular myths regarding Robin Hood, and Shakespearean intertexts about Jews. The result is a highly syncretic, highly resonant, and very distinctive brew in which various opposed and overlapping collective identities are brought into play.[20]

The new England that emerges at the end of the book is a hybrid one, embodied in the person of Ivanhoe. Born a Saxon and (hence) a defender of justice and liberty, the eponymous hero of the novel has also imbibed the chivalric values of the Normans to the point of joining the crusade under the command of Richard the Lionheart. Since he has fully assimilated both traditions, it is hard to say which of Ivanhoe's values came from which ethnic tradition, only that he is somehow a perfect hybrid combining the best of both cultures along with the best of England and Abroad. In some ways, then, the story also imagines a world in which it is possible to have one's cake and eat it: with the country firmly in the hands of Richard the Lionheart, supported by Ivanhoe, the novel exudes a confidence in the leadership of (modernizing, conquering) aristocrats if harnessed to more traditional, demotic, and local values. This 'one-nation'

Toryism was, in advance of Disraeli's coinage of that term, Scott's alternative to revolution: a way of supporting change that honoured traditions even if it did not always keep them intact in practice.

In 1820, Samuel Taylor Coleridge criticized *Ivanhoe* itself for being too remote ('for what Englishman cares for Saxon or Norman?') while predicting that Scott's work in general would continue to speak to later generations because of his reiterated preoccupation with the conflict between the forces of progress and the forces of tradition:

the contest between the Loyalists and their opponents can never be *obsolete,* for it is the contest between the two great moving Principles of social Humanity— religious adherence to the Past and the Ancient, the Desire and the admiration of Permanence, on the one hand; and the Passion for increase of Knowledge, for Truth as the offspring of Reason, in short, the mighty Instincts of Progression and Free-agency, on the other. In all subjects of deep and lasting interest, you will detect a struggle between two opposites, two polar forces, both of which are alike necessary to our human well-being, and necessary each to the continued existence of the other.[21]

Coleridge was wrong, as we will see, in assuming that temporal remoteness would preclude contemporary relevance. But his basic intuition was correct that Scott's preoccupation with the past reflected as much a fascination with progress as nostalgia for a bygone age. How can one become modern while preserving traditions? How to change while remaining the same? How can multiple groups be turned into one nation? These fundamental questions, forming the core of Scott's work, are particularly close to the surface in the case of *Ivanhoe*.

Scott's investment in depictions of former ages might at first sight be seen as a symptom of what Svetlana Boym has called 'restorative nostalgia': a reaction to modernity that takes the form of imagining the past, not as a foreign country, but as a homeland to which one can actually return.[22] Certainly Scott's critics regularly accused him of 'running away from contemporaneity' or as Hazlitt put it in a strongly worded indictment, of mocking the present and ignoring the future: 'he knows all that [the universe] *has been*; all that *is to be* is nothing to him.'[23] However, Scott's historicism can best be seen, not in terms of nostalgia, but as part of an apology for progress, a way of paving the way towards new prosperity while retaining some connection to the past. Although he went to great lengths to evoke the past and its romance, he usually did so in order to let bygones be bygones: in each case it is the modernizers who win the day, while the disempowered are given the greatest aesthetic force. A strong case can be made on the basis of his emplotments that he accepted the inevitability of 'Progression and Free-Agency' and even promoted it; that his work was about cherishing the past in the symbolic realm in order to live with its demise. Scott gave consolation prizes to the disempowered by revealing the fascination of their culture even as he showed the inevitability of their political emasculation: in the tantalizingly ambivalent world of the Waverley novels, the appeal of lost causes did not stop the fact that they were indeed lost. In the case of *Ivanhoe*, these ambivalences were compounded by the fact that the necessity for progress was embodied in representatives of a feudal order that had become *ancien régime* by 1819.

But one way or another, *Ivanhoe* was very much of its time at the level both of overall design and of detail.[24] Most obviously the novel was part of ongoing discussions, in which the Waverley novels and their dramatizations were important players, about the distinctiveness of the multiple nationalities on the British Isles and their relations within what Ina Ferris has called the 'awkward space of union'.[25] In presenting a hybrid model of nationality in his novel about the Middle Ages, Scott was repeating in a new guise the story of Waverley. As one of his French admirers Augustin Thierry put it, that novel had revealed the 'poetry' inherent in Scottish history by putting the dramatic conflict between Highlanders and Lowlanders/English at the core of the novel.[26] While some contemporary critics saw *Ivanhoe*, Scott's first excursion into English history and into the remote past, as a falling off with respect to his earlier novels (no one could have predicted how successful it would be), his recycling of *Waverley*'s two-nation model can be construed instead as proof of its usefulness as a narrative template: it helped other people to imagine and articulate the story of how one nation emerged from two. The fact that *Ivanhoe* was a variation on Scott's earlier stories may have meant a loss of critical acclaim, but it also meant that the template had become more powerfully visible and, in being linked to the Middle Ages for which there was growing Europe-wide interest, more generally applicable and transferable to other cases. Suffice it here to note that Ernest Renan, in his classic essay 'What is a Nation?' from 1882, presented nation-building as the challenge of imagining one community on the basis of several: this too can be seen as part of the long-term impact of Scott and, specifically, of *Ivanhoe*.

Within an even broader framework, the novel also fed into imaginations of multinationality and colonial relations. Whether Scott was dealing with Scotland or with England, the societies he depicted are struggling in one way or another to overcome divisions generated by conquest and by ethnic difference.[27] As Ian Duncan has noted with respect to *Ivanhoe*, for example, the conquest of England by the Normans is situated in the larger framework of European expansionism since the drama is set off by the return of the Norman lords from the Crusades in the company of several black slaves, their invasion of England mirroring that of Palestine. Seen from this perspective, Ivanhoe's participation both in the Crusades and in the resistance to Norman injustice at home exemplifies the emergence of a mobile generation skilled in crossing over between different cultural communities; something that in his case involved ceasing to be mono-culturally Saxon in order to become Norman as well.[28] In this way, Scott's work bears out Linda Colley's basic contention that, after the union of 1707, Scottish writers had a vested interest in imagining collective iden-tities within multinational frameworks, be that of Great Britain or the Empire, even if only to re-assert their own distinctiveness.[29] Scott's earlier articulations of Scottish distinctiveness within the broader British frame-work had passed over into articulations of Englishness as a distinctively hybrid identity. Indeed, Scott's shift from Scottish to English themes was itself a strategic choice to assert his identity as a Scottish-British writer with a multinational constituency both north and south of the Tweed.

However we interpret the contemporary resonance of the various oppositions running through the novel, it is clear that the narrative posits and then sublimates differences in imagining a new order. In all the variations of the story that we will encounter here, this basic conflict–resolution–happy end structure remains constant. So the first explanation for *Ivanhoe*'s longevity lies in the stabilizing effect of its narrativization of history around ethnic conflict and resolution. The underlying narrative design was arguably all the more visible because of the temporal distance it bridged and the relative unfamiliarity of the period being portrayed. Although for some people it was less schematic than this rendition suggests, as we shall see below, the two-nation model proved to be a very powerful template for shaping national histories that was adopted and adapted to a variety of other contexts.[30] It provided non-British groups with a model of remembrance to be filled in by their own local version of the basic Norman–Saxon opposition. The next chapter will provide abundant evidence for this. Suffice it to note here, that within England too, *Ivanhoe* was appropriated as an interpretive frame for recent history, from Benjamin Disraeli's view of the contemporary state of English society in *Sybil, or the Two Nations* (1845) to the jingoistic operatic version of *Ivanhoe* by Arthur Sullivan and Julian Sturgis from 1891. Dedicated to Queen Victoria, the opera celebrated the unity of all factions in the country under the leadership of Richard who (with Saxon vigour?) brings the rebellious Normans to heel: a comforting thought at a time when Britain and France were embroiled in imperial rivalry.[31]

INSTABILITY: DIFFERENTIAL MEMORY

The word ambivalence has already been dropped with reference to *Ivanhoe*. While it is true to say that the Norman–Saxon opposition had a fertile afterlife as a narrative template, and that the narrative had a stabilizing effect, this is only part of the story. As schematic as the novel might appear from the point of view of its overall plot, the closer one gets to it, the more fraught with ambivalence it becomes. The basic tension between modernization and tradition in the depiction of medieval chivalry has already been mentioned. Another type of tension has been analysed by Jerome McGann in some of the most impassioned critical engagements with the novel to date. Writing against the mistaken tendency to judge *Ivanhoe* according to the norms of what would later become realism, McGann demonstrates how the paratextual framing of the novel creates an 'ironic awareness' of the constructed character of the fiction that brings Scott more into line with postmodern writers than with some of his successors in the nineteenth century.[32] McGann's concerns are primarily with the tension between the immersive powers of the story with its colourful characters and high drama and Scott's self-reflexivity as a fiction-maker. But the basic opposition between realism and romance, between Scott's claims to portray things as they were and his admission that he is after all giving an idealized and imaginary picture of things that might have been, is another version of the ambivalence discussed earlier with reference to *The Heart of Mid-Lothian*.

Scott himself was the first to admit that the coherence he had projected onto the early history of Britain in *Ivanhoe* was an imaginary one: as he made clear in his dedicatory epistle and even in the subtitle, he was offering a historical romance to his readers in which he had taken liberties with historical information, but through which he nevertheless hoped to give a vivid sense of the lives of our medieval ancestors.[33] The romance element was even more egregiously present in *Ivanhoe* than in Scott's earlier novels, which had all dealt with well-documented and highly charged topics from the history of Scotland during the seventeenth and eighteenth centuries.[34] The tension between history and romance in the case of *Ivanhoe* is particularly interesting in light of Amy Elias' contention that there is a structural affinity between historical fiction and forms of *un*realism. In one of the most interesting re-assessments of the historical novel in recent years, Elias has drawn attention to the fact that historical fiction has been marked from its inception by a 'romance' streak, associating it with the ideal, the imaginary, and the uncannily ungraspable rather than with the documented and the real, and argues that this uneasy alliance between romance and realism accounts for its particular cultural power.[35]

What makes *Ivanhoe* distinctive in Scott's *oeuvre*, however, is the invention of a highly attractive character who, by personifying this under-lying tension, also becomes its lightning conductor: Rebecca. In his re-workings of the Norman yoke–Saxon liberties narrative, Scott had intro-duced a new level of complexity into the already hybrid origins of modern England by assigning a key role to a group of figures who fitted into neither category: the Jew Isaac and his beautiful daughter Rebecca, who was often depicted in Orientalist style as a way of underscoring her status as an outsider. Although the conflict between the Normans and Saxons provides the main frame for the novel, it is Rebecca's persecution by the Norman Bois-Guilbert and her subsequent rescue by Ivanhoe that provides its figurative focus. Ivanhoe, with his hyphenated identity as a Normanized Saxon, occupies a space between the two main groups, where Rebecca occupies a place outside the basic categories. Representing a mixture of Enlightenment philosemitism and traditional stereotypes, Rebecca and her father exemplify an irreducible alterity against which the common ground between Normans and Saxons is all the more easily highlighted. As such their appearance in Scott's novel fits into a larger tendency, highlighted by Michael Ragussis in *Theatrical Nation* (2010), to explore national identities in Britain through the figure of 'outlandish' outsiders.[36]

What makes the case so intriguing, however, is that Rebecca is not only an outsider, but also the moral and aesthetic centre of the story. The combination of old Jewish father and beautiful daughter clearly recalls Shakespeare's Shylock and Jessica, but with a twist. While the depiction of Isaac resonates with Shakespeare's moneylender, Rebecca is portrayed in more exoticizing terms than Jessica, but also as more of an empowered agent who is well educated and capable of taking action.[37] Most impor-tantly, where Jessica's inclusion into the body politic was made dependent on her conversion to Christianity, there is no question of Rebecca denying her religion and traditions. Most reviewers in 1820 and most commenta-tors since then have found Rebecca to be the most interesting character in the novel. It is a remarkable fact that every reviewer, almost without exception, cited the figure of Rebecca as a noteworthy feature of the novel (a consoling consensus in face of a tendency nowadays to think that, since readers differ, they have nothing at all in common).[38] As was mentioned earlier, the beautiful Jewess was also singled out for tributes on the part of engravers and painters, including major artists like Eugène Delacroix, who painted Rebecca's abduction in 1846 and again in 1858. In a particularly elaborate commentary from 1832, Harriet Martineau saw

Rébecca.

Figure 3.2: *Rébecca.* From Walter Scott, *Ivanhoé*; dessins par MM Lix, Marie, Riou et H. Scott (*c.*1852).

her as a powerful symbol of female potential in a world dominated by men, harnassing her memory to the cause of emancipation:

As a woman, no less than as a Jewess, she is the representative of the wrongs of a degraded and despised class . . . she wanders unemployed (as regards her peculiar capabilities) through the world; and when she dies, there has been, not only a deep injury inflicted, but a waste made of the resources of human greatness and happiness. Yes, women may choose Rebecca as representative of their capabilities: first despised, then wondered at, and involuntarily admired; tempted, made use of, then persecuted, and finally banished—not by a formal decree, but by being refused honourable occupation, and a safe abiding place. Let women not only take her for their model, but make her speak for them to society.[39]

One foot nearer & I plunge myself from the precipice.
Un pied plus près et je me plonge dans le précipice.

Figure 3.3: *Rebecca and the Templar.* Drawing G. Cruikshank; engraving J. Goodyear. From *Landscape-Historical Illustrations of Scotland and the Waverley Novels* (London, 1836–8).

Martineau was exceptional in the eloquent feminism of her identification with the marginalized Rebecca, but not in her enthusiasm for the well-educated and beautiful Jewess. Despite the centrality of Rebecca's role in the novel, and the nascent love between herself and Ivanhoe, the story ends with Rebecca removing herself to Spain while Ivanhoe marries the blond and bland Rowena. As in *The Heart of Mid-Lothian,* Scott used symbolic deportation as a way of upholding the fiction of a unified national culture. But in this case, upholding that fiction meant cutting across the emotional economy of the story. Rebecca, along with Bois-Guilbert (the passionate, ruthless, orientalized, byronic Templar who dies at the end of the story) is the one principal excluded from the reconciliatory ending. The national reconciliation between Saxons and Normans symbolized by the marriage between the Normanized Ivanhoe and the Saxon Rowena restores peace and harmony to England, but at the cost of losing the most interesting character to the ever-after of exile. Had Scott used his freedom to invent by having Rebecca marry Ivanhoe as the logic of the romance demanded, then this would have been at the cost of historical plausibility, as he pointed out to one of his critics, or at the cost of having forced her to convert as Shakespeare's Jessica had done.[40] If Rebecca is used as a foil to highlight the newly found national reconciliation, she also demarcates the artificial limits of the national frame. Through her, as Ian Duncan has put it, 'we glimpse the shadow of a post-national *imperium* that lies beyond the novel's official fiction of nationality.'[41] On the one hand, the novel proposes a view of nationality based on the sublimation of original differences; on the other hand, it performs the fact that differences remain.

History and poetic justice clash. There is perhaps no greater testimony to Scott's historical insight than in the uncomfortable ending of *Ivanhoe,* carrying as it does the harsh lesson that the past cannot be changed and that the historical marginalization of the Jews can never be retrospectively overwritten by romance. It is a lesson in historical necessity.[42] In the historical world of the twelfth century, Spain was indeed a safer place than England for Rebecca and the other Jews of York. But even if one takes into account that anti-Semitism was a historical fact, there is still something shocking about a romance that banishes its attractive female protagonist from its own happy end. Certainly, Scott's choice left readers uncomfortable, drawn to the story and, at the same time, drawn to re-right its structural imbalance.

Scott's genius in disturbing the basic symmetry between Normans and Saxons, and even to disturb the neatness of his own happy end, proved to be a powerful source of mnemonic *energeia*.[43] The story Scott offered to the public was at once highly schematic *and* charged with tension. Or, to use Michael Riffaterre's term, it was charged with an 'ungrammaticality' that made it difficult to merely consume, appropriate, and forget, and that invited correction, re-working, and puzzling through.[44] It is here in the clash between the imaginary and the historically probable that the depth of Scott's engagement with history becomes most apparent, and it is this ambivalence that explains *Ivanhoe*'s procreativity. Like the famous duck/rabbit drawing, it was two things at once: by being vivid and schematic it stuck in people's memory and invited replication; by being ungrammatical, it invited generations of readers to re-write it.[45] To begin with, on the stage.

STAGINGS

Dramatizations of *Ivanhoe* belonged, together with *The Heart of Mid-Lothian*, *Guy Mannering*, *The Bride of Lammermoor*, and *Rob Roy* to the top five of the Waverley novels in terms of its popularity on the stage. As we have seen in Chapter 2, the many productions of *Rob Roy* were based on a very limited number of scripts and, especially for theatre-goers in Scotland, their value lay in the ritual reiteration of the familiar rather than in the exploration of something new. *Ivanhoe* presents a very different picture. To begin with, it was relatively more popular in England than in Scotland while also enjoying a more significant afterlife in operatic form on the European stage. Its dramatization thus reflected the more international appeal of the story itself. Significantly, productions of *Ivanhoe* were based on multiple scripts, at least twenty-five of which were published (Bolton mentions in addition the existence of some forty 'penny dreadful' publications of the plays though it is unlikely that these chapbooks all offered different versions of the story).[46] New productions of *Ivanhoe* were thus quite likely to be based on a different version of the story with the story itself continuously changing in subtle ways. Although the existence of so many versions has been noted, this has usually been in passing as anecdotal evidence of the pliable character of popular theatre and, with the exception of George Soane's *The Hebrew: A Drama* (1820), there has been little attention to individual adaptations. More importantly, there has been no analysis until now of the *Ivanhoe* corpus as a whole. As I shall show, however, the proliferation of Ivanhoes offers a unique opportunity to study both the continuities and the transformations in the story as it travelled through the nineteenth century and beyond: what remained the same and what changed? Which were the 'sticky'

Figure 3.4: *Ivanhoe*, theatrical print. Engraving John Redington (1860–76).

aspects of Scott's story reiterated in all versions, which ones were regularly overlooked, and which ones transformed?

The published versions for the stage, which will be my principal source in what follows, represented a whole range of dramatic genres. There were multiple melodramatic versions, including Thomas Dibdin, *Ivanhoe: Or, the Jew's Daughter; A Romantic Melo-Drama, in Three Acts* (1820); W. T. Moncrieff, *Ivanhoe! Or, the Jewess; a Chivalric Play, in Three Acts*;

Founded on the Popular Romance of 'Ivanhoe' (1820); Samuel Beazley, *Ivanhoe: or, The Knight Templar* (1820); John W. Calcraft, *Ivanhoe, or the Jewess* (1820); A. Bunn, *Ivanhoe: Or, the Jew of York; a New Grand Chivalric Play in Three Acts* (1820); and W. H. Murray, *Ivanhoe: a Historical Drama, Founded on the Celebrated Romance of the Same Name, by the Author of 'Waverley'* (1823). There were multiple versions that can be broadly classified as international opera, including those by Emile Deschamps and Gustave de Wailly, *Ivanhoe: opéra en trois actes* (1826), Heinrich Marschner, *Der Templer und die Jüdin* (1829); G. M. Marini and Otto Nicolai, *Il templario* (1840); and the 'Romantic Opera' by Arthur Sullivan and Julian Sturgis mentioned earlier that was produced to a rather lukewarm reception in 1891.[47] Finally, as befits such a popular work, *Ivanhoe* had the honour of being the subject of multiple burlesques, including Robert B. and William Brough, *The Last Edition of Ivanhoe, with All the Newest Improvements; an Extravaganza in Two Acts* (1850); Henry J. Byron, *Ivanhoe in Accordance with the Spirit of the Times; an Extravaganza* (1858); and Thomas J. Plowman, *Isaac Abroad; or, Ivanhoe Settled and Rebecca Righted* (1878).[48]

The subtitle 'national', which so often appeared in productions of *Rob Roy* and the other Scottish novels, was missing in the case of *Ivanhoe*. In some cases, moreover, the actual scripts belied their generic titles. The version by Deschamps and de Wailly (1826) announced itself as an opera and was in fact a pasticcio in which they reworked a medley of tunes by Rossini.[49] Lacy's *The Maid of Judah; or the Knight's Templar* (1829), which Bolton considers the most successful one in terms of the number of times it was produced, presented itself as a 'serious opera' but was in fact a reworking of Deschamps and de Wailly's *Ivanhoe*, with music by Rossini (this accumulation of different authors and composers provides another good example of the sampling endemic to the theatre at this time). Marschner's *Der Templer und die Jüdin* (1829), with a libretto by Wohlbrück, was an internationally successful opera brought to London in 1840 and apparently produced there in German (without any of the controversy that surrounded productions of other Europeanized Scott plays).[50] But although all of these versions of *Ivanhoe* had a musical dimension, there was no fixed repertoire of songs associated with its dramatization as there so clearly was in case of *Rob Roy*.

In contrast, the playbills indicate that the theatrical productions of *Ivanhoe* in England were drenched through with the spectacular aesthetics of melodrama. Thus a prominent place was reserved on the playbills for enumerations of the scenery and stage props that the audience could expect (a tendency that was mocked in the many burlesque versions that appeared from the 1840s on).[51] The programme bill for an anonymous production at the Theatre Royal in Edinburgh on 3 June 1828, for example, promised the spectators in bold-capitals: 'THE GRAND TOURNAMENT...THE ATTACK AND DESTRUCTION OF TORQUILSTONE CASTLE...THE PROCESSION OF REBECCA TO THE STAKE, AND TRIAL BY COMBAT.'[52] On another occasion, the machinery deployed for the burning of Torquilstone was so elaborate that the audience was warned in advance that an extra interval was being planned in order to 'arrange the stage for this extraordinary spectacle'.[53] Equestrian performances, pageantry, and displays of sword play were also popular. A one-night revival of Dibdin's play at the Surrey Theatre in September 1834 featured the 'TOURNAMENT in which Mr Hill and an Amateur (his pupil) will give a GRAND ILLUSTRATION of the Elegant and Manly exercise of THE SMALL SWORD,' while *Ivanhoe; or, The Lists of Ashby* was a regular feature of Astley's circus up to at least 1859.[54] This emphasis on spectacle reflected the character of the novel, which, arguably more than the Scottish stories, is structured around richly graphic and colourful scenes packed with antiquarian knowledge and characters dressed in historical costume.

Even a cursory comparison of the twenty or so scripts published in the nineteenth century indicates that some characters and scenes were highly resilient.[55] To begin with, a hard core of characters turned up in almost every version: Ivanhoe the Saxon-turned-Norman crusader; his father, Cedric-the-Saxon; a group of Normans spear-headed by Brian de Bois-Guilbert; Cedric's fool Wamba and his servant Gurth; Robin Hood and Friar Tuck; Isaac and Rebecca.[56] Beyond these highly memorable core characters whose re-appearance had immediate recognition value, there were also a number of dispensable characters who figure in the novel, but were left out of some or all of the dramas. Most prominent among the dispensables is 'Athelstane the Unready'. The last representative of the Saxon Royal House was apparently also Athelstane the Forgettable since he was the character most consistently jettisoned, appearing in only two of the earliest adaptations (Dibdin, Moncrieff) and dropping out of view altogether after 1820. Rowena, the colourless Saxon princess and Ivanhoe's future wife, was also written out of several scripts, as was Prince John, the servant Elgitha, Ulrica the abused Saxon heiress, and even King Richard aka the Black Knight.[57] The resilience of a hard core of recognizable characters confirms the importance of individual 'figures of memory' as points of reference in cultural memory already discussed in relation to Jeanie Deans.

Inevitably the cast of characters had to be reduced in order to fit the novel into the confines of a stage performance, while keeping intact the basic intelligibility of the plot and its outcome. The fact that Thomas

Dibdin had stuck too closely to the novel and as a result ended up with the largest cast of characters may partly explain why his rather unwieldy version, which was the first to reach the stage within just a month of the novel's publication, did not become the standard one. The way in which the various dramatists went about reducing the number of characters reflects their understanding of the underlying logic of the plot and of the double conflict at the heart of the novel: between the Saxons and the Normans as they struggle to gain control of England; between Ivanhoe and Bois-Guilbert as they struggle to possess or protect Rebecca the Jewess. Demonstrating a structuralist understanding of narrativity *avant la lettre*, dramatists mixed and matched characters quite freely, apparently considering characters to be dispensable if their role in this double conflict could be taken over by someone else (Cedric could represent the Saxon world as well as Athelstane, Ivanhoe could take over from Richard the Lionheart as the champion of justice, and so on) or if their role was not actually necessary for the outcome of the story (thus the Norman castle of Torquilstone could be destroyed without Ulrica being the one to burn it down). In some cases, however, a character's resilience did not follow from the logic of the narrative. Wamba the fool, for example, has neither a dramatic role of any significance to play in determining the outcome of events nor a symbolic role as political representative of the Saxon order. Nevertheless, he kept turning up in the dramatizations, his memorability apparently a function of his value as local colour and of the amusement afforded by his appearance and his verbal plays rather than by his historical role.[58]

The point is reinforced by looking at the scenes selected for staging the novel. A comparison between the different versions again shows a certain amount of continuity with recurrent locations being Cedric's banquet hall at Rotherwood, the Forest where Robin Hood hangs out, the castle of Torquilstone, and the Priory at Templestowe where Rebecca is tried, threatened with execution, and then saved from the scaffold. The Tournament at Ashby featured in the earliest versions by Dibdin and Moncrieff and in the equestrian versions at Astley, but it was by and large overlooked by all of the other dramatists. Given the spectacular character of the tournament, which was picked up by others as we shall see later, it is all the more puzzling that most playwrights opted to drop Ashby as a scene and referred indirectly to it instead. The explanation probably lies in the fact that Ashby was less crucial to the plot than, for example, the banquet at Rotherwood where the basis of the story is laid out. There may also have been an element of what Daniel Dennett calls 'accumulated design' at work, meaning that the dramatists built on the work of their predecessors (sometimes explicitly so as the playbills made clear).[59] They not only referred back to Scott's text and often literally repeated passages of his dialogue; they also profited from some of the solutions earlier dramatists had found to the practical problems of putting the novel onto the stage.

Given the pressures on dramatists to be economic, it is all the more surprising that a scene that was unnecessary to the plot should have consistently returned in all the adaptations in English except the burlesques: the scene at the hermitage of Friar Tuck, when the brave Tuck receives a visitor and, having initially protested his asceticism to the stranger, ends up enjoying a rowdy eating and drinking session in his company. In half the plays, the visitor is the Black Knight, aka Richard the Lionheart; in the others, it is Ivanhoe. But the identity of the stranger was clearly less important than the fact that his arrival provided for a comic display of the Friar's devious pursuit of the pleasures of the flesh. (It was presumably because this scene was comic already that it failed to reappear in the burlesques.) The recurrence of the Friar Tuck scene also throws light on the stickiness of the comic figure of Wamba. As *einfache Formen*, to invoke Jolles' useful term, jokes and comic incidents (like the songs in *Rob Roy*) persist as discrete units that can be recycled in changing contexts.[60]

Underscoring this point, Stephen Knight has shown that Scott's novel was responsible for the popular image of Friar Tuck current today.[61] He had been a regular component of Robin Hood legends before the novel. But it was only with the advent of *Ivanhoe* that the friar became associated with Richard the Lionheart and that 'tuck' became synonymous with merry gluttony, with Scott's friar providing a model for later versions of the Robin Hood legend. Scott's reworking of the Robin Hood legend provides another fascinating illustration of the composite nature of his texts and of the intersection, against the background of increasing commercialization, between popular traditions and literate culture. As we have already seen in the case of *The Heart of Mid-Lothian* and *Rob Roy*, Scott worked many materials from oral traditions and ballad culture into his novels; the case of Friar Tuck provides a rare illustration of the subsequent influence of Scott's writings—probably as much through remediations on stage as through the book itself—on later popular tradition. More generally, *Ivanhoe* may also have helped in carrying over the legend of Robin Hood into modern cinema, where it has proliferated right up to the most recent version by Ridley Scott (2010) starring Russell Crowe.

The interaction between literary and popular culture also worked in the other direction: aspects of the Robin Hood legend neglected by Scott found their way back into the theatrical adaptations. The dramatists not only reduced Scott's narrative to dramatic proportions by cutting back on the number of characters and scenes, they also on occasion added to his repertoire of characters. Whereas Allan-a-Dale's name is only mentioned in passing in the novel, he himself appears on stage in several versions (Beazley, Bunn, Murray, Lacy, Brough). Moreover, the figure of Little John, well known from popular stories but missing from Scott's novel, reappeared as a character in Lacy's dramatization. These are minor details, bearing on marginal characters, but they speak volumes about the way in which stage versions of Scott's novel functioned as a vehicle for cultural memory, providing a platform for the public revival not only of the novel itself, but also of *other* stories—in this case, the large body of folklore relating to Robin Hood—with which it was associated. Again, a parallel can be drawn with the case of *Rob Roy* where, as we have seen, the novel and its stagings helped reinvigorate folkloric traditions relating to the Highland outlaw and helped carry them over into the age of screen culture.

This brings me again to the fact that *Ivanhoe*, unlike *Rob Roy*, was subject to such repeated re-writing. The need to avoid copyright claims and the dramaturgical difficulties in transposing a novel to the stage go some way towards accounting for the number of scripts along with the resonance of the story in popular legend.[62] But since these conditions applied to both novels, the explanation for the number of versions of *Ivanhoe* must be sought elsewhere: back to Rebecca.

RIGHTING REBECCA

Scott's achievement in creating a highly intriguing Jewess in the person of Rebecca was not only acknowledged, as we have seen, by the first generation of critics, but she continued to fascinate painters and dramatists for decades after her first appearance. As the titles of many of the plays indicate and several commentators have noted, she also literally upstaged Ivanhoe in the theatrical adaptations: *Ivanhoe: Or, the Jew's Daughter*; *Ivanhoe! Or, the Jewess*; *The Hebrew; a Drama*; *Ivanhoe: Or, the Jew of York*; *The Templar and the Jewess/Der Templer und die Jüdin*; *The Maid of Judah; or, the Knights Templar; a Serious Opera in Three Acts*; *Isaac Abroad; or, Ivanhoe Settled and Rebecca Righted*.[63] Given the main thrust of Scott's narrative towards national reconciliation, it is remarkable just how much attention was paid by his adaptors to Rebecca and, to a lesser extent, her evil pursuer, the Templar Bois Guilbert: orientalized characters who, through death or emigration, end up excluded from the new Britain. These new versions were attempts to resolve the tension between historical necessity and romance that Scott had brought into play.

This was most clearly the case in George Soane's *The Hebrew; a Drama* (1820), the play that has most frequently come onto the radar screen of literary critics. The most overtly philosemitic of all versions and the most radical in its re-working of the story, it was produced as part of the first wave of *Ivanhoe* adaptations in 1820. Eliminating all secondary characters except Robin Hood and the inevitable Friar Tuck and ignoring the whole political dimension relating to the return and restoration of King Richard, Soane's play re-focuses the drama so that maximum coverage is given to the trials and tribulations of Isaac and his daughter (and their servant Miriam, who had indeed figured in Scott but was usually overlooked on the stage). In doing so Soane activated a Shakespearean intertext designed to enhance Isaac's stature as a misused and tragic old man: the last act in particular is laden with quotations from *King Lear*.[64] In keeping with the memory of the earlier Shakespearean play and taking the sting out of Scott's novel at the price of killing off a character, the play ends with Isaac's dying for joy on hearing of the rescue of his daughter at the hands of Ivanhoe and not with a marriage.

Other versions of the play were not as narrowly focused on the Jewish characters; nor were they as obviously concerned with giving Isaac a good press. But they too reworked Scott's novel in such a way as to engage with its tensions rather than merely reproduce them in the same form (the only exception is Moncrieff, who tended to stick quite closely to the Scott script). Common to all other adaptations is that the ending focuses on the rescue of Rebecca and the restoration of Richard rather than on the imminent marriage of Ivanhoe to Rowena and the departure of Rebecca. Remarkably for a romance, Ivanhoe's bride was left off-stage in the final scene by almost all dramatists (Moncrieff again, along with Sturgis, was an exception to this rule). The final tableaux celebrate above all the national unity that has been achieved with the restoration of Richard's regal power and the up-beat saving of Rebecca from the stake, events that are usually made to coincide in a 'let's all be British' sort of sing-along (mocked in the Broughs' burlesque as a 'grand tableau of all nations, singing "Rule Britannia" '). Nowhere is there an explicit reference to the exile of Isaac and Rebecca in Spain and so their ultimate fate in the midst of the national reconciliation is left undetermined—but with variations. Most striking in this regard is Wohlbrück's ending where Ivanhoe, having saved Rebecca, expresses his thanks to her for her earlier rescue of him; she is then invited to speak her heart's desire, but just as the public might wonder whether she will declare her love for Ivanhoe, the music stops: the result is a suspended animation in which all possibilities remain open. Lacy (who in other respects follows Wohlbrück quite closely) has Rebecca fall in gratitude at Ivanhoe's feet, while Marini's *Il Templario* ends with the love-struck Rebecca swooning in the arms of her father. Deschamps and Wailly opted in 1826 for the extreme measure of turning Rebecca into a Muslim, who luckily and utterly implausibly turns out in the end to have been a Saxon all along so that she can marry Ivanhoe. The detail is different in each case, but Rebecca's departure from England is everywhere elided even as she remains the centre of the show, almost always a tragic one.

The fact that the story continued to be re-written suggests that none of the solutions proposed was felt to be satisfactory. Although the dramatists did borrow from each other in other respects, then, it is remarkable that no two endings were quite the same. In a satiric story called 'Rebecca and Rowena' (1850), William Makepeace Thackeray articulated and poked fun at the commonly held belief that 'by rights' Rebecca should have married Ivanhoe while Rowena was sent off to a convent, his story ending in the following way:

And who is that comes out of the house—trembling—panting—with her arms out—in a white dress—with her hair down—who is it but dear Rebecca? Look, they rush together, and Master Wamba is waving an immense banner over them, and knocks down a circumambient Jew with a ham which he happens to have in his pocket...As for Rebecca, now her head is laid upon Ivanhoe's heart, I shall not ask to hear what she is whispering, or describe further that scene of meetings: though I declare I am quite affected when I think of it. Indeed I have thought of it any time these five-and-twenty years—ever since as a boy at school, I commenced the noble study of novels—ever since the day when, lying on sunny slopes, on half-holidays, the fair chivalrous figures and beautiful shapes of knights and ladies were visible to me—ever since I grew to love Rebecca, that sweetest creature of the poet's fancy, and longed to see her righted.[65]

Although Thackeray's spoof articulated the underlying logic of the re-scripting of *Ivanhoe* and is regularly quoted, it was actually exceptional in its ceding to the desire to have Rebecca marry Ivanhoe. For although the 'longing to see Rebecca righted' persisted well beyond the first generation of Scott readers, it never simply meant that the Jewish Rebecca married the Christian Ivanhoe, either because this was unthinkable for people in the nineteenth century or because it would have betrayed the historicity of Scott's original.

As in the case of *Rob Roy* and *The Heart of Mid-Lothian*, stage productions of *Ivanhoe* dried up in the twentieth century. The silent movie *Ivanhoe* (1913), directed by Herbert Brenon and filmed on location at Chepstow Castle with the aid of hundreds of local extras, broke with the theatrical tradition by actually highlighting the exile of the two Jews and making their non-assimilation, rather than the national reconciliation, into the outcome of the plot: the hour-long film closes with the haunting image of Isaac and Rebecca looking out to sea as they prepare to leave England, which, according to one contemporary commentator, shows her thinking of the 'happiness that might have been hers had he but returned her love.'[66] In the same year, yet another film version by Leedham Bantock came out under the title *The Jewess*: although unfortunately only a fragment of this movie is extant and the precise ending is unknown, the section that does exist shows a beautiful and vigorous Rebecca expressing her passion for Ivanhoe and then being thwarted by Rowena. This may not be 'righting' Rebecca by giving her Ivanhoe, but it is 'righting' her in the sense of keeping her concerns centre stage.

In a well-documented case from 1946–7, a version planned by Paramount Studios based on a script by Aeneas MacKenzie again pursued the dream of 'righting Rebecca' in a new guise. This took place in the aftermath of the Holocaust and against the background of debates about the foundation of the state of Israel and the future of Britain as a colonial

Figure 3.5: Rebecca and Isaac, *Ivanhoe* (1913: dir. Brenon), still.

power. The film was to close with a 'Land of Hope and Glory' and, more interesting from our perspective here, with the marriage of Ivanhoe to Rebecca—initially conceived by Mackenzie as a Jewish wedding, and subsequently revised to a Christian one under a Jewish canopy and in the presence of a rabbi. As Jonathan Stubbs has pointed out in a fascinating discussion of the case, MacKenzie's screenplay had a utopian dimension, imagining a society based on racial harmony in the immediate aftermath of World War II.[67] Plans to produce the movie were scuttled, however, ostensibly because it was deemed 'sacrilege to rewrite a classic'; in fact, according to Stubbs, because Paramount became afraid that their anti-racism would be perceived as 'anti-American' against the background of the Hollywood witch-hunt that figured so prominently in the work of the House Un-American Activities Committee in those years.[68] In the event, when *Ivanhoe* was released as a major Hollywood film in 1952 based on Noel Langley's adaptation of MacKenzie's screenplay, Ivanhoe was back to marrying Rowena. Nevertheless, Rebecca, through the star Elizabeth Taylor, continued to hold centre-stage: her trial for witchcraft was the dramatic highpoint of the film, an anti-McCarthyite touch that predated Arthur Miller's better-known *The Crucible* (1953) by a year. More recently, the 1997 BBC mini-series (dir. Stuart Orme) realized the feminist potential indicated by Harriet Martineau when she called on women to allow Rebecca to 'speak for them to society' by portraying Rebecca as an independent woman who actively chooses to leave England and, in contrast to her counterpart in 1913, actively renounces a life with Ivanhoe.

This ongoing story of the re-writings of *Ivanhoe* shows how playwrights and script-writers have fixated on the figure of Rebecca and, in the process, adapted Scott's work in such a way as to reduce or resolve its tensions, occasionally at the cost of fidelity both to Scott's text and to history. In all these appropriations the classic was recalibrated in the light of contemporary values and concerns, be these related to current notions of Britishness or—reflecting the transnational portability of the story—Americanness and, increasingly since World War II, the fate of the European Jews. Instead of being a sacrilege as Paramount suggested, re-writing the classic was a way of articulating contemporary concerns and, to recall Jan Assmann's definition of cultural memory, a way of stabilizing and articulating one's self-image.

Recalibration has not been limited to dramatists and movie-makers. Literary critics too have tended to appropriate Scott's text by re-interpreting it and explaining its ambivalence in the light of contemporary concerns. This is very clear in the case of Philip Cox's extensive discussion of Soane's philosemitic adaptation of *Ivanhoe* in his *Reading Adaptations* (2000). In one

of the few analyses of this work, Cox focuses on the Lear-like rendition of
Isaac, and interprets this as a 'pointed reminder of the violent exclusions
upon which images of national and cultural unity are established'; indeed,
Cox writes, 'such is the power of the performance that it seems to offer the
spectator a more finished rendition of Isaac than the mere draft version
provided by Scott in his original novel; the play develops Isaac as a
protagonist in ways which, although perhaps unexpected, seem, retrospectively, entirely convincing.'[69] Convincing to whom? Convincing in the
first instance to the critic as he notes with approval the way in which Soane
has indeed worked through some of the tensions inherent in Scott's work.
But apparently not so convincing to Scott's own contemporaries (with the
notable exception of William Hazlitt): the play had a short run of some
eight performances at Drury Lane in March and April 1820, and was
never revived again.[70] This was arguably not, as Cox suggests, because the
public found the tragic figure of Isaac too painful,[71] but because—as the
reviewer from the *Times* suggested—the adaptation had strayed too far
from the original novel and, in doing so, had also become historically
implausible:

A preliminary objection will be felt by many spectators to this drama, in the
confusion it creates with the associations caused by the great popularity of the
novel. Any deviation from a story so constituted is in great danger, without
extreme caution, of becoming one also from consistency. The lawless love of the
Templar for *Rebecca*, and even the hopeless passion of the fair Jewess for *Ivanhoe*
are quite consistent with the time; but when *Ivanhoe* is made in the drama, to
propose an honourable union with a female, however beautiful, of a race it was
then deemed pollution to hold communication with, our ideas are diverted from
the period, and finding no other to rest on, lose all interest in the story.[72]

By intuition or design, Scott's writing raised thorny issues, promoting and
at the same time undermining the fiction of national unity. This does not
mean that *Ivanhoe* offered a 'pointed reminder of the violent exclusions
upon which images of national and cultural unity are established' (this
would make his work merely monologic and didactic) but rather that his
attempts to imagine a national narrative generated an *energeia* through
its own ambivalence and vividness. Ever since, people have been harness-
ing that energy as they engaged with the story within shifting historical
horizons.

In a study of the modes of transmission prevalent in traditional, oral
cultures Roman Jakobson and Petr Bogatyrev argued that stories in such
cultures are constantly adapted to meet the horizon of expectations of the
world in which they are reproduced.[73] They survive, not just because they
are retrievable, but because they are also adaptable. As the re-scriptings of

Ivanhoe discussed above suggest, the same principle of adaptability seems to apply unexpectedly to what might be described as the first modern best-seller.

INTERACTIVITY

In one of the most recent appropriations of the novel, Jerome McGann has used 'Ivanhoe' as a theoretical model for rethinking the (in)stability of texts with a view to developing new pedagogical and critical tools in interactive digital environments. The collaborative *Ivanhoe* game developed by McGann and his colleagues is designed as an interface for engaging with canonical texts interactively. Within a ludic framework, players re-write the original text so as to highlight and articulate some of the implicit, but unexplored narrative possibilities generated by the text. The choice fell on *Ivanhoe* as a flagship for this programme because it offered, according to McGann, a textbook example of a work with different 'narrative possibilities' and of a book that had accordingly been regularly re-written (to illustrate how fictions can be re-imagined, he himself offered an interesting Byronic reading in which Rebecca marries Bois-Guilbert). Referring to Victorian readers' unhappiness with Scott's decision to marry Ivanhoe to Rowena and not to Rebecca, and to present-day readers' discomfort with his handling of anti-Semitism, McGann challenged his contemporaries to be as proactive as earlier generations:

Everyone knows that an anti-Semitic strain runs through the novel...The question is: 'What are you prepared to DO about it?' Victorians rewrote and reimagined the book. Why are we so hesitant about doing the same thing?[74]

The analysis given above of the morphings of *Ivanhoe* bears out McGann's basic point about the performativity of reading: even where it is not acknowledged as such, reading is an active, and sometimes highly creative appropriation of an existing text in view of present-day values. My analysis also chimes in with his basic point that adaptations and reworkings should not be dismissed as derivative forms: they can be fruitfully taken as paradigmatic for reading as such. Nevertheless, his suggestion that Victorians unhesitatingly 'rewrote and re-imagined the book' gives the impression that this process of adaptation was unfettered by the original text. A closer look at the replication and transformation of *Ivanhoe* over time shows that script-writers indeed re-wrote the story, but that they did so while struggling with the limits set by historical plausibility, their own imaginative limits, the desire to be loyal to Scott, and the contours of the original text as a 'tool to think with'. Both readers and Scott were active agents in this process.

This is not to say that all of those who appropriated *Ivanhoe* were interested in engaging with its complexities. At a certain point the story, as we shall see in the next chapter, also became so well known that it could even be recalled and harnessed to contemporary agendas without any direct knowledge of the original.

4

Re-enacting *Ivanhoe*

The classics are the books about which you usually hear people saying: 'I am rereading...' and never 'I am reading.'
—Italo Calvino, *Why Read the Classics?* (1980)

Despite poor health, foreshadowing his death later that year, Walter Scott spent the spring of 1832 with his son and daughter in Naples. He was fêted by all and sundry, among others by the Austrian minister who organized a masquerade ball in his honour on the theme of the Waverley novels. The invitations to this literary masquerade apparently led to some commotion, Scott's son, Charles, describing how 'one beautiful Italian woman has been in tears for the last week because her family are too Catholic to allow her to take the character of Rebecca the Jewess.'[1] The anecdote shows how the Waverley characters had become household words even in Scott's lifetime and illustrates the international popularity of *Ivanhoe* (1819), especially the figure of Rebecca, among readers throughout Europe. Even more importantly here, it brings to light an 'embodied' form of remediation that, well in advance of computer role-playing games, involved people acting out stories and getting dressed up as their favourite characters. Refusing a Catholic permission even to make-believe that she is a Jewess betrays a striking belief in the power of role-playing.

The Naples episode was part of a fashion in the 1820s and 1830s for *tableaux vivants* and masquerades based on the Waverley themes. There are accounts of similar events taking place in Vienna, Paris, Calcutta, and Hertfordshire, while so-called Waverley balls also took place in Edinburgh in the early 1840s as a way of raising funds to build the Scott monument (see below, Chapter 6).[2] Obviously, a feeling for fashion was an important part of these games played by the European rich. But the reluctance to have a Catholic play a Jewess or, to invoke another incident related by Richard Barsham, the unwillingness of Englishmen to play Isaac indicates that this role-playing was also part and parcel of the everyday articulation of identities: it was a way of displaying a collective appreciation for Scott and, in the process, a way of temporarily identifying with one of his characters, or refusing to do so.[3] As such, it provides another illustration of the way Scott's readers incorporated their imaginative experiences into everyday objects and practices.

As mentioned earlier, the recent turn to performativity in Humanities research invites us to analyse remembrance as a form of action, as a way both of recalling things from the past and of doing something in the present. Whether in the form of interpreting, re-writing, remediating, or re-enacting, recollecting 'Ivanhoe' was a way for people to play roles in the present through the intermediary of a story from 1819. As the anecdote of the would-be Rebecca in Naples suggests, however, the word 'performative' can be used with respect to recollections of Scott's work both in the generalized sense of agency and in the more specific sense of theatricality and role-playing: remembrance as re-enactment. As Helen Solterer has shown in her studies of medieval theatricality in twentieth-century France, re-enactments of earlier scenarios, whether on stage or in daily life, represented a way of literally performing identities in the modern world: historical role-playing helped people to orient themselves and shape their own actions amidst the crises and complexities of twentieth-century history.[4] Taking its cue from Solterer's analysis of what she calls 'medieval roles for modern times', this chapter on the afterlife of *Ivanhoe* will reach beyond its critical reception on the part of professional readers and its remediations on the actual stage to the various re-enactments of the story in the form of embodied role-playing outside the theatre. In doing so I will be less concerned with how individuals identify with particular characters than with the ways in which appropriations of *Ivanhoe* were linked to the articulation of *collective* identities.

Studies of collective memory, especially those in the tradition of Maurice Halbwachs, have generally assumed that memories are shaped by the social frames (the family, class, religious community, nation) in which they are expressed and that these frames have an a priori existence.[5] While following Halbwachs in accepting the importance of social frames to memory, I depart from his belief in their prior existence by arguing instead that acts of remembrance do not so much give expression to identity as that they are agents in articulating it. Communities, including national ones, come into existence together with the stories about their emergence.[6] As recent comparative research on nationalism by Joep Leerssen has shown, one of the remarkable features about nation-building is what might be called the paradox of universal exceptionalism: national groups stake their claim to distinctiveness and shape their distinctiveness in comparable ways and following common transnational templates.[7]

Models of remembrance and of identity travel across the boundaries of languages, cultures, and territories along with the narratives in which they are articulated. The Waverley model and *Ivanhoe* in particular, as we shall see, was one of the templates that travelled in this way.

As we have seen, Scott's works offered graphic details about past lives embedded in narratives of conflict. His work inspired widespread interest among historians throughout the Western world in lived experience as an object of historical inquiry. But it also offered a model of remembrance for dealing with *other* events in which a comparable struggle between modernizers and traditionalists, or between intruders and natives, was played out. In the absence of many precedents at the time, the Waverley model worked as a catalyst for writing the story of other groups by providing a template for shaping national histories. As mentioned earlier, Scott had already performed a *translatio* in his own *oeuvre*, by applying the Waverley template, developed with respect to Scotland, to his narrative of England in the Middle Ages. What is more, the two-nation Waverley model had proved remarkably fruitful for other groups as they sought in the early nineteenth century to articulate their nascent national narratives both inside and outside the British Empire.[8] As a recent study of his European reception shows, Scott also provided an inspiration to other 'small' nations (the Poles, the Czechs, among others) seeking to establish their distinctiveness within a larger imperial framework.[9]

Scott's narrative matrix proved to be as portable as the novels themselves. The French historian Augustin Thierry, who had praised Scott for having brought out the 'poetry' of Scottish history, went on to adopt his basic model of ethnic conflict and conflict resolution in his own historical work on the early history of France.[10] The Belgian writer Hendrik Conscience produced a new version of *Ivanhoe* in his novelistic epic *De leeuw van Vlaenderen* (1838) about the struggle between French oppressors and the Flemish in the late Middle Ages; while the Polish writer Henryk Sienkiewicz also took the struggles of the Poles against successive foreign oppressors as the template for his historical fiction, most notably in his *Trylogia* (1884–8). Perhaps most remarkably since it involved a distinctiveness vis-à-vis England, the idea of Irishness put forward by the nationalist poet Thomas Davis also echoed the hybridizing terms of *Ivanhoe*. As he wrote in the 1840s, '[Irish nationality] must contain and represent the races of Ireland. It must not be Celtic, it must not be Saxon—it must be Irish.'[11]

This international appropriation of the basic Waverley model, especially as this became disseminated through the bestseller *Ivanhoe*, shows how Scott's work as a medium of remembrance crossed over the borders of mnemonic communities and, as importantly, helped create new ones by providing a language and a template for narrating hitherto marginalized or diffused topics. In the process of being adapted, as Murray Pittock has remarked, Scott's work was sometimes harnessed to causes more overtly nationalistic and separatist than those envisaged by the author himself.[12] *Ivanhoe* may have represented to a certain degree 'more of the same' in relation to the earlier Waverley novels, and accordingly enjoyed less critical acclaim. But the fact that its plotline was so strong and that it dealt with the Middle Ages meant that its applicability to other situations was broader than in the case of the specifically Scottish conflicts of the seventeenth and eighteenth centuries treated in other novels. Its portability ensured its further survival in the form of appropriations within a variety of national and cultural frameworks.

Where the previous chapter dealt with the adaptation of *Ivanhoe* to other media, my concern here will be with its travels to other constituencies; how the story passed across the borders of particular mnemonic communities and, in the process, helped create new lines of identification. I argue that the capacity to transfer memories and to mediate between groups underpins the role played by historical fiction in the formation of nineteenth-century identities.[13] I develop this point by analysing the appropriations of *Ivanhoe* in the United States, showing how its narrative of the British Middle Ages was adapted to local circumstances. How did the recollections of Scott's story reflect the changing social contexts in which it was recalled?

In addressing this question I build on some points already made with respect to *The Heart of Mid-Lothian*: namely, that Scott's work was characterized by a temporally convoluted combination of monumentality (persistence as is) and malleability (openness to appropriation by others). As a result, its reception did not evolve in a linear way: while the various interpretations of the novel worked accumulatively and the name Ivanhoe became more and more iconic, the original text continued to persist as a monumental point of reference to which people could always return in search of a new starting point.

JOUSTING: THE NOVEL AS CHIVALRIC SCRIPT

On 26 August 1842, a ring tournament was held at Fauquier Springs, Virginia, in which an Ivanhoe on horseback fought along with other 'knights' for the honour of crowning some lady the 'Queen of Love and Beauty'.[14] The event belonged to the contemporary fashion for literary masquerades among the upper classes already mentioned. Within the North American context, it also fitted in with a burgeoning tournament tradition that had been partially inspired by the spectacular medieval tournament organized in Ayrshire in 1839 by Lord Eglinton, news of which had spread across the Atlantic.[15] That extravagant event had itself been modelled on the Ashby-de-la-Zouche tournament in *Ivanhoe* and had possibly also been inspired by some of the equestrian versions of *Ivanhoe* mentioned in the previous chapter. While its main purpose was entertainment and the possibility for wealthy aristocrats to indulge in the make-believe that they were medieval knights, it was also construed by organizers and commentators alike as a political statement on the part of Tory aristocrats: the display of ancient traditions and rituals was a mark of opposition to a Whig government that had opted to ignore such outmoded traditions in the coronation of Victoria in April 1838. Not a trace of this contemporary context is to be seen, however, in the idealized representations of the tournament in circulation. As Alexander Tyrell shows, the event was also designed as a way for Lord Eglinton and his colleagues to court popular goodwill by providing a mass spectacle integrating tartan symbols of Scottishness and Highland games into the otherwise medieval event (these demonstrations of Scottishness formed the prelude to a mass celebration of the work of Robert Burns at the same location in 1844).[16]

Among the estimated hundred thousand spectators at the Ayrshire event was a William Gilmor from Maryland who, on his return to the United States, imported the Eglinton model in organizing a first tournament in 1840 at his estate in Baltimore. This was to prove the beginning of a fashion that was concentrated in Maryland and Virginia in the antebellum period, and became widespread after the Civil War in all of the Confederate states, only diminishing in popularity after the 1880s.[17] The combination of re-enactment, entertainment, and political performance evident in the Eglinton tournament also played into the development of a newly invented tradition in the Southern American states. Popular among the upper-class elite, tournament-going became the marker of aristocratic values in the slave-owning society. In playing out the roles of jousting knights, these southern gentlemen were following a nostalgic chivalric script, projecting a historical imagination fed by the works of Scott and Scott's own play-acting at Abbotsford into their own leisure activities.

These latter-day medievalist tournaments picked up on existing local traditions—'tournaments' involving cock-fighting and horse-racing and displays of horsemanship—and transformed them into 'chivalric' displays, albeit ones attended by people in top hats and crinolines. It was arguably because of this affinity with existing pastimes and with an honour-based ethos that the tournament became as popular as it did in the Southern states, where it was also coloured by various local touches (these included

Figure 4.1: *Tilting and the Grand Stand*. From J. Aikman and W. Gordon, *An Account of the Tournament at Eglinton* (Edinburgh, 1839).

at least one occasion on which the figure of an Indian was used as a shooting target).[18] The tournaments involved high-order pageantry, where gentlemen riders took on the name of a knight and, often dressed in an appropriate costume, ran jousting poles through rings so as to compete for the privilege of crowning some lady the 'queen of his heart' according to protocols that, within a short time, became quite formalized. The names adopted by the gentlemen-knights were regularly taken from literature—from Scott, but also from the works of Spenser, Tennyson, and Cervantes. This popularity underscores the point made earlier about the role of literature in providing a secular pantheon of characters and underscores more generally the importance of Literature to identity-building in the mid-nineteenth century: people defined who they were by defining their relationship to particular writers.

Especially in the later tournaments the frame of reference became wider and many of the adopted names were whimsical inventions or, after 1865,

Figure 4.2: *The Alabama State Fair: The Tilt* [from a Sketch by Nixon]. *Harper's Weekly*, 27 November 1858.

references to the Civil War. Scott was by no means the only inspiration, therefore, or the only point of reference. But running like a red thread through all the tournaments, his work seems to have had a privileged role, and Ivanhoe was the most popular of his characters.[19] The *Richmond Enquirer*, for example, provided a graphic account on 2 September 1845 of another tournament in Fauquier County, Virginia, in which local gentlemen engaged in tilting, jousting, and heralding, with all the trappings of medieval pageantry, and using the titles of Ivanhoe and Bois-Guilbert, but also comically joined at the last moment by a burlesque Don Quixote.[20] Such pageant-like jousting in imitation of literary models (sometimes accompanied by the Queen of Sheba, an 'Indian Chief', or even the comic 'Knight before last') took place at regular intervals in Virginia up to the Civil War and there are even reports of their taking place among the Confederate wounded in the closing years of the conflict.[21] The drawing by Léon Joseph Frémaux (1821–98), reproduced opposite, which was probably made in 1862 while he was a colonel in the Confederate army, literally projects the name of Rowena onto a military encampment and, in the process, reveals the extent to which the story of Ivanhoe had penetrated into hearts and minds of the age, into the very subjectivity of those looking at the world.[22] This foregrounding of Rowena is also remarkable: a local deviation from all other responses to the novel, it stands in stark contrast to the emphasis on Rebecca in the adaptations of the story by painters and dramatists in Great Britain and Europe. The post-war tournaments, which were often attended by former military leaders and used as fundraisers for monuments to the Confederate dead, saw the regular appearance of knights recalling specific events in the war along with figures from Scott.[23] At one such event in Holly Springs, North Carolina, in July 1866, the list of knights included a Knight of the Lost Cause, a Knight of Bull Run, and a Knight of the Potomac along with a variety of Scott figures from both the novels and the poetry: Coeur de Lion, Rob Roy, Snowdon, Rhoderic Dhu, James Fitz-James, Malcolm Graeme, Douglas, the last figures all recognizable from *The Lady of the Lake*.[24]

The Southern tournaments are interesting in themselves as a locally specific precursor of modern-day re-enactment societies. They are also interesting for what they reveal about the shaping of a regional identity and the cultural memory of the South. If the tournaments began as a pastime for the plantation-owning elite, they ended up as markers of a self-conscious tradition: the prominence of the Knights of the Lost Cause and the association with the Confederate army suggests that the tournaments, by being repeated annually, had become self-reflexive expressions of affiliation with a specifically Southern culture and its recent history. In playing out their tournaments the Southern ladies and gentlemen were not only having a good time. From a certain point on, they were actively shaping and publicly identifying with a particular tradition seen as a mark

Figure 4.3: *Confederate Encampment.* Drawing Léon Joseph Frémaux (*c.*1862).

of distinction with respect to their fellow Americans in the northern states.[25] What may have started as a ludic blow-over from Britain seems to have become fairly quickly established as a calibrator of local identity that was self-reflexively cultivated as such.[26]

The appropriation of 'Ivanhoe' in the form of local tournaments thus fed into a larger cultural movement in which the identity of the South was increasingly defined in its difference from the North and in opposition to the North's perceived progressivism. Particularly from the mid-century, the political differences between the North and South were translated into racial terms and construed as the manifestation of a deep-seated historical opposition between two different ethnic traditions. Here too Scott played an important role. Indeed, the reception of his work from the 1820s helped prepare the ground for the political imagination at work in the 1850s and helped transform opposing views on the future of the United States into the apparent reflection of immutable racial differences.[27] Scott's work provided some of the language with which the South identified itself, several of the key words regularly used to define the distinctiveness of southern culture being actually neologisms borrowed from Scott's earlier poetical work. 'Aristocratical', 'Southron', and 'the Chivalry' were all branded with Scott his mark. Indeed, behind the reception of *Ivanhoe* lay the popularity of Scott's poetry, which continued to figure prominently in the tournaments, as the example from 1866 illustrates. (The ongoing importance of the poetry is also illustrated by the fact that from the 1820s on, thanks to an 1812 dramatization of *The Lady of the Lake*, 'Hail to the Chief' had become the signature tune of American presidents.[28])

In ways less easy to pinpoint than lexical items, the Waverley model provided one of the blueprints for interpreting current political differences. It will be recalled how Coleridge had ascribed Scott's longevity to the fact that he had dealt with the perennial clash between Loyalists, bent on preserving tradition, and Progressives, bent on shaping the future. This underlying narrative matrix provided an imaginative resource for representing the current differences between North and South as a historical clash between two cultures with contrasting European roots (the black population was left out of the picture). Since Scott's own work was suffused throughout with a preoccupation with cultural differences and the power struggles between forward-looking and backward-looking groups, it resonated with many contemporary concerns in the United States and helped articulate them. Although his fiction dealt with Scotland or with medieval England, then, it provided a model for understanding what was going on in nineteenth-century America in terms of a historical clash between two 'races'. An article in the *Southern Literary Messenger* entitled 'The Difference of Race between the Northern People and the Southern People' (1860) described the current conflict as follows:

The people of the Northern States are more immediately descended of the English Puritans, who emigrated to this continent during the reign of James I...The Puritans at home constituted as a class the common people of England, at least a portion of it, and were descended of the ancient Britons and Saxons.

On the other hand, the Southern States were settled and governed, in a great measure, under supervision of the crown, immediately by and under the direction of persons belonging to the blood and race of the reigning family, and belonged to that stock recognised as CAVALIERS—who were the *royalists* in the time of Charles I, the commonwealth, and Charles II, and directly descended from the Norman Barons of William the Conqueror, a race distinguished, in its earliest history, for its warlike and fearless character, a race in all times since, renowned for its gallantry, its chivalry, its honor, its gentleness, and its intellect.[29]

In this sleight-of-hand genealogy, various historical oppositions were conflated with the Northerners implicitly identified with the Saxon–Puritan group (who have 'severe traits of religious fanaticism', p. 404), while the 'Southrons' (p. 406) are identified with the Norman–Cavalier aristocrats who, ever since the time of the Crusades, have been sallying forth to grandeur and victory: 'men, whose plumes have waved in triumph in all the martial scenes of modern Europe' (p. 407). The historical opposition between Roundhead and Cavalier had been very much in the air since the 1820s, and had its roots in the different patterns of settlement in New England and Virginia. It belonged to the commonplaces of the period where thought was saturated with racial and ethnic oppositions.[30] But the extension of this opposition back in time to the Saxons and Normans, in utter disregard of the niceties of historical fact, carries the definite mark of *Ivanhoe*. In this self-representation, and others like it, the Scott model was re-enacted as it were on the live stage of contemporary politics and used as one of the templates for interpreting the present in the light of other conflicts in which an aristocratic and highly civilized group had been pitted against levellers and newcomers. On both sides of the divide, historically nonsensical references to syncretic 'Norman cavaliers of the South' brought together various discursive sources, including *Ivanhoe*, in order to provide a common template for the expression of differences.[31]

To the extent that the identification with the Normans was a by-product of *Ivanhoe,* the case exemplifies the workings of prosthetic memory—but with a difference. In her elaboration of this concept,

Alison Landsberg gives the impression that prosthetic memory operates across cultural borders in an unproblematic and unselective way by the sheer power of the representation.[32] This was not borne out, however, by the antebellum appropriation of *Ivanhoe*: local filters were clearly active in providing a firewall against possible complexities. Thus appropriations of Scott's story in the Southern states, as elsewhere, were marked by the frame of reference and the current needs of those invoking it. While the figure of Ivanhoe was invoked, this was often in blithe and reductive neglect of the story as a whole, and was also fraught with contradictions. As indicated earlier, the outsider figure of Rebecca was entirely overlooked in favour of the (Saxon) Rowena: the clever Jewess never figured in any of the tournaments, according to a recent analysis, because of the value attached in Southern culture to submissive women.[33] Moreover, the ethnic conflict was reduced to an intractable binary opposition between North and South. The fact that Scott had actually portrayed the Normans and the Norman yoke in rather negative terms was ignored, as was the fact that, within the universe of the novel, the chivalric and feudal Normans stood for change rather than for tradition. Nor was there apparently much attention paid to the mediating role of Ivanhoe who helps bridge the gap between the warring parties and between the old order and the new.[34] In a highly selective way, then, the Southron re-enactment of Scott appropriated the novelist's fascination with ethnic differences and with honour-based aristocratic cultures, and used this as an imaginative tool with which to articulate Southern distinctiveness against the background of a growing gap between Northern abolitionists and Southern slave-owners.[35] But it was blind to the reconciliatory and indeed progressive logic of the original plot and, while extolling the virtues of aristocratic chivalry, overlooked the fact that Scott himself, although ready to evoke the chivalric tournaments in all their pomp and colour, had ended up by relegating both Norman and Saxon cultures in their unadulterated forms to the past and been quite critical of the more violent aspects of the medieval age.[36] We have had ample evidence that remembrance involves active engagement; in this case, however, remembering *Ivanhoe* also meant misreading it.

REFLECTING: THE NOVEL AS ICON

He did measureless harm; more real and lasting harm, perhaps, than any other individual that ever wrote. . . . But for the Sir Walter Scott disease, the character of the Southerner—or Southron, according to Sir Walter's starchier way of phrasing it—would be wholly modern, in place of modern and mediaeval mixed, and the South would be fully a generation further advanced than it is.

In this 1883 diatribe Mark Twain famously lashed out at Scott, accusing him of having turned back the tide of modernization in the South and misled people into a sham and outmoded medievalism. Scott had contributed as much as slavery to the recalcitrance of the South, Twain continued, because he had held people in the thrall of aristocratic and feudal values. Indeed, 'Sir Walter had so large a hand in making Southern character, as it existed before the war, that he is in great measure responsible for the war.'[37] As if to drive home his opinion about Scott's true value, Twain's *Adventures of Huckleberry Finn*, published two years later in 1885, included a suitably wrecked paddle-steamer called the *Walter Scott*. (Although this particular wreck was a fiction, its presence in Twain's novel can be read as yet another reflection of Scott's influence on practices of remembering through material culture since, as *Bradford's Guide to Merchant Steam Vessels* for the period 1830–70 shows, there had indeed been at least one paddle-steamer called *Sir Walter Scott*, which had snagged outside New Orleans in November 1838.[38])

More harm than any other individual who ever wrote? Responsible for the war? Twain's words have been regularly quoted, usually in agreement and as an anecdotal illustration of the impact of Scott. But the role of Scott and Twain's invocation of it has not been fully analysed, as I shall do here, as part of the workings of cultural memory. The evidence presented so far suggests that Scott's work was at most a facilitator, not a cause. But a facilitator it was. As we have seen above, it did inspire cultural practices in the South. More importantly, it provided a model for articulating a specifically Southern nationalism although this was more a matter of Scott's seed falling on fertile ground than of his dictating how people actually thought: whatever influence the Scottish writer had was contingent upon local filters and combined with that of other writers.[39] What was arguably as important as Scott's actual influence in the South was his value for Twain in formulating his post-hoc assessment of the causes of conflict. Scott's America-wide reputation offered the Yankee author a collective point of reference that crossed over between North and South. As Emily Todd has shown through a close scrutiny of publishing figures, Scott's novels were not only unprecedentedly popular in the United States: their very popularity led directly to the development of new distribution networks, linking Boston, New York, and Charleston around the common appreciation of this particular brand of literature.[40] There were ships named after Scott's characters made in Pennsylvania as well as in the South.[41] In short: 'Scott' and 'Ivanhoe' were recognizable figures, linking all parties by a common knowledge of literature.

Susan Manning has recently offered a compelling analysis of Twain's famous remarks in which she claims that Twain himself was guilty of misreading Scott's view of chivalry, of overlooking the fact that Scott too was dealing with civil war, and of reducing Scott's ambivalence to a one-dimensional nostalgia of the restorative kind which he could then parody.[42] Given Twain's critical acumen, Manning's argument continues, this misprision of Scott can only be explained by a certain anxiety of influence vis-à-vis the 'Great Enchanter' and, more generally, an anxiety about the fact that Twain's own division between North and South, modernizers and idealists, present and past, was constantly coming under pressure from a reality that was more complex and nuanced. He needed Scott as a kicking boy.

From the perspective of the politics of remembrance, however, other questions also arise. Why did Twain attribute so much influence to just one man? And why should Twain's comments have had such a tenacious afterlife as a commonplace? It recurs in most discussions of antebellum culture and continues to shape even the most recent critical discussions.[43] The return of Twain's judgement as commonplace exemplifies the power of writers, in this case through the use of hyperbole and personal charisma, in formulating collective views of the past. More fundamentally, Twain's focus on Scott and its reiteration by later writers draws attention to the fact that cultural remembrance, as I have argued elsewhere, works according to the principle of scarcity.[44] It tends to converge on a limited number of figures of memory, which are then continuously re-invested with additional meaning. These include the figure of 'authors', which Michel Foucault once aptly described as 'principles of economy' that limit the proliferation of meaning.[45] From a certain point on, Scott's work—or rather, 'the Sir Walter Scott disease'—became an icon or figure of memory, whose invocation provided a shorthand and semantically laden reference to an entire period and culture. But even more than Scott-the-author, in this case, it was *Ivanhoe* that acquired such an iconic function. Twain signalled out this particular novel as exemplifying 'the Walter Scott disease' even though Scott's other work, especially his poetry, was very influential throughout North America. Thus Twain rounded off his anti-Scott tirade with a shot in the direction of the novel that sums up everything that went wrong in the South and put a stop to the march of progress:

A curious exemplification of the power of a single book for good or harm is shown in the effects wrought by Don Quixote and those wrought by Ivanhoe. The first swept the world's admiration for the mediaeval chivalry silliness out of existence; and the other restored it. As far as our South is concerned, the good work done by Cervantes is pretty nearly a dead letter, so effectually has Scott's pernicious work undermined it.[46]

As a 'single book' the 'pernicious' *Ivanhoe* offered Twain a figure of memory with which to evoke a whole era for the American public and sum up the ethos of an entire generation. His reference indicates that he could trust his readers to recognize Scott and Ivanhoe as household names that needed no further explanation. *Ivanhoe*'s association with the highly visible tournaments presumably allowed it to serve this purpose more easily than the poetry or the other novels. Somewhere along the line, 'Ivanhoe' as a book and a media event had itself become a figure of memory, meaning that it recalled its reception in the southern states in the nineteenth century, and all the hype around it, as much as it did the green pastures of medieval England. In the process, the fact that the burlesque Don Quixote had sometimes appeared side by side with Ivanhoe at the tournaments (witness the Fauquier Springs event mentioned earlier) had been forgotten by all parties.

There is no evidence that the initial reception of Scott's work itself, to the extent that this can be reconstructed in any great detail, had been any more intense in the southern states than elsewhere in North America in terms of the number of books sold and or the frequency with which his stories were read.[47] Indeed, on the occasion of his centenary in 1871, the biggest celebrations were in Boston and New York (though this may just have reflected the disarray in the South). What makes the Southern reception of Scott so significant in the long term was the fact that it fed into the cultural politics of the later period, both becoming an icon of antebellum southern culture and, in its exploration of Lost Causes, providing an aesthetic model for the Confederate defeat.[48] Twain's remarks two decades after the end of hostilities have cast their retrospective light on all studies of the topic and muddied the view of the pre-war period. Nevertheless they do seem to have clinched a process that was already occurring and that involved public expressions of affinity with 'Ivanhoe' and, through its role as a figure of memory, to a specifically southern heritage. After a certain point, demonstrations of an affinity with Scott had become a marker of affinity with the cultural heritage of the antebellum South and later, drawing arguably on *Waverley* more than *Ivanhoe*, with the idea that a lost cause could be dignified and not just quixotic.

The process whereby 'Ivanhoe' became this highly charged icon can be illustrated by the popularity of naming persons and places after Scott's work. This was a way of publicly expressing a long-term allegiance to his writing and what it had come to stand for. Thus Ivanhoe had turned up from the 1830s onwards, as the assumed name of at least one writer in the *Daily Express* of Petersburg and as a given name among the children of Scott's first readers in Virginia, who were thus branded for life with their parents' tastes.[49] From the 1840s onwards, reflecting once again the movement of imagination into the material world, there were also Ivanhoe plantations to be found in the states of Georgia, South Carolina, Louisiana, Mississippi, and Virginia; and towns called Ivanhoe in North Carolina, Virginia, and Georgia.[50]

There were Scott towns elsewhere in North America, Waverley being particularly popular as I mentioned earlier. One critic has referred to the invention of American place names in the nineteenth century in terms of the projection of an 'unimaginative lamina of Greco-Scotch-English never-neverism on the surface of a land that seemed too new to would-be-cultured sensibilities.'[51] A more systematic study of the geographical distribution and dating of such implanted Scott names would be necessary before making any definitive judgement as to their relative popularity in the southern states.[52] But pending such a study, it is already clear that there are no Ivanhoe towns in New England (though there is a Waverley in Massachusetts) and that the occurrence of these Ivanhoes in the South was *interpreted* in the post-war period by both parties as symptomatic of the South's 'special relationship' with Scott. The use of Ivanhoe had become a way of performing in public an affiliation with a distinctively 'Southern' heritage (just as Twain's invocation of Ivanhoe in 1883 was a way of distancing himself from it). Thus the Virginian town of Red Bluff was changed to Ivanhoe in 1885 and in the same year, a Confederate veteran successfully moved to have the town of Hawkins Prairie in Texas renamed Ivanhoe.[53] It seems safe to assume that both instances of renaming were ways of recollecting an antebellum world that had now, like Scott's Highlanders, become a 'lost cause'. In light of this interpretive frame, it seems retrospectively fitting that one of the Civil War blockade runners, an iron-hulled steamer that ran aground off the coast of Alabama in June 1864 and was sunk by a Union force, should also have been called the *Ivanhoe*.[54]

Because Ivanhoe, helped on by Twain's egregious comments, later became synonymous with antebellum Southern culture, it is sometimes difficult to disengage the retrospective view of Scott's influence from what was actually happening in the South in the pre-war period. (The power of the Scott legend is illustrated by the fact that the website giving the history of Ivanhoe, Texas, simply points out that the name-giver was a 'Confederate veteran' and presumes that the significance of this fact in relation to a preference for the name Ivanhoe is self-evident.[55]) Whatever the actual importance of *Ivanhoe* in antebellum Southern culture—as I have been showing, there is evidence that it was important though not exclusively so—it certainly later became the most manifest figure of memory in representations of what happened: the shorthand version and icon of why the South was lost. As such it has figured in later historical fictions bearing on the South, often working in close conjunction with the memory of the tournaments. Allen Tate's *The Fathers* (1938), a historical novel set in Virginia in the second half of the nineteenth century, gives a prominent place to the description of a tournament and explicitly connects it to *Ivanhoe*. On hearing as a child that a tournament was to take place, the narrator recalls, he started imagining what it would be like:

I had never been to a tournament and I saw knights riding in armor, with fettered lances, clashing in mortal combat before pavilions gaily colored, in which lay beautiful ladies swooning in the anxiety of their delight. I saw the Black Knight charging down a dusty course and I rose and walked a few steps to the high bookcase with glass doors that stood in the far corner of the room. Opening the doors I tip-toed on the red ottoman to the tall brown volume of *Ivanhoe*.[56]

REVISIONING: THE NOVEL AS TOUCHSTONE

Given its status as a figure of memory, Ivanhoe became available to later writers as a shorthand way to invoke a cluster of commonplaces regarding the chivalric self-representations of the South and explain why indeed the South should have become a 'lost cause'. It comes then as no surprise that in Harper Lee's *To Kill a Mocking Bird* (1960), the book that the young Jem is forced to read to the scary old lady Mrs Dubose is *Ivanhoe*: the reference is brief, but the name says it all.[57] Once the book had gained such iconic notoriety, however, it also started to provide a focal point for generating a counter-memory of the same period and for reflecting critically on nostalgic commonplaces. As we shall see from the following cases, this meant bringing Ivanhoe back into play both as an *icon* of southern 'chivalry' (building on its reputation) and as a *story* about ethnic differences in the Middle Ages (building on Scott's original narrative).

Charles W. Chesnutt's novel *The House behind the Cedars* (1900), generally considered a landmark in African-American writing, can be seen in many ways as a new version of *Ivanhoe*. The fifth chapter is called 'The Tournament' and it describes the annual 'lists' organized by the Clarence Social Club and the impact this has on the emotional life of the young characters. This might just be considered a historical echo of the many tournaments that did take place, but Chesnutt carries the Scott reference further: not only does the name of the principal female character—Rowena or 'Rena'—recall *Ivanhoe* but on several occasions the characters at the tournament themselves draw parallels with Scott's fictional tournament at Ashby-de-la-Zouche. The narrator informs us, moreover, that the local bookseller had got in extra copies of *Ivanhoe* in preparation for the tournament because 'the South before the war was essentially feudal, and Scott's novel of chivalry appealed forcefully to the feudal heart. During the month preceding the Clarence tournament, the local bookseller had sold out his entire stock of "Ivanhoe".'[58] In this highly concentrated way, the character of southern culture is sketched as a background to the actual drama of the book: that of mixed-race siblings trying to pass for whites in a racially divided South. The title of Scott's novel serves in this way as an icon of the old South at the same time as Scott's original story provides a template for revising the historical view of southern culture: 'Rowena' is turned into the mixed-race Rowena/Rena, who, instead of living happily ever after with her Ivanhoe, ends up being tragically rejected by her all-white lover. In fact, one of the other characters remarks on hearing that R(ow)ena is 'dark, rather than fair, and full of tender grace', that she might well have been called Rebecca.[59] This particular comment was made with reference to the colour of her hair by a character still ignorant of the fact that Rowena has 'black blood' in her veins and hence, following the racial logic of the characters, that she belongs to 'them' rather than to 'us'. Within the larger framework of the story, however, Rowena's identity is indeed confirmed as being closer to that of the outsider Rebecca than to her novelistic namesake (with the one difference that Chesnutt's Rebecca/Rowena actually dies a victim to her outsider status). In this way, *The House behind the Cedars* invokes *Ivanhoe* as an icon of a particular southern heritage at the same time as it re-fashions elements of Scott's story in order to mark its difference from that heritage and to introduce a counter-memory highlighting the horrors of racism behind the chivalric facade. The outsider Rebecca, who was so prominent in the British reception of the novel and largely elided from the American,[60] thus re-emerged from the pages of the book as a central figure in Chesnutt's narrative, albeit in disguise. Re-writing *Ivanhoe* was used in this way in the margins of Chesnutt's story to recalibrate the collective memory of the South around the period of the Civil War, and to highlight those groups that never fitted at all into the Norman–Saxon or North–South divide. This reading was arguably closer to the 'ungrammaticality' of the original described in the previous chapter than it was to the polarizing appropriations by apologists for Southern distinctiveness described above. It bears out the principle of 'multidirectionality' in the dynamics of cultural memory, as discussed recently by Michael Rothberg: the idea that the story of one marginalized group can become a catalyst in articulating the hitherto overlooked story of other comparable groups.[61] In this instance of multidirectionality, the story of the Jewish Rebecca that had been recessive in the Southern appropriations of the novel became reactivated, providing an imaginative resource with which to narrate the story of racism in the United States.

Re-writing of another kind was carried out more recently by South Carolina writer Franklin Burroughs in an essay reflecting on his own recollections of a children's story called *Johnny Reb*. Although he has forgotten the name of the author of *Johnny Reb*, he admits, the details are branded in his memory: the book *Ivanhoe* figured as a material object in the story where it is given by a southern landowner to a poor white boy whom he adopts.[62] The boy's family, however, seize upon the book as an alien presence and burn it in an iconoclastic auto-da-fé that clearly reflects their rejection of this particular piece of heritage. Later on in the story, the boy finds himself on the Confederate side facing his own siblings, who, not surprisingly given their burning of *Ivanhoe* the book, have now joined the Union. In this way, the giving and burning of the novel are used to epitomize the struggle going on between the haves and the have-nots. Burroughs' reflections on this youthful reading experience provide him too with an occasion to introduce his own counter-memory of the South, no longer dominated by notions of the Gentleman (as in the original 'chivalry'), or by racial anxieties (as in Chesnutt), but by the experiences of poor whites, descendants of poor Scottish immigrants who had been victims of the Highland clearances and represented a significant percentage of the settlers in the South. Once again, re-visioning 'Ivanhoe' became a way of rewriting the memory of the South. Clearly for Burroughs (born in the 1930s) and his generation, *Ivanhoe* still works as an icon of the antebellum South. As such it could play a role as a mnemonic wedge making way for an oppositional memory: the recollection that the South was not only made up of plantation-owning, tournament-going, *Ivanhoe*-reading gentlemen but also of poorer folk who found every reason to fight for a different future. The canonical status of *Ivanhoe* allowed it to thus function as a measuring stick against which alternative perspectives on the past could be staked out.

MIXED LEGACIES

The novel persisted throughout all these different performances as a monumental point of reference against which new standpoints, and new visions of the past were calibrated. Even as *Ivanhoe* persists in this way, however, the nature of that reference keeps changing as the actual familiarity with Scott's own work recedes. A story about the Middle Ages, it became a title recalling a nineteenth-century media phenomenon and, in the case of Burroughs, a material object symbolizing ideological allegiances; finally it became, in its shrink-wrapped form in Franzen's *Corrections* (2000) mentioned earlier, an icon of pastness itself.

In *Race and Reunion: The Civil War in American Memory* (2001), David W. Blight argues that three dominant narratives emerged after 1865 as models for dealing with the troubled legacy of the brutal conflict between North and South.[63] The majoritarian narrative was that of 'Reconciliation' based on the common recognition both North and South of the honourable motives of the two sides in the conflict in defending the causes in which they believed. Blight suggests that this narrative, allowing room for an honourable 'Lost Cause', was promoted above all by Southerners in the first decades after the War and was later taken over by Northerners; while highlighting the communality between the warring parties, it tended to overlook the question of slavery and its abolition. The second major narrative was that of 'Resistance', based on the idea that the South was still locked in an ongoing struggle against foreign usurpers and their attempts to disturb the independence of the original population and their liberties; this uncompromising stance fed into White Supremacist discourses, most notably Thomas Dixon's *The Clansman: An Historical Romance of the Ku Klux Klan* (1905) and its later adaptation to the screen in D. W. Griffith's *Birth of a Nation* (1915). The third narrative was that of 'Emancipation': focused on the abolition of slavery as the key aspect of the Civil War and its outcomes it fed into an emerging black discourse linked to the ongoing struggle for equality in post-abolition America.

Blight refers only in passing to Scott and Twain while discussing the rather formal diction of the Confederate leaders. Surprisingly, he makes no mention of the fiction.[64] The evidence I have been presenting suggests, however, that the author of Waverley had a much bigger role to play in helping to shape all these different narratives and the mindsets behind them: from the 'Lost Cause' theme of reconciliation and the idea that there could be honour in defeat, to the emancipatory counter-memory offered by Chesnutt, to the idea of resistant Klansmen whom Dixon explicitly compared to the 'reincarnated souls of the Clansmen of Old Scotland' and whose manifestation on the original poster for the *Birth of a Nation* recalls in a malignant form the medieval tournaments of the mid-century.[65] Indeed, the fiery cross that entered Ku Klux Klan practices through Griffith and Dixon can be traced directly back to *The Lady of the Lake* and seen as the most recent, and most obnoxious morphing of Scott's work.[66] The very diversity of Scott's offspring, spanning as they do the ideological arc from White Supremacism to black liberationism, is testimony to the fertility of the original and to its cultural ubiquity by the second half of the nineteenth century. It also demonstrates how literary appropriations, while inspired by the original, may mutate in entirely different ideological directions.

Franzen's shrink-wrapping may be the end of the road for *Ivanhoe* as a medium for shaping collective identities. Its procreative power was fed by the combination of Scott's text, the many frameworks in which it was

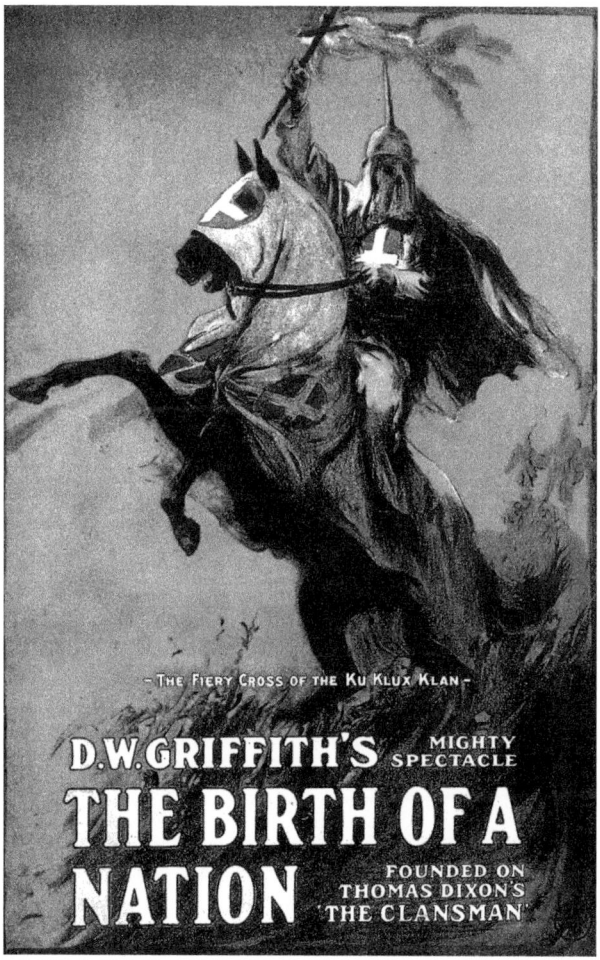

Figure 4.4: D. W. Griffith's *The Birth of a Nation* (1915), original poster.

appropriated, and the historical predominance of literature as a calibrator of values. The 1997 BBC television version mentioned earlier suggests that there is still life in Scott's story for those who can re-interpret it, for example, in a feminist or post-colonial direction. But it is unlikely that Scott's text will ever again be the subject of so many appropriations and provide such a readily recognized common point of reference for elaborating social and political differences as it did in the century after its publication.

This particular work of literature seems to be heading for obsolescence. Indeed, some would argue nostalgically that Literature as such will never again exercise the cultural power it enjoyed in the nineteenth century when it did not seem too absurd to suggest that a novel caused a Civil War. It is undeniable that the role of literature as a cultural medium and as a mediator of cultural remembrance is changing in the new media landscapes of the twenty-first century. However, since the struggle between the forces of tradition and the forces of progress and free agency is a permanent one, as Coleridge suggested, then the need for narrative mediators of collective memory remains unabated.

5
Locating Memory: Abbotsford

In Chapter XVI of *Waverley*, as young Edward is being led northwards through the remote mountain pass marking the border into the Highlands, his companion identifies the place and tells a tangential story about it:

'This', said Evan, 'is the pass of Bally-Brough which was kept in former times by ten of the clan Donnochie against a hundred of the low country carles. The graves of the slain are still to be seen in that little corri, or bottom, on the opposite side of the burn—if your eyes are good, you may see the green specks among the heather.'[1]

'If your eyes are good, you may see the green specks': the pictorial qualities of Scott's writing are here in full evidence in the depiction of the sublimely rugged spot, with its foaming stream and circling birds. This address to Waverley (and indirectly, to the reader) also exemplifies the way in which Scott could make places come alive aesthetically and, at the same time, appeal to an historical imagination. The location is displayed in the story, just as a museum might display everyday objects and, in the process, endow them with an aura.[2] In contrast to a museum, however, the frame here is one which is itself full of suspense. As narrative, it engages the emotions of characters and readers as they wonder what will happen next and try to imagine a massacre that had taken place on that same spot 'in former times'. In this description of Waverley's passage through Bally-Brough, the history of the Highlands in 1745 becomes linked with, or more accurately, contiguous with a massacre that took place at the same spot some hundred years earlier. Like a rock face marked by different geological upheavals, the palimpsestic site holds together various memory strata, becoming a material placeholder for the memory of events that are not necessarily causally linked.[3] By virtue of being physically there, Waverley is brought into physical contact with the past as well as initiated into its stories.

Bally-Brough was an imaginary location, but like other places in the Waverley novels it fed into a desire to pinpoint actual spots on the map of Scotland. To meet this demand, the novels were followed up by many supplementary publications giving more information about the locations that had figured in the fiction and, with the help of illustrations, another mode of virtual access to the locations described. Such remediating supplements, in whose appearance Scott colluded until his death in 1832, included the *Series of Sketches of the Existing Localities Alluded to in the Waverley Novels* (1829), *Landscape Illustrations of the Waverley Novels, with Descriptions of the Views* (1832), *The Book of Waverley Gems: In a Series of Engraved Illustrations of Incidents and Scenery in Sir Walter Scott's Novels* (1846), and *Landscape-Historical Illustrations to Scotland and the Waverley Novels,* produced between 1836 and 1838 with commentary by George N. Wright and drawings by William Turner and others.[4] In this last work, Scott's Bally-Brough figured once again, but now in visual form and accompanied by a commentary in which Wright identified the imaginary location with the pass of Glencoe:

If the author had any precise mountain glen in his 'mind's eye' when he described the Pass of Bally-Brough, his picture is such an exact copy of a dark defile in the wild vale of Glencoe, that, in conjunction with popular opinion, we have concluded this gloomy spot must have been his original. Let the description be compared with our illustration, which is faithful to nature, and the identity will immediately appear. 'The descent from the path to the stream was a mere precipice, with here and there a projecting fragment of granite, or a scathed tree, which had warped its twisted roots into the fissures of the rock, on the right hand the mountain rose above the path with almost equal inaccessibility; but the hill on the opposite side displayed a shroud of copsewood, with which some pines are intermingled.'[5]

Having established the connection between Bally-Brough and Glencoe through this appeal to popular opinion and to 'nature', Wright then went on to link the place to the infamous massacre of the MacDonald clan by the Campbells in 1692, concluding:

The desolation caused by the dagger of the assassin continues unchanged, and Glencoe seems scorned and shunned and solitary, as if the deeds of the by-gone days were never to be forgotten.

Where Scott had already used the location to link the world of Waverley to 'former times', Wright adds another layer to this temporal sedimentation so that the rising in the Highlands in 1745, as described by Scott, the slaughter of the clan Donnochie as narrated by his character Evan, and the massacre of Glencoe in 1692, as known from other sources, all converge on this particular place. In his commentary Wright also linked the place for good measure both to Ossian and to Macpherson, who likewise had been associated with the area around Glencoe. Through the mediation of the book, the illustrations, and the commentary, Scott's imagined pass

Figure 5.1: *The Pass of Bally-Brough.* Drawing H. Melville; engraving J. H. Kernot. From *Landscape-Historical Illustrations of Scotland and the Waverley Novels* (London, 1836–8).

became a symbolic node where different narratives converged. The place that was first displayed as a historically significant as well as aesthetically impressive location in Scott's novel went on to become, with the help of Wright and others, a potential destination for anyone in search of an enhanced experience of memory.

VIRTUAL MAPPING

Although the work of Walter Scott has traditionally been associated with historicism, and rightly so, the case of Bally-Brough/Glencoe serves as a reminder of the fact that his memory work was inextricably mixed up with imagining new relations to space and to landscape. As a growing body of criticism has demonstrated, his writings helped imagine the island of Britain as a spatial configuration cut through by roads and access routes, and cut across by physical, political, legal, and cultural borders that characters have to overcome, circumvent, or renegotiate.[6] Waverley characters are highly mobile, tracking routes from Edinburgh to London to the Highlands, from Glasgow to Stirling to Edinburgh, from Rotherwood to Ashby-de-la-Zouche to York, and so on.[7]

Since adventures-on-the-road are a basic design feature of the romance genre and of its modern variant, the picaresque, this is not in itself surprising. Indeed being away from home and trying to get back to it is one of the most basic narrative structures in existence. But in the early 1800s it had taken on a particular geopolitical resonance against the background of political and social change including the Highland clearances, urbanization, and migration. In the popular genre of the 'national tale' that Scott adapted freely, travelling to peripheral regions had acquired a distinctively temporal dimension: the farther from the centre, the further back in the past.[8] In Scott's Scottish novels in particular, movement from one region to another is equivalent to moving into a different 'chronotope', with the Highlands representing an earlier time period (a place 'outside of time' and now an object of display) that nevertheless coexisted *alongside* the contemporary world of Glasgow and Edinburgh.[9] Scott's work thus plays out the fact that modernization continuously produces what Joep Leerssen has called an 'allochronic periphery': regions that are imagined as belonging to an earlier era, as having 'not yet' changed or as needing to be preserved as a future reminder of how things used to be.[10] The movement of characters stages the existence of these heterogeneous time zones, making visible in the fabric of the story the fact that social developments are not unilinear or across the board and that not all people living at the same time are each other's contemporaries.[11] Although the novels inaugurate a new sense of contemporaneity as part of national reconciliation ('from now on everyone occupies the same time zone'), it is hard to forget that the actual stories told over hundreds of pages have depicted the unevenness of change on the part of people located in different areas within the imagined national territory.[12]

The recent spatial turn within the Humanities and specifically the exploration of heterogeneous temporalities from a postcolonial perspective has meant that these complexities in Scott's work have become more apparent.[13] The recent discussions summarized above have together built up a fascinating view of Scott's work as a response to geopolitical developments in the world around him: the Highland clearances and mass migration, which were still going on as he was writing *Waverley* and *The Heart of Mid-Lothian*; the emergence of Glasgow as a commercial centre, which formed the background to *Rob Roy*; and more generally, the expansion of Great Britain as a colonial power, which framed all of his fiction and to which, according to Katie Trumpener, he imaginatively contributed by inventing 'the novel of imperial expansion'.[14] In this way, Scott's virtual geographies have come to be seen as imaginative tools for rethinking the relations between people, territory, and movements.

In this chapter I build on these recent discussions, but take the analysis in new directions. To begin with, my concern is specifically with the role of memory in this expansive rethinking of space that Scott facilitated. Secondly, where other critics have concentrated on Scott's mapping of Great Britain and hence on the representation of contours, borders, and frontiers in his writings, the focus here is on the emergence of particular *locations* within those general maps. Such concentrated pockets of memory serve, I argue, both to intensify and to contain remembrance within a changing world. Finally, in keeping with the focus of this book, I will move beyond the analysis of Scott's virtual cartographies as such to examine their afterlife as guides to the actual movements of people, both tourists and migrants. The realization that the past had become a foreign country, to echo David Lowenthal, also entailed the belief that by going elsewhere you could go back and forward in time.[15]

I shall argue that Scott's work helped create a radically modern relationship between memory and place that fitted the changing conditions of his age, being based on a combination of portability (memory can be re-located and re-assembled) and hyper-locatedness (the past can be re-experienced in an immediate way by going to particular places).

MEMORY SITES

Given the intimate association between memory and time, the persistence of locative models in conceptualizations of remembrance is all the more striking. Ever since classical times, it has proven difficult to reflect on memory and mnemonic practices without doing so in spatial terms.[16] The concept of 'memory site', first introduced in Pierre Nora's *Lieux de mémoire* (1984–92), is the most recent manifestation of this tendency. As mentioned earlier with reference to Jeanie Deans, the term memory site is used here to mean actual locations or symbolic points of reference that serve as dense repositories of historical meaning and the focus of continuing semantic investment, becoming in the process communal orientation points in collective self-definitions and in the contestation of identities.

Nora's influential *Lieux de mémoire* was based on the historical claim referred to earlier that the importance of specialized memory sites grew as a result of modernization. Pre-modern societies, Nora claimed, were steeped in tradition and had no need to actively cultivate memory since it was all around them (they were embedded in an all-encompassing 'memory environment' or *milieu de mémoire*). But with modernization, people started to experience the past as discontinuous with the present, as a foreign country accessible only at particular locations (memory sites or *lieux de mémoire*) and only on particular occasions clearly demarcated from the everyday. The opposition evoked by Nora between traditional and modern societies is too black and white to stand the test of close historical analysis—the case of *Rob Roy* and *Ivanhoe* has already shown that there are traditions and continuities even within highly mediatized societies. Nevertheless, the basic idea holds true that memory sites were cultivated on an unprecedented scale in the nineteenth century and that they represented a principle of economy within collective memory. As I have argued at greater length elsewhere, the value of sites is related to their scarcity: once particular locations, events, or stories become invested with mnemonic significance, they attract more and more attention at the cost of sidelining other topics, thereby allowing for a greater concentration of meaning in a limited number of sites as part of what Jeffrey Olick has called a 'chronic differentiation' between temporal zones.[17] Because they receive repeated attention in a variety of media, moreover, they become household names in an ever-widening community.

In Nora's initial use of the term, the concept of memory site included both symbolic points of reference (such as the Declaration of Human Rights) and actual locations (such as Verdun). It would seem that in practice remembrance always gravitates towards actual locations that provide a material focus for larger issues. This was a point already made by Maurice Halbwachs, the grandfather of recent theories of collective memory, whose posthumous *La mémoire collective* (1950) ended with a long section on 'Collective Memory and Space'. Here Halbwachs argued that memory tends towards becoming located, like rainwater flowing to the lowest point, because particular places build a material bridge between past and present. Because they are unchanging, locations offer points of stability in a changing world. Space, Halbwachs wrote, 'is what allows a group to organize its actions and movements in relation to the stable configuration of the material world,' 'giving us the illusion of not changing across time and of finding the past in the present.'[18] The intense cultivation of memory sites in the physical form of particular locations allowed history to be given its due place, but not everywhere. It became a contained and demarcated place to visit, not one to inhabit. And as we shall see later with reference to Scott tourism, it was part of time off rather than of the everyday.

Locations offer the sensation of an authentic, embodied connection to the past, but it is nevertheless clear from the case of Bally-Brough/Glencoe that the significance of 'being in' a place is prepared by the stories and images shaping one's encounter with it.[19] Even though memory sites tend to be connected to actual locations, they are always thoroughly *synthetic* in character, in the sense both of being composite (bringing together various events) and of being artificial (the product of mediations). The result is a paradoxical, but very potent combination of authenticity and mediation. Indeed, the significance of location can be the result of mediation rather than of the fact that something happened there *in situ* without this taking from the authenticity of the embodied experience of being there. Aleida Assmann has distinguished usefully between locations that are in themselves carriers of meaning because something happened there (a battle, for example) and places that acquire meaning through symbolization (the cenotaph in Whitehall, for example), suggesting that *ex situ* memory locations, depending entirely on representations for their significance, became increasingly important in modern societies.[20]

In what follows, I use these theoretical reflections to argue that Scott's work as a writer, antiquarian, and homeowner helped reconfigure the territory of Scotland around particular memory-saturated locations. His stories not only helped to map space into distinct regions and designated routes, they also synthesized memory sites by virtually transplanting places and symbolically overlaying one place with another. The result was summed up by one commentator in a book entitled *Scott and Scotland*: 'the spots which the poet has enshrined in verse, and the events which the romancer has immortalized by weaving round them the silken web of fable and fiction, become hallowed places and sacred things.'[21] Scott had recreated Scott-land (the obvious pun has been repeatedly invoked since the nineteenth century, most recently in Stuart Kelly's eponymous set of vignettes on 'the man who invented a nation'[22]) as an imagined network of such spots in which aesthetic value was combined with historical depth. As the idea of 'spot' or site suggests, these locations were experienced as distinct from the surrounding territory. Their significance as 'hallowed places' and as possible destinations was linked to the fact that they were somehow set apart from the everyday—they were 'heterotopia', to borrow a term from Michel Foucault: bounded pockets of 'otherness' that were discontinuous with their surroundings and the contemporary world.[23] Remembering the past at designated spots and at designated times meant that it could be safely laid aside on other occasions: both honoured and quarantined.

SCRIPTED ITINERARIES

It is a truth generally acknowledged that Scott's procreativity extended to the development of tourism to Scotland. In a recent study, Nicola J. Watson has referred aptly to Scott's topographical imagination: his works, including prominently *The Lady of the Lake*, were designed as virtual itineraries for the would-be traveller, their influence later enhanced by the many illustrations they inspired.[24] He played into an existing interest in sublime landscapes and the nascent popularity of Highland travels, but he also gave that travel a new impulse by creating a discourse about locations in which memory and aesthetics were combined. Just as his narrativized depictions of location invited visualization, so too did they invite people to visit them in search of both history and beauty. Where Watson has emphasized the general ways in which private individuals sought to extend their imaginative life into literary tourism, I will examine the ways in which private reading and cultural memory worked together to produce the Scott experience.

For many of his fans, reading Scott's work, watching it on stage, or recollecting it through the many illustrations in circulation must have been a form of armchair travel. Mention has already been made of the importance of scenery to the dramatic productions. Moreover, his work also mobilized readers to travel to actual destinations to experience the places evoked in his work. Mentally and often physically armed with Scott's description, new generations of tourists sought out those places that he had so memorably described. Tourism to Lake Katrine is a case in point. As Watson has shown, the lake had already been something of a destination for romantic travellers in the eighteenth century, and Scott drew on earlier travel descriptions in the design of his poem.[25] But once the lake had figured prominently in Scott's bestselling *The Lady of the Lake* (20,000 copies sold within a year of publication), it became swamped with visitors from an early stage. Whereas the lake had previously seen on average about fifty carriages a year, within six months of the publication of the poem in 1810, numbers had swelled to almost three hundred.[26] Publishers helped in this process with the production of supplementary maps and pocket editions to help tourists find their way.[27] The interest of the place was heightened as of 1817 by the subsequent addition to its store of memories of the figure of Rob Roy. The outlaw's cave had long been associated with Lake Katrine (it has been suggested that this in itself was an extra reason for Scott to focus on him); but that association was at the very least reinforced by Scott's novel and its subsequent dramatizations. With the memory both of *Rob Roy* and of *The Lady of the Lake* converging on Lake Katrine, there would be all the more reason to travel to such a memory-laden spot. That the 'Lady of the Lake' was a fiction set in the sixteenth century and Rob Roy a historical figure from the eighteenth was apparently irrelevant to the resonance of the location that had been implanted by Scott's evocations of the place.

Thomas Cook, the first organizer of package tours, praised Scott for having given 'a sentiment to Scotland as a tourist destination'.[28] Cook's tours included both Lake Katrine and Oban, site of *The Lord of the Isles,* with tour-goers being apparently advised to carry along a copy of the relevant poems.[29] Tourism thus represented yet another performative appropriation of literature with the well-read traveller playing out a script (as such it is a variation on the Ivanhoe-inspired tournaments considered in Chapter 4). One of the many people to visit Lake Katrine was Queen Victoria, whose famous attachment to Balmoral and all things Scottish can be seen as a royal re-enactment in holiday form of the Waverley world.[30] In her journal Victoria described on several occasions how particular places reminded her of lines from Scott and how she would read out his poems in the appropriate places. In her entry for 2 September 1869 she described in particular an excursion to Lake Katrine and the adjacent MacGregor territory, of Rob Roy fame. Her enumeration of the familiar sites suggests that this excursion to Lake Katrine had the character of a ritual in which she performed her membership of a particular mnemonic community by visiting those spots that had already been invested with meaning by Scott. She recalled how she and her entourage took a 'clean little steamer called Rob Roy' across the lake with a copy of *The Lady of the Lake* at hand: 'The evening was lovely, and the lights and pink and golden sky as we drove through the beautiful Trossachs were glorious indeed,' she wrote, and then quoting Scott, continued: 'So wondrous wild, the whole might seem | the Scenery of a fairy dream' (p. 148). Her embodied, subjective experience of the particular moment was thus thoroughly shaped by her reading and presumably also by earlier visualizations of the scenery on the part of Turner, Horatio MacCulloch, and others:[31]

Emerging from this road we came upon the Loch Lomond Road, having a fine view of Loch Arklet, on the banks of which Helen MacGregor is said to have been born. The scene of our drive today is all described in Rob Roy. Loch Arklet lies like Loch Callater, only that the hills are higher and more pointed. Leaving this little loch to our left, in a few minutes we came upon Loch Katrine which was seen in its greatest beauty in the fine evening light. Most lovely!... It was about ten minutes past five when we went on board the very clean little steamer Rob Roy... We took a turn and steamed a little way up the bay called Glen Gyle, where there is a splendid glen beautifully wooded, which is the country of the MacGregors, and where there is a house which belonged to MacGregor of Glen Gyle, which, with the property, has been bought by a rich Glasgow innkeeper of the same clan. We turned and went on, and nothing could be more beautiful than the loch, wooded all along the banks. The rugged Ben Venue, so famed in the Lady of the Lake (which we had with us as well as several guide-books, of which we find Black's far the best) rises majestically on the southern side of the lake, and looking back you see the Alps of Arrochar, which well deserve the name, for they are quite pointed and most beautiful; their names are Ben Vean, Ben Voirlich, Ben Eim, and Ben Crosh. Next came the well-known 'Silver Stand' and 'Helen's Isle' which is most lovely, and the narrow creek so beautifully wooded below the splendid high hills, and the little wooden landing-place which I remembered so well.[32]

As the royal diary indicates and as is well-documented elsewhere, the nascent tourist industry was served by the development of railways and paddle-steamers. Indeed, Cook's excursions later gave way to ones organized directly by the railway companies; witness the title of a guide-book published around 1910 called *To the Homes and Haunts of Scott and Burns by the Caledonian Railway*.[33] As the terms 'beaten track' and 'package tour' suggest, the development of commercial tourism involved a further reduction in the number of historical sites celebrated by Scott and a concentration on an easily accessible few, increasingly well-serviced by hotels, guidebooks, and various modes of locomotion. The names of Scott characters also became literally inscribed in the landscape, in the names given to such beauty spots as Ellen's Isle and Roderick Dhu's hideout and, more recently, in the names of the hotels serving them, such as Abbotsford Lodge and the Waverley Hotel.[34] Moreover, from the mid-1800s tourists visiting Lake Katrine and environs were transported by a series of steamboats named from a variety of Scott novels, some of which had been associated with the lake, but others not. Their virtual re-location to the Trossachs was therefore a way of intensifying the Scott experience by maximizing the traces of his work at one particular (one-stop-shop) location. When Victoria steamed across the lake in the evening light she was aboard the *Rob Roy*, where later visitors would find a *Jeanie Deans*, a *Talisman*, a *Waverley*, and a *Lucy Ashton* (sometimes, in an intriguing amalgamation of different fictional worlds, these boats operated side by side).[35] Most prominent among the Lake Katrine steamers seems to have been the SS *Sir Walter Scott*, first launched in 1899 and replaced by a second *Sir Walter Scott* in 1946. And it is still sailing today. As a recent monograph called *Sir Walter Scott on Lake Katrine* puts it:

This has been a popular area with tourists ever since Sir Walter Scott described it in 1810 in his narrative poem *The Lady of the Lake*. It is fitting that the steamer that ventures into the deep Highland vastness on the sparkling waters of the beautiful Loch Katrine should be named after the author who also penned the folk hero Rob Roy MacGregor.[36]

The use of the name Sir Walter Scott for the steamer on Lake Katrine encapsulates the way in which narrative representation and tourism played into each other: having read the book you go to the real place and step on the steamer whose name recalls the author of the book (along with all his other books).[37] It is an ontological hybrid, but one that seems to exemplify a common pattern in the synthesis of memory sites: memories, and the figures associated with them, become reduced, shunted around, and amalgamated so as to provide ever more concentrated and localized experiences, and, in the long term, ever more eroded complexities. That tourism to Lake Katrine was structured by what John Urry has called a 'tourist gaze' is so obvious as to need no further elaboration.[38] Nevertheless, the appeal for the tourists would seem to have lain in the indisputable authenticity of actually being *in situ* and of performing a singular, embodied relationship to a place that had been endowed with literary and historical value. It can be described as the ultimate extension of the life of the imagination into everyday life, though one that is linked to the exceptionality of holidays rather than to the quotidian.

One of the main themes of the eulogies at the banquet held in Glasgow on the occasion of Scott's centenary in 1871 was that he had materially contributed to the modernization of Scotland since his mental routes and mappings had laid the foundations for actual roads, hotels, and steamers. As one eulogist put it: 'To him we chiefly owe the beautiful roads which conduct through our loveliest scenery: the splendid hotels which supply every comfort to the traveller, the magnificent fleet of steamers...But greater riches than these has he conferred. He truly made our wilderness rejoice.'[39] Truly, indeed. Scott had made this 'wilderness' accessible with the help of earlier representation and his literary imagination before commercially minded entrepreneurs made it materially accessible through the building of roads, hotels, and steamers. It is easy with the condescension of posterity to emphasize all that was synthetic about this packaging of Scott and Scotland. But the whole point about the case of Scott is that it makes the opposition between the prefabricated and the authentic ultimately irrelevant. The production of a 'tourist gaze' on Scotland was not a radical new departure from his own principles, but a continuation of his cultural work in creating a real and intimate relationship to an imagined past.

The packaging of Lake Katrine as described above is the most egregious manifestation of a radical refashioning of the relationship between location and memory that Scott helped produce, although he himself was surely disappointed, as at least one passage in his later *Chronicles of the Canongate* suggests, by the destruction of nature caused by mass tourism.[40] As we shall see, he spearheaded a thoroughly modern and manufactured form of cultural remembrance in which attachment to custom-made memory locations was closely intertwined with the mobility of media and with human mobility in the form both of tourism and of migration. In order to elaborate this point and show more of the continuities between the various aspects of his cultural work, I shall turn to Abbotsford, the Walter Scott memory site *par excellence*.

BUILDING ABBOTSFORD, RE-LOCATING OBJECTS

The name Abbotsford refers in the first instance to an actual location and building: the large country house located south of Edinburgh in the border area of Scotland where Scott lived with his family from 1812 to his death in 1832. But it was also much more than that: Scott's imaginative investment in his house means that Abbotsford should also be seen as part and parcel of his *oeuvre* and a key element in its global impact. Indeed, Trumpener has summarized the latter by referring to 'the novelistic institution of Abbotsford'.[41] Its dual character as both a located site and a portable monument means that his home can exemplify Scott's role in re-imagining the relationship between location and memory.

The home of Walter Scott is remarkable for its combination of lordly allure and comfort. It has something of a medieval castle with defensive turrets and crenellation, while the spacious drawing rooms at the back have large windows affording an open view down to the lawns and the river Tweed. With the exception of an extension, the house now standing is basically the one left by Scott, who, having acquired the property in 1811, rebuilt it in various stages, and at great cost, between 1817 and 1825.[42] The building advertises its link to history through its many neo-medieval features, while also being designed as a modern family home. This combination of the old and the modern tallies with the fact that Scott was at once a key figure in the development of Romantic historicism and, at the same time, as Virginia Woolf pointed out, a modernizer who installed gas-lighting and pneumatic bells in the house.[43] That those bells were suitably moulded in the shape of gargoyles, as I mentioned earlier, is a manifestation of the forward-looking historicism that Scott practised in so many cultural fields as well as his concern with integrating history into material life. Abbotsford is, in the first instance, a place you can visit in order to see where the famous Waverley works were written: the book-lined study is maintained as a shrine to the site of his literary creativity even though many of the major works were written elsewhere. When I first visited in 2005 there were postcards on sale of 'The Study' with pride of place given to the chair upon which Scott sat when working at his desk (this chair is a recurrent topic in the representations of Abbotsford arguably because it is the closest one can get to the physical presence of the man himself in the act of writing).[44]

The fact that such a major cultural figure from the nineteenth century lived, worked, and died here would be in itself enough to give the building and its contents a historical significance—although the word 'historical' here is ambivalent. Since Scott's reputation and the numbers of visitors to Abbotsford have waned in the course of the twentieth century, recent commentators like Stuart Kelly have under-scored its current character as an empty shell with an 'air of unreality',

Figure 5.2: Abbotsford (2005).

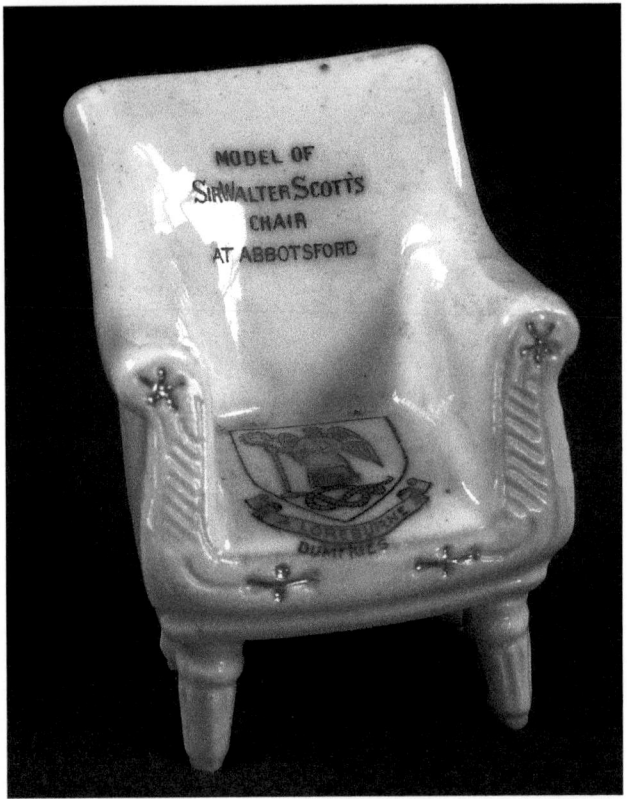

Figure 5.3: Scott's chair, porcelain (*c*.1930).

highlighting the fact that what was futuristic in the 1820s has now something grotesque about it, and suggesting furthermore that the whole place feels as if it has been left behind by history. It has an 'uncanny' (*unheimlich*) feel to it: a home that is a mockery of a home because of the fakeness of its medievalist composition and because Scott is no longer living in it.[45] Nicola Watson echoes these sentiments by describing the house as having an 'embarrassing Victorian fossilized quality'.[46] The very materiality of the place has meant that it has not been able to morph with the times as some of Scott's other works have. The house is currently undergoing renovation: having stayed with the Maxwell-Scott family until 2004, the house passed into the hands of the Abbotsford Trust in 2007. It will be interesting in the coming years to follow its appeal to a twenty-first-century public, but whatever the future will bring, its enormous significance as a memory site in the past calls for further analysis.

Abbotsford, a new version of Horace Walpole's eighteenth-century Strawberry Hill, was from the very beginning more than a mere backdrop to Scott's real life. The house itself, both its architecture and its furnishings, can be 'read' as another one of his creations and a tissue of references to his own work. Abbotsford's neo-gothic appearance set the example for a whole generation who sought to integrate a newly fired historical imagination into the architecture and interiors of their homes.[47] In his introduction to a collection of case-studies called *Writers' Houses and the Making of Memory* (2008), Harald Hendrix distinguishes between a house as a medium of self-fashioning (expressing the author's self-image) and houses that have become sites of memory because of their association with an author.[48] Abbotsford managed to be both these things at once because Scott's self-fashioning was so closely linked to his role as curator of collective memory. The posthumous recollections of Scott as Laird of Abbotsford, which I will discuss in greater detail in the next chapter, were adding just one more level of remembrance to that already at work in the very fabric of the building—and even in its name.

In fact Abbotsford was originally known by the more prosaic name of Cartleyhole. Having bought the fairly modest farm in 1811 and renamed it, Scott then proceeded to apply his literary fortune and his antiquarian interests to found an ancestral home, engaging in elaborate building works in 1816–19 and again in 1822–4.[49] Whereas Byron had inherited an ancestral home, the newly ennobled Scott set out to make one synthetically and in the process he practised an 'invention of tradition' on a par with his reception of George IV in Edinburgh in 1822.[50] This meant designing an historical home by filling it with models and objects from elsewhere, including ones associated with his written work.[51] In his pioneering study of Abbotsford as a cultural construct, Stephen Bann referred in this regard to a 'technique of transference and assemblage' being characteristic of Scott's approach to the building.[52] He recycled architectural elements from existing medieval buildings, using generic features such as crenellation and a tower, but also specific models which he then copied: the ceiling of the library, for example, reproduces the ornate ceiling of Rosslyn Chapel and has wood-grained plasterwork (the latter elicited Ruskin's particular contempt).[53] He also recycled actual building materials from elsewhere and incorporated these salvaged objects into the very fabric of the new building. Thus original Roman friezes were built into the wall of the garden alongside nineteenth-century reproductions. An original door from the Tolbooth in Edinburgh was built into the side of the house, while other pieces of wood from the same building were recycled in making the shelves that line the library (as was mentioned earlier, the Tolbooth prison, which figures prominently in the novel *The Heart of Mid-Lothian* (1818), had been demolished in 1817).[54] Interestingly, the Tolbooth door is inserted into the wall in such a way and at such a height that it is useless as a door but all the more striking as an object of display that recalls both the original prison and Scott's novel. The author's study also contains objects made from recycled wood with a more indirect historical significance but nevertheless with some sort of material link to great events: a chest made from one of the wrecks of the Spanish Armada along with a chair, with no more and no less historical significance, than that it was made from the wood of a tree that actually stood near the spot where William Wallace was betrayed. In all this recycling of models and materials, the boundary between original and copy, the historical and the aesthetic, the functional and the exhibited, was less relevant than the possibility of maximizing the symbolic presence of history through a multiplication of its material traces in particular locations in the house. In her *Destination Culture* (1998), Barbara Kirshenblatt-Gimblett linked the phenomenon of display to the framing that occurs when something is *re-located*: if an ordinary object is taken out of its everyday environment and exhibited in a museum or a special case, it takes on a new aura. No longer a mere functional object it invites a new type of attention and interpretation. In this light, one could say that Abbotsford not only exists as house, but also as 'display building': architectural features reminiscent of the Middle Ages were both used and displayed *as* historical remainders by virtue of being de-contextualized and relocated.[55] The crenellated house with its recycled building materials and architectural styles signalled 'oldness' in multifarious ways.

This was also true of the furnishings. Particularly in the reception rooms (the entrance hall and library), bits and pieces from the past are exhibited rather higgledy-piggledy in the manner of an old curiosity shop and of an age when the principles of modern museum design were still a thing of the future.[56] The sheer quantity and eclectic range of these objects reflects Scott's considerable achievement as a collector of antiquities, which was fed by his passionate interest in the material, touchable traces of the past: neolithic axes, several suits of armour, lots of small arms from different historical periods, the original key to the Tolbooth, various relics that he had picked up on the battlefield of Waterloo in 1815, a display case with various leftovers of Scottish history including a piece of oatcake purportedly found on the body of a Highlander after the battle of Culloden and a purse belonging to Helen McGregor, wife of Rob Roy, and several objects of colonial provenance sent to him by friends and admirers.[57] The objects on display range from prehistoric times to recent Scottish and European history, but the frame provided by the house allows for them to coexist side by side in the a-chronological way typical of collections. Scott's wide-ranging library on Scottish history and popular culture (including many pamphlets that are now proving to be of great interest) formed the bibliophile counterpart to this collection of objects.[58] In short, Abbotsford had all the marks both of a family home and of a public museum and library, with Scott as its curator. In bringing together in one place so many original relics and copied bits of history, Scott succeeded in turning Abbotsford, like the other more official museums that have emerged as custom-made *lieux de mémoire* since the beginning of the nineteenth century, into a place where disparate memories were made materially present in highly concentrated doses; where re-located objects found new meaning as part of a display. One of the reasons for going to Abbotsford, besides the interest of meeting Scott himself until his death in 1832, was the possibility of seeing many objects and styles brought there from *other* locations.

Figure 5.4: Entrance Hall, Abbotsford. Photograph George Washington Wilson (*c.*1880).

A ROMANCE OF A HOUSE

'The *Waverley* novels in stone': as a number of commentators have pointed out, Scott's imaginative investment in the building and running of Abbotsford (even down to the care with which he planted trees) was another variation on his other cultural work as historical novelist, poet, historian, antiquarian, public figure.[59] His innovations in the field of historical writing, as mentioned earlier, were closely linked to his antiquarian passion for the material aspects of past life and to his own imaginative involvement in the sensual texture of times past. His keeping an oatcake carried by an anonymous Highlander can be seen as a variation on his novelistic descriptions of what historical individuals ate and the clothes they wore. Since evidence for the actual provenance of this particular oatcake was at best flimsy, it may also have reflected Scott's willingness to suspend disbelief in favour of historical imagination even as he was ostensibly playing the role of antiquarian.[60] Certainly, Scott himself was highly conscious of the parallels between his various activities, referring repeatedly to Abbotsford as the 'romance of a house I am making'.[61] This romance dimension is reflected in the idealized depiction of the house by John Bower reproduced below which bears little resemblance to the actual building.

Figure 5.5: *Image of Abbotsford*, John Bower (1833).

The intimate link between Scott's novelistic work and his role as creator of Abbotsford is confirmed by *Reliquiae Trotcosienses*, a work written at the end of his life in which the persona of the antiquarian John Oldbuck (the protagonist of *The Antiquary* (1816)) sets out playfully the design for an imaginary house that bore many resemblances to the actual Abbotsford.[62] The Abbotsford project—fabricating as it did a physical retreat outside the currents of history—bore some resemblance, moreover, to the Highland retreat awarded to Jeanie Deans in *The Heart of Mid-Lothian* and possibly anticipated Wemmick's fantasy castle in Dickens' *Great Expectations* (1861).[63] In earlier chapters mention has been made of Scott's influence on the spread of the historical imagination to everyday life: the design of Abbotsford and the role he played there as 'laird' indicates that Scott himself remediated his novels in his own domestic life in a way that enhanced their impact.

These variant forms of literary production were not only linked thematically, but also in another, more concrete way. There is a general agreement among historians that the huge financial burden in building and maintaining Abbotsford provided an ongoing stimulus to him as novelist to keep producing new works for the market; that the novels subsidized the house with which he was passionately involved.[64] The 'timeless' character of Abbotsford had paradoxically been made possible by the modernization of the publishing industry that he had helped advance. The intimate connection between commercial life and the 'romance of a house' became even more apparent after the financial collapse of Ballantyne in 1826, whose impact on Scott's personal finances was aggravated by the heavy financial toll of Abbotsford—not just the initial outlay and restoration, but also the ongoing expenses incurred by his long-term performance as a Scottish laird.

At an age when self-fashioning was not the explicit issue it is today, it is remarkable how many different identities Scott assumed or had attributed to him. I shall come back to the figure of 'Walter Scott' in more detail in the next chapter. Suffice it here to point out that his many personae included, besides the Author of Waverley and the Wizard of the North, the title Laird of Abbotsford, which was the way he often styled himself in his letters. While the actual building was a materialized form of self-fashioning, his lifestyle as Laird of Abbotsford involved performing various related roles: curator of memory; protector of his family, servants, livestock, lands, and dogs (he was known for his extraordinary loyalty to canines and was often pictured with them);[65] and a host who showed hospitality on an almost feudal scale to the many friends and guests who regularly filled the house, and later, like Washington Irving wrote about their experiences.[66] His many documented acts of benevolence and patronage were no less real for being scripted in this way, but scripted they were according to the idea of a paternalist and honourable gentleman who lived up to his ideals and paid his debts (more on this in Chapter 6). Through both his life and his work he helped shape later views of the Victorian gentleman as a modern version of chivalry. Although he never dressed up himself as a medieval knight, there was nevertheless a certain kinship between his everyday role-playing and the chivalric re-enactments in the United States discussed earlier.

In short: Abbotsford had all the features of a synthetic memory site with high concentrations and layers of meaning. A placeholder for the historical objects that Scott had collected or incorporated into the building, the location thematized history and remembering as such. It also marked the actual spot where the Waverley novels had been written and where Scott himself had lived out his historicizing dreams, and his role as writer and Laird of Abbotsford. In a memorial layering typical of memory sites, its role as museum (recalling Scottish and European history) was overlaid by its role as a monument recalling the life and works of the maker of that museum, Sir Walter Scott. Indeed, as W. S. Crockett wrote of Abbotsford in 1905, the location was even more reminiscent of Scott than the custom-made memorial put up in Edinburgh in 1840: 'So far as monuments to Scott go, there is none to equal [Abbotsford], not even the most splendid and costly pile which is one of Edinburgh's proudest ornaments.'[67] As Crockett's reference to the human and financial *cost* of Abbotsford indicated, a certain tension existed between the various memorial layers: the fact that Scott had had to struggle financially to keep up Abbotsford highlighted its artificial character at the same time as it humanized it by linking this 'romance' to both the genius and the vulnerability of its maker. As this summary indicates, the place had more than enough ambivalence to make it fascinating for decades to come right up to those recent visitors, quoted earlier, who have seen it as an uncanny, haunted, or 'embarrassing' house.

PORTABLE 'ABBOTSFORD'

When Scott was travelling back home in 1832, on what was to be his last trip abroad, he happened to visit a bookseller in Frankfurt who, on hearing that there was an English speaker in the shop but not recognizing the man in question, hastened to offer this potential customer something that would be sure to interest him: a print of Abbotsford.[68] The anecdote illustrates the extraordinary popularity both of Scott's writings and of his home, a fame that in the form of a printed image had literally travelled the world in advance of its owner. Nor was the presence of this print in a Frankfurt bookshop an outrageous fluke: even within the lifetime of Scott, 'Abbotsford' had become the metonymic mark of Sir Walter Scott and everything associated with him, the material embodiment of his life and the Waverley world. Like his poetry and novels, his custom-built 'romance of a house' generated many visualizations that travelled widely throughout the British Isles, Europe, and North America. This interconnectedness between his writing and his house culminated in the richly illustrated Abbotsford edition of his novels (1842–7).

Images of Abbotsford were disseminated from an early stage in a variety of media and genres, from oil paintings (as Thomas Faed's *Sir Walter Scott and his Literary Friends at Abbotsford*, 1849) to the engravings of the house that were reproduced in popular magazines, to the photographs and magic lantern slides of the interior and exterior of the house that were mass-produced from the 1860s onwards (*Abbotsford: 12 Photos for your Album* (1900), for example), to the souvenirs depicting Abbotsford or porcelain miniatures of the writer's chair that are a feature of the last part of the century and that continue today. While the photographs made in the last decades of the century by George Washington Wilson are striking for their haunting realism, some of the earlier illustrations of Scott's comfortable house, as we have seen, underscored the romantic cast of the whole enterprise, erasing all signs of the modern and offering instead a decon-textualized view of a wondrous medieval castle.

The intimate connection between Abbotsford, Scott's life, and his other creative activities meant that tie-in publications dealing with the 'original' sites in Scott's novels and poetry were often supplemented by images or descriptions of Abbotsford as the site where the writing itself took place. *The Land of Scott: A Series of Landscape Illustrations, illustrative of real scenes, described in the novels and tales, of the author of Waverley* (1848) included a drawing of the study at Abbotsford alongside images of the various sites that had figured in his historical fiction, as if the writer's home were a natural extension of his writing.[69] Similarly, many items from the Abbotsford collections were included in the illustrations to the Abbotsford edition of the novels. An illustration to *The Heart of Mid-Lothian*, for example, featured two visitors pointing to the Tolbooth door that had been built into the sidewall of the house. This engraving was the outcome of a complex series of remediations in which the material and the imma-terial were intensely bound up with each other: Scott's inclusion of the Tolbooth both in the building of Abbotsford (as object) and in the novel *The Heart of Mid-Lothian* (as representation).[70] By the 1840s the novel could be evoked by an image of the door at Abbotsford as perceived by two visitors, indicating tourism as the natural outcome of reading and an intrinsic part of the circulation of stories. In Scott's multifarious *oeuvre*, the boundaries between the individual works and between the material and the immaterial were never fixed and his admirers took this lesson from his book, by crossing over easily from one aspect of Scott to another. At least one bibliophile edition of the novels was advertised as bound in wood that had grown in the grounds at Abbotsford.[71]

This ongoing symbolization of Abbotsford continued a process that the writer himself had set in motion: as we saw earlier, there never was an original Abbotsford beyond the modest house Scott moved into, but only a site where acts of remembrance were performed and where they continuously left their material traces. The intermedial convergence of objects and images relating to Abbotsford involved a good deal of mere repetition, but also an increasing self-referentiality. One of the Wilson photographs, which was designed as a souvenir to be brought to other people's homes, now hangs in the entrance hall of Abbotsford itself. A miniature of the colossal Scott monument in Edinburgh, made for the centenary exhibition in 1871, is also on display in the house. Thanks to the many images in circulation, the idea of 'Abbotsford' preceded later visitors and overlay their perceptions of the actual place—increasingly to their disappointment, as various accounts from the decades after Scott's death attest.[72]

'Abbotsford' also became portable to other locations: as a name that stood for Scott and all his works (or even: heritage itself) it was virtually relocated to multiple other houses and streets in the suburbs of British cities, particularly Scottish ones, in the second half of the nineteenth century. In this way, Abbotsford was literally mapped onto lived-in urban space, inscribing the memory of Scott's works and his romance of a house into Abbotsford Drives, Avenues, and Crescents in places as dispersed as Dundee, Falkirk, Perth, Paisley, Glasgow, Manchester.[73] In the process, it helped inscribe newly built-up city areas, which had hitherto been agricultural or park land, with an historical pedigree that they would have otherwise lacked. As many city maps show, Abbotsford often figured along with clusters of related Scott streets creating a new neighbourhood with a ready-made history. Used in this way, it was generally interchangeable with Scott's *oeuvre* and the Waverley world as a whole. Glasgow's Abbotsford Avenue, for example, is located near a Waverley Drive and alongside avenues called after a series of Scott-related sites—Jedburgh, Dryburgh, Melrose, and Kelso—actual places that are thus virtually relocated to other towns and cities. A similar Scott cluster can be found in Birmingham, where Abbotsford Avenue adjoins a Peveril Way, a Rokeby Road, a Marmion Drive, and, the implicit link between them all, a Scott Road.

Figure 5.6: *Abbotsford, with the Door of the Tolbooth that Opened on the Scaffold.*
Wood engraving William Dickes. From *The Heart of Mid-Lothian*, Abbotsford
Edition of the Waverley novels (Edinburgh, 1842–7).

Reference was made earlier to the spread of the place-name Waverley
across the settler colonies of the English-speaking world, from the United
States and Canada, to South Africa and Australia. Examples have also been
given of places called Ivanhoe, and the significance of their distribution in
the United States. Less obviously marked by partisanship, Abbotsford was
also used to name cities, neighbourhoods, and streets in Wisconsin,
Victoria, Dunedin, Johannesburg, and British Columbia among many

others (which also boasts a scenic Lake Katrine and a Roderick Dhu mountain). Not to mention the countless Abbotsford houses, baptized by proud homeowners with Scottish roots or otherwise with a literary appreciation of Scott. Many of these namings date to the 1870s, around the centenary of Scott's birth, and are concentrated in the period 1870–1900, but some are later: witness the case of Tallahassee, Florida, where a Scott suburb, including an Abbotsford Street, was built in the 1950s (as an act of Victorian nostalgia? Or as a sign of Anglo-Celtic gentility?).[74] Although Scott also enjoyed an enormous success on the European continent (witness the carnival in Naples discussed earlier or the availability of images of Abbotsford), it is a striking fact that the name Abbotsford was not carried over into the naming of streets and houses outside the British Empire and its former colonies. This suggests that, although Scott's texts were eminently exportable, there were limits to the extent to which his writings could subsequently be inscribed in the public spaces of other countries. Indeed, as I shall argue in greater detail in Chapter 6, Scott helped define and consolidate the very notion of a culturally unified English-speaking world through his inscription in public spaces in Great Britain, North America, and other colonies. As one commentator noted sardonically in 1903, the typical British official in Simla still lives in 'a ridiculous white-washed house made of mud and tin, and calling itself Warwick Castle, Blenheim, Abbotsford!'[75]

The inscription of Scott names in urban spaces of the Empire and the New World was part of a larger-scale transplanting of memories or, what might be called memorial colonization. This meant overwriting the landscape with imported references or, to recall words quoted earlier, creating a 'never-neverism on the surface of a land that seemed too new'. Particularly significant in this regard was the decision made by the New York authorities to allow the erection of a statue to Sir Walter Scott in Central Park, alongside Shakespeare and Columbus.[76] As the speech made in 1872 by the poet and liberal activist William Cullen Bryant on the occasion of the official unveiling revealed, Scott had been symbolically relocated in Central Park as a way of recalling Americans' connection with a long literary tradition, but also as a way of peopling the hitherto virgin ground of Manhattan with 'new memories' and 'old traditions'. He too linked Scott's legacy to the pantheon of characters he had created and that could now be used to help populate the wilderness (in Chapter 6 we will encounter a similar conceit with respect to the repopulation of the 'emptied' Highlands). As Bryant himself waxed forth in blithe neglect of pre-Columbian America:

Figure 5.7: Abbotsford Way, Tallahassee, FL.

And now as the statue of Scott is set up in this beautiful park, which, a few years since, possessed no human associations, historical or poetic, connected with its shades, its lawns, its rocks, and its waters, *these grounds become peopled with new memories.* Henceforth the silent earth at this spot will be eloquent of old traditions, the airs that stir the branches of the trees will whisper feats of chivalry to the visitor . . . . [Scott's characters] will pass in endless procession around the statue of him in whose prolific brain they had their birth, until the language we speak shall perish, and the spot upon which we stand shall be again a woodland wilderness.[77] [emphasis AR]

As this eulogy to the author of Waverley suggests, Scott's role in 'peopling' Central Park with memories was overdetermined: he was not only a sign of literature as such but, specifically, of a literature that was itself a memorial medium. Whoever put up a statue to Scott, or whoever inscribed his name in other ways into the landscape, implanted a whole package of history in a single gesture. With the name Scott or its metonym Abbotsford came a host of historical characters to instil memories into the spaces of Manhattan, Boston, and British Columbia (just as they had helped implant tradition in the new urban spaces of Glasgow and Birmingham).

Scott and Abbotsford did not just travel, then, as icons of a particular writer back in Scotland: they functioned as a ready-made icon of History or of pastness itself. In some cases the use of these names was linked to the desire of diasporic Scottish communities to publicize their identity by locating it in the public space. Both the Scott statue and the Burns one that followed it a few years later were offered to the city of New York on behalf of the Scottish community. But although Scott was indeed marked as Scottish, he also served a broader constituency of genteel literature lovers. Like Abbotsford, Scott was recognizable and cherished by a wider English-speaking audience for whom he symbolized a common past. The case of Ivanhoe showed that there were serious limits to the underlying consensus within the community of Scott lovers, but also that his work offered a common ground on which differences were played out.

ABBOTSFORD/'ABBOTSFORD' AS DESTINATION

Images carried Abbotsford abroad, but also mobilized people to go there. Scores of visitors found their way to the house even during Scott's lifetime: these included many illustrious literati with whom Scott had corresponded, but also more opportunistic travellers wanting to be in on the Scott phenomenon and ready to profit from a free lunch. The sheer number of visitors led Scott to complain in his journal in November 1825:

Abbotsford begins to be haunted by too much company of every kind. But especially foreigners. I do not like them ... I hate the impudence that pays a stranger compliments and harangues about his works in the author's house, which is usually ill breeding. Moreover they are seldom long in making it evident that they know nothing about what they are talking of excepting having seen *The Lady of the Lake* at the opera.[78]

Despite such reservations, Scott's entry for the next day mentions a visit from a Russian youth (whom he praises for being 'kind, modest and ingenious') and two Frenchmen ('whom I liked'): apparently his bonhomie regularly got the better of his desire for peace and quiet. His own reputation as a friendly host worked together with his literary fame to encourage this continuous stream of visitors.

After Scott's death Abbotsford became something of a nineteenth-century Graceland, a major pilgrimage destination for book-lovers from far and near: as one writer put it as early as 1833, it was 'the spot to which pilgrims from all parts of the civilised world will bend their footsteps'.[79] As we shall see in Chapter 6 there was a discussion after Scott's death about whether Abbotsford itself rather than a custom-made monument would not be the most suitable memorial to the great writer. The house still attracts significant numbers of visitors, though it has undoubtedly lost out relative to other tourist destinations.[80] In the Victorian period it attracted many literati, including the Brontë sisters, Charles Dickens, Harriet Beecher Stowe, Nathaniel Hawthorne, Theodor Fontane, Harriet Martineau, and Oscar Wilde, to name just a few of the names in the visitors' book kept since 1837.[81] Abbotsford was often also on the itinerary of visits by royalty, though usually the spouses, children, or cousins of reigning monarchs rather than the monarchs themselves (a notable exception being Scott-lover Queen Victoria, who visited in 1867 and left her signature on a copy of *Ivanhoe*).[82] From the late 1840s, however, as organized tourism got under way in Scotland and destinations were often defined in terms of their historical and literary interest, Abbotsford increasingly attracted a broader, genteel public often from overseas. The conditions under which these visitors were entertained changed quite radically, being no longer a matter of visitors staying several weeks 'on the house', as Washington Irving had done back in 1817, but of paying an entrance fee and receiving a guided tour of the house.

Visitors on organized tours often combined a trip to Abbotsford with a visit to Scott's grave at Dryburgh Abbey, and to the nearby Melrose Abbey, which had not only been evoked in the *Lay of the Last Minstrel* (1805) but was also historically interesting in its own right.[83] The proximity of these related sites increased the value of Abbotsford as a destination. As mentioned earlier, the growth of tourism in general to Scotland was enormously facilitated by the introduction of the railway, which helped create routes and destinations. This certainly applied to Abbotsford: several railway lines passed in the vicinity of Abbotsford, including the so-called Waverley line, which started in 1862, ran from Waverley Station in Edinburgh (built in 1848), had engines named after characters in Scott's *oeuvre*, and stopped near Scott's old home on its way to Carlisle.[84] As in the case of Lake Katrine and its steamers, visitors were offered an experience in which locations and the routes to them were Scott-saturated. In this way, tourism continued to reconfigure the imagined geography of Scotland in terms of routes and destinations or, to use the term Scott's contemporaries seem to have favoured, routes and spots.

As the visitors' books reveal, a significant portion of the visitors to Abbotsford in the nineteenth century came from North America, and the guide written by W. S. Crockett in 1905 specifically targeted 'the great congregation over the seas' for whom Scott's home had become a household name.[85] These included groups from Philadelphia and Cincinnati, but also noteworthies like the defeated leader of the Confederacy Jefferson Davis, who visited in 1869, followed by the victorious Union general

Ulysses S. Grant in 1883 (as if to keep up the tradition, General Omar Bradley turned up in 1947).[86] The appearance at Abbotsford of a party from Cincinnati in 1862 reflects what Benedict Anderson has called the 'long-distance nationalism' of diasporic communities.[87] Cincinnati was home to one of the oldest Caledonian Societies in North America (founded in 1827) and the local loyalty to Scott had expressed itself among other things in the number of Mississippi paddle-steamers registered in Cincinnati bearing Scott names. These included several *Sir Walter Scotts* whose fictional avatar, mentioned earlier, later figured in Mark Twain's *Adventures of Huckleberry Finn* (1885).[88]

Although the reception of Scott in North America deserves further study, it is already evident that the appropriation of his work was both intense and varied, spanning a social spectrum that ran from tournament-going gentlemen in the Southern states, to the genteel reading classes all over the continent, to members of the Scottish diaspora and emigrant organizations. It is a measure of Scott's cross-party appeal and the broad range of topics covered in his work that he could be construed as specifically Scottish, as specifically Southron, and as a 'non-aligned' writer: a purveyor of English poetry and narrative at a time when a distinctly American literature was still only emerging. The Southern reception focusing on *Ivanhoe* became infamous through Twain's intervention, but it was only a part of this much broader appeal. As the London *Times* noted in August 1871, Scott had transformed Scotland from a country people left to a destination to which they returned as pilgrims.[89] When they signed the visitors' books, tourists to Abbotsford in the 1880s regularly added locations such as Boston, Philadelphia, Guelph, the Cape of Good Hope, and New South Wales to their names.

In what follows, I want to describe in some detail one such visit to Abbotsford in 1882 by a member of the Ulster-Scots diaspora: Thomas Mellon (1813–1908), founder of the Mellon Bank and patriarch of the well-known family in Pittsburgh. The account he gave of Abbotsford in his autobiography is exceptional for being written by someone who was not himself a man of letters (most other accounts, starting with that of Washington Irving, were written by literati). Its particular interest here is that it demonstrates how Abbotsford functioned as a designated memory site within an imaginative mapping of Great Britain on the part of a returning migrant-now-tourist.

In 1882 Thomas Mellon retired from business and, together with his son, took what he called in his autobiography a 'trip to Europe'.[90] In fact, this trip to Europe was a return trip to the British Isles. With an Ulster-Scots background (this hyphenated identity the outcome of the settlement of Northern Ireland from Scotland in the seventeenth century), he had emigrated as a child from Northern Ireland to North America some 65 years earlier. Given this background, Mellon's trip to Europe had the character of a pilgrimage. His trip was mapped around various tourist sights and a number of memory sites ('spots'), which he describes at some length. In the course of two weeks he made a round trip from Queens-town (present-day Cobh) in Southern Ireland (the first port of call after the Atlantic crossing), up to Dublin and Ulster, over to Scotland, down to London and back to Queenstown. Having visited a couple of designated tourist spots such as Blarney Castle, near Queenstown, the affective high point of the whole trip came with his visit to the original family home near Omagh. His wandering around the cottage was tied up with his childhood memories of the area and with family stories. As he put it, this was really 'all he cared to see of Ireland'.[91] But having time on his hands and having made the entire trip across the Atlantic, he also took a trip over to Scotland. Here the focus of his visit, in terms of both the length of his description and the enthusiasm which it expresses, was his visit to the houses of two writers: that of Robert Burns near Glasgow and that of Scott at Abbotsford.

Mellon's account shows that he identified in a deeply felt and highly personal way with the figure and writings of Burns, whose humble house he saw as a copy of his own homestead in Ulster. He describes the visit to Ayrshire as a private 'pilgrimage'[92] in which his personal appreciation of Burns' poetry (he quotes large chunks of 'The Cotter's Saturday Night') fed into his appreciation of standing in the actual spot where the man who produced it had lived. Mellon's attitude to Burns resonates with a widely-shared image of the poet as a humble 'man of the people' with a great popular and egalitarian appeal (as distinct from the cult of Scott, who was more generally associated with upper middle-class gentility).[93] Having paid his tribute in Ayrshire, Mellon then moved east and went to Abbots-ford, describing in considerable length his excursion to Scott's home in terms that are generally enthusiastic, but also rather impersonal, evincing cultural curiosity rather than the very personal interest he had shown in the case of Burns. The day-long excursion by train to Abbotsford, which Mellon concluded was on balance worth the trouble, included visits to several interrelated spots associated with Scott's work or with his person.

Mellon's mood was adversely affected by the persistent rain and by his disappointment with Melrose Abbey, the first spot on the itinerary, which he found to be far less interesting than his reading of the *Lay of the Last Minstrel*, with its description of the ruins by moonlight, had led him to expect. At Abbotsford, he was also initially disappointed by the overly business-like character of the reception—as he had been dismayed by the overly tidy and modern appearance of the graveyard where Burns was buried. Despite such reservations, Mellon ended up impressed by the sheer range of historical objects on display, which made the excursion 'far more than the worth of our money and time and discomfort'.[94] The sense of having had cultural value for money and effort ('The labor and discomfort of the afternoon was richly repaid'[95]) was then reinforced by his subsequent visit to Scott's grave at nearby Dryburgh Abbey. Standing beside the actual spot where the great man was buried, this successful man of business felt for the first time that day that he had really travelled away from the modern age into what we would call another chronotope. Despite all the history that had been laid out for him at Abbotsford, apparently nothing could beat the authenticity of being *in situ*, all alone in the presence of the great man's material remains and in a real medieval ruin to boot. *Hic jacet*:

And here lies buried the remains of Sir Walter. . . . Those wild ruins in this solitary domain, with nothing of the modern world in sight or hearing to disturb the repose, afford a most appropriate resting place for what is perishable of so renowned a man.[96]

Having experienced this momentary sensation of being finally in physical touch with the past itself, Mellon completed the rest of his journey without visiting any other significant sites. Having made his way back to Cobh, he cheerfully headed back to the New World without the least trace of sentimentality:

With the prow of our great ship turned westward as the shades of evening came on, the barren lofty coasts of Ireland disappeared, and I bade it farewell forever, with a pleased feeling of satisfaction with my visit, but a consciousness that a repetition or more protracted stay would be undesirable.[97]

Mellon's itinerary expressed a personal memory-scape in which various social frameworks were embedded in each other. At the centre were his personal and familial memories linked to his recollections of the home-stead in northern Ireland, the highpoint of his journey (to the rest of Ireland he seemed indifferent); beyond that, there was the broader frame of Scotland (even after several centuries settlers to Ulster still identified with that country). Significantly, it was Burns and Scott who represented Mellon's point of imaginary access to Scotland and provided specific sites to shape his route through the country. His connection to Burns seems to have been based on an intensely personal identification with the values he stood for: the author of 'A Man's a Man for a' that' provided a link between Mellon's personal experience and public culture. In contrast, his visit to Abbotsford was a more abstract and distant affair with no evocation of his writings, as if Scott merely represented 'history' as such, and it was only at the grave in Dryburgh that he was truly affected by the experience. The excursion not only offered him this momentary historical sensation along with an impressive array of historical objects, it also led him to reflect on the difference between the American and the European approaches to ruins, noting that Europeans are ready to wait long enough for historical buildings to become so interesting that people will pay to see them, whereas Americans tidy up their ruins and replace them by buildings that will be immediately useful.[98]

That an excursion to Abbotsford should work as an access point to History for the returning emigrant entrepreneur is evidence of the power that Scott's work had acquired as a cultural symbol and as a model for engaging with the past. Mellon's trip was also suggestive of the erosion across time and space of the historical complexities with which Scott as a writer had dealt. What was perhaps most remarkable about Mellon's return to his homeland, however, is that it should have been so non-nostalgic: his unsentimental farewell ('been there and done that') is the very opposite of a romantic longing for an original homeland. However, it is in this willingness to visit the past and then continue on with the business of making the future that Mellon may have in fact been closest to the spirit of Scott. With the help of Scott he had acquired the possibility of experiencing briefly the imaginative force of 'wild ruins in this solitary domain, with nothing of the modern world in sight'. At the same time his reactions pointed to the limits of memory and to other possible modes of relating to the world: 'a more protracted stay would be undesirable.'

DISPLACEMENTS

Abbotsford as an actual location has from the very beginning been caught up with its representations. It has always been on the move, as it were, in the virtual sense that its meaning has shifted as time passed. Like other memory sites, it represents both an unchanging location and a crossroads where exchanges take place between mobile media and mobile people. In the course of such exchanges cultural memory has continuously been produced and continuously eroded. This erosion of complexity may be more acute in Scott's case than in that of other less popular writers. Precisely because he meant so much to so many people, as I shall show in the next chapter, he ended up being appropriated by attitudes he may have helped to shape, but that would nevertheless have surprised him.

6

Commemorating Scott: 'That Imperial Man'

The gigantic monument to Sir Walter Scott in Princes Street Gardens in Edinburgh has something of an albatross about it.[1] Built in the period 1840–4 and shaped like a gothic tower, it rises 200 feet 6 inches above one of the city's main thoroughfares. It is a dominant presence in the contemporary cityscape, although it seems to be more 'in the way' than an urban hub. Those enthusiastic enough may climb a vertiginous flight of 287 steps to enjoy the urban panorama from the upper floors, stopping perhaps to study the first-floor exhibition on Scott and the monument itself in the little museum that was part of the original building. From these upper reaches, one can also examine more closely the multifarious statues that, faithful to the neo-ecclesiastical design, fill the 64 niches built in among the arches. These statues include some thirty of the characters who had figured in Scott's work, both those who had sprung from his imagination, like Jeanie Deans and Flora McIvor, and those, like John Knox, Saladin, and Cromwell, whom he recycled from the pages of history. Surveying this array of characters is like seeing an abridged version of Scott's collected works: its syncretism reflects the mixture of the factual and the imagination that was his hallmark, while the emphasis on individual figures highlights his role as creator of a pantheon of literary characters.[2]

This towering pile of characters and arches in turn forms a canopy above the statue of the author: Sir Walter, calmly seated as becomes a sage, and yet wrapped in a plaid, with his faithful deerhound at his feet. The whiteness of the marble seems to accentuate the mildness and calmness of his features, especially in the contrast it forms to the hustle and bustle of the street in which this huge monument has alighted. The statue is twice life-size and still looks a bit too small to bear the size of the tower, though the mildness of Scott's features suggests that he is at ease with the colossal honour being done to him. Nevertheless the total effect is one of incongruity: as the double-decker buses trundle by and shoppers hurry to cross the street, the enormous monument seems a leftover from another age.

The fact that its blackened stone is well past its clean-me date (in 2010) seems to highlight its affinity to a bygone monumentalism when cultural value was correlated with physical size and weight. Despite its size, however, scholars have tended to overlook the Scott monument, at most mentioning its existence in passing as a petrified symptom of the enormous popularity that the Author of Waverley once enjoyed and of a now out-dated cult of the Great Man.[3]

Figure 6.1: Scott Monument, Edinburgh. Photograph George Washington Wilson (*c*.1864).

The monument to Scott is not only remarkable for its size, but also as a relatively early example of the nineteenth-century celebration of artist-heroes, which would end up by dotting the capitals of Europe with statues to national writers and artists. These illustrate the gravitation of collective memory towards particular places, discussed at greater length in the previous chapter, and its material location in custom-made memorabilia in the heart of the city. Precisely because of their petrified character and their chiselled materiality, many nineteenth-century monuments appear nowadays as belated relics of a bygone age. Their celebratory, and some-times triumphalist, character is uncongenial to our contemporary emphasis on the traumas of the past rather than its pleasures, and on the victims of history rather than on its heroes, a shift of paradigm that started with World War I. Most importantly, they are relics of a period in which the celebration of the memory of *cultural* heroes was at the heart of constructions of collective identity. It now takes an effort of historical imagination to understand this collective pride and positivity, and the monumentalism that expressed it.

Recent criticism has tended at the very least to work around (if not against) the Great Men. In the case of Scott, this has meant a concerted attempt to downsize the Author of Waverley and displace him from his predominant position by excavating lesser known writers and highlighting their achievements.[4] This is a legitimate way of undoing the earlier history of reception by allowing alternative voices to be heard, however belatedly, and by generating complexity in the intellectual landscape where there seemed to have been silence. The result has been many new insights into the qualities of writers like John Galt and James Hogg, and of alternative intellectual positions that were overshadowed by the success of Scott. The recent downsizing of the Author of Waverley in favour of these more radical thinkers, however, has not just involved highlighting these authors, but also criticizing Scott by associating him with imperialism. Most influentially, Katie Trumpener has admonished Scott for his 'national-imperial thinking', a phrase echoed by Douglas Mack, who has confidently referred to Scott's 'symbolic legacy in the master-narrative of the British Empire'.[5] There are good reasons, as we will see, for linking Scott to empire since this is what many of his readers did. But Scott can only in part be held responsible for the ways in which his readers appropriated his work.

In what follows, I propose to examine Scott's 'symbolic legacy in the master-narrative of the British Empire', not by simply re-reading his work for its traces, but by pursuing his legacy in the public celebrations of his memory. This will involve analysing a lot of occasional tributes to the Author of Waverley that have hitherto travelled below the radar of cultural analysis, but which provide more detailed insight into his subsequent role in the elaboration of collective identities. What was at stake in putting up that enormous monument and who were the stakeholders? Why literature? And what does it tell us about 'the master-narrative of the British Empire' and Scott's place in it?

In Chapter 1 I contrasted the portability of texts with the materiality and locatedness of monuments. It does not follow from the physical stability of monuments, however, that their symbolic meaning is also fixed once and for all. Although statues are part of an effort to stabilize memory by *locating* the appreciation for certain figures in the public space,[6] they only preserve their meaning if they are kept alive by commemorative acts in which their significance is articulated, reinforced, or redefined.[7] They are at once symbols of collective identity and, what Jan Assmann has called, a theatre for social interactions:

> Every group which wants to consolidate its existence as such tries to acquire and secure places which will not only provide a theatre for their interactions, but also symbols of their identity and points of reference for their memory.[8]

How then did 'Sir Walter Scott' emerge as a memory site? As important, how did the subsequent evocation of his memory play into the shaping of collective identities? I propose to address these questions by analysing the commemorative activities and discourses around Scott's funeral, the erection of the monument, the centenary of his birth in 1871, which represented the highpoint of his public role, and the centenary of his death in 1932, when it was almost played out. Despite their high public profile, these highly mediated events have received little scholarly attention. To the extent that critics have studied the reception of Scott's work, their attention has largely been confined to critical responses in the form of published reviews and evaluations, or to discussions of his influence on other writers or artists. But with the exception of Ian Duncan's *Scott's Shadow* (2007), there has been a general neglect of the fact that Scott was a dominant presence in Edinburgh in the first decades of the nineteenth century: retriever of the Scottish royal regalia in 1818, orchestrator of the Royal Visit in 1822, a practicing lawyer as well as an immensely successful writer, he was very much a public figure. Inevitably his reception extended far beyond the arts and calls for critical study beyond the field of literary criticism.[9] The public memorialization of Scott was part of a more general culture of commemoration in which writers played an extremely important role as locus of value and as calibrators of identity. Echoes of this at a personal level have already been heard in the case of Thomas Mellon.

The self-reflexive cultivation of synthetic sites of memory, as we have seen, was one of the by-products of modernization and a reaction to the ruptures it occasioned.[10] The enlargement of the scale upon which societies operated was also important to this development since local groups, as Benedict Anderson has influentially argued, were increasingly called upon by the media to associate with an 'imagined community' of people whom they would never meet face to face but with whom they shared a territory and identity.[11] The case of Scott shows that there was indeed a close link between nation-building, public remembrance, and literature, but it also complicates the usual picture. By highlighting the role of commemorative festivals, my analysis will argue that not all communities are imagined and, as is demonstrated by the discourses produced on such

Figure 6.2: Scott Monument, detail. Photograph George Washington Wilson (*c.*1864).

occasions, that not all imagined communities are national. It challenges the assumption that community-building in the nineteenth century always ran along national lines by showing how the reception of Scott's fiction brought other frameworks into play. In the decades after his death, Scott's cultural afterlife already took place amidst what Benedict Anderson elsewhere called 'the nomadism of modern life', under transnational conditions brought about by economic development, emigration, and empire.[12]

THE GREAT UNKNOWN: AN OPEN SECRET

It was no coincidence that the fashion for erecting public monuments to writers blossomed in a post-Romantic era that showed singular respect for individual genius and, in Carlylean form, for 'heroes and hero-worship'.[13] The nineteenth century gave rise to numerous pantheons of national culture and, in the field of cultural scholarship, to the (infamous) 'man and work' paradigm in whose emergence Lockhart's *Memoirs of the Life of Sir Walter Scott* (1837–8) played a prominent role. This emphasis on great men and their biographies is repugnant to many of the declared principles of contemporary literary criticism (even though much literary criticism still consists in practice of re-readings of canonical works). But biography was an integral part of the collective consciousness-raising endemic to nineteenth-century nationalism and ideas of citizenship. In this regard, secular hagiography was helped along by the practical usefulness of the individual as a 'figure of memory' in concretizing and narrating the collective past, and in embodying cultural values in material, humanized, and singular ways. Because 'heroes and hero worship' could be translated by painters and sculptors into iconic faces or bodies, as I have shown elsewhere, they had an especially important role to play in concretizing collective memory at a time when nation-building based on democratic principles (and hence on the affective involvement of all individuals) coincided with a predilection in the aesthetic realm for realism.[14]

Just as his work invited remediation, so too did Scott's life prepare the way for his later remembrance. By design or instinct, he turned himself into a living monument and displayed an extraordinary intuition as to how best to maximize his public profile as an author. As we have seen in discussing the design of Abbotsford, his own life was part and parcel of his collective works, an embodied addition to his Waverley series illustrating the blurring of the boundaries between imagination and everyday life that would be part of his legacy. The sheer variety of names by which he was known—Wizard of the North, the Shirra (or Sheriff, referring to one of his official functions), Laird of Abbotsford, the Enchanter, the Great

Unknown, and, of course, the Author of Waverley—is indicative of the multiple roles that he played as antiquarian, lawyer, patron of the theatre, editor, *pater familias*, landlord, poet, and novelist. The emergence of Walter Scott as a cultural icon was surely facilitated by his having brought together in his person so many fields of activity and then having turned his domestic life into a material showcase for his ideas. Immensely popular through his writings as well as multifaceted in his activities, Scott came to mean many things to many people.

The proliferation of names by which he was known was also arguably provoked by Scott's own long-term strategy as an author, which was to keep making his identity an issue. After all, one of the many remarkable achievements of his life was to have remained the anonymous Author of Waverley for so long even as his real identity was an open secret. It is generally understood that Scott, when making his career move in 1814 from extremely successful poet to a producer of 'mere' novels, wanted to protect his reputation and secure his cultural capital by remaining anonymous. He explained his choice in a private letter written in July 1814:

I shall not own Waverley; my chief reason is, that it would prevent me of the pleasure of writing again. . . . I'm not sure it would be considered quite decorous for me, as a Clerk of Session, to write novels . . . and what should I gain by it, that any human being has a right to consider as an unfair advantage? In fact, only the freedom of writing trifles with less personal responsibility, and perhaps more frequently than I otherwise might do.[15]

His decision not to reveal his identity in face of the overwhelming success of *Waverley*, but to publish the subsequent novels anonymously, only admitting his authorship in February 1827, turned out to be a major promotional strategy that helped brand the novels.[16] Scott's carefully orchestrated anonymity also paradoxically drew attention to the puppet-master behind the scenes who, as David Brewer has shown, was constantly asserting his 'parental control' in subtle ways.[17] Since it was generally understood from quite early on, however, that Walter Scott was indeed the Author of Waverley (as we saw earlier, playbills regularly named him as the progenitor of the stories), he enjoyed the double return of being personally famous as the Great Unknown.[18] Within the novels too, Scott carried out some polished shadow-boxing with his reader and, by introducing multiple narrators with playful names and frame stories, obfuscated the origins of the narrative.[19] All these strategies heightened the authorial presence while they made it difficult to pin the author down.

Not long after he had confessed publicly to being the Great Unknown Scott consolidated his status as the Author of Waverley by embarking on the revised edition of the novels—the so-called magnum opus edition—to which he added editorial comments and notes. According to Jane Millgate, the idea of producing a collected works of a living author, and a novelist to boot, was unique at this time and meant that the *oeuvre*, even before its actual completion (Scott continued to write new works right up to his death in 1832 even as he struggled against the sense of his own diminishing powers and showed less optimism about historical progress[20]), was already being monumentalized with the help of the author himself.[21] With the edited and revised edition of 1829–32, he already anticipated as it were on his posthumous existence as a dead author whose works would be collected and edited by another party (as he himself had done for his predecessors Dryden and Swift). His diary entry for 17 December 1827 included the following comment on the magnum opus edition: 'Death (my own, I mean), would improve the property since an edition with a Life would sell like wildfire.'[22] Future memory was already influencing real finance.

As we saw in the previous chapter, Scott combined a strong investment in his authorial persona with a high-profile public life.[23] A sociable man and by all accounts a very kind man, his image was the reverse of the artist-as-tortured-egoist or of the subversive imagination; the terms 'healthy' and 'cheerful' were regularly applied to him, indicating both approval and, in some cases we shall encounter, a whiff of the asinine.[24] His self-presentation in the early autobiographical sketch known as the Ashestiel fragment (1808) had emphasized above all his socialization and gentility.[25] He had been the first to comfort himself with the thought that he tried 'to unsettle no man's faith' and 'corrupt no man's principle', a sentence that resonated long in appreciations of his work and critiques of its limitations.[26] His life at Abbotsford, as we have seen in the previous chapter, was a performance continuously subject to comment and interpretation by others. Mention has already been made of the many images of Abbotsford in circulation along with the many portraits of Scott himself and, from 1824 on, copies of the Chantrey bust from the library of Abbotsford.[27] Images of Scott at home were also often included as illustrations to his work or circulated as stand-alones, suggesting a seamless transition between that work and the author's life and place of residence that was summed up in the Abbotsford edition of works (1842–7). Scott was, in short, a celebrity: someone who was not just famous for what he did, but also famous for being famous. To the extent that his actual life had become as fascinating as his fictions (despite the modesty he expressed in his early autobiography in face of the current 'rage' for the private history of public men), Scott ended up as part of the Romantic cult of the celebrity spearheaded by Byron. But Scott's celebrity and his self-representation had a very different character from that of his Byronic counterpart in that it emphasized above all his semi-public everyday life as a sociable, honourable gentleman rather than his intimate and genius-driven transgressions.[28]

That life would later be memorialized in the famous biography written by his son-in-law J. G. Lockhart, incorporating the journal Scott himself had kept from the financial collapse of 1826 onwards while framing it in such as way as to downplay Scott's vulnerabilities and highlight instead his productivity and achievements.[29] Published a mere five years after Scott's death, *Memoirs of the Life of Sir Walter Scott* (1837–8) was in many ways as much a monument to his memory as the colossus of Princes Street Gardens. It has regularly been hailed as a masterpiece on a par with Boswell's *Life of Samuel Johnson* (1791), providing a highly textured and detailed portrait of the writer and making generous use of letters and diary entries to show the interweavings of his physical, intellectual, domestic, and public lives. Ian Duncan has described Lockhart's biography as yet another variation on 'the romance of private patriarchy' which Scott had already unfolded in his literary works.[30] As if to underscore the principle that size matters, the work was originally published in seven volumes; even in the one-volume popular edition of 1893 it runs to more than 800 double-columned pages. Despite this awesome length, however, it was very popular so that multiple editions and abridgements appeared for the best part of a century, including a new Centenary edition to coincide with the celebrations in 1871.[31]

The *Life of Sir Walter Scott* was interesting, not just for revealing the man behind the literary work, but also because it had a classic tale to tell about struggle in face of adversity. Central to all later stories about Scott's life was the financial disaster that struck him in 1826 and that wrought a dramatic reversal from the status of immensely successful writer to someone who had to struggle courageously against exhaustion to pay off debts that he had not himself incurred but for which he felt morally responsible. This gave a new and highly narrativized dimension to his already multi-layered public profile. In his own person the author of Waverley came to embody both an aristocratic code of honour and a middle-class sense of the duty to earn one's keep, a winning combination that fed into emerging notions of the Victorian gentleman. A decade later, Lockhart would pick up on related themes within Scott's own work to construe his biography in terms of the interplay between the romance identity of chivalric largesse and modern economic realities.[32] Two decades later, Samuel Smiles would unsurprisingly depict Walter Scott in his famous *Self-Help* (1859) manual as an example of how far one could get with the typically Victorian virtues of hard work and regular habits.[33]

His failing health in his final years was construed by observers as the physical expression of his heroism, the embodiment of a personal tragedy that, despite his ongoing output, entailed declining creativity. In the accounts of his final days, when the state of his health was broadcast regularly in the national newspapers, the link was regularly made between his life story (extraordinary success, crisis, overcoming of adversity) and his physical demise.[34] The account of his funeral in the *Scotsman* (29 September 1832) ended with a rather gruesome reflection on the physical state of the great man's brain:

We understand that Sir Walter's head was opened on Sunday. The left side of the brain was found in a soft state, and there were globules of water under the left lobe, appearances which fully accounted for all the fatal symptoms by which he has been afflicted.[35]

This materialist interest in the body itself of the writer—the very texture of his brain—sticks out in an article that is otherwise loftily solemn in tone. It also stood in stark contrast to the highly poetic terms in which his death was officially registered: 'Weep, classic Tweed; pour out your floods of woe; | Your great magician's dead' was added to his death certificate.[36] Apparently those involved in the dissection believed that the public was 'due' an explanation of his final malady.[37] (It is all the more interesting to note that the *Edinburgh Evening Courant*, in summarizing the results, protected Scott for posterity by leaving out the final sentence of the physician's report: 'The brain was not large—and the cranium thinner than it is usually found to be.'[38]) As a contemporary newspaper account illustrated (see Figure 6.3), the Great Unknown had been reduced to 'the body'. The dissection itself expressed the marking of a radical transition between the living presence of the writer and 'Walter Scott and all his works' as a multilayered, semantically saturated site of memory whose interpretation would become a way of recalibrating collective identity and cultural value. The disintegration of the artist's body, linked to what was perceived as diminished creativity and excessive productivity, also gave a foretaste of an anxiety about the very possibility of being 'immortal'. Carlyle would refer later to Scott, in a distinctly unhagiographic piece, as having been in the general imagination a 'living mythological personage . . . ranked among the chief wonders of the world.'[39] What would happen when this living legend—this cultural icon—actually passed into memory?

PROSPECTIVE REMEMBRANCE

When reporting the death of Walter Scott on 21 September 1832, most newspapers in Scotland, many newspapers in England, and incidental newspapers elsewhere (in Paris and Richmond, Virginia, for example)

Head.
Major Sir WALTER SCOTT, eldest Son of the Deceased.

Right.	Left.
CHARLES SCOTT, second Son.	J. G. LOCKHART, Esq. Son-in-Law.
CHARLES SCOTT of Nesbitt, Cousin.	JAMES SCOTT, Esq. of Nesbitt, Cousin.
WILLIAM SCOTT, Esq. of Raeburn, Cousin.	ROBERT RUTHERFORD, Esq. W.S., Cousin.
Colonel RUSSEL of Ashiesteel, Cousin.	HUGH SCOTT, Esq. of Harden.

THE BODY.

Foot.
WILLIAM KEITH, Esq. of Edinburgh.

Figure 6.3: The Funeral of Sir Walter Scott, by an eyewitness [T. D. Lauder]. *Tait's Edinburgh Magazine* (1832).

were edged in black to indicate the loss of a public figure. His funeral on 27 September was reported in detail as an event of general significance, some of the reports coloured by all the pathos of a funeral dirge.[40] Scott's physical demise inevitably led to a spate of appreciations and obituaries in the media along with widespread public marks of mourning, including the covering up in black of all shop signs along the funeral route, the ringing of church bells in the bigger cities, and the hanging at half-mast of all the flags in the harbour of Glasgow.[41] Obituaries were almost without exception extravagantly laudatory, with comparisons to Shakespeare (apparently the gold standard for measuring greatness) in regular supply. There was inevitably much reminiscing about Scott's life and works, and what they meant for individuals and for society. But since Scott had been a public figure and memory-maker as well as a private man, reminiscences of the man himself were suffused from the outset with second-order reflections on the act of recollection itself and the responsibilities of those left behind. Given Scott's public significance, people were quick to take a long-term perspective: recollecting his life in 1832 was caught up in imagining how future generations would remember him and his achievements. The death of any author, since it makes the contours of his *oeuvre* definitive, inevitably calls for a critical assessment of his long-term significance and his chances of enjoying cultural longevity. Certainly in Scott's case, remembrance was as much a prospective matter as a retrospective one, as much a matter of the future as of the past. Would Scott be remembered as long as Shakespeare? And most importantly: what should people now do to protect, preserve, or shape that memory? With Scott himself dead, the ball was in the court of posterity and its stakeholders. The case was rendered all the more complicated, as we shall see, precisely because Scott had been so popular.

The idea that the moment had come not just to recall, but to predict the future of Sir Walter Scott's memory provoked many, more or less clichéd expressions of confidence in his long-term fame, if not indeed his immortality. After all, books are more durable than bronze, it had long been believed, and a writer who has written such 'immortal' books can, therefore, never really die. The fact that Scott had broken all records for popularity during his own lifetime added a new dimension to the discussion that was seen by some people as an extra guarantee of longevity (though not by everyone, as we shall see later). Thus the *Morning Chronicle* waxed lyrical on the day before the funeral:

There are some minds which, accommodating themselves to circumstances, appear only great to their contemporaries...but with the sons of true genius the reverse holds true. If ever, then, a human being could be classed among the latter, Sir Walter Scott, must: and 'if we write our annals true' generation and generation will be only, until the end of all time, gathering in to him the harvest of his fame. No writer that ever lived has possessed in his lifetime the extent of popularity which has been enjoyed by our countryman—his words have been translated into all the languages of Europe—are to be found in all quarters of the globe—and will cease to delight its inhabitants only when 'that globe and all that inhabit it shall dissolve'.[42]

The confidence expressed in the *Morning Chronicle* regarding the future permanence of Scott's memory was echoed by others who referred, for example, to the fact that his 'works are his monument';[43] that his 'immortal name' would be 'handed down to all succeeding generations';[44] that he was 'an immortal painter of men';[45] that the Waverley novels will be prized by Scotsmen as 'permanent depositories of their language and manners';[46] that Scott's voice will come alive every time his works are read out and be 'remembered fondly in the living voices of our loved ones as they read out his poetry'.[47] I will come back later to the accuracy of these intimations of immortality.

At the moment of his death in 1832, there seems to have been an overriding sense that it was incumbent upon those who knew and admired him to become guardians of his memory. Up to a point, the discussions recall Pierre Nora's notion of a memorial duty (*mémoire-devoir*), active intervention to keep a particular memory alive for the common good. In the case of Scott, however, the sense of duty was not linked to an injunction to preserve the memory of suffering 'lest it be forgotten', but to a cultural duty to pay tribute to achievement. With his death, the agency shifted away from Scott and his work to his admirers: how best to 'pay tribute to his memory',[48] to 'testify their respect', to 'render homage to the memory' of Scott?[49] These were recurrent phrases in the days and weeks following his death, and they indicate the extent to which remembrance was experienced in a proactive way and in communitarian terms. 'Scott dead, let Scotland be prepared to do her duty,' as one advocate of action put it.[50]

Paying tribute to Scott took a variety of forms in the following years: written appreciations, portrait paintings, and a slew of bad poetry.[51] It also included a theatrical production by Sheridan Knowles called the *Vision of the Bard*, first produced in Covent Garden in October 1832, a month after the actual funeral, and then revived at various venues in Scotland, London, and New York in the months following. Set at Scott's grave in Dryburgh by moonlight, the masque showed the figure of Immortality alongside figures representing the four continents, who then conjured up a series of tableaux representing locations and characters from Scott's work, ending with a gathering in the library at Abbotsford, recognizable as such by the presence of the familiar Scott icons (a copy of the Chantrey bust, his chair, and an unstrung harp).[52] The whole affair was larded with ponderous assertions of Scott's immortality and the fact that he would not be forgotten. Since it took someone who already knows Scott's work to understand the references in this masque, the evocations of his *oeuvre*, his life, and his reputation were clearly preaching to the converted. It was a ritualistic reminder of what people already knew that, as such, recalled the performances of *Rob Roy* discussed in Chapter 2. But in this case, the ritualistic replaying of Scott's work as a whole also offered a way of sharing the moment with fellow mourners in an age before television could broadcast funerals to those who could not attend them and the theatre had an important role as a public forum (mention has already been made of re-enactments of the death of Nelson). In the *Vision of the Bard*, personal memories of reading Scott were given a collective, social expression in the form of a theatrical tribute. As we shall see, commemorations of Scott were regularly suffused with personal recollections of reading pleasure suggesting that the combination of private pleasure with collective value may be the key to the importance of artistic figures in the memory cultures of the nineteenth century: they offered a point of intersection between the sentimental life and aesthetic experience of individuals and their public life as citizens.

Although the masque took the form of a theatrical spectacle, it anticipated in some ways the design of the monument that would be erected in
1840: in both cases, the memorial is organized around the figure of the
author and a select number of characters, whose identities are presumed
known. The production of the masque also seems to have anticipated
explicitly on the future of Scott's memory by ending with an evocation of
future commemorations of the dead writer: the final scene of the masque
figures *tableaux vivants* of Scott's characters set in Abbotsford on the
occasion of a jubilee in memory of the bard taking place in the year
3664 (that is, exactly 1,832 years in the future). Remembering and
shaping future remembrance went hand in glove.

ACCELERATED MEMORIALIZATION, EAGER STAKEHOLDERS

The most extravagant public tribute to Scott's memory nevertheless
remains the monument in Edinburgh, whose contours were sketched at
the beginning of this chapter. It was not only remarkable for its size, but
also for the speed with which moves were made to have it erected, a speed
that seems of a piece with the accelerated character of much that is
associated with Scott. Thus, on 27 September 1832, the day of Scott's
funeral, the *Edinburgh Evening Courant* reported that a preparatory
meeting had already taken place the day after Scott's death, and that
another public meeting would take place on 5 October 1832 'to consider
the propriety of erecting a national testimonial of respect for his memory,
and of gratitude for the honour Sir Walter Scott had conferred on his
country.' That meeting duly took place and, after some prolix speech-
making, those present resolved to seek donations for the purposes of
putting up a memorial, possibly inspired by the monument to Robert
Burns erected in 1831.[53] Although it was generally acknowledged that
Scott had ensured his own lasting memory through his works, the need
was nevertheless felt to put up a concrete mark of appreciation for the man
who had put Edinburgh on the map: 'True, that monument cannot
prolong his memory, but it is to be erected as an expression of gratitude,
and as an act of reverence.'[54] A public monument, it was believed, would
also provide a communal repository for the many private memories of
reading pleasure evoked in eulogies of Scott.[55] Committees were then
appointed in Edinburgh, Glasgow, and London to raise funds to 'testify
by some public and permanent mark, their respect for his memory'.[56]
Even before the close of the meeting, donations began to be pledged, and

notices were subsequently distributed throughout Great Britain, Ireland, and the colonies. Admirers in England raised no less than £10,000 (part of this ended up embezzled), a generosity indicating that Scott's fan base extended beyond Edinburgh and Scotland.[57]

As it turned out, the foundation stone for the monument would only be laid in 1840. The delay was initially caused by a lack of consensus on the most appropriate way to 'testify their respect' for his memory—an interesting phrase in itself suggesting that the erection of the monument was not just the means to recall the past, but a way of actively bearing witness to their present-day enthusiasm. Others expressed their confidence that the country 'will do itself justice by its tribute to his memory'.[58] One dissenting group of admirers, most notably those in London, were adamant that the best mark of respect would consist of financial support to the family at Abbotsford, on the grounds that this would continue Scott's own heroic endeavours to balance his books after the financial catastrophe of 1826 and that Abbotsford, in any case, already constituted the best monument to Scott because he had built it himself.[59] At a certain point the London group split away while the Glasgow group decided to put up its own monument (which it did in 1837) along with Selkirk and Perth, leaving the Edinburgh committee to go ahead with its own plan for a memorial located in the new city centre. The lack of consensus between the different groups is indicative of the distributed character of Scott's fan base and, linked to this, the stakes involved in fixing on a particular location for the memorial to him. While the discourse among his Scottish fans was often couched in national terms, it is clear that civic rivalries and competing local claims to be guardians of Scott's memory were also at work.

Once the decision had been taken to erect a monument in Edinburgh, problems arose. Though people agreed that the proposed memorial should be big and include a statue of the man himself, they became divided on the actual design, specifically, on whether it should take the more classical form of an obelisk or the more medievalist form of a Gothic cross.[60] After a series of competitions, the choice fell on a Gothic design on the grounds that this was the style most congenial to the historicizing Scott and that it echoed Melrose Abbey with which he had been so long associated. The design also allowed room for accommodating other statues, as described above, along with a central statue of the man himself so that the whole could bear testimony to the author, to the pantheon of characters he had depicted, and to the public value attached to all of these.

As a custom-built site of memory, the monument both recalled Walter Scott in multiple ways and gave expression to a collective memory habitus that he had helped generate. If the monument's design echoed some of the features of Abbotsford, so too did the theatricality of the ceremony in 1840 recall other aspects of Scott's cultural work. The foundation stone was laid on 15 August 1840 (the sixty-ninth anniversary of Scott's birth) with much pomp and pageantry, with a procession of 2,000 Freemasons in full regalia, a twenty-one-gun salute, and a detachment of dragoons, all reminiscent of Scott's orchestration of the be-tartaned visit of George IV, as one observer noted, and the tournament at Eglinton a year earlier. In this regard, the celebrations surrounding the monument also represented a unique conjunction between cultural status and popularity: in 1840 there was a free day all round in Edinburgh, 'all classes vying with each other in expressions of sympathy in the grand national movement, and joining in one universal [*sic*] and harmonious tribute to the memory of the illustrious dead.'[61] Both in 1840 on the occasion of the laying of the foundation stone and in 1846 on the occasion of the inauguration of the finished monument, enormous crowds gathered along the hillsides and housetops overlooking the site, many of whom had been brought to the Scottish capital by train.

Although frequent reference was made in speeches to Scott's 'national' significance, there was nevertheless a remarkable lack of typically Scottish markers such as tartan and bagpipes. The two celebrations around the monument in 1840 and 1846 were very much top-down, Edinburgh-centred affairs, dominated by the elite and by officials representing the institutions of the city.[62] The ceremony in 1840 was closed off with the band's playing of 'Rule Britannia', thereby clearly placing the event within a broader framework than that of Scotland.[63]

After the festive laying of the foundation stone, the project ran into some financial hiccups (the total cost would run finally to the phenomenal sum of £16,154.7s.11d.), requiring some new fundraising that involved among other things the house-to-house sale of the engravings of the future monument and a series of Waverley balls held in London and Edinburgh. On 17 August 1846, however, the monument was finally inaugurated, though the addition of statuettes in the niches would only be completed several decades later. The end result of this long process was the colossal monument that we see today which recalls both Scott's *oeuvre*, by depicting his characters, and the private man of flesh and blood who thought it all up, now present in the gleaming form of the marble statue (the statue to Scott in Central Park, mentioned in the previous chapter, was a copy of the Edinburgh one).

From the outset there had been a dual motivation behind the plan: to honour the writer and provide evidence of his fellow-citizens' admiration. As one of those present at the first meeting in September 1832 had put it, the monument 'is to be erected as an expression of gratitude, and as an act of reverence—it is to tell posterity that his contemporaries were not insensible to the glory of having had among them the foremost man of all this world.'[64] The same duality—the desire of the living to communicate their respect and gratitude to later generations being as powerful a motive as the desire to remember Scott as such—also ran through the speech made by Sir William Rae on the occasion of the laying of the foundation stone:

I trust I may announce it as the united and earnest wish of all whom I now see around me, that there may be erected in this spot a testimonial truly worthy of the great name which it is meant to celebrate—worthy of the metropolis of Scotland, and of the conspicuous site in which it is to be placed—worthy of the subscribers who have given their money for its erection—and not unworthy of the humble individuals who have undertaken to be the instruments of carrying the wishes of their countrymen into effect.[65]

Obviously one should be wary of reading too much into occasional speeches like these, especially since those who made them were not theorists of memory or necessarily systematic thinkers. But the rhetoric and turns of phrase follow a similar logic in explaining their memorial practices: that the monument was a highly public, and large-scale expression of a collective pride and that, in paying tribute to Scott, the city and its leading inhabitants sought posthumous fame for themselves by latching on to his greatness.

The latter is borne out by one of the invisible features of the monument. In the foundation stone of the two-hundred-foot Gothic pile, the organizers took care to place a jar containing an almanac for 1840, copies of the six Edinburgh newspapers, the coins of the realm, a plan of the city and county of Edinburgh, a medal struck for the occasion, the names of the subscribers, and a 'backup' copy of the plaque on the monument, which reads:

This Graven Plate | deposited in the base of a votive building | on the fifteenth day of august, in the Year of Christ 1840, and never likely to see the light again, | till all the surrounding structures are crumbled to dust | by the decay of time, or by human or elemental violence, may then testify to a distant posterity that | his Countrymen began on that day | to raise an Effigy and Architectural Monument | TO THE MEMORY OF SIR WALTER SCOTT, BART., | whose admirable writings were then allowed | to have given more delight and suggested better feeling to a larger class of readers, in every rank of society, | than those of any other Author, | with the exception of Shakespeare alone; And which were therefore thought likely to be remembered | long after this act of gratitude | on the part of the first generation of his admirers | should be forgotten.

With this prolix epigraph, 'the first generation of his admirers' ensured they themselves would not be forgotten. Why not put a copy of Scott's works under the monument in lieu of the 1840 newspapers and the other traces of life in contemporary Edinburgh? Ironically, the almanac and newspapers would only ever appear to the light of day in the unlikely event that the monument were ever destroyed, hence outliving even the statue of Scott himself. The last to go would be the relics of the monument-builders and their world, while Scott's works were presumed to be able to take care of themselves.

Amidst all this high-minded symbolism, there is much that was plain silly (a fact to which apparently some of those present were sensitive since the appearance of so many Freemasons in their robes elicited some laughter from the bystanders.[66]) But the case itself, anecdotal though it may be, illustrates a more serious point: that monument-building, as Reinhart Koselleck recognized, is a way for survivors to shape their own lives, and is more a source of identity for the survivors (*Identitätsstiftungen der Überlebenden*) than for the deceased.[67] It is also a way of communicating with posterity and hence of creating an imagined community—more specifically an imagined 'mnemonic community' to use Zerubavel's term[68]—that stretches across generations and into the future. In the Scott case, the members of this community were drawn together by their common gratitude to the writer as a purveyor of interesting works and as a benefactor who had increased the citizens' prosperity by attracting tourists from 'the whole enlightened world'.[69] Remembering Scott was first and foremost a way of celebrating present and future prosperity, and civic pride. In light of this, it makes sense that replicas of the monument in the form of silver cruets later figured as symbols of the city at civic banquets in Edinburgh.

Behind all of this rhetoric and posturing was an apparent trust in the possibility of collecting all the writer stood for in one single site, along with an apparent confidence in Scott's 'immortality'. So while the design of the monument echoed Scott's work in many ways, its full-blown monumentalism, and the confidence in permanence expressed on the part of 'the first generation of his admirers', was in fact curiously at odds with the idea of historical *dis*continuity that underlined Scott's own writings.

THE CULT OF COMMEMORATION, 1871

The scale of the inauguration of the monument provides a reminder of the fact, already encountered in the case of theatre, that the nineteenth century was not only the era of newspapers and imagined communities, but also of huge gatherings, mass spectacles, assemblies, and exhibitions that were often facilitated by the railways. In recent years there has been a heightened awareness of the significance of these mass events in shaping citizenship through performance, particularly in the second half of the nineteenth century.[70] The importance of such mass assemblies challenges the assumption that large-scale social bonding had become wholly reliant on media, and that the media had somehow made all forms of embodied communality redundant. The ceremony in 1840 surrounding the erection of Scott's monument was a forerunner of the civic theatricality that would become widespread in British cities later in the century, but also part of a more widespread fashion for performances of collective identity through public acts of remembrance.[71]

From the late eighteenth century onwards, commemorations had become a regular feature of civic life across Europe, from the festivals of the French Revolution (examined by Mona Ozouf in her ground-breaking study *La fête révolutionnaire, 1789–1799* (1976)), to less well-known celebrations such as the tercentenary of Columbus' landing in the New World in 1792 and the tercentenary of Luther's posting of his theses in Wittenberg in 1817.[72] The organization of remembrance to the calendrical rhythm of centenaries and anniversaries, which persisted in the post-Napoleonic world, formed a temporal counterpart to the 'chronic differentiation' of memory into a limited number of designated locations that was discussed in the previous chapter.[73] Commemorative festivals helped shape public life in an increasingly urbanized and increasingly mediatized world by providing periodic occasions, not only for putting up durable monuments, but also for bringing people together in civic spaces in order to perform their loyalties in a pleasurable way: in the streets of Paris (as in the Revolutionary festivals), the streets of Berlin (as in the many festivals that helped prepare the unification of Germany in 1871), or the streets of British cities (as in the feasts organized in celebration of Queen Victoria's jubilee in 1897).[74] They provided occasions for orchestrated acts of public remembrance based on the principle of collective pride and face-to-face conviviality. As such, the parades organized by civic authorities and public figures can also be seen as controlled versions of the street demonstrations and riots that periodically erupted in a society deeply divided along class and economic lines. Many of these festivals were linked, for reasons that need further elucidation, to the celebration of writers and artists, beginning with the celebration of Handel in 1764 and Shakespeare in 1769 and going on to the commemorations of Goethe (1849), Schiller (1853, 1859), Handel (1857), Tasso (1857), Burns (1859), Shakespeare (1864), Dante (1865), Petrarch (1875), Rousseau and Voltaire (1878), Camões (1880), Pushkin (1880), and, of course,

Walter Scott, whose hundredth birthday occurred in 1871, at the height of this fashion.[75]

Scott's centenary provided an occasion, as the funeral had done, for an epidemic of occasional poems in which private citizens gave more or less clichéd expression both to their own literary ambitions and to their appreciation of Scott.[76] The Waverley novels were relaunched in a 25-volume centenary edition and commemorative medals were struck, while a slew of commemorative essays appeared in the periodicals. The *Illustrated London News* provided extensive Scott coverage in the first three weeks of August, publishing engravings both of the festival and of various objects and places associated with the writer (including once again the famous Tolbooth door that had been integrated in the side wall of Abbotsford). But undoubtedly the main event was the 'National Festival in Celebration of the Centenary of the Birth of Sir Walter Scott' that took place in Edinburgh, with satellite events in other locations spread across the British Isles, North America, and the Antipodes: Glasgow, London (with a Scott festival at Crystal Palace attracting more than 15,000 visitors), Dundee, Galashiels, Melrose, Belfast, New York, Boston, Toronto, Montreal, Melbourne, and Dunedin among others.[77] The national festival was planned on 9 August, in fact a week ahead of the actual centenary, the choice of an earlier date apparently dictated by the desire to have the celebrations tie in with the annual meeting of the British Association, also to take place in Edinburgh, and the opening of the hunting season. This fiddling with the dates was not without its critics since, in the eyes of some, changing the day contradicted the very idea of a centenary while the desire to increase the turnover of hotels cast a suspiciously mercenary light on the whole proceedings.

The festival on 9 August 1871 was a 'day long to be remembered' in which 'the eyes of the world are now looking to the citizens of Edinburgh' (as C. S. M. Lockhart wrote in his memorial of the occasion).[78] The festival was organized by a committee of leading citizens and it would appear from several accounts that while the festival did draw big crowds, there was no widespread and heartfelt support among the inhabitants of the city, bunting being confined to the big shops and hotels. Given the number of precedents by 1871, it was possible for some commentators to dismiss the event as a rather vulgar spectacle that was merely following a trend or 'invented tradition':

The custom has, however, been established. In our own day, England has honoured Shakespeare, Scotland, Burns, and Germany, Schiller; and now in his turn Scott, as another national writer of acknowledged pre-eminence, is to receive the homage of a celebration. Putting aside whatever of mere tawdriness and vulgarity inevitably attends manifestations of this sort, we may yet accept them as genuine tributes of admiration, and in the case of Sir Walter Scott as an assurance that his fame is destined to no speedy eclipse, but will be lasting as it has been world-wide.[79]

The rather muted enthusiasm evinced here indicates that a certain commemorative fatigue had set in, with Scott only third in a row after Burns and Shakespeare. The earlier celebrations, particularly the extraordinarily widespread celebration of Burns in 1859, were still very much present in the minds of the participants in 1871. Indeed, up to a point these festivals were interchangeable since they were as much about celebrating literature and cultural achievement as such as they were about any particular writer. Thus the *Edinburgh Evening Courant*, while noting that only large hotels and businesses had gone to the trouble of decking out their premises with appropriate flourishes in August 1871, commended the Edinburgh Hotel for its decorations, which included busts not only of Scott, but also of Burns, Shakespeare, and Byron. It was literature as well as Scott that was being celebrated against the background of Victorian appreciations of genteel literacy.

But there were also significant differences between the events, and the contrast with the Burns centenary of 1859 was particularly striking within the Scottish context. Where the discourse about Burns was one of global fellowship, egalitarianism, and love for his poetry, the discourse surrounding Scott was more distant, marked by pride in what the Author of Waverley had achieved and concern with what this achievement meant for Edinburgh, Scotland, and the wider world. Moreover, the celebration of the 'ploughman poet' in 1859 had been organized in a bottom-up manner through a circulated appeal to all interested parties to pay tribute to Burns, with the result that small and large-scale events took place at more than eight hundred different locations, a diversity and decentralization that meant that the financial and social threshold for participation was relatively low.[80] In contrast, the 'national festival' for Scott in 1871 was very much a top-down and centralized affair, clearly pitched towards the paying classes and spearheaded by members of the establishment. In that respect it resembled more the celebration of Shakespeare in 1864, which had taken the form of large-scale, fee-paying banquets at Crystal Palace and Stratford. These financial and social barriers had led to street protests on the part of working-men's groups angry at being excluded from the celebration of the so-called national bard.[81] There were no such protests in Edinburgh in 1871 despite the de facto exclusion of workers who had not been given a day off, probably because Scott's fan base was above all genteel. To be sure: there were many popular versions of Scott's work in circulation (chapbooks and ballads were mentioned earlier along with the vitality of his work in the popular theatre). There is also some evidence to show that Scott's work was also popular among working-class readers.[82] Yet, it would appear from the centenary that his work enjoyed neither the populist appeal of Burns nor the deep-rootedness of Shakespeare; and that as a *public* figure he was above all celebrated by the upper classes.[83] The National festival provides ample support for the link that would be made by Edwin Muir on the occasion of the 1832 centenary between Scott's work and the 'vice of gentility'.[84] The general mood in the Scottish media was celebratory, but one London commentator denounced the whole event as a whited sepulchre, a screen memory designed to draw attention away from the squalor and poverty that subsisted in modern Edinburgh at a stone's throw from the monument.[85]

Although they mobilized somewhat different constituencies, the centenaries of Scott in 1871, Burns in 1859, and Shakespeare in 1864 were all part of an ongoing triangulation between literature, collective self-fashioning, and modernization in the second half of the nineteenth century. The cultivation of 'Walter Scott' as a figure of memory helped articulate the participants' self-image as members of different communities positioned variously across Scotland, the British Isles, and the (former) colonies. Whereas the inauguration of the monument by the 'first generation of his admirers' in the 1840s had focused on Scott's relation to Edinburgh, the emphasis of the second generation was more on his national and international significance and on his place in a broader meta-narrative of progress and global expansionism. At the same time, economic progress and global expansion were being placed under the edifying aegis of Scott's cultural achievement.

The celebrations took a variety of forms. A centenary exhibition was held in the National Gallery throughout the months of July and August, and attracted some 12,000 visitors despite the 1s. entrance fee. The exhibition, which was modelled on the Dante exhibition in Florence in 1865, brought together Scott portraits held in private collections, along with other visual materials relating to Abbotsford and his funeral, manuscripts, and, finally, illustrations of his work.[86] In order to prolong the memory of the event, the catalogue contained many photographic illustrations of the exhibits themselves. One of these photographs is of the first hall of the exhibition, which shows in pride of place, along with various portraits and the famous Chantrey bust, a large maquette of the monument together with another engraving of the monument on the wall. This recursivity provides a striking illustration of how a limited repertoire of figures tended to be repeated over and again. The reproduction of images was presumably also, in this pre-television age, a way of giving a visual sense of the events to those who could not themselves make the journey to Edinburgh.

The day of the festival saw among other things widespread bunting in the city centre and a parade of some two hundred people dressed up as Scott characters in the tradition of the Waverley balls of the 1830s and 1840s (described by one sardonic commentator as a 'straggling procession' of a 'second-rate circus troupe').[87] That evening there was also a gala production of *Rob Roy* at the Theatre Royal—a not unexpected choice of play given its privileged status in the Scott repertoire and the fact that it had already figured in 1822 on the occasion of George IV's visit. But the high point, and the focus of the most reporting, was the toast-filled banquet held at 6pm in the Corn Exchange at the Grassmarket. A large illuminated transparency of Scott was on public display outside the venue, suggesting a split between the genteel banqueters inside who had paid one guinea for the pleasure and the rest of the population outside.[88] Inside, the banquet hall was lavishly decorated with Scott's portrait and with the titles of his works and the names of characters and locations. These were festooned around pillars interlocking with shields displaying the arms of Scott, the triple-towered castle of Edinburgh, and the shields of Scotland, England, Ireland, France, and America. The list of diners indicates this was an event for those with wealth and status beyond the borders of Scotland, and confirms Scott's image as the darling of the genteel and the aristocratic rather than of 'ordinary' working people (traces of this attitude could also be seen in Thomas Mellon's contrasting views of Scott and Burns). The appearance in the newspapers on the following day of the names of those present or who had offered apologies (later supplemented by additions presumably at the behest of the men involved) suggests that 'being there' was a way of enhancing one's own prestige—even of those who had not gone to the trouble of showing up in person. As it was, the evening began with the Chairman (the Earl of Dalkeith) reading out apologies from a long list, including that of Prime Minister Gladstone, who sent his regrets in the form of an extensive eulogy to Scott.[89] The list of notable absences read like a who's who of Victorian culture and, crossing party-political lines, included the names of Thomas Carlyle, Ralph Waldo Emerson (who was however present at the Boston event), Harriet Martineau, Benjamin Disraeli, John Motley, Matthew Arnold, Lord Lytton, John Stuart Mill, Anthony Trollope, John Ruskin, along with many lords (notably the Duke of Argyll and the Marquis of Lothian), baronets, and high-ranking officials. There were also many notable presences from various parties and walks of life, as we shall see, a variety that seems to bear out Scott's reputation as someone who had a certain cross-party appeal despite his own avowed Toryism.

Figure 6.4: The National Festival, Edinburgh, 19 August 1871. *London Illustrated News*, 19 August 1871.

The evening progressed through various courses interspersed with music that had largely been inspired by Scott's work and recycled from the theatrical versions of his novels along with several evergreens from the Burns' repertoire (*Auld Lang Syne, Green Grow the Rashes O*) which by this time seemed to have become standard fare at festive events in Scotland and had also figured regularly in the *Rob Roy* productions. But key to the formalities was that Victorian genre *par excellence* and the key to its conviviality: the toast. The list of subjects at Edinburgh indicates the multiple social frames in which the event was embedded and shows again how remembering Scott was caught up, like the erection of the monument, with inscribing stakeholders into a public memory that crossed national boundaries. Following the obligatory toasts to the Queen and the Prince of Wales came ones to 'The Memory of Sir Walter Scott',[90] 'Our National Literature', 'The Visitors', 'the City of Edinburgh', 'The Roof Tree of Abbotsford', the University, the Chairman, Sister Celebrations, the Ladies, and the Committee. The 'Sister Celebrations' referred primarily to Glasgow, where a similar banquet was taking place that evening, but also to the various other gatherings in Scotland, London, and North America, which had been planned around or on that date. It is symptomatic of the workings of canonicity that the occasion for celebrating Scott

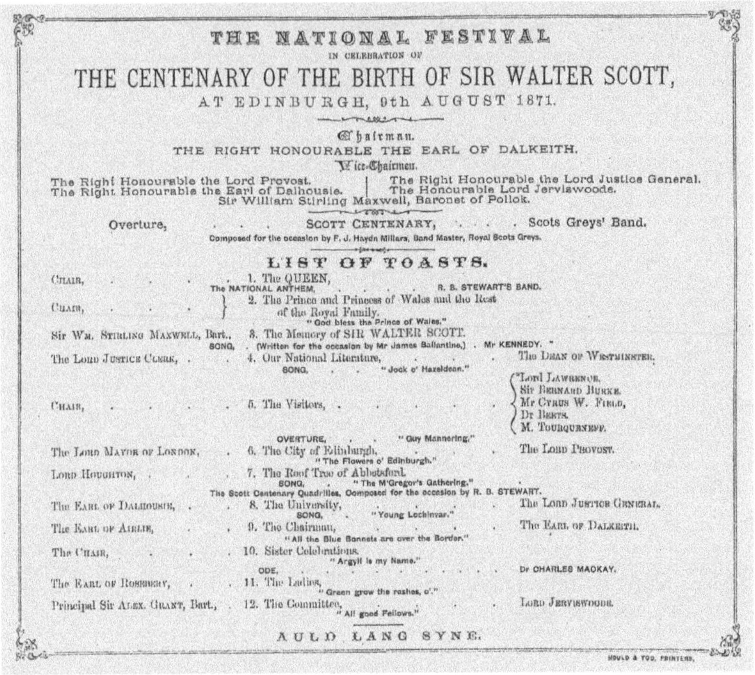

THE NATIONAL FESTIVAL
IN CELEBRATION OF
THE CENTENARY OF THE BIRTH OF SIR WALTER SCOTT,
AT EDINBURGH, 9th AUGUST 1871.

Chairman.
THE RIGHT HONOURABLE THE EARL OF DALKEITH.
Vice-Chairmen.
The Right Honourable the Lord Provost. | The Right Honourable the Lord Justice General.
The Right Honourable the Earl of Dalhousie. | The Honourable Lord Jerviswoode.
Sir William Stirling Maxwell, Baronet of Pollok.

Overture, . . . SCOTT CENTENARY, ... Scots Greys' Band.
Composed for the occasion by F. J. Haydn Millars, Band Master, Royal Scots Greys.

LIST OF TOASTS.

Chair, ... 1. The QUEEN,
The NATIONAL ANTHEM, ... R. B. STEWART'S BAND.
Chair, . . . } 2. The Prince and Princess of Wales and the Rest of the Royal Family.
" God bless the Prince of Wales."
Sir Wm. Stirling Maxwell, Bart., 3. The Memory of SIR WALTER SCOTT.
SONG, . (Written for the occasion by Mr James Ballantine,) . Mr KENNEDY.
The Lord Justice Clerk, . . 4. Our National Literature, . . . The Dean of Westminster.
SONG, . . " Jock o' Hazeldean."
Chair, ... 5. The Visitors, ... { Lord Lawrence. Sir Bernard Burke. Mr Cyrus W. Field, Dr Beets. M. Tourgueneff.
OVERTURE, . . " Guy Mannering."
The Lord Mayor of London, . 6. The City of Edinburgh, . . . The Lord Provost.
" The Flowers o' Edinburgh."
Lord Houghton, . . . 7. The Roof Tree of Abbotsford.
SONG, . " The M'Gregor's Gathering."
The Scott Centenary Quadrilles, Composed for the occasion by R. B. STEWART.
The Earl of Dalhousie, . . 8. The University, ... The Lord Justice General.
SONG, . " Young Lochinvar."
The Earl of Airlie, . . 9. The Chairman, ... The Earl of Dalkeith.
" All the Blue Bonnets are over the Border."
The Chair, . . . 10. Sister Celebrations.
" Argyll is my Name."
ODE, ... Dr CHARLES MACKAY.
The Earl of Rosebery, . . 11. The Ladies,
" Green grow the rashes, o'."
Principal Sir Alex. Grant, Bart., . 12. The Committee, ... Lord Jerviswoode.
" All good Fellows."

AULD LANG SYNE.

NOULD & TOD, PRINTERS.

Figure 6.5: Programme, The National Festival, Edinburgh, 9 August 1871.

spilled over into the celebration of other related objects of value and the persons who valued them. In some instances, the topics were related to Scott, but in other cases, their only relevance was the fact that they were also valued by the people doing the remembering. The toasts directed to the visitors, the sister celebrations, and the committee also foregrounded the stakeholders in Scott's memory and the ties that connected them. The various groups celebrating his memory at different locations were all self-reflexively linked in imagination as part of a global community of Scott fans.

The importance of transnational links was manifest in the physical presence of 'The Visitors', a group that included among others Sir Bernard Burke representing Ireland, Mr Cyrus W. Field representing the United States, Ivan Turgenev representing Russia, Nicolaas Beets representing Holland, and finally, as delegate from England, the former viceroy of India, Lord Lawrence.[91] Although Scott was honoured in a 'national festival', the national frame of remembrance overlapped with other frames and was positioned in the broader arena of the British Isles and, extending further outwards, Europe, the British Empire, and the English-speaking world. The latter was underscored by the use of telegrams to create a sense of simultaneity between the events being held at various locations across the British Isles and North America, a sort of video-conferencing with the technology of 1871 (this may sound very innovative, but was in fact an imitation of the Burns' festival some twelve years earlier where the telegrams had been used even more extensively). In the run-up to the Edinburgh banquet in 1871 telegrams had been sent to the various sister celebrations in New York and Glasgow, among other places. Congratulatory replies were received from Glasgow along with expressions of readiness 'to join with us in paying a tribute to the memory of Sir Walter Scott'. The Edinburgh telegram to New York had similarly expressed the wish that the 'the links that unite us be as lasting as the memory to which we this month do common homage'. In the course of the festival banquet, the chairman announced that the Atlantic telegraph, the 'connecting bond of union between the two countries', had just delivered a telegram from the chairman of the Scott Centenary Festival in New York expressing the 'sense of national pride' felt by himself and his associates (presumably both as Americans and as being of Scottish descent) in their common celebrations. A week later, the foundation stone of the Central Park monument would be laid to the musical accompaniment of Highland bands and in the presence of representatives of the Scottish diaspora (its inauguration a year later would elicit the speech by William Cullen Bryant quoted earlier).[92] The ceremony in Central Park led the *London Quarterly Review* to comment in its turn on 'how powerful a popular and noble-minded literatus can be in knitting men together' and that the enthusiasm with which New Yorkers of all backgrounds had joined in the centenary festivities made it now hard 'to imagine such a hideous event as an Anglo-American war' (no mention is made of the much more recent Civil War and the Southern appropriations of Scott).[93] A telegram was also sent personally to President Grant by the Edinburgh committee congratulating 'the American people' (no less) on the birthday of the Scottish poet and inviting a response, presumably in the hope that this high-level connection to the United States would shed additional lustre on the Scottish capital (the president only managed to reply, however, a fortnight later because he had been away in California, a delay that rather spoilt the hi-tech *coup de théâtre* the organizers had hoped for).[94] Like the Burns' celebrations in 1859, Scott's centenary provided an occasion for both local and long-distance bonding, bearing out Peter Burke's contention that commemorative occasions are as much about forging present-day links as they are about recollecting the past.[95]

The extensive, almost blow-by-blow newspaper account given of the banquet on the following day includes much evidence of civic pomp along with some intriguing details (the chairman admitted not having been able to hear one of the speakers because of the size of the room, suggesting that the newspaper account of the speeches may have been of interest not only to those who were not in a position to attend the event, but also to those who were actually present but, given the absence of amplification, unable to hear what was being said by the speechmakers[96]). Much of the toasting was in the hands of statesmen and administrators rather than fellow-writers, and only extensive quotation can capture their flavour. The eulogies rarely show much sensitivity to the complexities of Scott's writings and there is little direct quotation, perhaps because the poetry had been largely overshadowed by the fiction. Nevertheless, several themes running through the centenary, both in the speeches and in the reporting, deserve further elucidation here as an indication of the discourses surrounding Scott's memory almost a generation after his physical demise and the types of appropriation to which he was subject. Two strands in particular stand out: the idea that Scott's writings laid a foundation for progress, and the idea that his eminently portable works had a distinct resonance for English-speakers all over the world.

PROGRESS: HOW SCOTT HAD REPOPULATED SCOTLAND

On 11 August, the *Edinburgh Evening Courant* republished an article from the *Times* of London devoted to the Scott centenary. Comparing the present state of Scotland with the age of Boswell, it waxed fulsome on Scott's achievements:

Scotland was then a country to leave, and even to forget. It is now the favourite haunt of pilgrims not merely from England, but from every country to which the literature of our race has penetrated, and to be a Scotchman is now a title of a kind of nobility of the imagination. . . . The choice of a Scottish residence by the Queen and Prince Consort is at once an example and consequence of this creation of *a new world beyond the Tweed.* . . . A history which was once regarded as in great part composed of 'battles of kites and crows' has become an embodiment of our most chivalrous conceptions. All this had been done by Scott, and by Scott alone. Burns indeed charmed the world by his lyric revelations of Scotch pathos, humour, tenderness, and vigour; but the feelings he aroused were even more personal and human than national.[97] [emphasis AR]

This association between the influence of the writer and the emergence of Scotland as a 'haunt for pilgrims' resonates with the imaginative geographies discussed in Chapter 5, and particularly with the case of Thomas Mellon. The idea that Scott had turned Scotland into a tourist destination (or from the English perspective expressed by the *Times*: had created 'a new world beyond the Tweed') had already figured in 1832 and 1840, but became dominant in the 1871 proceedings. The relationship between Scott and Scotland was linked in the first instance to the growth of tourism and what has been called Balmoralism on the part of English visitors.[98] Reference was already made in the previous chapter to the praise meted out to Scott at the Glasgow celebrations for his having 'made the wilderness rejoice' with the addition of new roadworks and steamers making the Highlands accessible to tourists. In various ways, the Glaswegians expressed their gratitude for his direct contribution to material prosperity through tourism—an interesting continuation of the interactions between the economic life of the city and the romantic Highlands which Scott himself had already thematized in *Rob Roy*.[99] In an interesting variation on the persistent connection between Scott and economic development, one orator exclaimed (ingenuously, ironically?): 'He made us love our country more than money.' Paying tribute to Scott as a prime locus of cultural value, and as symbol of what Scotland had become, provided a counterweight to the everyday preoccupation with making money.[100] One commentator somewhat ominously remarked in the *Gentleman's Magazine* that Scott's ambition to combine chivalrous behaviour with a head for business was of a 'kind which touches the heart of the Englishman and Scot alike' and 'is most serviceable to the state'.[101] A poet serviceable to the state?

For Scott had not only turned Scotland into a tourist destination, he had also created a new image of Scottishness for local consumption as well as for export to its neighbours and the outside world. In fact, many of the tributes to him in 1871 paid more attention to this benign influence on modern economic life than to his innovations in the field of historical writing. There was a sense that Scott had made economic development possible by turning the messiness and violence of history into a romantic landscape peopled by fictional characters; that he had found a way of dealing with history by consigning it safely to the past. His historical imagination had transformed a disturbing past into 'the embodiment of our most chivalrous conceptions', as the *Times* put it, and hence exorcized its ghosts.

This idea was echoed in strikingly demographic terms in a centenary article in *Blackwood's Edinburgh Magazine*:

Could we go back to that Scotland of 1771, into which a new Scott was born...
how strangely different we would find it! The people we should meet would be
more entertaining in themselves, more original, less like everybody else, no doubt.
They would remember the '45, and still feel in their hearts some remnant of that
thrill of doubt and fear and hope which must have run through the island before
the ill-fated prince turned on his way to London. But in their recollections there
would have been no Vich-Van-Vohr, no Evan Dhu, no Flora...And Loch
Katrine and her isles would have lain hidden in the darkness, with no courageous
Ellen to bring them to human ken. What a strange, what an incredible difference!
No Highland emigration could so depopulate those dearest hills and glens as they
are depopulated by this mere imagination. A hundred years ago they were bare
and naked—nay, they were not, except to here and there a wandering, hasty
passenger.[102]

According to this convoluted reasoning, Scott had counteracted the
Highland clearances by his imaginative repopulation of these emptied
areas, meaning that to forget his characters would be to empty the Highlands once more. Scotland was not 'there' before Scott (to echo Gertrude
Stein's famous comments on Oakland as having no there, there), but
empty. Thanks to his writings the landscape had been populated with
imaginary figures who, it is implied, not only took the place of those who
had left but in fact surpassed them in interest.

   This link between Scott's stories and virtual colonialism would be
echoed by William Cullen Bryant in his inauguration of the statue in
Central Park a year later when he described Scott and his characters as
peopling the empty space of Manhattan. Although Scott himself did not
formulate things quite this way, his work appears to have been congenial
to this blithe colonialism in which purportedly empty spaces were populated with poetic figures while the world got on with its business elsewhere.[103] In Chapter 1, we have already seen a clear example of this virtual
re-settlement in the re-location of Jeanie Deans to the Highlands as a
reward for her steadfast virtue. Intended or not, his work provided a
repository of colonial figures of thought and, as we saw in the previous
chapter, an imaginative tool for rethinking the relations between people,
places, and memories.

   Across the sea in Belfast, the relation between memory and material
prosperity was also a major theme in the celebrations of Scott. The main
speaker was Lord Dufferin, a native of northern Ireland and prominent
civil servant, who would later go on to become governor-general of
Canada and Viceroy of India, and whose triumphantly imperialistic statue
now stands outside Belfast City Hall. After a series of predictable comments on the bard's immortality and 'the beauteous array of breathing
men and women' with which he had 'peopled the realm of fiction',

Dufferin went on to echo the point made in the *Times*, to the effect that Scott had recreated Scotland by replacing 'the harsh elements of Scotch history' by the 'romantic associations which now haunt every vale'. It was such a pity, Dufferin continued, that Ireland had not yet found her own Scott with whose help 'many of the distressing elements which now discolour and disturb the current of Irish sentiment would disappear'. From this Ulster perspective, Scott provided a model for the exorcism of unhappy histories by converting the relationship to the past into the definitive form of an agreeable story. Were Ireland to find her Scott, who would display the materials of Irish history under the 'genial and impartial auspices, to which the past of Scotland owes so much of its celebrity', then the way would be open to future-building: 'that restless, uneasy longing for a more gratifying retrospect' would disappear and 'with a calmer spirit we might proceed to tread that career of industrial and material prosperity which lies before us (applause).'[104] The unwitting echo of Thomas Mellon's non-nostalgic turning towards and then away from the past is striking.

In these various ways, Scott was construed as a pathfinder to future prosperity who had anchored the present in the past, while neutralizing its distressing bits. All of this emphasis on modernity may be surprising in view of the commemorative nature of the event. But it bears out Peter Fritzsche's contention that the historical culture of the nineteenth century paradoxically represented one of the ways for people to discover their common identity as contemporaries.[105] The narrative of progress linked to the celebration of the contemporary in the Scott centenary represents in many ways a gross simplification of Scott's writings, eliding the complexities and tensions that we have seen at work. By 1871 too, Scott's power to generate reproductions and adaptations of his work was diminishing—the theatrical appropriations analysed earlier passed their highpoint in the 1860s at the latest. Nevertheless, one of Scott's most enduring legacies was still operating powerfully in these pontificating speeches, however unpalatable to our contemporary frame of reference; namely, the belief that for progress to occur the past must be honoured, but honoured *as* past so that it will not continue to disrupt the future. Investing in the past is a way of defusing it. After all, in the great struggle between Progress and Tradition, to recall Coleridge's assessment of Scott's central theme, progress always won out against tradition, even if its victory was packaged in emotionally and aesthetically ambivalent ways. At the 1871 celebrations this basic message, without the ambivalence, was being re-enacted in the dinner-table performances of Victorian administrators and leaders as they raised their glass to the 'immortal memory'.

TRANSNATIONAL LITERATURE

It is clear from the presence of 'The Visitors', from the exchanges of telegrams with the 'Sister Celebrations', and from the shields displayed in the banqueting hall that Scott had a privileged relation to Scotland, but that he also operated as a figure of memory within other social frameworks that were both multinational and transnational. The case thus provides for interesting variations on the idea of imagined communities put forward in 1983 by Benedict Anderson: remembering Scott was indeed linked to the shaping of imagined communities, but ones that were both national and transnational in character. As a figure of memory, Scott became a hub in a global network of admirers where the movement of people (emigrants, colonials, tourists) and the movement of stories about British history (his novels, poems, biography) intersected.[106] As we shall see, his memory helped articulate collective identity in Scotland, the British Isles, the United States, and the Empire, seen as distinct if overlapping spheres within the larger framework of an English-speaking world. It is a remarkable fact that although Scott's writings were enormously influential in France (as in other parts of Europe), he never acquired the same role in that country as a figure of collective memory as he did in the English-speaking world.[107]

Scott's double role as both a national and an international figure of memory was borne out in the Edinburgh festival when the Author of Waverley was celebrated along with various other Scotsmen who had played a role on the global stage. The American Mr. Cyrus Field, for example, used the occasion to voice his praise for Sir William Thompson, whose work in electricity had made the laying of a transatlantic telegraph cable possible five years earlier (the connection was no coincidence since Field himself was a director of the Atlantic Telegraph Company).[108] This invocation of Scottish engineering fitted in with the general sense that the Author of Waverley was a thoroughly modern figure who had contributed to economic prosperity and to the globalization of Scotland. Field also eulogized another prominent man of Scots descent, the then President of the United States, Ulysses S. Grant, and celebrated his progressive influence on American society. Speaking as a self-appointed delegate 'in the name of the United States', Field recalled the important Scottish influence on American culture and linked it by association both to the abolition of slavery and to victory over the slave-owning South in the Civil War. His remarks just six years after the war thus make for an ironic counterpart to Mark Twain's accusation that Scott had caused the same war and confirm the fact that Scott's fan base crossed the North–South divide:

We are profoundly grateful to Scotland for all that she has done to refine the tastes, expand the intellects, and build up the material civilisation of the human race—benefits in which my country has largely participated. I cannot forget that while a Scotchman, in the person of the distinguished Lord Brougham, was the first to secure the statutory prohibition of the African slave trade—(cheers)—President Grant, a Scotchman by descent, was the indomitable commander whose arm guided by Providence struck down slavery in its last great stronghold. (Cheers).[109]

Field was not himself of Scots descent, so the fact that he was there to celebrate the Author of Waverley (and other great Scotsmen) serves as a reminder that Scott's fan base was not exclusively Scottish and that his work belonged to different constituencies. This point needs to be emphasized in face of the tenacious methodological nationalism that still dominates literary scholarship, and that has already been mentioned as a point of concern in the Introduction. It has meant that criticism has not yet fully addressed the fact that Scott, while being intensely involved with shaping Scottish identity, also wrote about histories taking place outside of Scotland and was widely read in other places. He both helped advance the use of tartan as a marker of Scottishness and treated non-Scottish topics, in particular ones from English and Welsh history: besides *Ivanhoe*, *Kenilworth* (1821), *Fortunes of Nigel* (1822), *Peveril of the Peak* (1822), *The Betrothed* (1825), and *Woodstock* (1826). With the exception of *Ivanhoe*, none of these was as successful or as well known as his major Scottish novels, but they did extend Scott's imaginative jurisdiction into other parts of the British Isles (and in the case of *Quentin Durward* (1823), *Anne of Geierstein* (1829), and *Count Robert of Paris* (1832), to other parts of Europe).[110] Moreover, Scott's work operated outside the borders of Scotland in a way that was also partly independent of subject matter; indeed, it is one of the more remarkable features of his imaginative power that his work could appeal as prosthetic memory to so many readers in the British Isles, Europe, and the colonies with no ancestral link to Scotland. The tournament-goers discussed in Chapter 4 are an obvious case in point.

Underscoring this broad appeal, Hazlitt once claimed that Scott's Scottish novels were more popular outside of Scotland than north of the border, implying thereby that the novelist had turned his country into a virtual export product.[111] There is certainly abundant evidence of his cultural significance within a larger British context, exemplified in the monument erected to him in Westminster Abbey in 1897 as a mark of respect for his contribution to the literature and culture of Great Britain at large. Indeed for many commentators in Britain in 1871, Scott belonged to *English* (and American) literature along with Shakespeare even as he was clearly marked by his Scottish nationality. This enthusiasm had been reflected a few decades earlier in the many English subscriptions to the erection of the Scott monument. Although Edinburgh was the principal venue for the centenary, the *Leisure Hour* wrote in 1871, 'English states-men and English writers will also countenance the festival, for is it not to English literature that Sir Walter Scott belongs?'[112] Given the slipperiness endemic to 'English' at this period, which Robert Young has recently analysed, the use of the term here can be read as a way of designating the common cultural ground within the multinational British archipelago and the English-speaking world.[113] The 'English' in English Literature re-ferred less to the nationality of Scott's subject matter than to the language of communication, a point I shall come back to.

It has become widely accepted by now that Britishness as a concept carries a distinctively Scottish stamp since it was above all the Scots who invested in the principles of subsidiarity and multinationality so as to guarantee their own cultural distinctiveness even after the political union with England. Mention has already been made of this with reference to *Ivanhoe* in Chapter 3. One of the main themes of criticism in the past twenty years has been the ways in which Scott opened up an imaginative space for positioning Scottish history within a broader British framework of multiple, rather than singularly English, identities. Robert Crawford argued notably in his *Devolving English Literature* (1992) for seeing Scott as 'attempting to ensure and articulate Scotland's distinctive place in Britain' and as highly conscious of the need 'to construct and reconstruct images of cultural identity that are other than Anglo-centric'.[114] There are differences in emphasis among critics with respect to Scott's relations to his fellow Britons and to the world at large. Where Crawford stresses Scott's awareness of cultural multiplicity (and more recently, his European spirit), others have highlighted variously his awareness of Scottish distinc-tiveness, and his willingness to countenance political union with England on the basis of that cultural distinctiveness. Nevertheless, there is an underlying consensus that Scott's creative work was involved in creating an imagined community of Scotsmen within a larger framework. His work negotiated the border between Scotland and England as much as that between Highlanders and Lowlanders, and he was therefore a key player in the creation of the British nation and the literary negotiation of political realities on the ground. In the words of Leith Davis: 'Far from being constituted by a single Act of Union, Britain was forged, in all of the variant senses of that word, from multiple acts of union and dislocation.'[115]

These discussions have yielded a wealth of new insights into the multiple identities articulated within Scottish literature and what this means for our understanding of Britain and the Empire at large. In light of this, it is all the more striking how little attention has been paid so far to Scott's actual reception outside Scotland—as if being British (or not) was indeed a matter of how Scotsmen viewed the world (and not, for example, how others viewed Scotsmen or Scott).[116] But Scott did not just evoke multiple identities; it is a fact of cultural history that he himself operated as a cultural influence and as a figure of memory in a transnational British, Imperial, and Anglophone framework.

GLOBALLY POSITIONED SCOTT

Scott's transnational reach can be illustrated with reference to another centenary banquet held in Edinburgh on 15 August 1871, Scott's actual birthday. It was presided over by William Hepworth Dixon, an Englishman who had been involved in the centenary celebrations at the Crystal Palace for both Scott and Shakespeare, and included a delegation from the London Branch of the Caledonian Society. In that company, it was above all Scott's role as a 'reconciler' and 'amalgamator' in the literary negotiation of the Union that the chairman highlighted:

We hold by him for what he was—the reconciler, the amalgamator. We acclaim him as the man who made the Scotch and English nations know and love each other—as the man who changed the union of these kingdoms from a legal fiction to a social fact.[117]

The idea that Scott should have turned a 'legal fiction' into a 'social fact' is highly suggestive of the power of literature to build imagined communities (the fiction) and hence lead to the actual amalgamation of peoples on the ground (the social fact). Not everyone would have agreed with this speaker in 1871 regarding either the desirability or the reality of the union between England and Scotland. But it is clear from the celebrations in 1871 that Scott did function in 'social fact' as a mediator between the two main national groups on the island.

By 1871, moreover, the geographical frame within which Scott was situated had stretched beyond the British Isles and had expanded along with the empire. Hepworth Dixon's praise for Scott's role in consolidating the union was preceded by the apodictic statement that 'his place is in the empire' and he brought it to a climax by his giving the toast in the following terms:

I give you this imperial writer—this imperial man—'the Memory of Walter Scott'. (Loud and continued cheering).[118]

Scott: an imperial writer? This seems at first sight a surprising conclusion since Scott depicted British expansionism only in the margins of his major fiction (as when the good-for-nothing son of Effie Deans takes himself off to North America, or Ivanhoe returns from the Crusades) or in less known works such as *The Talisman* (1825) or *The Surgeon's Daughter* (1827). It can be safely presumed that Hepworth Dixon was not thinking of these minor works when he praised Scott as 'imperial man'. The link made between Scott and imperialism may simply have been another way of expressing the speaker's appreciation of both. But within the context of the centenary, the association ran deeper than mere coincidence and was explicitly linked to Scott's role as 'amalgamator' and 'reconciler', the underlying belief that it was possible to overcome historical ruptures by remembering them as a story (or, to recall the speaker from Belfast: to turn into literature 'the distressing elements which now discolour and disturb' the present). Scott's literature and a legitimization of conquest fed into each other as Scott was appropriated in an imperialist discourse that was all pervasive by 1871. Not surprisingly in view of this, many of those celebrating Scott's centenary also held high office in the imperial administration.

Already in 1832 the *Edinburgh Courant* had referred to grief at Scott's death 'in every part of the civilised world', while Harriet Martineau had depicted the community of Scott readers extending far beyond his native kingdom to include, along with various European locations, 'the spicy bowers of Ceylon...the verandahs of Indian bungalowes...the perfumed dwellings of Persia...groups of sellers at the Cape...the pine-woods and savannahs of the Western world.'[119] At the inauguration of the Edinburgh monument in 1846 the Lord Provost had extended Scott's reach even further beyond the reaches of the known world: 'Continents as yet unexplored will be taught by the wisdom of Scott, and enlivened by his wit; and rivers unknown to song will resound with the lays of his minstrelsy.'[120] By the time the centenary came around, this idea of 'continents unexplored' had become salient with regular reference being made to Scott's turning up in the outer reaches of the empire. While some of these references merely reflect the importance of empire in British life at this period, others reveal more about Scott's procreativity as an imaginative resource in dealing with its realities.

Thus the Reverend McCleod, speaking at the Glasgow celebrations, recalled how a friend of his had met a 'twice-born Brahmin boy in India who was passionate about Scott's poetry' and—picking up again on the idea of the amalgamator and reconciler—urged his listeners to be 'grateful to have such a man as this to bind even Hindustan to us by the bonds of a great human sympathy'.[121] This anecdote in itself fits in with other incidental evidence regarding the popularity of Scott in India, stimulated among other things by the fact that copies of his work were standard in the library collections of the colonial service.[122] Where McCleod's Brahmin boy showcases Scott as bridge-builder between East and West, the more common view of his place in empire was as a home from home, offering solace to Britons on duty in far-flung places. Exemplifying in a very literal way the role of literature as a 'portable fatherland', Scott provided colonial exiles with a memory of Britain and its imagined landscapes, along with a memory of the pleasures they had experienced when first encountering his romances and poems. In the main speech at the Edinburgh festival on 9 August 'To the memory of Scott', Sir Maxwell Stirling recalled that:

[The] songs of Scott have made the tour of the world with the songs of Burns, and haunt the memory of most men who love poetry and speak English. They are the very songs to be sung in a strange land by exiles not much given to weeping and hanging their harps on willows, and who yet at Vancouver or Hongkong, very steadily think of Scotland, knowing, or perhaps not knowing, how greatly the Scotland to which their hearts turn is the intellectual creation of Scott. It is the poet's best reward, we are told by Longfellow, to find his song in the heart of a friend. One of the latest of his stranger friends whom I have met with turned up in North-Eastern Siberia. If you will look into the pleasant Tent Life in that country of Mr George Kennan, an American surveyor, you will find him discovering analogies between the scenery around him and the Western Highlands of Scott's poetry, and recording how he and his party made the woodlands of Kamtchatka re-echo to the wild and unaccustomed war-notes of 'Bonnie Dundee'.[123]

The idea that Scott's text could 'haunt the memory' of English-speakers in far-flung places and so provide them with an imaginary homeland, was also the primary focus of the speech made by Lord Lawrence, former viceroy of India, who presented the works as providing comfort in face of adversity:

In a long and varied career in a distant land, I had always beside me a copy of Sir Walter Scott's novels—(Cheers)—and I can tell you with truth, that on the bed of sickness, racked with fever and pain, when I could bear nothing else, I read his works with delight and profit (Cheers).[124]

Although there may be an unwitting suggestion here that Scott's work was as anodyne as chicken broth, the ostensible intention of the speaker was to emphasize its importance as a home from home in the adverse circumstances of empire, and to assign Scott a role in the master-narrative of the empire as one of the British-made things that made it a bit easier to carry the white man's burden—though more as a sweetener in times of distress than a heavy-weight source of civilization and edification such as would be offered by Shakespeare or the Bible.[125]

The association between Scott, empire, and exile turned up again in the speech given at the Toronto celebrations by Professor Daniel Wilson, at one of several meetings organized by Scottish communities in Canada. Picking up on passages in *Lay of the Last Minstrel* (1805) and *Marmion* (1808), and with unusually little references to the novels and lavish references to the poems instead, Wilson praised Scott as bard of the Scottish diaspora:

[The idea] of emigration to such a land as this in which we now recall his name and fame, involved all that is most tragic in an enforced exile: and he gives expression to it in words wonderfully suggestive to me now. As . . . Eustace's response to Marmion's call for some lay to beguile the time, the poet exclaims: 'such have I heard in Scottish land . . . of wild Ontario's boundless lake/when heart-sick exiles in the strain/recalled fair Scotland's hills again.'

And here now, by the shores of wild Ontario's boundless lake, in no swampy jungle . . . but amid all the appliances of modern civilization, a century after that poet's birth, we recall fair Scotland's old historic landscape in association with the poet's name who in the young hey-day of pride and hope exclaimed in the familiar lines of his minstrel—'Breathes there the man.'[126]

'Wild Ontario' is a long way from India, and Lord Lawrence and Professor Wilson occupied quite different positions in the British Empire: where the former was a high-ranking official in the Indian administration, the latter was a scholar and permanent emigrant to Canada. But both men presented Scott as a source of comfort by reminding the emigrant of an imagined home and by articulating the losses that emigration entailed. Wilson highlighted the tragedy of enforced exile (which presumably applied to many of the Scots in Canada, though not to himself), while also intimating that the pains of emigration could be mitigated by the memory of 'Scotland's old historic landscape' furnished by Scott. Interestingly from the perspective of what was said earlier about the narrative of progress, Wilson suggested moreover that exile was mitigated by the more immediate comforts (the 'appliances of modern civilization') offered by life in metropolitan Canada. Indeed, Wilson's speech displays a fascinating proliferation of colonialist analogies, applied unsystematically but lavishly to the case of Scott so that his work as memory-maker is construed in terms of discovery and conquest. At one point, Wilson likened Scott to a 'Columbus' who had discovered the past; at another point he compared his work to a Peruvian goldmine. 'Born in an age of progress', he argued, Scott had used his genius to capture fashions that were becoming as obsolete as the 'era of the mastodon' and in the process had created a treasure-trove that was both the equivalent of imperial booty and a source of 'Anglo-Saxon' confidence in their own worth. Amidst the rhetorical flourishes, the basic message would seem to have been that Scott, in discovering the past, had facilitated the creation of a new world order by adding fresh wealth in the form of literature:

It is fitting that here, in the capital of this young Canadian province, as through-out the world-wide Empire won to itself by the Anglo-Saxon race . . . we gather to commemorate the birth, one hundred years ago, of one who, by his writings, had added to the world's true wealth, an El Dorado more precious than that of Ophir and Peru.[127]

The term 'Anglo-Saxon' was another one of the umbrella labels used at this period to designate the world of all English-speakers, independent of their ethnic background. Wilson referred elsewhere to 'the world-wide empire of our English race and tongue'.[128]

In *The Idea of Greater Britain: Empire and the Future of World Order, 1860–1900* (2007), Duncan Bell has characterized the last four decades of the nineteenth century by an intense preoccupation with reimagining the relations between the nations on the British Isles, the settler colonies, the British Empire, and the United States.[129] As Bell shows, various ideas of federation and confederation emerged among political theorists as imagi-native responses to the foreshortening of distance made possible by the new technologies and by the increasingly urgent need to rethink political connectedness across the long distances of empire in the face of the increasing desire of the colonies to become more independent. Bell identifies J. R. Seeley's *Expansion of England* (1881–2) as a key text in this discussion, but makes no reference to the role of writers in providing support to the idea of a common culture. In *The Idea of English Ethnicity* (2008) Robert Young covers similar ground and also locates the emer-gence of the idea of an Anglo-Saxon federation in the last decades of the nineteenth century. Although Young briefly refers to the importance of Shakespeare as a figurehead of this English-speaking world, he does not expand on this idea and also ignores the role of other writers. There is evidence to suggest, however, that the distillation of this confederative concept began earlier and that it was a key feature of the celebrations of Burns in 1859 and Scott in 1871.[130] As we have seen in the case of Wilson and others, Scott's fans positioned themselves within multiple social frames that reflected this emerging discourse on the relations between the nations of Britain and her (former) colonies, and on what Bell has called 'the global political imagination' of this period.

An American-inflected Scott within an over-arching English-speaking world was certainly evoked in 1871 at the Boston celebrations organized by the Massachusetts Historical Society. Ralph Waldo Emerson, whose sentiments were echoed by Longfellow and Oliver Wendell Holmes, began his eulogy to the Scottish writer with reference to 'the exceptional debt which all English-speaking men have gladly owed to his character and genius'.[131] But he then proceeded to suggest that Scott belonged to another era and that he stood for feudalism rather than for revolution. He was part of a heritage that should be honoured and cherished; but he was not a guide to the future. He was, in Emerson's words, the 'delight of boys', someone to look back to fondly rather than an inspiration for the future (more on this in Chapter 7).[132]

The tributes made in Boston thus resonated with the evocations of transatlantic bonding made a week earlier in Edinburgh. As acts of cultural diplomacy they also resonated with the remarks made a couple of decades earlier by another American fan, the Reverend John McVickar, who, at a memorial service held in New York soon after Scott's death, had referred to the latter's role in creating a 'global citizenship' that stretched from America to Scotland: his work had forged bonds of a transatlantic brotherhood between those who had never seen each other or who did not share the same territory.[133] It was in the same spirit that a telegram was sent from Glasgow to New York on 9 August 1871 expressing the hope that the links that united the two cities might be 'as lasting as the memory to which that night they did common homage'.[134]

As is well known, the federation of English-speaking peoples, bringing the global British Empire together with the United States into a 'special relationship', would become important in twentieth-century diplomacy and military alliances. The active participation of the American Ambassador John Hay at the unveiling of the monument to Scott in Westminster Abbey in 1897 underscored the idea of a special relationship based on a common canon of 'English' literature and a reverence for the English language. In the speech he delivered on that occasion, Hay repeated the notion that Scott had 'peopled' the hills of old Scotland with 'engaging phantoms' and at the same time introduced a new twist by insisting on the 'robust, athletic spirit of his tales of old' that made him particularly congenial to the young American nation with its 'civilization of slender resources but boundless hope' where there was not too much time to spend on the past.[135] These various appropriations by Americans indicate that Scott's work, along with that of Burns and Shakespeare, had a vital role to play as a transnational platform: it provided both a lingua franca and a resource for developing local inflections.

CULTURAL DIPLOMACY

The commemorations of Scott illustrate once again how memory and social frameworks are co-produced: public performances of memory allowed people to define themselves as members of a community by displaying and interpreting their relationship to a particular object of value; or, to recall the words of Jan Assmann, by 'conveying' their self-image. What makes the commemorations of Scott particularly interesting is that they involved both embodied communities at city level and an imagined national and transnational community of Waverley lovers. While the centenary provided a consensual occasion for a certain transnational simultaneity in which all heads were turned for a fortnight in the direction of Scott, a closer look reveals that the various groups involved used the occasion to display their distinctiveness and calibrate their position with respect to a common reference point. The collective dimension of this commemorative ritual was not a matter of everybody remembering in the same way, then, but involved instead the existence of common points of reference allowing people to parade their distinctiveness. Wilson in Toronto highlighted involuntary emigration from Scotland; Emerson in Boston portrayed him as a man of the old world rather than of the new; Glaswegians used the occasion to express their pride in both their material prosperity and the arts of Scotland; the VIPs in Edinburgh emphasized his role in increasing the prosperity and international status of Scotland, and his role as amalgamator and reconciler between peoples within the framework of British expansionism. These public manifestations were part of an evolving relationship between geopolitical developments, memory, and imagined communities in which literature played a key role in offering an idea of citizenship based on the shared appreciation of cultural values rather than on common origins.[136] Arguably, the arts had a more important part to play in forging alliances in the nineteenth century than did the remembrance of military and political victories. Where the latter was almost guaranteed to be divisive and set one group over against the other, the commemoration of literature could operate as a form of cultural diplomacy that worked *between* communities and built on the shared appreciation of certain authors. This is what in my opinion sustained the cult of authorship and made of literature and the arts such powerful instruments in nation-building and in the forging of transnational alliances in the late nineteenth century. Even as the shared memory of Scott was being celebrated, it was the idea of shared values rather than of a shared lineage or pedigree that was paramount.

The question, of course, still remains after this survey of speechifying: would Scott have turned in his grave had he heard what was being said about him? At the beginning of this chapter, I referred to the link made by Trumpener and others between Scott and 'national-imperial' thinking, based on the idea that Scott's view of nationality lent itself to appropriation for expansionist purposes:

The empirewide influence of the Waverley novels lies in their ability to harmonize Scottish materials with British perspectives, as they reconstruct the historical formation of the Scottish nation, the simultaneous formation of the Britain that subsumes it, and a cultural nationalism that survives because it learns to separate cultural distinctiveness from the memory of political autonomy and can therefore be accommodated within the new imperial framework.[137]

There is much in the celebrations of 1840 and 1871 to suggest that Scott had imaginatively prepared the way for his own appropriations within an imperialist–progressivist discourse: by depicting the violence of the past in such a way as to 'make it safe' within the present; by depicting characters acting in worlds in which border-crossing and intercultural trafficking were part of daily reality; by offering a social imaginary that was both locally specific and yet portable to other situations; by providing an icon of Literature that could act as a guarantor of civilization elevated above economics. Those commemorating him in later decades, and particularly in 1871, were in a sense replicating a gesture that they had already practised as readers of his work: recollecting the past in a way that facilitates future building and renegotiates the borders of the world by imaginatively incorporating other territories and other groups. Scott the reconciler and the amalgamator, to recall the words of Hepworth Dixon, provided a symbolic underpinning for later amalgamations and reconciliations whether under the label of Britishness, of empire, or of English-speaking 'global citizenship'. In short: there is much in the various commemorations of Scott that can be seen as re-enactments in the mode of public discourse of his imaginative legacy and geopolitical procreativity.

But there are also features of these discourses that tell us more about the world of 1832, 1840, and 1871 than about the imaginative world of Scott himself. At each step along the way, we have seen how remembering Scott in public was both about Scott and about the stakeholders in his legacy, from the citizens of Edinburgh who erected the monument in Edinburgh to the many well-heeled people around the world who celebrated his centenary in 1871. Unlike the other Scottish writers whom he overshadowed (to the chagrin of recent critics), Scott's immense popularity meant that he functioned as a communal site of memory for at least two generations. At a certain level, he was even interchangeable with

Shakespeare and Burns, since the important thing for many of the celebrants was the presence of a canonical writer and the occasion he afforded them to perform their collective appreciation of his work in public. In view of this, it is reductive to see Scott's 'symbolic legacy' only 'in the master-narrative of British empire'. Overemphasizing the imperialist substratum of his work obscures the parallel role Scott played in providing a liberationist model for smaller nations across Europe trying to establish their own identities within various Empires. More fundamentally, it also makes him the victim of the many eager readers who, at the highpoint of his fame in 1871, were themselves saturated in imperialism: people coming and going to the colonies and North America was part of everyday life. In that regard, writers like John Galt and James Hogg, who are now being brought out from behind the shadow of Scott as examples of alternative views of the world, have actually been protected by their very obscurity from the pompous appropriations of prosperity to which Scott was subject. That the imperialist appropriations of Scott resonated with his work, which they clearly did, does not mean to say that they exhausted its complexities or actualized all of its potential meanings. To begin with the fact, noted in the 1930s by Lukács and others, that Scott was one of the first writers to depict individuals as thoroughly social and historically constituted beings acting in circumstances that were not of their own choosing; or that Scott, as Ian Duncan has recently argued, was also keenly aware of the persistent shadow-side of modernization.[138]

In making this point, I do not wish to deny that Scott lent himself to such reductive appropriations, as the celebrations prove. Nor is it to deny the fact that Scott's work helped imaginatively prepare some of the ground for later imperialism by offering resources for thinking about culture as distinct from power, for honouring those things that are to be dispossessed, for turning literature into a 'robust, athletic' item of consumption. But it is to indicate the importance of thinking in much more nuanced terms about the relation between a literary work and its multiple appropriations, between the procreative power of the original text and its more malignant offshoots.

7

How Long Was Immortality?

In living memory he lives for ever.
—Lord Provost, Glasgow, 9 August 1871[1]

Immortality, like diamonds, is meant to be forever. When it comes to making claims about the immortality of writers or artists, counting out the future years seems to be as much beside the point as in declarations of unending love. When people in 1832 called Scott immortal they were mainly just expressing appreciation for his work in the pompous and by now outdated terms of a literary cliché. But it was also an implicit way of universalizing their aesthetic judgement by assuming that it would still hold true for future generations. 'Immortal' was basically an admission that one couldn't imagine a time when things would be different. When the Lord Provost at the banquet in Glasgow in 1871 claimed that Scott would live forever 'in living memory', he was both being tautologically vacuous and expressing succinctly a profound truth about the workings of cultural memory: that the 'immortal memory' of Scott would stay alive just as long as people remembered him, that 'forever' means for 'as long as it will last', and that it is hard to imagine the future.

It may be assumed that the provost himself was not thinking that a time would actually come when Scott would no longer be 'in living memory'. But since Scott himself had thematized cultural dynamics and helped generate a memory habitus premised on the reality of change, there was an underlying contradiction in supposing that his own status would be immutable. And indeed, a suspicion that Scott's immortality might itself be subject to curtailment began to run like a red thread through the nineteenth-century celebrations of his work. Beginning as a minor disturbance in the background, an anxious concern with his transience became a dominant theme. An all-pervasive historicism that he had helped foster along with the reality of cultural change inspired commentators into quantifying eternity and replacing phrases like 'until the end of time' by a more specific calculation of how long exactly Scott might be remembered. This yielded some curious predictions. Harriet Martineau, for example, assumed in 1832 that the influence of Scott was 'just beginning its course of a thousand years'.[2] To be sure, a millennium is very long and Martineau intended it as a compliment, but the figure of a thousand years did bring the 'immortal memory' into the realm of the secular and the countable. Bulwer Lytton was even more specific when he claimed, again as a compliment, that Scott's work would be irreplaceable for at least a 'hundred ages hence' and that only a 'remote generation' would bring forth his successor.[3] Implicit was the belief that canonicity works by replacement rather than accumulatively and that the baton of greatness would pass between the select number of writers who managed to survive the threshold of three generations.

On the eve of Scott's funeral in 1832, the *Morning Chronicle* pronounced his immense success to be a sure sign of his immortality ('generation and generation' will be praising him 'to the end of all time'), while the funeral masque, as we have seen, featured prominently the allegorical figure of Immortality.[4] But attempts to estimate Scott's future innings as an immortal were complicated from the outset by the fact of his unprecedented popularity both as poet and then as novelist. In an essay written as early as 1833, W. B. O. Peabody referred to a widespread suspicion that his 'unusual popularity' meant that he would not be read for long into the future.[5] His enormous appeal had opened up an awkward gap between contemporary taste and future longevity, between popularity and critical value that has been growing ever since. Scott was well loved, but was he great? Or to put this in terms of the underlying suspicion: since he was well loved, he probably was not so great since the public could not possibly have the discriminating foresight of serious critics.

Among those who went against the flow of public enthusiasm in predicting Scott's future was Thomas Carlyle, who, in his dyspeptic but extremely prescient review of Lockhart's biography in 1838, pointed out that Scott's present-day popularity might actually be in inverse proportion to his longevity, that 'by the nature of it, such popularity is transient.'[6] In his opinion, Scott remained a rather superficial writer with no philosophical vision reaching beyond present-day experience into the future. It was for this reason that he had appealed so vividly and immediately to his contemporaries and, for the very same reason, that he would fail to survive in the future. At best, Scott was 'sempiternal', Carlyle predicted, and would last one or more generations at most:

Buff-belts and all manner of jerkins and costumes are transitory; man alone is perennial. He that has gone deeper into this than other men, will be remembered longer than they; he that has not, not. Tried under this category, Scott, with his clear practical insight, joyous temper, and other sound faculties, is not to be accounted little,—among the ordinary circulating library heroes he might well pass for a demigod. Not little; yet neither is he great; there were greater, more than one or two, in his own age... What then is the result of these Waverley Romances? Are they to amuse one generation only? One or more. As many generations as they can; but not all generations: ah no, when our swallow-tail has become fantastic as trunk-hose, they will cease to amuse![7]

Carlyle's application of the language of sartorial fashion to Scott was indicative of an emerging perception that the Author of Waverley had not only changed people's relations to the past by providing stories they could imaginatively identify with. He had also profoundly affected their relationship to time itself by introducing the possibility both of immediate fame and, its shadow side, rapid obsolescence. Hence the paradox at the heart of the Waverley phenomenon: at the same time as Scott stimulated the belief that collective identity was linked to a memory that could be fixed in locations and monuments, he had also introduced the principle of rapid turnovers into cultural production and hence implicitly into the idea of collective memory itself. One of the first writers of bestsellers, and a writer of multiple bestsellers to boot, the very popularity of his work raised the possibility that cultural tastes might be as intense and as transient as sartorial trends; that his work itself, and certainly the hype surrounding it, would pass into the past as the eighteenth century had done.

Since those first optimistic predictions on the occasion of his death, Scott too has become as multistable as some of his works. With a magnificent ambivalence that places him in the centre of concerns about collective memory in the modern period and ensures his continuing fascination, he stands on the one hand for memory and monumentality; on the other hand, for the ephemeral and mutable. As John Henry Raleigh was to put it in 1963:

In the nineteenth century Scott was ubiquitous; in the twentieth century he virtually disappears. Never before or since in Western culture has a writer been such a power in his own day and so negligible to posterity. All writers' reputations. . . undergo vicissitudes, but none can equal the meteoric rise and fall of Scott.[8]

In this chapter, I analyse the changing perceptions of Scott's longevity, before going on to reflect on its implications for our understanding of both his particular legacy and the mutability of cultural memory. I shall concentrate here on the critical discourses around his *oeuvre* as these evolved in the hundred years after his death. The term critical discourses is used here as an umbrella word to cover a range of commentary by opinion makers, from occasional speeches by statesmen to professional assessments on the part of creative writers and literary critics. The ways in which later commentators assessed Scott's longevity, as we will see, bears out Jeffrey Olick's claim that cultural memory can best be understood in 'process-relational' terms as the changing outcome of the interplay between particular figures of memory and multiple players in the cultural field.[9] This interplay led to Scott's long-term prospects being continuously revised in retrospect within a narrative of cultural change that reflected attempts to re-assess his legacy and, in the process, to influence future generations.

In a book significantly titled *The Great Divide* (1986), Andreas Huyssen argued that modernism was permeated by the fear of mass culture and that its aesthetics were paradoxically formulated in opposition to the immediate desires of the public: popularity was suspect in the age of consumerism and the culture industry even as influence was passionately desired.[10] In retrospect Scott's work can be seen as a harbinger of the modern mass culture which is the subject of Huyssen's analysis, in that his writing and publishing strategies were directed towards stimulating the desire of an ever-widening public for new stories, new sensations, and in the case of books and related tie-ins, new possessions. From an early stage, as we have seen, the very enthusiasm shown by his readers earned him the disapproval of some literary critics and the arbiters of taste. At least one commentator complained in the 1820s that Scott's work threatened to make reviewing superfluous since the public in their greed for everything produced by the Author of Waverley would probably already have read the story by the time his mature assessment of its merits had appeared.[11] Later assessments of his work reflected this anxiety about the influence of criticism in a commercialized world that appealed directly to readers and bypassed cultural gatekeepers.

The afterlife of Scott indicates that well in advance of our present-day participatory culture, a gap emerged between the attempts to control taste on the part of opinion-makers and the desire of the public to follow writers and appropriate them as their enthusiasm saw fit. In *Janeites* (2000) Deidre Lynch has pointed to a comparable tension between critics and readers in the case of Jane Austen and her twentieth-century fan base.[12] The reception of Austen's works followed a very different trajectory from that of Scott in terms of both the curve of his popularity (Austen's star rose as Scott's declined) and the very public character of his role as memory site.[13] But the two cases are similar in showing readers' investing large scale in a writer's work outside the control of the arbiters of good taste and hence meeting with the latter's disapproval or condescension. Lynch refers in this regard to literary criticism as an institution that is 'invested in narratives about the legitimate transmission of a patrimony' and hence suspicious of procreativity outside 'the official mechanisms of cultural transmission and cultural memory'.[14] One might call this the anxiety about influence, an anxiety compounded by the uncomfortable realization on the part of professional critics that they might also be simply missing the point about works that patently had the power to mobilize other people. As Lionel Trilling pointed out with reference to Austen, the apparently excessive enthusiasm of admirers might not just be a mark of their inability to monitor the borders between fiction and real life; it might also be a reflection of some quality in the work itself that had hitherto eluded critics: 'in some unusual promise that it seems to make, in some hope that it holds out.'[15] The extent to which Scott's novels were remediated and incorporated into private life in the multiple ways that have been discussed in earlier chapters can be seen as proof of his vitality as an imaginative resource. In the eyes of some intellectuals, however, this seemed to prove instead Scott's failure to be a true artist. Precisely because of his popularity, as we shall see, Scott has enjoyed a complex, and not always comfortable, relationship with the (self-appointed) custodians of patrimony as they have attempted to impose their values on a public that did not necessarily want their guidance and on a commercialized publishing industry subject to the laws of the market as well as the creativity of authors.

NARRATIVIZING TASTE

Generationality has become a key issue in cultural memory studies and, as some of the quotations given above show, already figured prominently in the reception of Scott's work. While his contemporaries generally expressed their confidence that his work would be 'handed down to all succeeding generations', as the *Edinburgh Evening Courant* put it in September 1832, or that it would last at least for several generations, the notion of generation itself changed as the decades passed. It is generally understood that the nineteenth century, under the influence of revolution and economic modernization, saw a shift in the meaning of 'generation' from a genealogical model based on biological succession to a narrative model based on conflict, difference, and evolution.[16] The genealogical model had been premised on continuity, and the idea that the cultural and biological baton was simply handed over from parents to children to form an unbroken chain within a *milieu de mémoire*, while the evolutionary model supposed rupture, discontinuity, and hence narrativity as well. Scott himself had contributed to this narrative understanding of history based on the articulation of differences between parents and children, ancestors and descendants. Thus the subtitle *'Tis Sixty Years Since* that he had used for *Waverley* flagged both the historical distance between generations and the desire to overcome it, while his *Tales of a Grandfather* (1827–31), addressed to his grandson John Hugh Lockhart, who tragically died before the series was complete, foregrounded generationality in a direct manner.[17] By highlighting in multiple ways the differences between the worlds successive generations inhabit, Scott anticipated on recent research into family memory by showing that stories tend to pass directly from grandparents to their grandchildren across temporal spans of sixty years. Already within Scott's *oeuvre*, then, storytelling was intimately linked to the duties, pleasures, and challenges involved in transmitting imaginative resources and values to the coming generation.

Between 1832, 1871, and the commemoration of the centenary of his death in 1932, a gap between successive generations of Scott's readers also emerged. Behind all of the posturing and pageantry of 1871 was a shared familiarity with the work of Scott, a private memory of reading his poetry and novels that was regularly invoked as the foundation for participation in the public celebration. However, cracks were beginning to appear in this collective fan base. At least one critical observer noted that some of the American visitors attending the National Festival in Edinburgh seemed to have been more acquainted with Scott by reputation and by tourist guides than by any primary knowledge of his work; another wondered whether the visitors to the Crystal Palace celebrations had actually read Scott at all.[18] On the same occasion, the London *Times* mingled its effusive insistence on Scott's longevity with the suggestion that the Author of Waverley would not have the same value for the upcoming generation as he had had for earlier ones:

The successive appearances of the Waverley novels were important events. In days before the invention of circulating libraries they were passed from hand to hand, and read aloud in country villages, that every one might have his share in them. They formed the most indispensable part of a liberal education, and no one was counted fit to be heard in society who was not familiar with their most minute incidents and most obscure characters. How far are they similarly read in the present day? To judge by their countless editions, exhausted almost as soon as they are published, it is clear they are deemed indispensable in the most modest libraries; yet it must be owned *they hold a different place in the mind of the rising generation from that which they occupied with the elder or even the middle-aged among us*. New writers of a genius diverse from Scott's have arisen in the interval, and the present is, above all things, the age of science. Yet we believe the essential influence of the poems and tales of the author of 'Waverley' survives, and is perhaps less perceived because it has become natural and familiar to us. Time, probably, will tend to sift his works like all others, and he may be chiefly read in the future for his masterpieces. But he has riveted too firmly the chains of his imagination, his human sympathy, and his historical insight ever to lose his hold upon the world. He has ceased to exert the charm of novelty, but he retains the deeper charm of truth. There never, in short, was a man whose memory less needed a centenary celebration, and there never was one who more deserved it.[19] [emphasis AR]

One of the striking things about this commentary is that it historicizes Scott and, in the process, makes him aesthetically inert in the present. Rather than view his writings as still vibrant stories or texts that were as fresh in 1871 as when they were first written, the *Times* narrated the Scott phenomenon as a series of events in the past tense, as historical contributions at a moment in time that has been superseded by other things into which Scott has been absorbed. In other words, the memory of Scott belonged to the 'elder or even the middle-aged among us' rather than to the 'rising generation' and, linked to this, he was part of their youth and not of their present. Public eulogy had become permeated by a generational narrative in which temporal succession was articulated according to divisions between fathers and sons, ancestors and successors, romance and science that sat uneasily with earlier predictions that Scott would enjoy a timeless and undifferentiated immortality. Although the *Times* concluded with the assertion that Scott's memory did not need any celebrations, since the books will survive by themselves, doubts seem to have crept in that shake the very basis of this argument: on the one hand, only a few masterpieces would make it into the future; on the other hand, Scott had become so omnipresent and absorbed into everyday culture, through the many appropriations described in earlier chapters, that his own contribution had become invisible.

The generational discourse that informed the *Times* report produced a regular hum in the background to the celebrations of 1871, be this in a reference to Scott's having enchanted 'three generations of readers' or in a reference to his having made such a profound impression on his 'own generation' that 'there are men still—'tis sixty years since they were young—who feel that a large part of human genius perished with him.'[20] These intergenerational differences had already been flagged in an important survey written by Walter Bagehot in 1858 on the occasion of the publication of no fewer than six different editions of the collected Waverley novels, the hard-backed staples of Victorian parlours and family bookshelves. In a convoluted but fascinating passage, Bagehot recalled that great works of art are usually only recognized as such one generation after their appearance: contemporaries are not yet ready for them, since they bring to new books 'formed minds and stiffened creeds'. In Scott's case, however, the normal order had been inverted. Reflecting the accelerated pace of his memorialization discussed in the previous chapter, his works had appealed immediately and intensely to his contemporaries, but rather less to those who came later:

Their plain, and, so to say, cheerful merits, suit the occupied man of genial middle life. Their appreciation was to an unusual degree coincident with their popularity. The next generation, hearing the praises of their fathers in their earliest reading time, seized with avidity on the volumes; and there is much in very many of them that is admirably fitted for the delight of boyhood. A third generation has now arisen into at least the commencement of literary life, which is quite removed from the unbounded enthusiasm with which the Scotch novels were originally received, and does not always share the still more eager partiality of those who, in the opening of their minds, first received the tradition of their excellence. New books have arisen to compete with these; new interests distract us from them. The time, therefore, is not perhaps unfavourable for a slight criticism of these celebrated fictions; and their continual republication without any criticism for many years seems to demand it.[21]

Bagehot's essay brings together in a concentrated way many of the themes that would become salient in appreciations of Scott's works in the next half-century, central among them the idea that Scott's value needed to be appreciated in historical terms (it belonged to an earlier moment rather than to eternity) and that by now a critical distance had opened up between the first generation of readers and contemporary commentators. Value had become translated into generational terms with appreciation for Scott linked to 'youthfulness', either in the sense that he belonged to the childhood pleasures of those who were now middle-aged or that he offered 'cheerful' pleasures to people who were now young.[22] In other words, Waverley was becoming juvenile in the double sense of appealing both to an earlier generation and to children, but not to the mature reflections of present-day adults. The point was expressed very clearly in the *Saturday Review* in 1871: 'We ought to consider not only what [Scott's work] is to us, but what it was to the generation for whom it was produced. We ought also to forget, if possible, that we [are] critics, and to remember that we were once boys.'[23] This somewhat backhanded tribute to Scott's enchantments ended up again historicizing his work as something that, even if it was not culturally obsolete, nevertheless belonged to the readers' autobiographical past rather than to their present preferences as adult critics. Enjoyment of Scott and adulthood were apparently incompatible.

Reference was made earlier to Ralph Waldo Emerson's contention that Scott was the 'delight of generous boys' and that 'when we reopen these old books we consent to be boys again', sentiments echoed by Henry James, who believed that Scott's readers must 'become as credulous as children at twilight'.[24] These childlike, if not childish pleasures were regularly linked to the idea that Scott's work was 'healthy', 'clean', 'uncomplicated', and so little designed to unsettle any man's beliefs (Scott's own words were often quoted back at him) that it could be safely given by parents to children or, to recall some of the speeches made at the centenary, indulged in by adults suffering from illness or isolation.[25] They were perfect books for the sick-room and for freshening morbid minds, Bagehot suggested, giving a compliment that almost bordered on a snub. Scott's works were being paternistically declared safe (healthy, robust, athletic) for the next generation of boys while being divested of any power to be taken seriously in the present as challenges to think different-ly. The person Scott not only now belonged to an earlier generation, but the reading of his works had moved back as it were in developmental terms to that of childhood, a phase that by definition meant that they were set for being overtaken. The growth of this evolutionary narrative ran to a certain degree parallel to the production of children's versions of Scott's works, particularly *Ivanhoe*, which, as we saw earlier, had come to occupy a key place in the Scott canon and in the multiple remediations of his work.[26] His poetry was also given a fixed part in school curricula in Britain from the 1870s onwards, while the fiction seems to have been reserved for leisure time.[27]

Whereas fans in 1832 and 1840 were so concerned that future genera-tions would accuse them of not having honoured Scott enough that they insisted on erecting an enormous monument to him as soon as they could, thirty years later—even as the public celebrations of Scott reached their high-point in 1871—some critical minds had become self-conscious about what had now become an intergenerational tradition of remember-ing. They were beginning to be a bit concerned as to how *their* posterity would judge them if they continued for much longer to share the enthu-siasm of their predecessors, at least in public. Leslie Stephen, who believed that books were classics if they were still read after a century and that this happened rarely, surmised that people in the future would look back on the popularity of Scott and wonder if an entire generation had not been deluded by his enchantments: 'Will our posterity understand at least why he was once a luminary of the first magnitude, or wonder at their ancestors' hallucination about a mere will-o'-the-wisp?'[28] Stephen had some reason for concern about the views of the next generation—to begin with, those of his own daughter Virginia Woolf, who in an essay on *The Antiquary* (1924) would firmly pronounce Scott to be culturally dead, claiming that there are 'some writers who have entirely ceased to influence others' and 'among them is Scott'.[29] Her subsequent comments are quite appreciative of Scott's skill in dialogue ('he is perhaps the last novelist to practise the great, the Shakespearean art, of making people reveal themselves in speech'), but they also clearly relegate Scott to the past, dissociating him from current literary values in which the narration of interiority was more important than dramatic presentation. At the same time, Woolf recognized that her critical discriminations might in fact be entirely irrelevant for the thousands of readers who were probably at that very moment 'brooding and feasting in a rapture of uncritical and silent satisfaction' over Scott's works. This dissociation between critical value and private feasting echoed other commentators from the last decades of the nineteenth century, for whom the pleasures of reading Scott's novels had become something people continued to indulge in private, as if it had become the intellectual equivalent of irresponsibly eating a tub of ice cream.[30]

While increasingly dismissed as non-contemporary, Scott's work had acquired the nostalgic appeal of an earlier time when things were less complicated or the enduring appeal of uncritical pleasure. Varying from nostalgic reminiscences of youthful pleasures, to patronizing compliments, to downright dismissals of Scott's work as fit only for juveniles and the uncritical, historicizing comments abound in the many periodical articles and occasional tributes written once 'the first generation of his admirers' had passed. In the interstices of the public celebrations of the writer discussed earlier and running parallel to his appropriations as a cultural icon within the English-speaking world, a new narrative of cultural evolution was emerging in which Scott was generally honoured, but at the cost of being declared definitively *passé* or relegated to a naïve phase in people's development as readers. The latter was a gesture that Scott himself might have ironically appreciated as a variation on his own depictions of lost causes representing earlier phases of social development and, as such, destined to be surpassed (in the Hegelian sense of *aufgehoben*) by evolution. One way or another, by the time a hundred years had passed, the 'immortal memory' anticipated by admirers in 1832 had become a past future.

1932: MEMORY DIVIDED

In 1924 Virginia Woolf still supposed that thousands of people were regularly 'feasting' on Scott and, at first sight, his importance as a public site of memory seemed undiminished in 1932. The centenary of his death was celebrated in style in Edinburgh with the Prince of Wales in full attendance, reflecting the perceived Britishness of Scott's legacy. However, there were significant differences with respect to earlier celebrations.

Where the 1871 event had been organized by a coalition of well-heeled admirers of Scott and involved large numbers of Victorian worthies, the 1932 affair seems have been more a matter for city authorities and states-men with a procession to the monument on 21 September headed by the Prince and, in order of rank, all the officials of the city, followed by a pageant of school children. The celebration also included a church service, an exhibition at the National Gallery, and an official luncheon, accom-panied by toasts to the King, City, Sir Walter Scott, and the Chairman, and followed later that evening by an illumination of the monument, using power equivalent to that of three million candles.[31] Despite the high-profile attendance, this commemoration was a more scaled-down affair than that of 1871, in terms of the range of groups and locations involved, and the extent of the media attention. The fact that various schools in Scotland organized their pupils into pageants and *tableaux vivants* suggests an association with Scott that was being imposed by educationalists on the next generation rather than the more spontaneous, if orchestrated enthusiasm of the earlier events on the part of civil soci-ety.[32] By the time of the bicentenary in 1971, the chief stakeholders in Scott's memory and curators of the celebrations would be professional heritage managers: academics, archivists, and librarians.[33]

In fact Scott's public status as a cultural icon, as reflected in the very official character of the celebrations in 1932, formed a sharp contrast to what was in fact his declining popularity. Although there were undoubt-edly many people who continued to read Scott's works as Woolf believed, popular taste was in fact evolving in different directions. Although it is hard to identify an exact turning point in Scott's afterlife, it is clear that by World War I a corner had been turned and an irreversible decline had set in with respect both to his readership and to his public role as memory site. Reference has already been made to the fact that theatrical appro-priations of Scott's work, which had been such an integral part of his cultural presence, effectively dried up after 1914 although some of his works continued to procreate in the new media of cinema and radio. It is difficult to establish actual sales figures for individual novels, given the fact that they were no longer under copyright, but it is clear that the Victorian era of the collected works gracing all genteel parlours was a thing of the past by the 1920s. The canon of his works was also reduced (as the *Times* in 1871 had predicted) to his principal Scottish novels and *Ivanhoe*, while his poetry disappeared almost entirely from view. Indeed, there has been no new collected edition since the early 1900s, although one is now in preparation—an extraordinary eclipse of works that had been so im-mensely popular in the 1810s and, as we have seen in the case of the United States, so immensely influential. Although his works continued to be sold and read, it was on quite a different scale compared to a century earlier.[34] Despite the best efforts of his admirers, poems like *The Lady of the Lake* and novels like *The Heart of Mid-Lothian* had apparently become old-fashioned in a world where cinema and 'modern thrillers' were offering other forms of popular culture.[35] To be sure, widespread familiarity with Scott's pantheon of characters did not disappear overnight: an advertisement from 1950 indicates that Scott was still enough of a brand more than a century after his death to be harnessed, along with Burns, in the promotion of a cleaning agent called By-Prox. These incidental manifestations of familiarity with Scott's work or with his icon were marginal phenomena, however, and need to be seen as part of what Chris Anderson would call the 'long-tail' of cultural knowledge rather than as markers of its cutting edge.[36] In 1935, the *Scotsman* noted as symptomatic of the neglect of Scott in more recent times, the fact that Christie's had failed to sell a very large painting by Daniel Maclise illustrating the *Fair Maid of Perth* (1846). Scott had literally passed his sell-by date. No wonder then that one commentator at the 1932 centenary should refer to an unbridgeable 'gulf between the young and the old'.[37] Or that another would protest that the best way to honour Scott would be to actually take one of his books off the shelf and read it: the celebrations highlighted the fact that he had become the great Unread.[38]

Nevertheless, the 1932 centenary too, like the one in 1871, provided an occasion for recalibrating collective identities and gave rise to a flurry of publications assessing Scott's legacy in essays that combined platitudes with historical insights in often unequal measure.[39] The thrust of many of the interventions in 1932 suggests a perceived need to inform a new generation of the basic facts of Scott's life and achievements and provided multiple variations on the theme of Scott's cultural marginalization and the collective amnesia surrounding the figure that had towered over the nineteenth century. Reflecting the radical change in Scott's fortunes among the reading nation, moreover, public commentaries in the British media after World War I became split between nostalgic evocations of a time when he used to be so popular and impatience to get rid of a has-been.

On the one hand, the centenary provided an occasion for a renewed interest in Scott in the form of biography and criticism, while giving expression to what was becoming a growing need to defend his legacy. The latter was expressed in rhetorical headlines: 'Why Apologise for Sir Walter Scott' (1951), 'The Neglect of Scott's Novels is Deplorable' (1953), 'By General Consent Scott is Unread Today' (1953), 'Immortal Memory? Is Sir Walter Scott Forgotten?'(1956).[40] These were often the prelude to a well-meaning defence of the virtues of Scott and, in some cases, to an invocation of those virtues as a bulwark against the presumed

Figure 7.1: Advertisement, *Scotsman*, 4 August 1950.

decadence of modernist novels and, by implication, of modern society. A systemic concern with the threats to the primacy of reading and Literature in face of the rise of other media also ran through these laments. Indeed, many of these rearguard interventions in the press after World War I were themselves occasioned by the incidental appearance of new adaptations of Scott's novels for the cinema and for the radio.

On the other hand, 1932 also provided an occasion *par excellence* for a new generation of writers to engage in Waverley-bashing and mark a definitive rupture with a Scott-dominated past. In opposition to the many pious, platitudinous, and sometimes well-balanced eulogies in praise of the Wizard of the North, the centenary also saw the appearance of some vocal dissidents in Scotland who seized the moment to challenge Scott's right to be remembered and, specifically, to be remembered as a figurehead for Scottish culture. Symbolically killing off Scott as belonging to the generation of 'sixty years since' provided an opportunity of formulating a new modernist and a new nationalizing agenda that offered a counterpoint to the self-fashioning endemic in the multiple appropriations of Scott discussed in earlier chapters. Thus the appropriately named *Modern Scot* published a review article entitled 'Sir Walter Scott and the Scotsman's Heritage' in its spring issue of 1932 which attacked some of the recent eulogies. The familiar image of 'Scott the reconciler' was echoed, but in order to argue that 'he reconciled warring elements only by gelding them' and that he represented a superficial 'bogus Celticism' and 'pseudo-Scottishness' that was typical of the artificial culture of Edinburgh rather than of the 'Modern Scot'.[41] The *Modern Scot* renewed its charge that summer with a centenary issue entirely devoted to Scott, but one designed less to praise the Great Well-Known than to bury him. As the editorial put it, the contributors wanted to break with the tradition of merely celebrating Scott's *historical* significance (for this was undisputed), and to scrutinize instead his 'present artistic value'. As on earlier occasions, the commemoration was used to mark out differences and stake out claims for the future. In this case, however, the starting point was openly contestatory rather than celebratory. It did not involve an alternative 'counter' memory highlighting forgotten events and agents, but rather an *oppositional* act debunking a national idol while using the traction given by his memory to stake out a new position and a new direction for the future.

The opening article was called 'Why Scott is Neglected', with the neglect thus taken as incontrovertible. Its author, Donald Carswell, wittily contrasted the 'pumpkinification' of Scott through official ceremonies (there are always hierophantic ex-cabinet ministers and academics ready to make speeches about him, he complained, a point borne out by some of the eulogies analysed earlier),[42] with the fact that people quietly, but firmly refused to read him and that those who did try found him a total bore. He then pronounced not only the man but also his works to be dead from over-exposure and over-memorialization:

Scott, in fact, is no longer regarded as a living artist. *He is not forgotten, but he is gone.* Nothing is commoner in the history of literature than the overthrow of figures that were idols in their own generation, but here we have an idol that remains colossal and intact, but is become a museum piece instead of an object of worship.[43] [emphasis AR]

This view of Scott as a museum piece rather than memory site capable of generating new interpretations rendered all efforts to revive interest in his work completely misplaced. If people no longer read him, this was because he simply had nothing more to say. He was culturally speaking obsolete, at best a highly cherished relic and leftover of an earlier generation. In a subsequent article in the same issue, A. C. Cunninghame referred to Scott in similar terms as a 'national idol' accepted on trust by 'successive generations of uncritical readers' whose original popularity at best bore testimony 'to the sheer bêtise of an earlier generation'.[44] In a subsequent article, Edwin Muir accused Scott with equally high-minded condescension of never having been worth much in the first place and indeed of having actively lowered the standards of literature, with a 'clean conscience' to boot:

With his enormous prestige he helped to establish the mediocre and the trivial. . . . Scott was a man of great native genius and of enormous inventive powers. But has any other writer of equal rank ever misused his gifts and indefatigably lowered the standards of literature with quite such a clean conscience?

With critical volleys like these, the modernist–nationalist Muir and his associates (ironically, few of whom are particularly well remembered nowadays) used the occasion of the centenary to mark their Oedipal insurrection against a petrified tradition in Scottish culture.[45] This was not the first time Scott had been criticized. Hazlitt and Carlyle had pulled no punches either.[46] But it was arguably the first concerted, *collective* effort to revise Scott's public standing and empty him of significance, while imagining a future which would be different.[47]

The recollections of Scott in the *Modern Scot*, while ostensibly deploying the rhetoric of aesthetic judgement, were clearly also about negotiating cultural and political capital in the contemporary world where artistic value, to recall Huyssen's notion of the Great Divide, was being increasingly posited in opposition to popular success. In this case, the point was made by using the classic struggle between the forces of tradition and the forces of free agency and progress in order to relegate the (popular) Scott in no uncertain terms to the past. This was all the easier for a commentator in 1932 to do since, as we have seen above, Scott's popularity was already on the decline at this point. In 1954, *Punch* would ask whether Scott had not joined the 'extinct bestsellers' like Tom Moore and Bulwer Lytton, echoing an earlier reference to him in the *Irish Times* as a 'lost cause'.[48] That particular echo of Scott was yet another paradoxical reminder that it was the author of Waverley who had first conceptualized modernity as the obverse of its lost causes and hence helped provide the imaginative tools for his own replacement.[49]

BAD AND GOOD TRADITIONS

The rise of academic literary criticism as of the late nineteenth century coincided more or less both with the demise of Scott's popularity and cultural presence and the rise of a modernist aesthetic. Walter Raleigh, Regius chair of English Literature at Oxford and a key figure in the institutionalization of English studies, brought out a history of the romance tradition in 1894 that was designed to culminate with *Waverley* and 'the Greatness of Scott'.[50] Although a tradition of specialist scholarship around Scott can be dated to the 1932 centenary, with important editorial work by Herbert J. C. Grierson, he lost his place within the core canon of English literature.[51] Where Raleigh still talked in terms of Scott's greatness and saw him as the highpoint of a tradition, this status was not carried over into the influential surveys of fiction that were published in the twentieth century and widely used for decades in academic programmes. Thus E. M. Forster's *Aspects of the Novel* (1927) presented the Author of Waverley in unflattering terms as someone who was indeed famous, but who was definitely not great. If he had become famous, Forster continued condescendingly, this was only because of his 'primitive power of keeping the reader in suspense and playing on his curiosity'. Having thus reduced Scott to the level of a 'primitive' storyteller, Forster did admit that the general attraction of Scott's work was enhanced by its association with happy childhoods and with parents reading stories out loud: but, he asked rhetorically, is Sir Walter Scott anything more than 'a reminder of early happiness'?[52] He was surely only someone who at best could remind you of the romance of youth or offer comforts when you were too old to engage with life's complexities. In the meantime, Forster advised, you should look for 'great literature' in works whose characters had more psychological depth and brought a greater intensity of experience into play. In his privileging of subjective experience and psychological depth, Forster was clearly operating from a distinctly modernist aesthetic and, linked to this, passing aesthetic judgements on texts detached from the historical context in which they were written. But in passing judgement on Scott, he too was in fact positioning himself in a by now familiar generational narrative that relegated Scott to the past in order to make way for something new. In the process, the 'primitive power' of the Waverley novels supplied Forster with a whipping boy with which to promote a contemporary aesthetic that was implicitly coded as 'adult' and set over against popular taste.

Nor did Scott fare much better in F. R. Leavis' *The Great Tradition* (1948). By now relegated to a mere footnote, Scott figured as an 'inspired folk-lorist' and as a 'great and very intelligent man', backhand compliments that served only to preface the subsequent comment that he had no qualifications as a writer since he lacked (*nota bene*) 'the creative writer's interest in literature'. For this reason, Leavis went on, Scott not only had failed to break away from the 'bad tradition' of eighteenth-century romance, but he had had a negative influence on other writers. In short: 'Out of Scott a bad tradition came.'[53] As Leavis' distinctions between 'bad' and 'great' traditions indicates, his criticism was a way both of promoting certain aesthetic values and of monitoring cultural memory by promoting one past over another. In his particular narrativization, literary history became a struggle between the bad traditions (represented by Scott) and the great ones that did not dwell on the past, but instead promoted 'awareness of the possibilities of life' through the portrayal of complex characters and moral emotions.[54]

In the next and final chapter, I will come back to the role of literary critics as custodians and directors of cultural memory. Suffice it here to recall the fact that it took yet another generation for the intellectual conditions to emerge in which Scott's cultural importance could be reassessed outside of a modernist aesthetic and, linked to this, outside of a generational dynamics that relegated him with a certain animus to the ranks of a *passé* writer who as a 'reminder of early happiness' or as an 'inspired folk-lorist' merely represented the opposite of the contemporary world. By the time this change occurred, however, Scott had also become much less well known among the public at large and was no longer the cultural presence and cultural force he had been before World War I. And given the low critical status sketched above, there was little to stop this decline. Thus where in the 1870s Scott street names in new suburbs across the Empire could be presumed to ring a bell with the inhabitants and even in the 1900s locomotives could be named after minor characters from his *oeuvre*, this familiarity could no longer be supposed in 1950. When the City of Edinburgh decided then to give Scott names to the streets in a new housing estate in Inch, the motive given was not to celebrate a writer with

whom people were presumed familiar. It was to remind the next generation of a figure of historical importance for Scotland rapidly disappearing
from public memory even as, I would argue, his covert influence was daily
evident on cinema screens in the form of historical epics such as *Gone with
the Wind* (1939) and *Ivanhoe* (1952), and in the very idea that cultural
memory should be a feature of the lived environment.[55]

In retrospect the predictions of his admirers in 1832 that Scott's work
would be his own durable monument and that his fame would last a
thousand years were premature indeed. Having thematized cultural transience, he himself had become in part its victim. Forgotten perhaps, but
not gone.

Epilogue: Cultural Memory, Cultural Amnesia

> I do not know what meaning classical philology would have for our age if not to have an untimely effect within it.
>
> —Friedrich Nietzsche, *On the Advantage and Disadvantage of History for Life* (1874)

Old Mortality (1816) begins with a frame narrative about a man who used to be regularly spotted in the closing years of the eighteenth century in graveyards across the Lowlands of Scotland. Known as Old Mortality, this lonely figure travelled with his horse from one burial spot to the next with the aim of chiselling out afresh the inscriptions on the gravestones of the Presbyterians who had died in the civil wars that had torn apart Scotland in the seventeenth century:

Their tombs are often apart from all human habitation, in the remote moors and wilds to which the wanderers had fled for concealment. But wherever they existed, Old Mortality was sure to visit them when his annual round brought them within his reach. In the most lonely recesses of the mountains, the moor-fowl shooter has been often surprised to find him busied in cleaning the moss from the grey stones, renewing with his chisel the half-defaced inscriptions, and repairing the emblems of death with which these simple monuments are usually adorned. Motives of the most sincere, though fanciful devotion, induced the old man to dedicate so many years of existence to perform this tribute to the memory of the deceased warriors of the church. He considered himself as fulfilling a sacred duty, while renewing to the eyes of posterity the decaying emblems of the zeal and sufferings of their forefathers, and thereby trimming, as it were, the beacon-light which was to warn future generations to defend their religion even unto blood.[1]

Although he lent his name to Scott's novel, the figure of Old Mortality in fact only makes a very brief appearance in its opening pages. The prefatory story closes with the information that the old man had one day been found dying of exhaustion by the roadside and that, since then, the inscriptions on the gravestones had deteriorated: 'the monuments which were the

P. 4.

Figure Ep.1: *Old Mortality.* Drawing Frank Dodd; engraving J. D. Cooper. From Walter Scott, *Old Mortality*, The Dryburgh Edition of the Waverley Novels (London, 1893).

objects of his care are hastening, like all earthly memorials, into ruin or decay.'[2] Although his appearance is brief, the image of the lonely old man chiselling away at the inscriptions of those persecuted for their religious beliefs captures the imagination. Based as it is on the historical case of a certain Robert Paterson, it bears testimony again to Scott's extraordinary skill in spotting potential 'figures of memory'—Helen Walker/Jeanie Deans is another case in point—that stick in the mind. It is also a reminder of the complexity of Scott's narrative compositions and of his keen self-reflexivity as a memory-maker. Even today, he continues to provide readers not only with prosthetic images of a deeply materialized past, but also with imaginative resources for thinking about cultural memory and why it is important to identity. Thus the lonely figure of Old Mortality/Robert Paterson helps Scott's readers to think about collective remembrance in post-conflict societies by exemplifying the determination of minority groups to keep martyrdom and suffering alive as a warning and inspiration to future generations.[3]

As a meta-comment, the figure of Old Mortality is also a refraction of Scott's own role in taking up the baton where the old man left off. Where the latter had kept the memory of the Covenanters alive by chiselling out their names in stone, *Old Mortality* would offer an immaterial and eminently portable memorial in the form of a book in which the events at the close of the seventeenth century are imaginatively reconstructed. Once again, stone memorials and texts are variants of each other. As was his wont, moreover, Scott shaped the story that was to be passed on to future generations so as to smooth over the divisions of the past and mark a new beginning. If his account of the religious wars entered quite sympathetically into the viewpoint of the Covenanters, his interpretation of their struggle and its viability in the modern world was nevertheless ultimately at odds with the unquestioned devotion to their cause propounded by Old Mortality. In typical manner, Scott entered imaginatively into the mindset of the disempowered while nevertheless showing the inevitability of their being superseded by the forces of change; they were given a place in the present as part of memory rather than of contemporary reality. In this particular case, Scott was evoking the ghosts of a traumatic conflict that was still quite resonant at the time of writing, as the heated reactions to his novel demonstrated. Where Paterson/Old Mortality felt a 'sacred duty' to the memory of the Covenanters so that future generations would continue their struggle into the future with the 'zeal and sufferings of their forefathers' in mind, Scott's narrativized recollection of those events was instead an attempt to de-activate that charge precisely by evoking the Covenanters' cause as part of the *past*.[4]

Much more could be said about this novel in relation to contemporary discussions on trauma, memory, and post-conflict reconciliation with which it resonates in the post-World War II world where these issues have been at the heart of memory cultures. But at the close of this study, it is above all its status as quasi-monument that is of interest. As I have been arguing throughout this book, novels have a certain monumentality as well as a capacity to procreate: they enjoy longevity, stability, and normativity, and, either in their original version or in some derivative form, they link people to the past. But as the vignette of Old Mortality reminds us, memorials suffer from erosion and need to be continuously re-inscribed if they are to remain legible and, to the extent that texts resemble monuments, the same susceptibility to erosion applies. Despite Scott's having taken up the baton where the old man left off, the novel *Old Mortality* has largely ceased to be an active force in shaping collective remembrance in Scotland and, more generally, in the English-speaking world. To be sure, it persists intact and in pristine state as a 'monumental' text that has recently re-appeared with Edinburgh University Press in the latest collected edition of the Waverley novels.[5] But like its companion novels, Scott's *Old Mortality* no longer enjoys the same status and public profile that it did when it first appeared almost two centuries ago. It would appear that erosion and illegibility also affect literary works and not just moss-covered gravestones. So can they too be re-inscribed? And what is at stake in making them legible again?

REMEMBERING/FORGETTING

After several decades of research in the field of cultural memory it has become apparent that the key issue is not really how societies remember but how societies (learn to) forget. But is forgetting always the same thing? Is it always to be feared? Is it ever desirable? At the very beginning of this study, I referred to Andreas Huyssen's attribution of an intense fear of amnesia to the current preoccupation with memory in the academy and in public life. Echoing these concerns, Paul Connerton has referred recently to a 'systemic forgetting' within modernity.[6] Although forgetting has traditionally been seen in negative terms as something to be avoided at all costs, recent discussions have also started to explore it in its own right, as something that may be as complex, as multifarious, and as necessary as remembering. A glimpse of this was given earlier in my discussion of *The Heart of Mid-Lothian*.

The umbrella term 'forgetting' (along with related terms like amnesia and oblivion) in fact applies to a whole range of things: the repressive erasure of traces, benign neglect, overwriting by other priorities, self-imposed silence, mutation, obsolescence, and the particular form of obsolescence that Olick and Robbins refer to as 'inertia' whereby topics remain in the archives but have ceased to inform new acts of remembrance.[7] Behind this recent exploration of forgetting is the Nietzschean realization that it is neither possible nor desirable to remember everything and that to do so would be to become as paralysed as 'Funes the Memorious', the character in Jorge Luis Borges's story who is incapable of forgetting anything and hence is also incapable of living in the present or imagining a future.[8] Investigating amnesia as an active ingredient of memory-making is not just a matter of acknowledging its inevitability, therefore, but of scrutinizing how new futures can be shaped by the interplay between recollecting and leaving behind.

In this study we have seen the multiple ways in which Scott and his novels worked as agents of remembering. His stories about British and European history were just one part, albeit a key part, of a complex dynamic involving different media, multiple actors, and multiple locations. In the first chapter I discussed, with reference to *The Heart of Mid-Lothian*, the social life of the Waverley novels across time: on the one hand, their monumentality as unchanging texts that could be continuously reproduced in ever new material forms; on the other hand, their procreativity and 'portability' as stories that were carried over into different media and experiential domains, planted in new locations, and appropriated in different social frameworks and sometimes from opposed ideological positions. In later chapters I have shown this procreativity at work: in re-writings, in adaptations to paintings, the theatre, material culture, in transpositions to the theatre of politics, to museums and monuments, to commemorative ceremonies, to the practices of everyday life, and via a feedback mechanism, back into the reproduction of the original texts in the form of collective editions for family display. I have shown how the peculiar tension in Scott's work between a stabilizing narrativity and a de-stabilizing ambivalence served to generate an extraordinary mnemonic *energeia* that travelled like a tidal wave throughout nineteenth-century culture, gradually losing power in the process but with ripples that extended well into the twentieth century. Scott's cultural power arguably reached its high point in 1871 when direct and indirect knowledge of his works came together at a point when Literature was the primary resource for identity-constructions in the rapidly expanding English-speaking world. As such Walter Scott played a key role in linking the sphere of the cultural and the social, exemplifying the role of a specifically *cultural* memory, based on common appreciation of the arts, in articulating and conveying collective self-images within a broader transnational framework.

The marked decrease in interest in the original works in the twentieth century, outlined in the previous chapter, was due to the convergence of multiple factors, not least of them being the appearance of new writers and new media that drew attention away from the works of Scott and, in that sense, 'overwrote' his memory. But the erosion of his memory had also to do with the fact that Scott no longer fed into community-building as he had done in the nineteenth century when Confederate soldiers were remembered through re-enactments of *Ivanhoe*, when *Rob Roy* could provide a rallying cry for Scots, *Abbotsford* a port of call for Scots-Irish emigrants, and 'Sir Walter Scott' a point of common reference for those in the service of the British Empire. World War I brought about a shift of emphasis in public remembrance from celebration to mourning that was intensified after World War II and continues to the present time. In the shadow of two World Wars and the prevalence of what has been called a traumatic paradigm, the narrative of progress that fed into nineteenth-century celebratory remembrance lost much of its credibility and, with it, its ability to sustain collective identity. The idea put forward by Ernest Renan in 1882 that communal suffering in fact binds people more strongly than triumphs was borne out in the memorializing practices of the twentieth century.[9] The pride and confidence in cultural achievement and economic progress behind the centenary of 1871 was simply less congenial to the commemorations of the twentieth century. This meant that, even beyond questions of literary taste, Scott could no longer mobilize individuals and communities in the same way as he did a generation earlier. This gradual loss of collective purchase underlay the relegation of his works to the realm of the 'juvenile' that was discussed in the previous chapter.

By the time the bicentenary of 1971 came round, it was evident that Scott's memory no longer mobilized passions beyond those of intellectuals and heritage professionals. But then, how newsworthy was the bicentenary of Scott's birth as opposed to the news of his death in 1832 and his funeral, when all the shops in Edinburgh closed and all the ships in Glasgow harbour lowered their flags to half-mast? And how long could Scott have been expected to arouse passions in the twentieth century given his own description of himself, which was regularly echoed by others, as a consensual figure who had tried 'to unsettle no man's faith' and 'corrupt no man's principle'. Paradoxically, the case of Scott provides support for the idea that communal sites of memory can only survive in the long term if they feed into the preoccupations of later generations, that is, if something is at stake for the future in appropriating them in one way rather than another. The moral of the tale may well be that the public consensus about Scott's towering value generated indifference after the highpoint had been passed in 1871. At another level, Scott may himself have also helped the emergence of such indifference by working hard to smooth over the conflicts of history and turn them into objects of imaginative display rather than legacies to be passionately disputed. Turning the past into an imaginative comfort zone and a platform for romance was a way of containing its power to disrupt the present, but also deprived it of its power to inspire a changing world in the long term. It is all the more remarkable, then, that Scott did have a relatively long innings. This was thanks to the fact, as I have been arguing, that his works never offered straightforward comfort but were also fraught with ambivalence and ironies.

While this study shows how 'Walter Scott' or 'Waverley' lost their power as cultural icons and became instead icons of has-beens, it has also provided evidence for Scott's long-term cultural procreativity outside of any direct connection to his *oeuvre*. There is good reason to believe that Scott lives on in multifarious and unacknowledged ways as a component of contemporary culture, albeit no longer a dominant one and not easy to isolate from other influences. This applies to the importance of experientiality in museum practices as well as to the resurgence of historical fiction as a dominant genre in contemporary literature: novels as diverse as Vonnegut's *Slaughterhouse Five* (1969), Ismail Kadare's *Chronicle in Stone* (1971), Caryl Phillips' *The Nature of Blood* (1997), and W. G. Sebald's *Austerlitz* (2001) can all be seen as distant descendants of *Waverley*. It also applies to his resonance in the cinema, which should be seen as one of the successors to the nineteenth-century novel. The influence of Scott on Griffith's *Birth of a Nation* (1915) and his sinister offspring in the practices of the Ku Klux Klan has already been noted. But more generally, his influence can also be discerned in historical films from *Braveheart* (Mel Gibson, 1995) to Ken Loach's *The Wind that Shakes the Barley* (2006) and Andrzej Wajda's *Katyn* (2007).[10] Even less obviously, but more fundamentally, Scott's legacy can be detected in the by now generally accepted belief that collective identity is tied to a collective memory that can be experienced by individuals in an intimate and imaginative way. It also informs the general belief that representing troubled pasts is a way of exorcizing their ghosts and putting them to rest so that people can move on. It is very difficult of course to establish particular links with absolute certainty, but it has been one of the arguments of this book that Scott not only offered stories about the past, but created the memory habitus of several generations.

Whatever the importance of this indirect influence, it is undoubtedly true that the Waverley novels as such have lost much of their popularity and their prestige and the figure of 'Scott' no longer plays the same role in community-building as it did in the nineteenth century. His poetry has in effect disappeared from public view—there will be few people in the United States who still connect 'Hail to the Chief' with a poem from the beginning of the nineteenth century. His books are still there in libraries and book shops, although they occupy a less prominent position than they did almost two hundred years ago and have been joined by more recent writings and art forms that too demand attention. They are read by some amateurs and on university courses, but no longer by the educated public at large. In short: Scott's works are extant and an established part of what Aleida Assmann has called 'archival memory'.[11] But having become largely 'illegible' to the common reader, they no longer generate the same cultural energy they did when they first appeared.

In a recent article, Ann Stoler has used the concept of 'aphasia' as an alternative to 'forgetting' to describe those situations where information about the past is available but we have lost the ability to make sense of it. Stoler discusses aphasia with respect to the collective remembrance of colonialism. But her basic point also applies to books from another period that are still available, but have simply lost their capacity to be meaningful.[12] They are culturally speaking inert. Stoler's idea of 'aphasia' seems particularly applicable to the fate of literary works that were once enormously popular but whose fascination most non-professionals can no longer imagine. Is this reversible?

PHILOLOGY AS COUNTER-AMNESIAC

With the fading of Scott's public role since 1932, custodianship of his memory passed into the hand of professionals, which brings us back to literary criticism, or more specifically to philology, as a distinct factor in the dynamics of cultural memory. In outlining Scott's afterlife, I have generally gone with the flow of cultural history, tracing the transpositions and transformations of the memory of his work across several generations, tracing too the rise and fading of his role as a figure of memory to the point where he was 'forgotten, but not gone', to recall Carswell's phrase. But philology represents a potential counter-force to the dynamics I have been describing, and a potential remedy to aphasia. I use 'philology' here in preference to 'criticism' to indicate an engagement with literary texts that is historically informed and, as such, a reflexive intervention in cultural memory rather than merely a purveyor of an ahistorical aesthetic judgement or philosophical insight. Like Old Mortality, philologists can 're-inscribe' books so that they become readable—in the sense of worth reading—again. Within the dynamics of cultural memory, philology is potentially a counter-amnesiac force that works against the erosions brought about by cultural change and helps re-awaken the interest of the next generation. It does so both by elucidating obscure passages and, to recall the words of Gumbrecht, by generating complexity where there seemed to be none. It roughens up surfaces that had been worn smooth by over-exposure or indifference so as to make old texts readable again, both followable and fascinating.

This is not the place to give a detailed account of twentieth-century academic criticism of Scott as it emerged from the 1930s onwards. As we have seen in the previous chapter, Scott's place in the critical canon has fluctuated. Given the different priorities within modernist writings and the rhetoric of radical renewal that characterized their interest in psychological complexity, it was only in the past decades that an interpretive framework could re-emerge in which Scott's work made sense again, in new ways taking into account both their aesthetic and their historical character. Following the translation of Lukács' influential work in the early sixties, his social and historical perspective on Scott's characters has proven very fruitful as an interpretative approach even as the emphasis has shifted from the issue of class struggle, so central to Lukács' reading, to the postcolonial and post-imperial perspectives offered by more recent critics on whose work I myself have drawn in previous chapters along with recent work in memory studies.[13] Working against the erosion of Scott's work and its reduction to the juvenile, recent critics have shown how Scott's work was a highly creative attempt to deal with the complexities and contradictions within modern society, and with the possibilities and limits of historical representation and romance in relation to deeply divided pasts. At its best, such criticism shows (in the first instance, to other critics) that works written two hundred years ago still belong to the present because they deal with issues that continue to challenge us today.

As I indicated earlier, the custodianship of Scott's memory has passed into the hands of professionals who generally write for each other. But they also teach, and teaching too is a counter-amnesiac force and an active intervention in cultural memory. Indeed, as we have seen in the previous chapter, shaping the next generation has been a key feature of the dynamics of remembering Scott since his death in 1832. A recent collection of essays suggests that getting students involved in Scott's novels at the present time poses particular didactic challenges: because of their length, extensive descriptions, and relative lack of pace, because of the need to know a lot of historical background, and because the extensive use of dialect makes them, in a more literal way, simply illegible. Where readers almost two centuries ago had apparently no problem, present-day readers need help in being able to make sense of Scott's stories. The essays in *Approaches to Teaching Scott's Waverley Novels* (2009) provide many inspired suggestions for bridging the gap between young readers today and Scott's novels. These include showing his covert influence on recent movies and other works of fiction, reading aloud passages in dialect, and, above all, exploring the novels from the perspective of their relevance to such contemporary concerns as multiculturalism, transnationality, colonialism, gender, civil war, and the politics of reconciliation.[14] If successful, both criticism and pedagogy can work together against cultural amnesia by making old writings 'legible' to the next generation and by showing that they provide imaginative resources for thinking about contemporary concerns and yet, as importantly, remain tantalizingly fraught with the alterity that comes from historical and cultural distance.

Lest we forget. Like Old Mortality many a teacher feels it to be a 'sacred duty'—or to use Pierre Nora's more recent term, a *mémoire-devoir*[15]—to recollect works from the past and, by broadening the historical horizons of their students, to give them new conceptual and imaginative tools with which to think critically about their own age and where it is heading. And this duty remains as an ideal, even as the most enthusiastic of the contributors to the MLA collection, and the most committed of teachers, must admit that, in the case of Scott, the most they can hope for is to pass on an interest in a very select number of works from his enormous *oeuvre*.

Philological counter-amnesia has a special role to play in contemporary cultures when it comes to teaching and to the transfer of historically imaginative reading skills to new generations. Its potential importance, although not necessarily its actual effectiveness, has arguably grown in what has been called our age of amnesia. But although Scott's *oeuvre* is indestructible as long as there are archives around, some cultural changes are irrevocable, and there is no taking from the fact that Scott and his work will never again occupy the central place they did in the nineteenth century. Many other interesting narratives have been produced in the past two hundred years that also deserve attention and there are aspects of Scott's world, including his optimism, that are (still) too outdated to speak to the present generation and help meet the challenges of dealing with our world. Above all his role has changed because literature itself is no longer the source of collective identity and the focus of cultural values that it was three generations ago when the Abbotsford editions of the collected works graced parlours and school libraries. But why be nostalgic?

In considering the cultural afterlife of Scott, one is torn between a sense of disappointment—that his cultural importance and the excitement generated by his work should have been so short-lived—and amazement: at the scale of its importance, the fact that it did indeed last for three generations, and that it created all sorts of cultural continuities that link us to the beginning of the nineteenth century and beyond. In the end, it is the amazement that prevails. Scott's most durable legacy may be precisely in teaching us the necessity of having to let go in order to go ahead: the awareness of the need for both memory and the need to accept its mutability in a world that continues to change.

Notes

INTRODUCTION

1. Information regarding the towns called Waverley was compiled from the following sources: Saul B. Cohen (ed.), *The Columbia Gazetteer of the World* (New York: Columbia University Press, 1952); *The Times Comprehensive Atlas of the World*, 10th edn (London: Times Books, 1999); *The Times World Index-Gazetteer* (London: Times Publishing, 1966). Information regarding districts, streets, and other public venues was gleaned in addition from Internet searches.
2. Stuart Kelly, *Scott-Land: The Man Who Invented a Nation* (Edinburgh: Polygon, 2010). Kelly's work, which appeared as this book was nearing completion, originated as a series of radio broadcasts and offers a series of brief, personalized reflections on 'Scott' as a cultural phenomenon, particularly in relation to Scotland.
3. For general background see Stephen Bann, *The Clothing of Clio: A Study of the Representation of History in Nineteenth-Century Britain and France* (Cambridge: Cambridge University Press, 1984); Stephen Bann (ed.), *Romanticism and the Rise of History* (Twayne: University of Nebraska Press, 1995). Specifically on the cultivation of heritage and the historical imagination as one of the lynchpins of nationalism: Joep Leerssen, *National Thought in Europe: A Cultural History* (Amsterdam: Amsterdam University Press, 2006); Joep Leerssen, 'Nationalism and the Cultivation of Culture', *Nations and Nationalism* 12 (2006). For a more detailed exploration of Scott's influence on historiography, see further Ann Rigney, *Imperfect Histories: The Elusive Past and the Legacy of Romantic Historicism* (Ithaca, NY: Cornell University Press, 2001).
4. Walter Scott, *Waverley*, ed. Andrew Hook (London: Penguin, 1972), 34.
5. Recent scholarship has shown that there were in fact several precedents, including ones for the name Waverley itself: the name did in fact have a precedent in the ruined (though not particularly famous) Waverley Abbey in Surrey. On generic precedents, see esp. Ina Ferris, *The Achievement of Literary Authority: Gender, History, and the Waverley Novels* (Ithaca, NY: Cornell University Press, 1991). On earlier literary uses of the name 'Waverley', see Katie Trumpener, *Bardic Nationalism: The Romantic Novel and the British Empire* (Princeton, NJ: Princeton University Press, 1997), 139–40.
6. See Chapter 6 for a more detailed discussion of Scott's authorial strategies and relevant sources.
7. William St Clair, *The Reading Nation in the Romantic Period* (Cambridge: Cambridge University Press, 2004).
8. In a letter dated 3 August 1818, Archibald Constable complained that his opinion 'is of little consequence, as the public seems quite crazy for the novels of this author'; Thomas Constable, *Archibald Constable and his Literary*

Correspondents, 3 vols (Edinburgh: Edmonston & Douglas, 1873), II: 97; quoted in http://www.british-fiction.cf.ac.uk/.

9. Ian Duncan, *Modern Romance and Transformations of the Novel: The Gothic, Scott, Dickens* (Cambridge: Cambridge University Press, 1992), 178, 80.

10. From the 1860s on, Scott's poetry was part of the elementary school curricula and his work also figured in Civil Service examinations in Britain; Richard D. Altick, *The English Common Reader: A Social History of the Mass Reading Public, 1800–1900* (Chicago: University of Chicago Press, 1957), 160, 83–4.

11. St Clair, *The Reading Nation in the Romantic Period*, 427. For a fuller discussion of Mark Twain's accusations in the direction of Scott, see Chapter 4 below.

12. John Henry Raleigh, 'What Scott Meant to the Victorians' (1963), in Harry E. Shaw (ed.), *Critical Essays on Sir Walter Scott: The Waverley Novels* (New York: G. K. Hall, 1996), 49.

13. Peter Fritzsche, *Stranded in the Present: Modern Time and the Melancholy of History* (Cambridge, MA: Harvard University Press, 2004). See also Richard Terdiman, *Present Past: Modernity and the Memory Crisis* (Ithaca, NY: Cornell University Press, 1993).

14. Pierre Nora, 'Entre mémoire et histoire: la problématique des lieux', in Pierre Nora (ed.), *Les lieux de mémoire*, 3 vols (Paris: Gallimard, 1997), I: xvii–xlii.

15. Andreas Huyssen, 'Present Pasts: Media, Politics, Amnesia', *Public Culture* 12 (2000), 31. See also Andreas Huyssen, *Twilight Memories: Marking Time in a Culture of Amnesia* (New York: Routledge, 1995).

16. The most thorough-going readings of Scott's work as a response to modernization can be found in Ian Duncan, *Scott's Shadow: The Novel in Romantic Edinburgh* (Princeton, NJ: Princeton University Press, 2007), 96–115; Andrew Lincoln, *Walter Scott and Modernity* (Edinburgh: Edinburgh University Press, 2007). For other important contextualizations, see esp. Bann (ed.), *Romanticism and the Rise of History*; James Chandler, *England in 1819: The Politics of Literary Culture and the Case of Romantic Historicism* (Chicago: University of Chicago Press, 1998); Duncan, *Modern Romance*; Richard Maxwell, *The Historical Novel in Europe, 1650–1950* (Cambridge: Cambridge University Press, 2009), 9–112. On Scott's elaboration of Scottish identity against the background of his own time and its continued resonance in the discourses of Scottish politics, see Caroline McCracken-Flesher, *Possible Scotlands: Walter Scott and the Story of Tomorrow* (Oxford: Oxford University Press, 2005).

17. Alison Landsberg, *Prosthetic Memory: The Transformation of American Remembrance in the Age of Mass Culture* (New York: Columbia University Press, 2004). The term 'imagined memory', meaning memory not grounded in lived experience, is borrowed here from Huyssen, 'Present Pasts: Media, Politics, Amnesia', 27.

18. The most extensive and most explicit treatment of the dynamics of cultural remembrance to date remains Jeffrey K. Olick and Joyce Robbins, 'Social

Memory Studies: From "Collective Memory" to the Historical Sociology of Mnemonic Practices', *Annual Review of Sociology* 24 (1998). See also Jeffrey K. Olick, *The Politics of Regret: On Collective Memory and Historical Responsibility* (London: Routledge, 2007), 175–92; Jeffrey K. Olick (ed.), *States of Memory: Continuities, Conflicts, and Transformations in National Retrospection* (Durham, NC: Duke University Press, 2003); Susannah Radstone and Kate Hodgkin (eds), *Contested Pasts: The Politics of Memory* (London: Routledge, 2003).

19. Huyssen, 'Present Pasts: Media, Politics, Amnesia', 31.

20. Virginia Woolf, *To the Lighthouse* (London: Penguin, 1989 [1927]).

21. Bertrand Russell, *Introduction to Mathematical Philosophy* (London: Routledge, 1996 [1919]), 178. With thanks to Albert Visser for this example.

22. Murray Pittock (ed.), *The Reception of Sir Walter Scott in Europe* (London: Continuum, 2007). Indicating the growth of interest in reception studies, see also Anika Bautz' recent comparative study of the long-term reception of Jane Austen and Walter Scott. This study traces through publication figures and a selection of critical responses the opposing trajectories the two writers have followed: Scott from fame to relative neglect, Austen the other way around; Annika Bautz, *The Reception of Jane Austen and Walter Scott: A Comparative Longitudinal Study* (London: Continuum, 2007). An early study is confined to his influence on other writers: J. H. Alexander and David Hewitt (eds), *Scott and His Influence: The Papers of the Aberdeen Scott Conference, 1982* (Aberdeen: Assn for Scottish Lit. Studies, 1983).

23. Arjun Appadurai, *Modernity at Large: Cultural Dimensions of Globalization* (Minneapolis: University of Minnesota Press, 1996), 4.

24. Ferdinand de Saussure, *Cours de linguistique générale* (Paris: Payot, 1995 [1916]).

25. By including the impact of relations to texts on social relations, my 'social life of texts' is also inspired by Arjun Appadurai (ed.), *The Social Life of Things: Commodities in Cultural Perspective* (Cambridge: Cambridge University Press, 1986). One of the rare examples of such a longitudinal study is provided in Isabel Hofmeyr, *The Portable Bunyan: A Transnational History of* The Pilgrim's Progress (Princeton, NJ: Princeton University Press, 2004).

26. My use of the term methodological nationalism, and the variant methodological textualism, is based on Andreas Wimmer and Nina Glick Schiller, 'Methodological Nationalism and Beyond: Nation-State Building, Migration and the Social Sciences', *Global Networks* 2 (2002).

27. My view of cultural dynamics in terms of the circulation of energy is broadly inspired by Stephen Greenblatt, *Shakespearean Negotiations: The Circulation of Social Energy in Renaissance England* (Oxford: Clarendon Press, 1988). Greenblatt's work draws on Warburg's highly suggestive, but notoriously diffuse theory of cultural reproduction; see Aby Warburg, *Der Bilderatlas Mnemosyne*, ed. Martin Warnke (Berlin: Akademie Verlag, 2000 [1924–9]). For background, see Philippe-Alain Michaud, *Aby Warburg and the Image in*

Motion, trans. Sophie Hawkes (New York: Zone Books, 2004 [1998]), 67–93.

28. My use of reception as 'appropriation' is inspired by Michel de Certeau, *The Practice of Everyday Life*, trans. Steven Rendall (Berkeley: University of California Press, 1988 [1980]).

29. Ibid.

30. According to Assmann memory is concretized (made representable) by being tied to specific figures of memory; Jan Assmann, *Das kulturelle Gedächtnis: Schrift, Erinnerung und politische Identität in frühen Hochkulturen* (München: C. H. Beck, 1997 [1992]), 37–8.

31. Sir Walter Scott, *The Lady of the Lake* (Milton Keynes: Dodo Press, n.d. [1810]); Sir Walter Scott, *The Talisman* (Milton Keynes: Dodo Press, n.d. [1825]).

32. St Clair, *The Reading Nation in the Romantic Period*, 430.

CHAPTER 1

1. The Internet has proved an invaluable resource in locating all of these Jeanie Deans; for the four-master ship, see http://ist.uwaterloo.ca/~marj/genealogy/ships/ships1843.html; for the potato, presented at Burnley Horticultural Gardens in 1986, Redcliffe N. Salaman, *The History and Social Influence of the Potato* (Cambridge: Cambridge University Press, 1985 [1949]), 168; for the rose, cultivated by Lord Penzance in 1896, http://www.rosegathering.com/penzance.html; for the hospital unit, opened as recently as 1998, http://www.helensburgh.info/Community_Info/Health_Services/health_services.html.
There is an extensive literature on Jeanie Deans the paddle steamer and Jeanie Deans the locomotive; for example, O. S. Nock, *Great Locomotives of the L.N.E.R.* (Wellingborough, North Hampshire: Patrick Stephens, 1988), 260; Fraser G. MacHaffie, *Jeanie Deans 1931–1967: An Illustrated Biography* (Coatbridge: Jeanie Deans Publications, 1977). Jeanie Deans the lounge-bar figured on board the paddle-steamer *Waverley*; see Fraser G. MacHaffie, *Waverley: The Story of the Last Seagoing Paddle-Steamer in the World*, 4th edn (Glasgow: Waverley Excursions, 1982), 181.

2. On Scott's inauguration of the 'heroic age of the literary character', and his creation of a secular pantheon of fictional characters that was 'produced by history yet transcending and incorporating it, to form a living tradition reaching back to Shakespeare and Chaucer', see Ian Duncan, *Modern Romance and Transformations of the Novel: The Gothic, Scott, Dickens* (Cambridge: Cambridge University Press, 1992), 181.

3. My use of the term 'stickiness' is inspired by the discussion of how ideas 'stick' in Malcolm Gladwell, *The Tipping Point: How Little Things Can Make a Big Difference* (New York: Little, Brown, 2000).

4. An excellent survey of basic issues and discussions is provided in Jeffrey K. Olick and Joyce Robbins, 'Social Memory Studies: From "Collective Memory" to the Historical Sociology of Mnemonic Practices', *Annual Review of Sociology*

24 (1998). Overviews of current debates can be found in Astrid Erll and Ansgar Nünning (eds), *Cultural Memory Studies: An International and Interdisciplinary Handbook* (Berlin: de Gruyter, 2008); Jeffrey K. Olick et al. (eds), *The Collective Memory Reader* (New York: Oxford University Press, 2011); Susannah Radstone and Bill Schwarz (eds), *Memory: Histories, Theories, Debates* (New York: Fordham University Press, 2010).

5. For historical surveys of shifts in memory practices, see among other works, Philippe Ariès, *L'homme devant la mort*, 2 vols (Paris: Seuil, 1977); Mary Carruthers, *The Book of Memory: A Study of Memory in Medieval Culture* (Cambridge: Cambridge University Press, 1990); Peter Fritzsche, *Stranded in the Present: Modern Time and the Melancholy of History* (Cambridge, MA: Harvard University Press, 2004); Patrick J. Geary, *Phantoms of Remembrance: Memory and Oblivion at the End of the First Millennium* (Princeton, NJ: Princeton University Press, 1994); Patrick H. Hutton, *History as an Art of Memory* (Hanover, NH: University Press of New England, 1993), 91–105.

6. Paul Connerton, *How Societies Remember* (Cambridge: Cambridge University Press, 1989), 39. My conceptualization of cultural memory is especially indebted to the social-constructivist accounts offered in Aleida Assmann, *Erinnerungsräume: Formen und Wandlungen des kulturellen Gedächtnisses* (München: C. H. Beck, 1999), 133–45; Jan Assmann, *Das kulturelle Gedächtnis: Schrift, Erinnerung und politische Identität in frühen Hochkulturen* (München: C. H. Beck, 1997 [1992]); Astrid Erll, *Kollektives Gedächtnis und Erinnerungskulturen* (Stuttgart: Metzler, 2005).

7. Maurice Halbwachs, *La mémoire collective* (Paris: Albin Michel, 1997 [1950]); Maurice Halbwachs, *Les cadres sociaux de la mémoire* (Paris: Albin Michel, 1994 [1925]).

8. Benedict Anderson, *Imagined Communities: Reflections on the Origins and Spread of Nationalism* (London: Verso, 1991 [1983]). The concept of 'mnemonic community' is taken from Eviatar Zerubavel, 'Calendars and History: A Comparative Study of the Social Organization of National Memory', in Jeffrey K. Olick (ed.), *States of Memory: Continuities, Conflicts, and Transformations in National Retrospection* (Durham, NC: Duke University Press, 2003). See also Eviatar Zerubavel, *Time Maps: Collective Memory and the Social Shape of the Past* (Chicago: University of Chicago Press, 2003).

9. Pierre Nora, 'Entre mémoire et histoire: la problématique des lieux', in Pierre Nora (ed.), *Les lieux de mémoire*, 3 vols (Paris: Gallimard, 1997), I: 38. For a further elaboration of Nora's concept of memory site that emphasizes its generative power, see further Ann Rigney, 'Plenitude, Scarcity and the Circulation of Cultural Memory', *Journal of European Studies* 35 (2005).

10. Jan Assmann, 'Collective Memory and Cultural Identity', *New German Critique* 65 (1995), 132.

11. Rigney, 'Plenitude, Scarcity and the Circulation of Cultural Memory'.

12. A preliminary discussion of the interplay between the social and the cultural dynamics of memory can be found in Ann Rigney, 'Divided Pasts: A

Premature Memorial and the Dynamics of Collective Remembrance', *Memory Studies* 1 (2007).

13. For the growing literature on forgetting, see the Epilogue, n.7.

14. Contemporary variations on the historical novel are discussed in Amy J. Elias, *Sublime Desire: History and Post-1960s Fiction* (Baltimore, MD: Johns Hopkins University Press, 2002); Linda Hutcheon, *A Poetics of Postmodernism: History, Theory, Fiction* (London: Routledge, 1988). The idea that literature has a structural role to play in meta-reflection on collective memory is taken from Erll, *Kollektives Gedächtnis*, 165–6; Astrid Erll, *Prämediation–Remediation: Der indische Aufstand in imperialen und post-kolonialen Medienkulturen (1857 bis zur Gegenwart)* (Trier: WVT, 2007).

15. For discussions of literature as a medium for the expression of personal memories of traumatic collective events, see among many others Cathy Caruth, *Unclaimed Experience: Trauma, Narrative, and History* (Baltimore, MD: Johns Hopkins University Press, 1996); Shoshana Felman and Dori Laub, *Testimony: Crises of Witnessing in Literature, Psychoanalysis, and History* (London: Routledge, 1992); Lawrence L. Langer, *The Holocaust and the Literary Imagination* (New Haven, CT: Yale University Press, 1985).

16. An initial survey of the multiple roles played by literature in the production of cultural memory is given in Ann Rigney, 'The Dynamics of Remembrance: Texts between Monumentality and Morphing', in Astrid Erll et al. (eds), *Cultural Memory Studies: An International and Interdisciplinary Handbook* (Berlin/New York: De Gruyter, 2008).

17. Reginald Heber, DD, Lord Bishop of Calcutta, *Narrative of a Journey through the Upper Provinces of India, from Calcutta to Bombay, 1824–1825 (with notes upon Ceylon)*, ed. Amelia Heber (London: John Murray, 1828), I: 189. Quoted in Nigel Leask, *Curiosity and the Aesthetics of Travel Writing, 1770–1840* (Oxford: Oxford University Press, 2002), 191n.

18. H. Heine, quoted in Assmann, *Erinnerungsräume*, 306. In his study of German literary culture during World War I, Wolfgang Natter provides a fascinating discussion of the way in which the production of paperback editions of canonical works was linked to the notion that literature was a form of portable heritage; Wolfgang Natter, *Literature at War, 1914–1940: Representing the 'Time of Greatness' in Germany* (New Haven, CT: Yale University Press, 1999).

19. The Corson collection at Edinburgh University Library includes amongst its 'realia' a cassette with the complete Waverley novels in miniaturized form, designed for those moving to holiday residences; with thanks to Paul Barnaby. The multi-volume Abbotsford Miscellany, published by A&C Black in 1855, was advertised as 'Tales for Travellers'; see Nicola J. Watson, 'Scott's Afterlives', in Fiona Robertson (ed.), *The Edinburgh Companion to Sir Walter Scott* (Edinburgh: Edinburgh University Press, 2012).

20. David Hewitt and Alison Lumsden (eds), *The Heart of Mid-Lothian*, Edinburgh Edition of the Waverley Novels (Edinburgh: Edinburgh University Press, 2004), 474.

21. Duncan, *Modern Romance*, 110.

22. On the transition between 'communicative' and 'cultural' memory, see Assmann, *Das kulturelle Gedächtnis*, 48–66; Erll, *Kollektives Gedächtnis*, 27–9. Marianne Hirsch has also proposed the term 'post-memory' to designate the transition from first-hand accounts to inherited memories; Marianne Hirsch, *Family Frames: Photography, Narrative, and Postmemory* (Cambridge, MA: Harvard University Press, 1997).

23. Catherine Jones, *Literary Memory: Scott's Waverley Novels and the Psychology of Narrative* (London: Associated University Presses, 2003).

24. The gravestone is described in W. S. Crockett, *The Scott Country*, 5th edn (London: A&C Black, 1920 [1905]); W. S. Crockett, *The Scott Originals: An Account of Notables and Worthies; the Originals of Characters in the Waverley Novels* (London: T. N. Foulis, 1912), 234–8. See also Ann Rigney, *Imperfect Histories: The Elusive Past and the Legacy of Romantic Historicism* (Ithaca, NY: Cornell University Press, 2001), 13–58.

25. Mrs Goldie, quoted in Sir Walter Scott, *The Heart of Midlothian*, ed. Claire Lamont (Oxford: Oxford University Press, 1982 [1818]), 5. Unless stated otherwise, further references to the novel will be to this edition, which includes the supplementary material added by Scott to the 1830 edition.

26. Edgar Johnson, *Sir Walter Scott: The Great Unknown*, 2 vols (London: Hamilton, 1970), II: 1128.

27. On Scott's use of the available sources, see Hewitt and Lumsden (eds), *The Heart of Mid-Lothian*, 588–92.

28. John McDiarmid, *Sketches from Nature* (Edinburgh: Oliver Boyd, 1830). 'Her sister was tried, condemned, and sentenced to be executed at the termination of the usual period of six weeks. The result is well known, and is truly as well as powerfully set forth in the novel' (p. 385). More information relating to the novel's sources can be found in Crockett, *The Scott Originals*, 588–92; Hewitt and Lumsden (eds), *The Heart of Mid-Lothian*; Mary Lascelles, *The Story-teller Retrieves the Past: Historical Fiction and Fictitious History in the Art of Scott, Stevenson, Kipling, and Some Others* (Oxford: Clarendon Press, 1980), 88–102. The most recent account of Helen Walker's life is by Deborah Symonds, who offers the rather implausible suggestion that the old woman whom Mrs Goldie had met was Isobel rather than Helen; Deborah A. Symonds, *Weep not for Me: Women, Ballads, and Infanticide in Early Modern Scotland* (University Park: Pennsylvania State University Press, 1997), 199.

29. On the possible influence of Sophie Cottin's *Elizabeth; or, the Exiles of Siberia* (English translation, 1807), see Peter D. Garside, 'Walter Scott and the "Common" Novel, 1808–1819', *Cardiff Corvey: Reading the Romantic Text* 3 (1999). Certainly the link between the two stories was already made by Charlotte Yonge in 1864 when she narrated as parallel acts of heroism the

story of Helen Walker (again her account is closely modelled on Scott's Jeanie Deans) and the story of Prascovia Lopouloff, the prototype for Cottin's novel; Charlotte Yonge, *A Book of Golden Deeds of All Times and All Lands, Gathered and Narrated by the Author of the 'Heir of Radcliffe'* (London: Macmillan, 1864). In turn Scott's novel seems to have inspired other 'recollections' of heroines-going-in-quest of royal pardons, from Alexander Pushkin's fictional *Captain's Daughter* (1836) to the historical Mrs Campbell whose unsuccessful attempts to gain a pardon for her husband in 1808 were remembered in a recent issue of *The Scott Newsletter* under the title 'Another Jeanie' (1996).

30. The concept of premediation is used here, following Erll, to mean the way earlier narratives inform later ones; Erll, *Prämediation–Remediation*.

31. Francis Cairns, 'Orality, Writing, and Reoralisation: Some Departures and Arrivals in Homer and Apollonius Rhodius', in H. L. C. Tristram (ed.), *New Methods in the Research of Epic [Neue Methoden der Epenforschung]* (Tübingen: Narr, 1998).

32. Regarding the interpenetration of oral and print cultures at this period, see further Penny Fielding, *Writing and Orality: Nationality, Culture, and Nineteenth-Century Scottish Fiction* (Oxford: Oxford University Press, 1996), 22–48.

33. The coincidence between the writing of *The Heart of Mid-Lothian* and the reactions to *Old Mortality* is noted in Hewitt and Lumsden (eds), *The Heart of Mid-Lothian*, 473, 85. The controversy surrounding *Old Mortality* was first analysed extensively from the point of view of generic expectations in Ina Ferris, *The Achievement of Literary Authority: Gender, History, and the Waverley Novels* (Ithaca, NY: Cornell University Press, 1991), 137–60. A supplementary analysis from a historiographical perspective is offered in Rigney, *Imperfect Histories*, 45–53. In that study I argue that Scott's novel, to the extent that it was seen as history, provoked other people into writing counter-histories; *The Heart of Mid-Lothian* was part of the same ongoing colloquy about the interpretation of Scottish history of the seventeenth century. On the continuity in concerns between the two novels, see also Andrew Lincoln, *Walter Scott and Modernity* (Edinburgh: Edinburgh University Press, 2007), 156–83.

34. Scott's ambivalent relationship to popular novel forms is well described in Ferris, *The Achievement of Literary Authority*, and Fiona Robertson, *Legitimate Histories: Scott, Gothic, and the Authorities of Fiction* (Oxford: Clarendon Press, 1994).

35. Elsewhere I have examined in greater detail Scott's correspondence with his readers: Rigney, *Imperfect Histories*, 31–58.

36. Anderson, *Imagined Communities*; Jonathan Culler, 'Anderson and the Novel', *Diacritics* 29 (1999). My interpretation of the novel's role in community-building is also inspired by Patricia Meyer Spacks' linking the genre to the most traditional form of social networking—gossip: Patricia Meyer-Spacks, *Gossip* (Chicago: University of Chicago Press, 1985).

37. Victor Hugo: 'L'historien des moeurs et des idées n'a pas une mission moins austère que l'historien des événements. Celui-ci a la surface de la civilisation, les luttes des couronnes, les naissances des princes, les mariages des rois, les batailles, les assemblées, les grands hommes publics, les révolutions au soleil, tout le dehors; l'autre historien a l'intérieur, le fond, le peuple qui travaille, qui souffre et qui attend, la femme accablée, l'enfant qui agonise, les guerres sourdes d'homme à homme [. . .] toutes les larves qui errent dans l'obscurité'; Victor Hugo, *Les misérables*, 4 vols (Paris: Nelson, n.d. [1862]), III: 282. More on the influence of novelists on the agenda of historians in Rigney, *Imperfect Histories*, 59–98. Recent research has made clear that Scott was also appropriating for his own purposes an emerging female literary tradition, which he subsequently upstaged; see esp. Ferris, *The Achievement of Literary Authority*; Ina Ferris, 'Writing on the Border: The National Tale, Female Writing, and the Public Sphere', in Tilottama Rajan et al. (eds), *Romanticism, History, and the Possibilities of Genre: Re-forming Literature 1789–1837* (Cambridge: Cambridge University Press, 1998); Robertson, *Legitimate Histories*.

38. Geoffrey H. Hartman, 'Public Memory and its Discontents', in Marshall Brown (ed.), *The Uses of Literary History* (Durham, NC: Duke University Press, 1995), 80.

39. The idea of a principle of scarcity is drawn from Michel Foucault, *L'archéologie du savoir* (Paris: Gallimard, 1969), 156. For a more elaborated version of this argument in relation to remembrance, see Rigney, 'Plenitude, Scarcity'.

40. Jane Austen, *The Novels*, ed. R. W. Chapman, 5 vols (London: Oxford University Press, 1923), V: 108.

41. Scott's reworking of different stories and discourses (particularly legal ones) in his fiction reinforces Mikhail Bakhtin's well-known argument regarding the fundamentally 'heteroglossic' character of novels; M. M. Bakhtin, 'Discourse in the Novel', in *The Dialogic Imagination*, ed. Michael Holquist (Austin: University of Texas Press, 1981). In the playful preface to *The Heart of Mid-Lothian* Scott has one of his characters sing the praises of the Scottish judiciary as a source of novelistic stories; Scott, *The Heart of Mid-lothian*, 19–23. More generally, on the connection between public trials and novels, see Sarah Maza, *Private Lives and Public Affairs: The Causes Célèbres of Prerevolutionary France* (Berkeley: University of California Press, 1993). Since the beginning of the nineteenth century not only has the novel changed status and film emerged as a new medium, but historians have been changing their priorities in ways that inevitably have a knock-on effect on what's 'left over' for novelists and film-makers; see further Ann Rigney, 'Fiction as a Mediator in National Remembrance', in Stefan Berger et al. (eds), *Narrating the Nation: The Representation of National Narratives in Different Genres* (Oxford: Berghahn Books, 2009).

42. James Colston, *History of the Scott Monument, Edinburgh; To which is prefixed a biographical sketch of Sir Walter Scott, Bart.* (Edinburgh: Printed for the Magistrates and Town Council, 1881), 101.

43. For discussions of the mobility of Scott's characters, see further Chapter 5, n. 6–7.

44. This point builds on my earlier discussion in Rigney, *Imperfect Histories*, 31–58.

45. Anon. *Tales of My Landlord, Second Series. Blackwood's Edinburgh Magazine*, August (1818): 569. See also Judith Wilt, *Secret Leaves: The Novels of Walter Scott* (Chicago: University of Chicago Press, 1985), 130.

46. On Scott's complicated relationship to the Jacobite tradition and the political context of his depiction of Culloden see esp. Murray G. H. Pittock, *The Invention of Scotland: The Stuart Myth and the Scottish Identity, 1638 to the Present* (London: Routledge, 1991), 73–98; *The Myth of the Jacobite Clans: The Jacobite Army in 1745*, 2nd edn (Edinburgh: Edinburgh University Press, 2009).

47. This summary of events is based on *Criminal Trials, Illustrative of the Tale Entitled 'The Heart of Midlothian,' Published from the Original Record: with a Prefatory Notice, Including Some Particulars of the Life of Captain Porteous* (Edinburgh: Archibald Constable, 1818); Hewitt and Lumsden (eds), *The Heart of Mid-Lothian*, 585–8; William Roughead (ed.), *Trial of Captain Porteous* (Glasgow: William Hodge, 1909). Scott came back to the Porteous affair in his *Tales of a Grandfather* (1828–31), where he described it as a 'strong and powerful display of the cool, stern, and resolved manner in which the Scottish, even of the lower classes, can concert and execute a vindictive purpose'; quoted in Scott, *The Heart of Midlothian*, 10. Scott's treatment of the Porteous riots has also been read as symptomatic of a more general unease, one year in advance of Peterloo, with potential social unrest and popular protests; Ian Duncan, 'Primitive Inventions: *Rob Roy*, Nation, and World System', *Eighteenth Century Fiction* 15(1) (2002), 165–6. For general background, see also James Chandler, *England in 1819: The Politics of Literary Culture and the Case of Romantic Historicism* (Chicago: University of Chicago Press, 1998), 309–20.

48. On the orderliness of Scott's version of events, see Hewitt and Lumsden (eds), *The Heart of Mid-Lothian*, 587.

49. The article called 'Remarks on the Tumult at Edinburgh, Commonly Called the Porteous Mob' appeared in the *Edinburgh Magazine and Literary Miscelleny* in June 1818; cited ibid. 483.

50. 'Between the eventful years of 1715 and 1745 the affair of the Porteous Mob forms a memorable and striking chapter in the history of Scotland. That few incidents of that history are more familiar to modern readers is due to the genius of Sir Walter Scott, who, with an artist's appreciation of its romantic value, has made it the basis of one of his happiest tales' (Roughead (ed.), *Trial of Captain Porteous*, 1).

51. On the importance of dislocation in the making of museum collections, see Barbara Kirshenblatt-Gimblett, *Destination Culture: Tourism, Museums, and Heritage* (Berkeley: University of California Press, 1998).

52. Roman Jakobson, 'Closing Statement: Linguistics and Poetics', in Thomas A. Sebeok (ed.), *Style in Language* (Cambridge, MA: MIT Press, 1960).

53. The title of the novel indicated a desire to commemorate the disappearance of the actual 'Heart of Mid-Lothian' demolished in 1817 as part of the renovation of the old city. Presumably from a similar impulse, Scott also made a point of recycling some of the wood from the old building in constructing bookshelves in the library at Abbotsford; see anon. [McVickar], 'Abbotsford', *Dublin Weekly Journal: A Repository of Music, Literature, and Entertaining Knowledge* 22, March (1833). See further Chapter 5 below.

54. Criticism of the plot was voiced by anonymous reviewers in anon., '*Tales of My Landlord. Second Series*', *British Critic* 10, July–December (1818); anon., '*Tales of My Landlord. Second Series*', *New Monthly Magazine and Universal Register* 10, July–December (1818); [Francis Jeffrey], 'Novels, by the Author of Waverley', *Edinburgh Review* 65, January (1820). In the *Monthly Review*, for example, the reviewer was generally very positive about the novel, but complained of the 'tedious detail' with which the happiness of Jeanie and her husband was related and the 'impropriety' of having turned Effie into Lady Staunton, while denouncing the denouement as 'inconsistent with the tenor of the previous narrative' (pp. 366–7).

55. Scott's campaign to retain the legal distinctiveness of Scotland is discussed in Colin Kidd, 'Sentiment, Race and Revival: Scottish Identities in the Aftermath of Enlightenment', in Laurence Brockliss et al. (eds), *A Union of Multiple Identities: The British Isles, c.1750–c.1850* (Manchester: Manchester University Press, 1999), 112.

56. Oscar Wilde, *Oscar Wilde: Plays, Prose and Poems* (London: Macdonald, 1982), 340.

57. Hayden White, 'The Value of Narrativity in the Representation of Reality' [1981], in *The Content of the Form: Narrative Discourse and Historical Representation* (Baltimore, MD: Johns Hopkins University Press, 1987). For surveys regarding the role of narrativity in historical representation, see Ann Rigney, 'The Concept of Narrative in Historical Theory', in Nancy Partner et al. (eds), *The Sage Handbook of Historical Theory* (New York: Sage, 2013). Also Hans Kellner, 'Narrativity in History: Post-Structuralism and Since', *History and Theory* 26 (1987); Paul Ricoeur, *Temps et récit*, 3 vols (Paris: Seuil, 1983–5).

58. Duncan, *Modern Romance*, 110.

59. Patricia Meyer-Spacks, 'Private and Social Reading', *Ideas* 5 (1998).

60. Alison Landsberg, *Prosthetic Memory: The Transformation of American Remembrance in the Age of Mass Culture* (New York: Columbia University Press, 2004).

61. Lady Louisa Stewart, quoted in Johnson, *Sir Walter Scott*, I: 623; J. G. Lockhart, *The Life of Sir Walter Scott, Bart.; New Popular Edition* (London: A&C Black, 1893 [1837–8]), 376.

62. 'L'oubli, et je dirai même l'erreur historique, sont un facteur essentiel de la création d'une nation'; Ernest Renan, 'Qu'est-ce qu'une nation?' [1882], in

Oeuvres complètes d'Ernest Renan, ed. Henriëtte Psichari (Paris: Calmann-Lévy, 1947–61), 284–5.

63. Rigney, *Imperfect Histories*, 30–1. According also to Ian Duncan, Scott's novels 'discover history in order to discover the horizon at which—as for the individual subject, so for the nation—history comes to a stop' (Duncan, *Modern Romance*, 53). Elsewhere I have shown the interplay between fore-grounding and neutralizing in the case of nineteenth-century narrative his-torians, and argued that this should be seen as a structural feature of historical writing since it involves by definition grappling with events not of the author's own choosing; Ann Rigney, *The Rhetoric of Historical Representation: Three Narrative Histories of the French Revolution* (Cambridge: Cambridge University Press, 1990), 90–101.

64. Murray Pittock, *Scottish and Irish Romanticism* (Oxford: Oxford University Press, 2008), 189.

65. Duncan, *Modern Romance*, 15.

66. Assmann, *Erinnerungsräume*, 249–50.

67. This argument continues in a new direction my exploration of 'imperfection' as the driving force behind the constantly renewed desire to re-write history (Rigney, *Imperfect Histories*).

68. Hewitt and Lumsden (eds), *The Heart of Mid-Lothian*, 500–12. One must of course be careful in speaking of new editions as merely reproductions of the original text since textual variations occur between editions, particularly between the original edition of 1818 and Scott's magnum opus edition of 1830 to which he added authorial footnotes and an introduction. This edition has been the standard one and my point of reference in this analysis. The novel was also published in abridged form at an early stage: D. Stewart, *The Heart of Midlothian; or, The Affecting History of Jeanie and Effie Deans; Abridged from the Original* (Newcastle upon Tyne: Mackenzie and Dent, 1833).

69. Information about the translations of Scott's works has been gleaned from the excellent database BOSLIT (Bibliography of Scottish Literature in Transla-tion) at the National Library of Scotland.

70. The British Museum Catalogue of Printed Books to 1955 (1967) lists 39 editions of the Waverley novels, including an Abbotsford edition (1842–7), a centenary edition (1871), a 'handy volume' edition (1877), an Edinburgh edition (1887), a popular edition (1890–2), and the Century Scott (1898). On the genesis and import of the magnum opus edition published by Cadell in 1829–33, see Jane Millgate, *Scott's Last Edition: A Study in Publishing History* (Edinburgh: Edinburgh University Press, 1987).

71. For a discussion of Scott's influence on Victorian novelists, including *The Heart of Mid-Lothian*, see Wilt, *Secret Leaves*, 1–18; also Jay Clayton, 'The Alphabet of Suffering: Effie Deans, Tess Durbeyfield, Martha Ray, and Hetty Sorrel', in Jay Clayton et al. (eds), *Influence and Intertextuality in Literary History* (Madison: University of Wisconsin Press, 1991); Jerome McGann, *The Scholar's Art: Literary Studies in a Managed World* (Chicago: University of

Chicago Press, 2006), 71–4. Thomas Carlyle was a notable critic of Scott (see Chapter 7 below), and yet it is hard not to see parallels between his depictions of the revolutionary crowd in his *French Revolution* (1837) and Scott's depiction of the Porteous riot.

72. For more details of contemporary reactions to the Waverley novels, see Rigney, *Imperfect Histories*, 30–58.

73. For early appreciations of Scott's success in portraying Scottish manners of the period see, for example, the anonymous reviews in the *Edinburgh Magazine, and Literary Miscellany* (August 1818), 107–17 (esp. 109); the *London Literary Gazette, and Journal of Belles Lettres, Arts, Sciences, Etc* 81 (August 1818): 497–500 (esp. 498); *Blackwood's Edinburgh Magazine* (August 1818), 564–74 (esp. 570); and in the survey article by Francis Jeffrey, *Edinburgh Review* (1820), 3–4.

74. For some nineteenth-century assessments, see H. J. C. Grierson, *Sir Walter Scott 1832–1932* (New York: Columbia University Press, 1933); Herbert Grierson (ed.), *Sir Walter Scott To-day: Some Retrospective Essays and Studies* (London: Constable, 1932).

75. Georg Lukács, *The Historical Novel*, trans. Hannah and Stanley Mitchell (Harmondsworth: Penguin, 1962 [1936–7]), 56.

76. Regarding the recent popularity of the novel among academic critics, see Mark Weinstein, 'The Millennial Scott Popularity Poll', *Scott Newsletter* 35 (1999).

77. For studies of the plight of the novel from a gender perspective, see Clayton, 'The Alphabet of Suffering', 123–6; Caroline McCracken-Flesher, 'Narrating the (Gendered) Nation in Walter Scott's *The Heart of Midlothian*', *Nineteenth-Century Contexts* 24 (2002); Wilt, *Secret Leaves*. Wilt also admits the oddity of the last volume, but then manages to integrate it into her reading of gender relations in the novel (pp. 140–1). A reading of the novel from the perspective of intergenerational tensions, with special attention to the last volume, is offered in James Kerr, 'Scott's Fable of Regeneration: *The Heart of Midlothian*', *English Literary History* 53 (1986). For an interpretation of the last section of the novel in the light of the mass emigration from Scotland in the eighteenth century see Charlotte Sussman, 'The Emptiness at *The Heart of Midlothian*: Nation, Narration, and Population', *Eighteenth-Century Fiction* 15 (2002).

78. Lincoln, *Walter Scott and Modernity*, 26.

79. Hans U. Gumbrecht, *The Powers of Philology: Dynamics of Textual Scholarship* (Urbana: University of Illinois Press, 2003), 62.

80. Edwin A. Barber, 'Printed Textiles', *Bulletin of the Pennsylvania Museum* 9 (34) (1911); Lourdes M. Font, 'Five Scenes from a Romance: The Identification of a Nineteenth-Century Printed Cotton', *Metropolitan Museum Journal* 22 (1987). Wedgwood produced ceramics based on Ivanhoe (though not apparently *The Heart of Mid-Lothian*) between 1880 and 1913: http://www.wedgwoodmuseum.org.uk/collections/online/2219/object/2693.

81. Examples of independently published engravings illustrating the novel include Fred Bromley, *Companion to the Trial of Effie Deans* (Philadelphia: J. Hedenberg, *c*.1850); Thomas Miles Richardson, *The Death of Captain Porteous in the Porteous Riots in Edinburgh in 1736* (London: Fisher, 1836).

82. For general reactions on the part of visual artists to Scott's work: Catherine Gordon, *British Paintings of Subjects from the English Novel: 1740–1870* (New York: Garland, 1988), 286–358. See further Chapter 2 below.

83. A production of *The Heart of Mid-Lothian* at the Princess Theatre, London, in 1849 was publicized as including the 'following scenes . . . painted by Mr. Cuthbert and Mr. Nichols: The Farm of David Deans, Reception Chamber of the Duke of Argyle, and Avenue leading to the Court of Justice, the Tolbooth, Canongate, with a Part of the City of Edinburgh in Flames'; Robert Giddings, 'Scott and Opera', in Alan Bold (ed.), *Sir Walter Scott: The Long Forgotten Melody* (London: Vision, 1983), 196. Also entry 2661 in H. Philip Bolton, *Scott Dramatized* (London: Mansell, 1992), 285.

84. Bolton, *Scott Dramatized*, 259–96. The versions reviewed here are (in alphabetical order) Joseph Bennett, *Jeanie Deans: An Opera in Four Acts and Seven Tableaux; Written and Composed Expressly for The Royal Carl Rosa Opera Company. Words by Joseph Bennett. Music by Hamish MacCunn* (London: Phipps and Connor, 1894); Dion Boucicault, *Jeanie Deans or The Heart of Midlothian; A Drama in Three Acts* (ms.; Harvard Theatre Collection [act 1 only], n.d. [1860]); Thomas Dibdin, *The Heart of Midlothian: A Romantic National Drama; Founded on the Popular Tale of the Same Name* (Edinburgh: James L. Huie, 1823); Thomas Hailes Lacy, *The Heart of Mid-Lothian; or, the Sisters of St. Leonard's: A Drama, (with unregistered effects,) in Three Acts. Adapted from Sir Walter Scott's admired novel, with introductions from T. Dibdin's play, W. Murray's alteration of the same, Eugène Scribe's opera, and Dion Boucicault's amalgamation of the above; Colin Hazlewood's adjustment and re-adjustment, J.B. Johnstone's appropriation, and other equally original versions, together with a very small amount of new matter* (London: Thomas Hailes Lacy, n.d. [*c*.1863]); George Dibdin Pitt, *The Whistler!: The Fate of the Lily of St. Leonard's, a Melo Drama, in Three Acts* (London: J. Duncombe, n.d. [1833]); Daniel Terry, *The Heart of Mid-lothian, a Musical Drama, in Three Acts; First Produced at the Theatre Royal, Covent Garden, Saturday, 17th April, 1819* (London: William Stockdale, 1819). The variation in the use of the hyphen in 'Mid-Lothian' in the play titles reflects the printed versions.

85. My thanks to Yuko Matsui for drawing my attention to Judy Steel's *The Journey of Jeannie Deans*, produced by the Rowan Tree Theatre Company in 2008.

86. Bolton, *Scott Dramatized*.

87. Ibid. 262–4.

88. See 'Women in History of Scots descent': http://www.electricscotland.com/ history/women/walker_helen.htm. The distinction made between 'storage'

(archival memory) and 'active memory' is made in Assmann, *Erinnerungs-räume*, 130–45.

89. The life of Helen Walker is discussed at some length in, for example, Lascelles, *The Story-teller Retrieves the Past*.

90. It also gave rise to an irreverent spin-off by John Galt called 'Jeanie Deans in Love' (1821), mentioned in Ian Duncan, *Scott's Shadow: The Novel in Romantic Edinburgh* (Princeton, NJ: Princeton University Press, 2007), 38.

91. The ballad is available through the National Library of Scotland: http://www.nls.uk/broadsides/broadside.cfm/id/15101/transcript/1.

92. For an example of a chapbook version produced as a 'tie-in' to Dibdin's theatrical version, see *Heart of Midlothian; or the Lily of St. Leonard, A Caledonian Tale of Great Interest, on which is Founded the Piece of that Name, Performed with Unbounded Applause at the Different Theatres* (London: Printed for the Company of Booksellers, 1822). With thanks to Alison Lumsden.

93. Erll, *Kollektives Gedächtnis*, 158.

94. David Brewer, *The Afterlife of Character, 1726–1825* (Philadelphia: University of Pennsylvania Press, 2005), esp. 189–206.

95. There was also a paddle steamer of 238 tonnes called *Effie Deans* operating from Louisville, Kentucky, in 1863; all ships listed in C. Bradford Mitchell (ed.), *Merchant Steam Vessels of the United States 1790–1868* (Staten Island, NY: Steamship Historical Society of America, 1975).

96. The steamship seems to have been the most famous of a series of Jeanie Deans, including the four-masted sailing ship in the 1840s and a motor yacht registered in Brisbane as recently as 1973 (http://www.amsa.gov.au/shipping_registration/list_of_registered_ships/Page_28.asp). A history of the Craigendoran steamers is given in Ian McCrorie, *Clyde Pleasure Steamers: An Illustrated History* (Greenock: Orr, Pollock, 1986). For an affectionate 'biography' of the steamship, see MacHaffie, *Jeanie Deans 1931–1967*. The steamship has by now become celebrated in its own right, but the Scott model is incidentally recalled; for instance, when MacHaffie contrasts the positive outcome of Jeanie's trip to London with the neglect and destruction awaiting the ship there: 'In "Heart of Mid-Lothian" Jeanie Deans journeyed to London to plead the cause of her sister Effie imprisoned in the Tolbooth, Edinburgh. The satisfactory outcome of the mission was not matched by *Jeanie Deans*' visit to the capital city' (MacHaffie, *Jeanie Deans 1931–1967*, 29). On the *Waverley*, see MacHaffie, *Waverley*.

97. On the different generations of 'Scott' locomotives, see Nock, *Great Locomotives of the L.N.E.R.*, 80–8. On the Waverley line, see Roger Siviter, *Waverley: Portrait of a Famous Route* (Southampton: Kingfisher Railway Productions, 1988).

98. Nock's comments on the Scott class of locomotives in his history of the Northern railways again reflects memory loss: 'Even at this early stage

[1909–12] in the naming of this ultimately numerous group of locomotives, it would need a specialist quiz contender to identify some of the personalities involved in those North British engine names! Who, for example, was "Madge Wildfire" and who was "Vich Ian Vohr"?' (Nock, *Great Locomotives of the L.N.E.R.*, 87). The fact that this recent historian of the railways is apparently not familiar with minor characters from *The Heart of Mid-Lothian* and *Waverley* shows that the work of Scott is much less well known nowadays than in 1909.

99. Michael Billig, *Banal Nationalism* (London: Sage, 1995).

100. Juri M. Lotman, *Universe of the Mind: A Semiotic Theory of Culture*, trans. Ann Shukman (London: I. B. Tauris, 1990), 264.

101. J. Assmann discusses the 'acculturation' of new groups in the evolution of cultural memory: Assmann, *Das kulturelle Gedächtnis*, 145–51.

102. The Heart of Midlothian football club was founded in 1874; the name of the club originated in the name of a dance hall that the players frequented and that may have originated in Scott's novel or in the memory of the 'Heart of Mid-Lothian', the popular name for the prison demolished in 1817. Whatever the exact origin of the name of the dance hall, the official history of the football club links the name to the work of Scott: 'The Tolbooth of Edinburgh, which was demolished in 1817, was known locally as the Heart of Midlothian. Sir Walter Scott immortalised the name in his writings and many institutions were named after this old jail' (Heart of Midlothian Football Club, *Heart of Midlothian Football Club* (n.p.: Tempus Publishing, 1998), 9). Since its foundation the football club has acquired its own history, which is celebrated in such publications as the Graham Blackwood et al. (eds), *The Hearts Quiz Book* (Edinburgh: Mainstream Publishing, 1987). It is worth noting as an indication of memory loss that the quiz book, focusing on the goals and penalties of famous players, includes no reference to Scott.

103. MacHaffie, *Jeanie Deans 1931–1967*.

104. While the *Monthly Review* saw the use of dialect as one of the attractions of the novel, the *New Monthly Review* was more negative, dismissing it as a Scottish affair—of interest to the Scots because 'recalling to their minds the traditionary facts of their early days' but relatively inaccessible to the English reader (p. 250).

105. On the idea of the 'national' at this period, see further Ina Ferris, *The Romantic National Tale and the Question of Ireland* (Cambridge: Cambridge University Press, 2002); Pittock, *Scottish and Irish Romanticism*.

106. For a complete listing of productions, mentioning venues and quoting advertisements, see Bolton, *Scott Dramatized*, 262–96.

107. Going on the number of theatrical productions, *The Heart of Mid-Lothian* would appear to have been relatively less popular than other Scott works among American audiences; ibid. 260.

CHAPTER 2

1. Details taken from entry 2426; H. Philip Bolton, *Scott Dramatized* (London: Mansell, 1992), 263. References are to the popular composer Henry Bishop (1786–1855) and the landscape painter Alexander Nasmyth (1758–1840). On the importance of Nasmyth's paintings to the success of *The Heart of Mid-Lothian* as a play, see James C. Dibdin, *The Annals of the Edinburgh Stage; With an Account of the Rise and Progress of Dramatic Writing in Scotland* (Edinburgh: Richard Cameron, 1888), 294. A recent study has shown the influence of Nasmyth's scenes both on the dramatizations of the novel and on later illustrated editions; Richard Hill, *Picturing Scotland through the Waverley Novels: Walter Scott and the Origins of the Victorian Illustrated Novel* (London: Ashgate, 2010), 133–62.

2. On media convergence in the digital age, see Henry Jenkins, *Convergence Culture: Where Old and New Media Collide* (New York: New York University Press, 2006). For a wide-ranging reflection on medial convergence in the nineteenth century, see Martin Meisel, *Realizations: Narrative, Pictorial, and Theatrical Arts in Nineteenth-Century England* (Princeton, NJ: Princeton University Press, 1983).

3. David Brewer, *The Afterlife of Character, 1726–1825* (Philadelphia: University of Pennsylvania Press, 2005), 97, 100.

4. John Ellis, 'The Literary Adaptation: An Introduction', *Screen* 23 (1982), 4.

5. The scarce research on Scott's readership, while admittedly dealing with a somewhat later period, suggests a serial consumption pattern; thus library records for Richmond, Virginia, in the 1840s show borrowers devouring the novels in intense and rapid succession; see Emily B. Todd, 'Walter Scott and the Nineteenth-Century American Literary Marketplace: Antebellum Richmond Readers and the Collected Editions of the Waverley Novels', *Papers of the Bibliographical Society of America* 93 (1999). There is evidence that other writers also tried to profit from the appetite for new Waverley novels by publishing their own writings as purportedly by the 'author of Waverley'. With thanks to Paul Koopman, I now own two Dutch novels allegedly by Sir Walter Scott: [Walter Scott], *Aymé Verd: of De opstand der Hugenooten in de 16e eeuw: Onuitgegeven roman van Sir Walter Scott naar de derde Fransche uitgave*, 2 vols (Gorinchem: A. Van der Mast, 1843); [Walter Scott], *Moredun. Een verhaal van omstreeks 1210 door Sir Walter Scott: Voorafgegaan door eene inleiding behelzende de geschiedenis van het handschrift. Uit het Engelsch vertaald door J. B. Rietstap*, 2 vols (Rotterdam: H. Nigh, 1855).

6. The Russian Formalists, whose hyper-modernist theories have been so influential in literary studies, did make room in their models of cultural dynamics for a regularly recurring 'secondary' phase in which less creative writers (the value judgement was implicit) imitated and gave widespread currency to the techniques and themes brought into play by the great innovators. See for example, Juri Tynjanov, 'On Literary Evolution', in Ladislaw Matejka et al. (eds), *Readings in Russian Poetics: Formalist and Structuralist Views* (Cambridge, MA: MIT Press, 1978 [1927]). On the aesthetics of modernism,

with its predilection for defamiliarization and its discomfort with mass culture, see Andreas Huyssen, *After the Great Divide: Modernism, Mass Culture, Postmodernism* (Bloomington: Indiana University Press, 1986). The value attached to novelty in criticism has been such that, as Matei Calinescu has observed, even our theories of reading are premised on the idea that the first defamiliarizing encounter with a book is defining, and that re-reading is something abnormal rather than a pleasure in its own right; Matei Calinescu, *Rereading* (New Haven, CT: Yale University Press, 1993).

7. Juri Lotman distinguished between the 'aesthetics of identity' (dominant in European culture until Romanticism) and the 'aesthetics of opposition', which has been dominant ever since; Juri Lotman, *The Structure of the Artistic Text*, trans. Ronald Vroon (Ann Arbor: University of Michigan, 1977 [1970]). The classic critique of originality is Roland Barthes, 'La mort de l'auteur' [1968], in *Le bruissement de la langue* (Paris: Seuil, 1984).

8. On Scott tie-ins as a marketing strategy, see Emily B. Todd, 'Establishing Routes for Fiction in the United States', *Book History* 12 (2009), 119.

9. Linda Hutcheon, *A Theory of Adaptation* (London: Routledge, 2006). This work forms a logical continuation of Hutcheon's long-standing fascination with 'derivative' forms of literature and their aesthetic value: Linda Hutcheon, *A Theory of Parody: The Teachings of Twentieth-Century Art Forms* (New York: Methuen, 1985); Linda Hutcheon and Mario J. Valdés, 'Irony, Nostalgia, and the Postmodern: A Dialogue', *Poligrafías* 3 (1998–2000). Another survey of recent discussions, which focused on re-working as a critical and aesthetic tool, is provided by Julie Sanders, *Adaptation and Appropriation* (London: Routledge, 2006). A seminal text for all recent discussions, despite its being hampered by the excessive emphasis on typologizing characteristic of structuralism, is Gerard Genette, *Palimpsestes: La littérature au second degré* (Paris: Seuil, 1982).

10. For an account of the Waverley textiles and furnishings (with thanks to Simon Waegemakers for having drawn my attention to it), see Lourdes M. Font, 'Five Scenes from a Romance: The Identification of a Nineteenth-Century Printed Cotton', *Metropolitan Museum Journal* 22 (1987). The Scott-inspired fashions, including children's 'Highland' outfits, were to be seen in *Ackermann's Repository of Arts, Literature, Fashion* (London, 1809–28); examples reproduced in Font, p. 123. Frescoes at Buckingham Palace were decorated with Scott illustrations; see Richard D. Altick, *Paintings from Books: Art and Literature in Britain 1760–1900* (Columbus: Ohio State University Press, 1985), 430. For more information on the *tableaux vivants*, see Chapter 4 below.

11. Alongside the popularity of costume balls, Scott's influence also extended to parlour games; for some fascinating examples, see Nicola J. Watson, 'Scott's Afterlives', in Fiona Robertson (ed.), *The Edinburgh Companion to Sir Walter Scott* (Edinburgh: Edinburgh University Press, 2012).

12. Ivanhoe tableware and tiles, designed by Thomas Allen around 1881, continued to be produced by Wedgwood up to the early years of the twentieth century; http://www.replacements.com/museum/images/ivanhoe. jpg; The Wedgwood Museum online also includes an Ivanhoe vase from 1913; http://www.wedgwoodmuseum.org.uk/collections/search/title/ ivanhoe. With thanks to Lynn Miller.

13. In making this point, I am drawing on William Uricchio's argument that media forms have long prehistories and that cinema, for example, had first to be imagined in other media; see 'Television's First Seventy-Five Years: The Interpretive Flexibility of a Medium in Transition', in Robert Kolker (ed.), *The Oxford Handbook of Film and Media Studies* (Oxford: Oxford University Press, 2008), 286–305.

14. Quoted in Beth S. Wright, ' "Seeing with the Painter's Eye": Sir Walter Scott's Challenge to Nineteenth-Century Art', in Murray Pittock (ed.), *The Reception of Sir Walter Scott in Europe* (London: Continuum, 2006).

15. The full quote runs: 'Lord Byron et Walter Scott... ont dessiné, vous savez avec quel bonheur et quelle exactitude, toutes les scènes principales de leurs romans et de leurs poèmes. Chacune de leurs pages est un tableau qu'on n'a qu'à reproduire', in Beth Wright, 'Walter Scott et la gravure française: A propos de la collection des estampes "scottesques" conservée au Département des estampes, Paris', *Nouvelles de l'estampe* 93 (1987), 6.

16. Walter Scott, *Waverley; or, 'Tis Sixty Years Since*, ed. Claire Lamont (Oxford: Clarendon Press, 1981), 175–6.

17. Hill, *Picturing Scotland through the Waverley Novels*.

18. Gerald Finley, *Landscapes of Memory: Turner as Illustrator of Scott* (London: Scolar Press, 1980); Hill, *Picturing Scotland through the Waverley Novels*; Richard Maxwell, 'Walter Scott, Historical Fiction, and the Genesis of the Victorian Illustrated Book', in Richard Maxwell (ed.), *The Victorian Illustrated Book* (Charlottesville: University Press of Virginia, 2002).

19. *The Waverley Gallery of the Principal Female Characters in Sir Walter Scott's Romances. From original paintings by eminent artists. Engraved under the superintendence of C. Heath* (London: Tilt and Bogue, 1841); George Newenham Wright et al., *Landscape-Historical Illustrations of Scotland and the Waverley Novels; from Drawings by J.M.W. Turner, Professor R.A. etc.*, 2 vols (London: Fisher, Sons, 1836–8). Many such collections of engravings, often based on earlier paintings, appeared from the 1820s on: *The Book of Waverley Gems: In a Series of Engraved Illustrations of Incidents and Scenery in Sir Walter Scott's Novels* (London: Henry G. Bohn, 1846); William Allen, *Illustrations of the Novels and Tales of the Author of Waverley: A series of portraits of eminent historical characters introduced in those works. Accompanied with biographical notices* (London, 1823); James Skene, *A Series of Sketches of the Existing Localities Alluded to in the Waverley Novels, Etched from Original Drawings* (Edinburgh: Cadell, 1829).

20. On Scott's huge influence on French painters, see Beth S. Wright, *Painting and History during the French Restoration: Abandoned by the Past* (Cambridge:

Cambridge University Press, 1997); Wright, '"Seeing with the Painter's Eye"'.

21. Altick, *Paintings from Books*, 69. This tradition of landscape painting was perpetuated and transformed in the photographs illustrating *The Lady of the Lake* made by George Washington Wilson in 1866; Helen Groth, *Victorian Photography and Literary Nostalgia* (Oxford: Oxford University Press, 2003).

22. Altick, *Paintings from Books*, 424–36 (p. 430); Catherine Gordon, *British Paintings of Subjects from the English Novel: 1740–1870* (New York: Garland, 1988); Wright, '"Seeing with the Painter's Eye"'; Beth S. Wright and Paul Joannides, 'Les romans historiques de Sir Walter Scott et la peinture française, 1822–63', *Bulletin de la société de l'histoire de l'art français* (1983).

23. On the aesthetics of historical painting during this period, see esp. Stephen Bann, *The Clothing of Clio: A Study of the Representation of History in Nineteenth-Century Britain and France* (Cambridge: Cambridge University Press, 1984).

24. Altick, *Paintings from Books*, 43.

25. Examples of images inspired by theatrical representations are given ibid. 428.

26. Information from http://www.rijksmuseum.nl/aria/aria_assets/SK-A-1902?lang=en

27. J. David Bolter and Richard Grusin, *Remediation: Understanding New Media* (Cambridge, MA: MIT Press, 2000), 55.

28. Examples of early Scott photography and of magic lantern shows are given in Chapter 5 and Chapter 6.

29. Astrid Erll, *Prämediation—Remediation: Der indische Aufstand in imperialen und post-kolonialen Medienkulturen (1857 bis zur Gegenwart)* (Trier: WVT, 2007). Grusin too has used the term 'premediation' in more recent publications, but does so with reference to the way in which future events are being 'premediated' rather than with reference to the presence of past stories in new ones; Richard Grusin, *Premediation: Affect and Mediality after 9/11* (London: Palgrave Macmillan, 2010); Richard A. Grusin, 'Premediation', *Criticism* 46 (2004).

30. Tracy C. Davis and Peter Holland (eds), *The Performing Century: Nineteenth-Century Theatre's History* (London: Palgrave Macmillan, 2007).

31. In the early years of cinema, film-makers looked to writers, not just for stories, but also for respectability; Willliam Uricchio and Roberta E. Pearson, *Reframing Culture: The Case of the Vitagraph Quality Films* (Princeton, NJ: Princeton University Press, 1993). The intense interaction between the novel and theatre goes back at least to Richardson; see Thomas Keymer and Peter Sabor (eds), *The Pamela Controversy: Criticisms and Adaptations of Samuel Richardson's Pamela, 1740–1750*, 6 vols (London: Pickering and Chatto, 2001).

32. Barbara Bell, 'The Nineteenth Century', in Bill Findley (ed.), *A History of the Scottish Theatre* (Edinburgh: Polygon, 1998), 157.

33. For example, Eliza Flower, *Musical Illustrations of the Waverley novels, etc.* (London: Jos. Alfred Novello, c.1831).

34. Ellis, 'The Literary Adaptation', 3.

35. Only towards the close of the century were the lights dimmed in the theatre so as to focus attention on the stage and quieten the audience; Allardyce Nicoll, *A History of English Drama 1660–1900*, 4 vols (Cambridge: Cambridge University Press, 1955), IV.

36. David Worrall, *Theatric Revolution: Drama, Censorship and Romantic Period Subcultures 1773–1832* (Oxford: Oxford University Press, 2006).

37. The battle of Waterloo was displayed as a panorama from 1815 on: Philip Shaw, *Waterloo and the Romantic Imagination* (London: Palgrave Macmillan, 2002). Among the historical events re-enacted on stage were *The Battle of the Nile* (1815), *The Battle of Trafalgar; or, The Death of Nelson* (1824), *The Naval Victory and Triumph of Lord Nelson* (1805); Nicoll, *A History of English Drama 1660–1900*, IV: 14. According to a bill circulated on 2 April 1804 the Siege of Gibralter offered 'a grand Naval Spectacle . . . with real Men of War and Floating Batteries'; new bills issued on 28 May further emphasized the accuracy of the show, drawing attention to 'real ships of 100, 74, and 60 guns, &c, built, rigged, and manoeuvred in the most correct manner, as every nautical character who has seen them implicitly allows . . . the conflagration of the town in various places, the defence of the garrison, and attack by the floating batteries, is so faithfully and naturally represented, that when the floating batteries take fire, some blowing up with a dreadful explosion, and others, after burning to the water's edge, sink to the bottom . . . the effect is such as to produce an unprecedented climax of astonishment and applause' (ibid. 42).

38. On the Victorian culture of spectacle and sensationalism in relation to drama, see Lynn M. Voskuil, 'Feeling Public: Sensation Theater, Commodity Culture, and the Victorian Public Sphere', *Victorian Studies* 44, Winter (2002). With reference to the earlier decades of the century, Worrall emphasizes in particular the theatricalization of politics and public life rather than sensationalism as such; David Worrall, *The Politics of Romantic Theatricality, 1787–1832* (London: Palgrave, 2007).

39. Reviewer in *The Atlas* (15 October 1826); quoted in paragraph 25 of Christina Fuhrman, 'Scott Repatriated?: *La Dame blanche* Crosses the Channel', *Opera and Romanticism*, Praxis Series, Special issue, ed. Gillen D'Arcy Wood (2005), http://www.rc.umd.edu/praxis/opera/index.html.

40. J. C. Dibdin, *Annals of the Edinburgh Stage* (1888); quoted in Barbara Bell, 'Sir Walter Scott and the National Drama', in J. H. Alexander et al. (eds), *Scott in Carnival* (Aberdeen: Ass. for Scottish Lit. Studies, 1993), 459.

41. On Scott's support for the theatre: Edgar Johnson, *Sir Walter Scott: The Great Unknown*, 2 vols (London: Hamilton, 1970), II: 322–4; Michael Ragussis, *Theatrical Nation: Jews and Other Outlandish Englishmen in Georgian Britain* (Philadelphia: University of Pennsylvania Press, 2010), 140–1. His one attempt at a 'dramatic poem' was a failure; Johnson, *Sir Walter Scott,* I: 787.

42. Ian Duncan, *Scott's Shadow: The Novel in Romantic Edinburgh* (Princeton, NJ: Princeton University Press, 2007), 7–8. For an interesting discussion of the occasion in terms of 'cross-dressing', see Kenneth McNeil, *Scotland, Britain, Empire: Writing the Highlands, 1760–1860* (Columbus: Ohio University Press, 2007), 76–82. Many recent analyses of the occasion are responses to Hugh Trevor-Roper, 'The Invention of Tradition: The Highland Tradition of Scotland', in Eric Hobsbawm et al. (eds), *The Invention of Tradition* (Cambridge: Cambridge University Press, 1983). An extensive account of the visit is also given in John Prebble, *The King's Jaunt: George IV in Scotland, August 1822; 'One and twenty daft days'* (Edinburgh: Birlinn, 1988).

43. Philip Cox, *Reading Adaptations: Novels and Verse Narratives on the Stage, 1790–1840* (Manchester: Manchester University Press, 2000), 80; Johnson, *Sir Walter Scott*, I: 514.

44. On the adaptation of other novelists, see further Cox, *Reading Adaptations*, esp. 121–62 (on Dickens); Patsy Stoneman, *Brontë Transformations: The Cultural Dissemination of Jane Eyre and Wuthering Heights* (London: Prentice Hall, 1996).

45. Bell, 'Sir Walter Scott and the National Drama'.

46. Ibid. 464.

47. Jane Moody, *Illegitimate Theatre in London 1770–1840* (Cambridge: Cambridge University Press, 2000); Jane Moody and Daniel O'Quinn (eds), *The Cambridge Companion to British Theatre, 1730–1830* (Cambridge: Cambridge University Press, 2007).

48. Some contemporary anxieties about the threats to literary drama from melodrama are described in Cox, *Reading Adaptations*, 11–19. Worrall attributes a politically subversive role to some of the popular theatres (in his terms: the 'plebeian public sphere of drama'); Worrall, *The Politics of Romantic Theatricality, 1787–1832*, 207. It is difficult to identify a subversive strain in the many Scott productions, though they did have political dimensions as will become apparent below and in Chapter 3.

49. John Russell Stephens, *The Censorship of English Drama 1824–1901* (Cambridge: Cambridge University Press, 1980), 5–16.

50. Bell, 'Sir Walter Scott and the National Drama', 458–9. This point is also made in Cox, *Reading Adaptations*, 4.

51. Peter Brooks, *The Melodramatic Imagination: Balzac, Henry James, Melodrama, and the Mode of Excess* (New York: Columbia University Press, 1985).

52. On dramatists and the piracy of novels, see John Russell Stephens, *The Profession of the Playwright: British Theatre 1800–1900* (Cambridge: Cambridge University Press, 1992), 97–8.

53. The Bernard C. Lloyd Sir Walter Scott Collection at Aberdeen University Library includes a large number of Waverley-related songbooks. With thanks to Alison Lumsden.

54. Bolton, *Scott Dramatized*. This catalogue builds on, while going far beyond, earlier surveys: Richard Ford, *Dramatisations of Scott's Novels: A Catalogue*

(Oxford: Oxford Bibliographical Society, 1979); Jerome Mitchell, *More Scott Operas: Further Analysis of Operas Based on the Works of Sir Walter Scott* (Lanham: University Press of America, 1996); Jerome Mitchell, *The Walter Scott Operas: An Analysis of Operas Based on the Works of Sir Walter Scott* (Tuscaloosa: University of Alabama Press, 1977); Henry Adelbert White, *Sir Walter Scott's Novels on the Stage* (New Haven, CT: Yale University Press, 1927).

55. The European reception of Scott's operas is discussed in Jeremy Tambling, 'Scott's "Heyday" in Opera', in Murray Pittock (ed.), *The Reception of Sir Walter Scott in Europe* (London: Continuum, 2006). There is no evidence in the survey edited by Pittock that non-operatic versions of Scott 'travelled' in significant numbers to other language areas.

56. Fuhrman, 'Scott Repatriated?'.

57. Bolton, *Scott Dramatized*, 272, 273.

58. Ibid. 289. See also ibid. 183 for other examples of multiple occurrences of Scott plays during the Edinburgh season in 1825.

59. In contrast to the operatic versions, which have received some attention within the framework of music history, critical discussions of the melo-dramatic versions have so far been restricted in scope; see Cox, *Reading Adaptations*; Anastasia Nikolopoulou, 'Historical Disruptions: The Walter Scott Melodramas', in Michael Hays et al. (eds), *Melodrama: The Cultural Emergence of a Genre* (New York: St. Martin's, 1996); White, *Sir Walter Scott's Novels on the Stage*. The emphasis of the study by Nikolopoulou is on the purportedly subversive dimensions of melodrama, which in the case of Scott dramatizations seems overstated.

60. Cox, *Reading Adaptations*, 110–11.

61. Quoted in Bolton, *Scott Dramatized*, 222.

62. Prefatory remarks to Isaac Pocock, *Rob Roy MacGregor; or, Auld Lang Syne* (London: Oxberry, 1820); quoted ibid. 165. Another playbill from 1821 [entry 1504] announces a drama 'founded on a novel of the same name, written by Walter Scott, Esq.' Bolton, *Scott Dramatized*, 175. Comparable references can be found in entries: 3418, 3345, 3388, 3342, 2268, 3336, 3358.

63. The pressure to be faithful to Scott's originals diminished after his death in 1832; Ford, *Dramatisations of Scott's Novels*, viii.

64. Quoted in Bolton, *Scott Dramatized*, 289. Despite such critical acclaim, the Boucicault version was never published and only a manuscript version of the first act remains extant (available through the Houghton Library, Harvard University).

65. Quoted ibid. 290. This production is also discussed in Voskuil, 'Feeling Public'.

66. Mitchell, *The Walter Scott Operas*, 35.

67. The 2005 movie *Waverley* (dir: Piers Thompson) listed in the IMDB is a psychological drama about ageing and is not an adaptation of Scott's novel: http://www.imdb.com.

68. Although it has since been overshadowed by other Scott works in academic criticism, *Guy Mannering* was immensely successful on the nineteenth-century stage and was produced more than 800 times between 1816 and 1912. There were at least five Guy Mannering operas, including *La Dame Blanche* (1825) by librettist Eugène Scribe and composer Adrien Boieldieu, which, second only to *Lucia di Lammermoor* in terms of its international success, had been performed no fewer than 1,675 times by 1914; see Mitchell, *The Walter Scott Operas*, 36–7. Also Fuhrman, 'Scott Repatriated?' *Guy Mannering* did not survive into the era of film and television, though BBC Scotland did produce a radio version in 1948; Bolton, *Scott Dramatized*, 58.

69. Ibid., 177–78.

70. Dibdin, *Annals of the Edinburgh Stage*, 301.

71. Bolton, *Scott Dramatized*, 256.

72. This tallies with Bell's suggestion that Scott plays were treated later in the century above all as cultural monuments rather than 'as a living force for change in the theatre'; Bell, 'Sir Walter Scott and the National Drama', 476.

73. The relative frequency of *Rob Roy* productions in the Scottish theatres is brought out ibid. 465–71. For Great Britain and North America, see Bolton, *Scott Dramatized*, 162–258.

74. Ibid., 56.

75. Ibid. 168. See also entries 1516 and 1890; and further variations in entries 1465, 1501, 1517, 1519, 1504, 1533, 1596, 1604. Interestingly a playbill from 1821 announces a drama 'founded on a novel of the same name, written by Walter Scott, Esq.', thereby identifying the still anonymous 'Author of Waverley' [entry 1504].

76. Entry 2331, ibid. 250.

77. Eight editions are listed ibid. 166. The Houghton library has identified with Pocock another edition of the play, published by The Crystal Palace Company, Sydenham, in 1875, which is not included in Bolton's list.

78. Walter Scott, *Rob Roy*, ed. David Hewitt (Edinburgh: Edinburgh University Press, 2008 [1817]), 274.

79. Bolton, *Scott Dramatized*, 162.

80. Stephen Knight, *Robin Hood: A Mythic Biography* (Ithaca, NY: Cornell University Press, 2003); Stephen Knight (ed.), *Robin Hood: An Anthology of Scholarship and Criticism* (Cambridge: D. S. Brewer, 1999).

81. Regarding ballads and other spin-offs: Scott, *Rob Roy*, 274.

82. George Soane, *Rob Roy, the Gregarach; A Romantic Drama, in Three Acts; as Performed at the Theatre Royal, Drury Lane* (London: Richard White, 1818). In his *History of the English Stage, 1600–1830* (1832), John Genest complained of this play that it 'is founded on the popular novel, but so many changes are made that one is disappointed, and consequently disgusted'; in Bolton, *Scott Dramatized*, 168.

83. Quoted from the *Glasgow Theatrical Observer* (1824); in Bolton, *Scott Dramatized*, 164.

84. See entries 1474, 1497, 1508, 1512; Bolton, *Scott Dramatized*, 171, 174, 175, 176.

85. Ibid., 163.

86. For the Dublin production see entry 2151, ibid. 235. Around 1841 a querulous critic in Glasgow complained that the Miss Sheriff, who had played Diana Vernon, should come better equipped in future when coming to the 'meridian of Scotland' by having a 'more popular selection of songs than what have yet appeared' (ibid. 224; entry 2007). On occasion foreign airs were also included, for example, the 'celebrated Bacchanalian Song' from *Der Freischutz* in Liverpool in 1827; Bolton adduces this example to suggest that revivals of *Rob Roy* were sometimes used merely as decor for the singers (ibid. 189; entry number 1638). Supplementary songs in other cases included Burns' 'A Man's a Man for a' That' [entry 1877], Moore's 'Last Rose of Summer' [entry 1570], and Moore's 'Oft in the Stilly Night' [entry 1878]; see Bolton, *Scott Dramatized*, 213, 182, 213.

87. Entries 1624, 1844, 1962; ibid., 188, 210, 220.

88. Bolton's comments relate specifically to *Guy Mannering*, but there is no reason to think that it does not also apply to the case of *Rob Roy*; ibid. 57. On the high rate of both internal migration and emigration in Scotland, see McNeil, *Scotland, Britain, Empire*, 12.

89. For a rare discussion of aural memory, see Caroline Bithell, 'The Past in Music: Introduction', *Ethnomusicology Forum* 15 (2006).

90. On recitation as a mode of remembrance, see also Ann Rigney, *Imperfect Histories: The Elusive Past and the Legacy of Romantic Historicism* (Ithaca, NY: Cornell University Press, 2001), 121–30.

91. Entry 1460, Bolton, *Scott Dramatized*, 169. On one occasion when Moore and Scott turned up together at the theatre, the crowd went wild and the band struck up a series of Irish and Scottish melodies; Dibdin, *Annals of the Edinburgh Stage*, 317–18.

92. Ragussis, *Theatrical Nation*, 14.

93. Entry 1499, Bolton, *Scott Dramatized*, 174.

94. For other uses of the term 'national' to describe theatrical works, see ibid., entries 1483, 1521, 1542, 1570, 1620, 1624, 1617, 1593, 1574; 1492, 1820; 1513, 1553, 1499, 1542, 1875, 1885, 1903, 1906, 2028, 2057, 2109, 2111, 2281, 2309, 2353, 2373, 2383, 2390, 2407; for an exception use of 'national' outside Scotland, see also 1641, 1844, 1962.

95. Entries 2138, 1624, 1798, 1475; Bolton, *Scott Dramatized*.

96. Bell, 'Sir Walter Scott and the National Drama', 474–5.

97. Quoted in Bolton, *Scott Dramatized*, 171–2.

98. Friedrich Schiller, 'Die Schaubühne als eine moralische Anstalt betrachtet' (1784) (http://gutenberg.spiegel.de).

99. Barbara Bell discusses the general rise of the term 'national' in the Scottish theatre in the 1820s, while noting the return of 'Scotch' in the 1850s as a way of proclaiming distinctiveness within the broader context of British politics

and against the background of renewed discussion of Scottish rights; Bell, 'Sir Walter Scott and the National Drama', 475–6.

100. Peter Burke, 'Performing History: The Importance of Occasions', *Rethinking History* 9(1) (2005); Diana Taylor, *The Archive and the Repertoire: Performing Cultural Memory in the Americas* (Durham, NC: Duke University Press, 2003). With specific reference to poetry and performance, see also Ann Rigney, 'Embodied Communities: Commemorating Robert Burns, 1859', *Representations*, 115 (2011).

101. Benedict Anderson, *Imagined Communities: Reflections on the Origins and Spread of Nationalism* (London: Verso, 1991 [1983]). The continuing importance of rituals in community-building has also been discussed extensively in Eviatar Zerubavel, *Hidden Rhythms: Schedules and Calendars in Social Life* (Berkeley: California University Press, 1985 [1981]).

102. Bell, 'The Nineteenth Century', 143.

103. *The Edinburgh Dramatic Review* 3 (31 March 1825), 449; quoted in Bell, 'Sir Walter Scott and the National Drama', 477.

104. Ernest Renan, 'Qu'est-ce qu'une nation? [1882]', in *Oeuvres complètes d'Ernest Renan*, ed. Henriëtte Psichari (Paris: Calmann-Lévy, 1947–61).

105. On the remediation of literary classics in early cinema, see Uricchio and Pearson, *Reframing Culture*.

106. On the political background to the 1995 film version, see Janet Sorensen, '*Rob Roy*: The Other Eighteenth Century?', in Robert Mayer (ed.), *Eighteenth-Century Fiction on Screen* (Cambridge: Cambridge University Press, 2002).

107. In J.G. Lockhart, *The Life of Sir Walter Scott, Bart.* (London: H&C Black, 1893 [1837–8]), 347.

CHAPTER 3

1. Jonathan Franzen, *The Corrections* (New York: Farrar, Straus and Giroux, 2001), 80.

2. Kurt Vonnegut Jr., *Slaughterhouse-Five: or The Children's Crusade, A Duty-Dance with Death* (St. Albans, Herts: Panther, 1972 [1969]), 114.

3. On *Slaughterhouse-Five* as a variation on the classic historical novel in the manner of Scott, see Ann Rigney, 'All This Happened More or Less: What a Novelist Made of the Bombing of Dresden', *History and Theory* 48 (2009).

4. Multiple children's versions are listed in Nicola J. Watson, 'Scott's Afterlives', in Fiona Robertson (ed.), *The Edinburgh Companion to Sir Walter Scott* (Edinburgh: Edinburgh University Press, 2012).

5. Extensive evidence of the impact of Scott's writings, first his poetry and then his novels, on the publishing scene is provided in William St Clair, *The Reading Nation in the Romantic Period* (Cambridge: Cambridge University Press, 2004), *passim*.

6. Paintings inspired by *Ivanhoe* are discussed especially in Paul deGategno, *Ivanhoe: The Mask of Chivalry* (New York: Twayne, 1994), 96–9.

7. An illustration of how even television can become a medium for traditional practices: since its first appearance almost three decades ago, it has become an annual ritual on New Year's Day for the 1982 film version of *Ivanhoe* (dir: D.Camfield) to be broadcast on Swedish television; with thanks to Niklas Bernsand. According to one Dutch commentator the generation who grew up in the 1960s in the Netherlands are linked too by their shared memory of the 1958 television series; http://vorige.nrc.nl/kunst/article1517119.ece/Roger_ Moore?service=Print [April 2011].

8. The idea of 'collective text' is borrowed here from Astrid Erll, *Kollektives Gedächtnis und Erinnerungskulturen* (Stuttgart: Metzler, 2005), 158–61.

9. For lists of translations, see Scottish Literature in Translation (BOSLIT) at the National Library of Scotland. With thanks to Yoriko Koyabashi-Sato for the reference to Kaise Hideo, 'The World of Ivanhoe Written by Walter Scott' (Tokyo: Asahki-Shuppan, 2009).

10. 'J'ai lu très jeune Ivanhoé, le roman de Walter Scott, qui m'a passionné. Je crois que c'est à partir de là que tout a commencé', François Busnel, 'Entretien avec Jacques Le Goff', *Lire.fr*, May 2005.

11. Stuart Kelly, *Scott-Land: The Man Who Invented a Nation* (Edinburgh: Polygon, 2010), 166–70.

12. Ann Rigney, 'Plenitude, Scarcity and the Circulation of Cultural Memory', *Journal of European Studies* 35 (2005).

13. On the link between recollection and shifting expectations, see Reinhart Koselleck, *Futures Past: On the Semantics of Historical Time*, trans. Keith Tribe (Cambridge, MA: MIT Press, 1985 [1979]), 261–86.

14. Walter Scott, *Ivanhoe*, ed. Ian Duncan (Oxford: Oxford University Press, 1996 [1819]), 29. Unless otherwise indicated, all further references are to this edition.

15. Ibid. 47.

16. Thomas Carlyle, *Critical and Miscellaneous Essays*, 7 vols (London: Chapman and Hall, 1872), VI: 71–2.

17. On the background to the novel in antiquarian research, and especially in the work of Sharon Turner's *History of the Anglo-Saxons* (1799–1805), see especially Clare A. Simmons, *Reversing the Conquest: History and Myth in Nineteenth-Century British Literature* (New Brunswick, NJ: Rutgers University Press, 1990), 53–63.

18. Scott's impact on the style and focus of historians such as Macaulay is discussed in greater detail in Ann Rigney, *Imperfect Histories: The Elusive Past and the Legacy of Romantic Historicism* (Ithaca, NY: Cornell University Press, 2001).

19. Thomas Babington Macaulay, *Critical, Historical and Miscellaneous Essays*, 3 vols (New York: A. L. Burt, n.d.), I: 307–8.

20. On Scott's addition of Robin Hood to the myth of the Norman yoke, see Marjorie Chibnall, *The Debate on the Norman Conquest* (Manchester: Manchester University Press, 1999), 53. For the background on racial origins, see Patrick J. Geary, *The Myth of Nations: The Medieval Origins of Europe* (Princeton, NJ: Princeton University Press, 2003).

21. Letter to Thomas Allsop (8 April 1820); Samuel Taylor Coleridge, *Collected Letters of Samuel Taylor Coleridge*, 6 vols (Oxford: Oxford University Press, 1959–71), V: 35. See also George Dekker, *The American Historical Romance* (Cambridge: Cambridge University Press, 1987), 34–5.

22. Svetlana Boym, *The Future of Nostalgia* (New York: Basic Books, 2001).

23. William Hazlitt, 'Sir Walter Scott', in *The Spirit of the Age* (Oxford: Woodstock Books, 1989 [1825]), 131. The idea that Scott 'spent his life running from contemporaneity' was echoed in A. T. Cunninghame, 'Scott in 1932', *Modern Scot*, Summer (1932), 115.

24. Given that the novel appeared just months after the Peterloo massacre the comparison drawn between the onlookers at Rebecca's would-be execution and spectators at a 'riot, or a meeting of radical reformers' had contemporary overtones; Scott, *Ivanhoe*, 479. This reference to contemporary riots elicited scathing criticism in Hazlitt, 'Sir Walter Scott', 150–1. Contemporary resonances of the novel are also discussed in James Chandler, *England in 1819: The Politics of Literary Culture and the Case of Romantic Historicism* (Chicago: University of Chicago Press, 1998), 84, 224–5.

25. Ina Ferris, *The Romantic National Tale and the Question of Ireland* (Cambridge: Cambridge University Press, 2002), 1–7. See further Laurence Brockliss and David Eastwood (eds), *A Union of Multiple Identities: The British Isles, c.1750–c.1850* (Manchester: Manchester University Press, 1997).

26. 'Sur l'histoire d'Écosse, et sur le caractère national des Écossais', in Augustin Thierry, *Dix ans d'études historiques* (Brussels: J.P.Meline, 1835), 175.

27. Robert Crawford, *Devolving British Literature* (Edinburgh: Edinburgh University Press, 2000), 132–33.

28. Duncan, in Scott, *Ivanhoe*, xix.

29. Linda Colley, *Britons: Forging the Nation 1707–1837* (New Haven, CT: Yale University Press, 1992), 130. For more recent developments following from Colley, see especially Evan Gottlieb, *Feeling British: Sympathy and National Identity in Scottish and English Writing, 1707–1832* (Lewisburg, PA: Bucknell University Press, 2007); Kenneth McNeil, *Scotland, Britain, Empire: Writing the Highlands, 1760–1860* (Columbus: Ohio University Press, 2007). The degree to which Scott's assertions of Scottish distinctiveness implied the desirability of political independence for Scotland is still hotly debated; but the fact that his world was a multinational one is undisputed.

30. I discuss the importance of 'models of remembrance' in greater detail in: Rigney, 'Plenitude, Scarcity'.

31. The jingoistic colouring of Sullivan's opera and its political implications are discussed in deGategno, *Ivanhoe*; Robert Giddings, 'Scott and Opera', in Alan Bold (ed.), *Sir Walter Scott: The Long Forgotten Melody* (London: Vision, 1983), 204, 215. A detailed description of this opera is given in Jeff S. Dailey, *Sir Arthur Sullivan's Grand Opera* Ivanhoe (Lampeter: Mellon Press, 2008).

32. Jerome McGann, *The Scholar's Art: Literary Studies in a Managed World* (Chicago: University of Chicago Press, 2006), 87. See also Jerome McGann, 'Walter Scott's Romantic Postmodernity', in Leith Davis et al. (eds), *Scotland and the Borders of Romanticism* (Cambridge: Cambridge University Press, 2004).

33. Scott, *Ivanhoe*, 17–18.

34. The reception of his Scottish novels shows that historical novelists do not always exercise their imaginations with impunity; for a fuller discussion, see Rigney, *Imperfect Histories*, 13–58.

35. Amy J. Elias, *Sublime Desire: History and Post-1960s Fiction* (Baltimore, MD: Johns Hopkins University Press, 2002). Scott's affinities with the tradition of Gothic romance are also highlighted in Fiona Robertson, *Legitimate Histories: Scott, Gothic, and the Authorities of Fiction* (Oxford: Clarendon Press, 1994).

36. Michael Ragussis, *Theatrical Nation: Jews and Other Outlandish Englishmen in Georgian Britain* (Philadelphia: University of Pennsylvania Press, 2010), esp. 196–203. The case provides a variation on Colley's contention that 'Britishness was superimposed over an array of internal differences in response to contact with the Other, and above all in response to conflict with the Other' (Colley, *Britons*, 30).

37. On the evolution of stereotypes, see Joep Leerssen, 'The Rhetoric of National Character: A Programmatic Survey', *Poetics Today* 21 (2000). The background of *Ivanhoe* in contemporary views of Jewishness has been discussed in Michael Ragussis, 'The Birth of a Nation in Victorian Culture: The Spanish Inquisition, the Converted Daughter, and the "Secret Race"', *Critical Inquiry* 20 (1994); Ragussis, *Theatrical Nation*; Michael Ragussis, 'Writing Nationalist History: England, the Conversion of the Jews, and *Ivanhoe*', *English Literary History* 60 (1993). On the ambivalence of Scott's liberalism with regard to Rebecca's Jewishness, see Nadia Valman, *The Jewess in Nineteenth-Century British Literary Culture* (Cambridge: Cambridge University Press, 2007), 33.

38. For earliest reactions to the novel: Anon., 'Ivanhoe, a Romance', *Blackwood's Edinburgh Magazine* 31 (1819); Anon., 'Ivanhoe, and The Monastery', *The British Review, and London Critical Journal* 15 (1820); Anon., 'Ivanhoe, by the author of Waverley, Etc', *The Edinburgh Magazine, and Literary Miscellany* 85, January (1820); Anon., 'Ivanhoe: A Romance', *The New Monthly Magazine and Universal Register* January–June (1820); Anon., 'Ivanhoe: A Romance', *Literary Gazette; and Journal of Belles Lettres, Arts, Sciences, etc. for the Year 1819*, 25 December (1819); Anon., 'Ivanhoe: A Romance, by the Author of Waverley', *Ladies Monthly Museum; or, Polite Repository of Amusement and Instruction; being an assemblage of whatever can tend to please the fancy, interest the mind, or exalt the character of the British Fair* 11 (1820); Anon., 'Ivanhoe: a Romance. By the Author of "Waverley"', *The Monthly Review; or Literary Journal* 91, January–April (1820); Anon., 'Ivanhoe: A Romance. By the Author of

'Waverley"', *Western Review and Miscellaneous Magazine*, May (1820); Anon., 'Ivanhoe: A Romance. By the Author of "Waverly"' [*sic*], *Literary Chronicle and Weekly Review* 33, January (1820).

39. Harriet Martineau, 'The Achievements of the Genius of Scott', *Tait's Edinburgh Magazine* 9 (1832), 456–7.

40. Scott, 'Author's Introduction' [1830], *Ivanhoe*, 544–5.

41. Ian Duncan, 'Introduction', in *Ivanhoe*, xxv.

42. Compare Umberto Eco's comments on *War and Peace* and the impossibility of Natasha ever marrying Andrej, as a lesson on the 'severe law of necessity'; in Umberto Eco, 'From Internet to Gutenberg', in *Italian Academy for Advanced Studies in America* (1996).

43. The term 'mnemonic *energeia*' is borrowed from Erll, *Kollektives Gedächtnis und Erinnerungskulturen*, 19–22; Aby Warburg, *Der Bilderatlas Mnemosyne*, ed. Martin Warnke (Berlin: Akademie Verlag, 2000 [1924–9]).

44. Michael Riffaterre, *Semiotics of Poetry* (Bloomington: Indiana University Press, 1978).

45. I am grateful to Laura Basu for this image which she also uses to describe the generative power of memory sites (what she calls 'dispositifs') in Laura Basu, *Remembering an Iron Outlaw: The Cultural Memory of Ned Kelly and the Development of Australian Identities* (Unpublished PhD thesis, Utrecht University, 2010).

46. H. Philip Bolton, *Scott Dramatized* (London: Mansell, 1992), 342. For a complete list of the published versions, see 345–6. For an example of a chapbook version, on sale for sixpence, see *Ivanhoe; Or, the Knight Templar, and the Jew's Daughter. An Ancient Tale of English Chivalry: From the Celebrated Romance of 'Ivanhoe' by the Author of 'Tales of my Landlord'* etc. (London: J. Bailey, 1821).

47. Mitchell also lists several more international operatic works more or less loosely based on the novel: Thomas Sari, *Ivanoé* (Ajaccio, 1863); Attilio Ciardi and Cesare Bordiga, *Ivanhoe* (Prato, 1888); Giovanni Pacini, *Ivanhoe* (Venice, 1832); Bartolomeo Pisani, *Rebecca* (Milan, 1865); A. Castegnier, *Rébecca* (Trouville, *c.*1886); Jerome Mitchell, *More Scott Operas: Further Analysis of Operas Based on the Works of Sir Walter Scott* (Lanham: University Press of America, 1996), 169–79; Jerome Mitchell, *The Walter Scott Operas: An Analysis of Operas Based on the Works of Sir Walter Scott* (Tuscaloosa: University of Alabama Press, 1977), 145–200.

48. Thomas Dibdin, *Ivanhoe: or, The Jew's Daughter; A Romantic Melo-Drama; in Three Acts* (New York: Samuel French, n.d. [1820]); William Thomas Moncrieff, *Ivanhoe! or, The Jewess; A Chivalric Play, in Three Acts; Founded on the Popular Romance of 'Ivanhoe'* (London: John Lowndes, 1820); Samuel Beazley, *Ivanhoe: or, The Knight Templar: Adapted from the Novel of that Name; First Performed the 2nd of March, 1820 at the Theatre Royal, Covent Garden* (London: W. Smith, 1820); John William Calcraft, *Ivanhoe, or the Jewess* (Leith: A. Allardice, n.d.); George Soane, *The Hebrew: a Drama*

(London: J. Lowndes, 1820); Alfred Bunn, *Ivanhoe: or, The Jew of York; a New Grand Chivalric Play in Three Acts* (Birmingham: Beilby and Knotts, 1820); [William Henry Murray], *Ivanhoe*, The Waverley Dramas, from the Novels of Sir Walter Scott, Bart. (London: George Routledge, 1845 [1824]); Emile Deschamps, *Ivanhoe: Opéra en trois actes imité de l'anglais par MM [E. Deschamps et G. de Wailly]* (n.p.: n.p. [c.1826]); G. M. Marini and Ottone Nicolaj, *Il Templario: melodramma in tre atti di G.M. Marini, musica del maestro Ottone Nicolaj, da rappresentarsi al regio teatro alla Scala, il Carnevale 1866* (Milano: Franceso Lucca, 1866 [1840]); Heinrich Marschner, *The Templar and the Jewess/Der Templer und die Jüdin* (New York: Metropolitan Opera House, n.d. [1829]); Robert Brough and William Brough, *The Last Edition of Ivanhoe, with All the Newest Improvements; an Extravaganza in Two Acts, as Performed at the Theatre Royal, Hay-Market* (London: Webster [1850]); Henry J. Byron, *Ivanhoe in Accordance with the Spirit of the Times; an Extravaganza* (London: Samuel French [1858]); M. Rophino Lacy, *The Maid of Judah; or, The Knights Templar; A Serious Opera in Three Acts* (London: Davidson [1833]); Fox Cooper, *Ivanhoe: A Historical Drama in Three Acts, Dramatised from Sir Walter Scott's Novel*, Dicks' Standard Plays and Free Acting Drama (London: John Dicks [1859]); Julian Sturgis, *Ivanhoe: A Romantic Opera; Adapted from Sir Walter Scott's Novel; words by Julian Sturgis; music by Arthur Sullivan* (London: Chappell, 1891). Thomas F. Plowman, *Isaac Abroad; or, Ivanhoe Settled and Rebecca Righted* (Oxford: Slatter and Rose, 1878) is listed in Bolton, *Scott Dramatized*, 345.

49. Mitchell, *The Walter Scott Operas*, 145–56.

50. See entry 3472 in Bolton, *Scott Dramatized*, 360. More information on the Marschner/Wohlbrück opera in Mitchell, *The Walter Scott Operas*, 156–66. On the controversy surrounding 'foreign' versions of Scott, see Chapter 2 above.

51. See entry 3513 on the Brough brothers' *The Last Edition of Ivanhoe with All the Newest Improvements* (1850) in Bolton, *Scott Dramatized*, 363.

52. See for example entries 3379, 3385; ibid., 352–3.

53. Entry 3447; ibid., 358.

54. Entry 3426; ibid., 357. For details of such an equestrian version of *Ivanhoe*, see entries 3370 and 3529 ibid. 364.

55. Bolton includes in the list of published versions several twentieth-century dramatizations geared towards schools (by Connell, Findlay, and Rau) that I leave out of my analysis here; Bolton, *Scott Dramatized*, 344–5.

56. Most remarkably in view of my argument later, Rebecca and Isaac were elided in a play from 1820 that was revived in 1821 (see Bolton entries 3336, 3350); ibid. 346, 349.

57. Rowena is missing from Calcraft, Soane, Deschamps, Lacy; King Richard is missing from Beazley, Soane, Bunn, Murray, Deschamps, Lacy; Prince John

from Beazley, Calcraft, Bunn, Murray, Deschamps, Marschner, Lacy; Ulrica from Moncrieff, Soane, Marschner, Lacy, Brough, Byron.

58. Another recurring scene is the one in which Wamba exchanges clothes with Friar Tuck and, reciting *pax vobiscum*, penetrates the Castle of Torquilstone in order to liberate Cedric (Moncrieff, Beazley, Calcraft, Bunn, Murray, Lacy, Cooper). Since the liberation of Cedric does not materially affect the outcome of events, the persistence of this scene presumably lies in its comedy.

59. Daniel C. Dennett, *Darwin's Dangerous Idea: Evolution and the Meanings of Life* (New York: Simon and Schuster, 1995), 68.

60. I use the term 'einfache Formen' (simple forms) following Jolles to refer to small textual units like jokes, proverbs, and anecdotes that have cultural sticking power; see further André Jolles, *Einfache Formen: Legende, Sage, Mythe, Rätsel, Spruch, Kasus, Memorabile, Märchen, Witz* (Halle: M. Niemeyer, 1930).

61. Stephen Knight, *Robin Hood: A Mythic Biography* (Ithaca, NY: Cornell University Press, 2003), 41.

62. Barbara Bell, 'The Nineteenth Century', in *A History of the Scottish Theatre*, ed. Bill Findley (Edinburgh: Polygon, 1998), 163.

63. The 'Knight Templar' was used as a subtitle in, for example, entries 353, 3352, 3360, 3369; variations on 'Jew's Daughter' and 'the Jew of York' were used in, for example, entries 3401, 3396, 3433, 3438, 3451, 3434, 3435; see Bolton, *Scott Dramatized*. The re-writings of the story on the stage are also briefly discussed in Duncan, 'Introduction', xxii–xxiii.

64. Soane, *The Hebrew*, 52, 53, 62.

65. William Makepeace Thackeray, 'Rebecca and Rowena: A Romance upon Romance by Mr. Michael Angelo Titmarsh', in *A Shabby Genteel Story; Novels by Eminent Hands; Rebecca and Rowena; The Rose and the Ring* (Moscow: Raduga, 1985), 300.

66. Lewis Roach, 'The Story of Ivanhoe: Sir Walter Scott's Great Story as Picturized in the Universal Film; Pictures Storyized by Lewis Roach', *The Photoplay Magazine* 4 (1913), 34. An extensive account of the production at Chepstow Castle is given in Anon., '"Ivanhoe": The Imperial Film Company's Great Production', *The Bioscope*, July 24 (1913); Anon., 'Producing "Ivanhoe" at Chepstow', *The Bioscope*, July 13 (1913).

67. Jonathan Stubbs, 'Hollywood's Middle Ages: The Development of *Knights of the Round Table* and *Ivanhoe*, 1935–53', *Exemplaria* 21 (2009).

68. An article in the *Weekly Scotsman* on 8 February 1947 reported on the controversy at Paramount but attributed the rejection of the script rather vaguely to the fear that it would be 'distasteful to the British'. Whether this distaste was linked to the deviation from a 'classic' or to the inclusion of Jews in the national narrative was not explained.

69. Philip Cox, *Reading Adaptations: Novels and Verse Narratives on the Stage, 1790–1840* (Manchester: Manchester University Press, 2000), 115, 111.

70. Bolton, *Scott Dramatized*, 342. On the reaction of Hazlitt, see Cox, *Reading Adaptations*, 111–12.

71. Cox, *Reading Adaptations*, 115.

72. Quoted in Bolton, *Scott Dramatized*, 347.

73. Roman Jakobson and Petr Bogatyrev, 'On the Boundary between the Studies of Folklore and Literature', in Ladislaw Matejka et al. (eds), *Readings in Russian Poetics: Formalist and Structuralist Views* (Cambridge, MA: MIT Press, 1971). In the case of *Ivanhoe*, the adaptations have only a tenuous relationship to the original; this applies to the popular television series from 1958, starring Roger Moore, that bears little resemblance to Scott's original beyond the name, the medieval setting, and the central character.

74. Jerome McGann, 'Ivanhoe: Education in a New Key', http://www.rc.umd. edu/pedagogies/commons/innovations/IVANHOE.html. See also Jerome McGann, 'Like Leaving the Nile: IVANHOE, a User's Manual', *Literature Compass* 2 (2005). The theory of interactive textuality underpinning the Ivanhoe project is elucidated in Jerome McGann, *The Point is to Change It: Poetry and Criticism in the Continuing Present* (Tuscaloosa: University of Alabama Press, 2007); McGann, *The Scholar's Art*, 135–71.

CHAPTER 4

1. Edgar Johnson, *Sir Walter Scott: The Great Unknown*, 2 vols (London: Hamilton, 1970), II: 1232.

2. A detailed account of a Waverley masquerade is given in Martha Wilmot, *More Letters from Martha Wilmot: Impressions of Vienna, 1819–1829*, ed. Marchioness of Londonderry, et al. (London: Macmillan, 1935), 234–41. The Duchesse de Berry was organizing similar events in Paris in 1826; Maurice Samuels, *The Spectacular Past: Popular History and the Novel in Nineteenth-Century France* (Ithaca, NY: Cornell University Press, 2004), 163. The Marchioness of Salisbury commissioned the painter Wilkie to provide sketches upon which the *tableaux vivants* at Hartfield House, Hertfordshire, would be based; Richard D. Altick, *Paintings from Books: Art and Literature in Britain 1760–1900* (Columbus: Ohio State University Press, 1985), 431. Masquerades in Calcutta are described, with passing reference to a Scott-themed event in 1826, in Bradley Shope, 'Masquerading Sophistication: Fancy Dress Balls of Britain's Raj', *Journal of Imperial and Commonwealth History* 39 (2011), 375–92 (esp. 385). Waverley masquerades apparently took place in Edinburgh and London as late as 1844: James Colston, *History of the Scott Monument, Edinburgh; To which is prefixed a biographical sketch of Sir Walter Scott, Bart.* (Edinburgh: Printed for the Magistrates and Town Council, 1881), 77–8. Some additional references to balls can be found in Nicola J. Watson, 'Scott's Afterlives', in Fiona Robertson (ed.), *The Edinburgh Companion to Sir Walter Scott* (Edinburgh: Edinburgh University Press, 2012).

3. On the reluctance to play the role of Isaac, see Richard Harris Barham, *Personal Reminiscences by Barham, Harness, and Hodder*, ed. Richard Henry Stoddard (New York: Scribner, Armstrong, 1875), 122.

4. Helen Solterer, *Medieval Roles for Modern Times: Theater and the Battle for the French Republic* (University Park: Pennsylvania State Press, 2010); Helen Solterer, 'The Waking of Medieval Theatricality, Paris 1935–1995', *New Literary History* 27 (1996).

5. See the basic argument in Maurice Halbwachs, *Les cadres sociaux de la mémoire* (Paris: Albin Michel, 1994 [1925]).

6. This point is elaborated in Ann Rigney, 'Plenitude, Scarcity and the Circulation of Cultural Memory', *Journal of European Studies* 35 (2005).

7. On the transfer of models of nation-building across the Western world in the early nineteenth century, see especially the major comparative project directed by Joep Leerssen: http://www.spinnet.eu. Also: Joep Leerssen, *National Thought in Europe: A Cultural History* (Amsterdam: Amsterdam University Press, 2006).

8. A more detailed discussion of the recycling of narrative models as a feature of collective remembrance is given in Rigney, 'Plenitude, Scarcity'. With respect to the historical novel, see specifically Ann Rigney, 'Fiction as a Mediator in National Remembrance', in Stefan Berger et al. (eds), *Narrating the Nation: The Representation of National Narratives in Different Genres* (Oxford: Berghahn Books, 2009). A more general discussion of racial opposition as a template for remembrance is given in Clare A. Simmons, *Reversing the Conquest: History and Myth in Nineteenth-Century British Literature* (New Brunswick, NJ: Rutgers University Press, 1990); Robert J. C. Young, *The Idea of English Ethnicity* (Oxford: Blackwell, 2008).

9. Murray Pittock (ed.), *The Reception of Sir Walter Scott in Europe* (London: Continuum, 2007).

10. On Thierry, see Ann Rigney, *Imperfect Histories: The Elusive Past and the Legacy of Romantic Historicism* (Ithaca, NY: Cornell University Press, 2001), 82–8. For more examples of the export of the Waverley model, see Pittock (ed.), *The Reception of Sir Walter Scott in Europe*. A more critical view on the 'export' of the Waverley model as a form of cultural colonialism is offered in Katie Trumpener, *Bardic Nationalism: The Romantic Novel and the British Empire* (Princeton, NJ: Princeton University Press, 1997), 242–91. The transposition of the model to South Africa and the South Seas is discussed in Douglas S. Mack, *Scottish Fiction and the British Empire* (Edinburgh: Edinburgh University Press, 2006), 169–203.

11. Thomas Davis, *Literary and Historical Essays* (Dublin: James Duffy, 1846), 222.

12. Pittock (ed.), *The Reception of Sir Walter Scott in Europe*, 1–9.

13. Rigney, 'Fiction as a Mediator'.

14. Esther J. Crooks and Ruth W. Crooks, *The Ring Tournament in the United States* (Richmond, VA: Garrett and Massie, 1936), 34. While it provides the most extensive information to date about the tournaments and is clearly based on extensive research in local archives, the authors regrettably do not list their sources in detail.

15. Ian Anstruther, *The Knight and the Umbrella: An Account of the Eglinton Tournament 1839* (London: Geoffrey Bles, 1963). The political background to the tournament is described in Marc Girouard, *The Return to Camelot: Chivalry and the English Gentleman* (New Haven, CT: Yale University Press, 1981), 88–110. That Ivanhoe provided a model for the tournament is made clear by a tie-in publication with a very wordy subtitle: *Tournament at Ashby-de-la-Zouche; As described by Sir Walter Scott, in the popular novel of 'Ivanhoe,' containing the best account of the Ancient and Chivalrous feat of Arms in our Language, and admirably Illustrative of the approaching Tournament at Eglington [sic] Castle* (n.p.: n.p., 1839). For more examples of tournaments in Britain, see Barbara Bell, 'The Performance of Victorian Medievalism', in Lorretta M. Holloway et al. (eds), *Beyond Arthurian Romances: The Reach of Victorian Medievalism* (London: Palgrave Macmillan, 2005). There were precedents for latter-day tournaments going back at least to 1778 to British troops stationed in Philadelphia; see Linda Colley, *Britons: Forging the Nation 1707–1837* (New Haven, CT: Yale University Press, 1992), 147. For general background to the tournament in Victorian medievalism, see Alice Chandler, *A Dream of Order: The Medieval Ideal in Nineteenth-Century English Literature* (London: Routledge & Kegan Paul, 1971); Girouard, *The Return to Camelot*.

16. Alex Tyrell, 'Paternalism, Public Memory and National Identity in Early Victorian Scotland: The Robert Burns Festival at Ayr in 1844', *History: A Quarterly Magazine and Review for the Teacher, the Student and the Expert* 90 (2005).

17. For extensive detail see Crooks and Crooks, *The Ring Tournament*; Guion Griffis Johnson, *Ante-Bellum North Carolina: A Social History*, electronic edn (Chapel Hill: University of North Carolina Press, 1937); Alex Tyrell, 'The Queen's "Little Trip": The Royal Visit to Scotland in 1842', *Scottish Historical Review* 82 (2003).

18. Crooks and Crooks, *The Ring Tournament*, 3, 101. On the value accorded duelling, see Ritchie Devon Watson, *Normans and Saxons: Southern Race Mythology and the Intellectual History of the American Civil War* (Baton Rouge: Louisiana State University, 2008), 6–7.

19. Ivanhoe was present, among other places, in Blakistone's Pavilion, MD, in 1857 (p. 12); at Point Outlook, MD, in 1860 (p. 13); Huguenot Springs, VA, in 1950 (p. 34); at Harper's Ferry, WV, in 1865 (p. 59); Bunker Hill, WV (p. 63). Other Scott knights include Peveril of the Peak (p. 58), Rob Roy (p. 109), Rhoderick Dhu (pp. 58, 109), and Waverley (p. 68). All references to Crooks and Crooks, *The Ring Tournament*. For several examples of Southern *tableaux vivants* based on Ivanhoe, see Watson, 'Scott's Afterlives'.

20. Quoted in Rollin G. Osterweis, *Romanticism and Nationalism in the Old South* (New Haven, CT: Yale University Press, 1949), 4–5.

21. Grace Warren Landrum, 'Sir Walter Scott and His Literary Rivals in the Old South', *American Literature* 2 (1930).

22. I am very grateful to Patrick J. Geary for having drawn my attention to this sketch and making it available to me.

23. Connections with confederacy fundraising are mentioned in Crooks and Crooks, *The Ring Tournament*, 15, 19, 51, 101, 107, 111, 130. For the presence of 'Knights of the Lost Cause', see ibid. 19, 51, 59, 81, 107, 152. The cult of the 'Lost Cause' in the period before 1880 was closely associated with the southern elite; see Gaines M. Foster, *Ghosts of the Confederacy: Defeat, the Lost Cause, and the Emergence of the New South, 1865 to 1913* (New York: Oxford University Press, 1987), 5–6.

24. Crooks and Crooks, *The Ring Tournament*, 108–9.

25. The extensive diary that Mary Chesnut kept during the war years reveals the extent to which literature was a formative influence on her generation and the educated class to which she belonged: Scott's *oeuvre*, along with that of other writers, provided multiple quotations and parallels for her description of the world around her; C. Vann Woodward, *Mary Chesnut's Civil War* (New Haven, CT: Yale University Press, 1981).

26. This discussion of the 'cultivation' of local traditions draws here both on Jan Assmann (see Chapter 1) and on Joep Leerssen's analysis of the link between identity-formation and the self-reflexive cultivation of culture; Joep Leerssen, 'Nationalism and the Cultivation of Culture', *Nations and Nationalism* 12 (2006).

27. This account of the general influence of Scott's poetry and the emergence of the concept of the Southron is based on Osterweis, *Romanticism and Nationalism*, 47.

28. Information on the Library of Congress Performing Arts Encyclopedia; http://lcweb2.loc.gov/diglib/ihas/loc.natlib.ihas.200000009/default.html (December 2009). The fact that *The Lady of the Lake* in particular had percolated into everyday life is vividly thematized in Margaret Atwood's novel *Alias Grace* (1996) in which Scott's poem takes the form of both a traditional quilt design and a ferry.

29. Anon., 'The Difference of Race between the Northern and Southern People', *Southern Literary Messenger: A Magazine Devoted to Literature, Science and Art* 30, June (1860), 403–4, 407. Quoted in Osterweis, *Romanticism and Nationalism*, 110.

30. William R. Taylor, *Cavalier and Yankee: The Old South and American National Character* (Cambridge, MA: Harvard University Press, 1979). On 'cavaliers' as a self-identifying label among students in Virginia, see Marshall Fishwick, 'F.F.V.'s', *American Quarterly* 11 (1959), 149. A recent survey of the evolution of the Cavalier/Roundhead opposition in nineteenth-century discourses about American identity confirms the general trend; see Ritchie Devon Watson, '"The Difference of Race": Antebellum Race Mythology and the Development of Southern Nationalism', *Southern Literary Journal* 35, Fall (2002). More generally on the discourse of racial oppositions, see Young, *The Idea of English Ethnicity*, 40–70.

31. A newspaper editor from Louisville, Kentucky, declared in 1862 that the 'slave oligarchs' had framed the Constitution of the United States, ran the government until 1861, and controlled the Yankees, just as 'Our Norman kinsmen in England, always a minority, have ruled their Saxon countrymen in political vassalage up to the present day.' The editorial expressed further the opinion that 'the Norman cavalier of the South cannot brook the vulgar familiarity of the Saxon Yankee'; quoted in Osterweis, *Romanticism and Nationalism*, 101. For more examples and a general account of the development of the opposition, see Watson, *Normans and Saxons*.

32. Alison Landsberg, *Prosthetic Memory: The Transformation of American Remembrance in the Age of Mass Culture* (New York: Columbia University Press, 2004).

33. Watson, *Normans and Saxons*, 62–5. Watson basically concurs with Mark Twain's view of Scott's influence (see below) while the main thrust of his analysis of the impact of *Ivanhoe* (pp. 47–71) is with showing that since Southern appropriations of *Ivanhoe* were based on misreadings of Scott's original, they could not be interpreted as symptomatic of a kinship with Scott's progressivism—*pace* Michael O'Brien, *Rethinking the South: Essays in Intellectual History* (Baltimore, MD: Johns Hopkins University Press, 1988).

34. The novel shows a 'non-transfigured' world rather than a romantic idealization; see the comments by Ian Duncan in his introduction to Walter Scott, *Ivanhoe* (Oxford: Oxford University Press, 1996 [1819]), xxvi.

35. On the increasing polarization between forward-looking abolitionists and 'backward'-looking Southerners, see Watson, *Normans and Saxons*, 52–3.

36. My argument here builds on Susan Manning's analysis of Scott's anti-chivalric traits: Susan Manning, 'Did Mark Twain Bring Down the Temple on Scott's Shoulders', in Janet Beer et al. (eds), *Special Relationship: Anglo-American Affinities and Antagonisms, 1854–1936* (Manchester: Manchester University Press, 2002). That *Ivanhoe* was actually critical of chivalry was already noted in 1878: 'The spirit of chivalry, on its harsher side, was never more adequately condemned than by Scott, in the very romance which has made the manners of chivalry familiar to us'; Julia Wedgwood, 'Sir Walter Scott and the Romantic Reaction', *Contemporary Review* 33, Aug./Nov. (1878), 535–6.

37. Mark Twain, *Life on the Mississippi* (1883), in *The Unabridged Mark Twain*, vol. II, ed. Lawrence Teacher (Philadelphia: Running Press, 1979), 422–3.

38. C. Bradford Mitchell (ed.), *Merchant Steam Vessels of the United States 1790–1868: 'The Lytle-Holdcamper List'* (Staten Island, NY: 1975).

39. Osterweis, *Romanticism and Nationalism*, 50–1. Although major, Scott's influence should not be seen as exclusive; see Landrum, 'Sir Walter Scott and His Literary Rivals in the Old South', 263.

40. Emily B. Todd, 'Establishing Routes for Fiction in the United States', *Book History* 12 (2009).

41. There were paddle-steamers named after Scott characters built between the 1830s and 1860s, including multiple *Ivanhoe*s, that operated both in the Union and in the Confederate states. There were also several vessels called *The Jewess* registered between 1839 and 1862 (in Pittsburgh, Baltimore, Cincinnati) though it is unclear whether there was a Scott connection; for details see Mitchell (ed.), *Merchant Steam Vessels*.

42. Manning, 'Did Mark Twain Bring Down the Temple on Scott's Shoulders'. Robert Crawford similarly portrays Twain as suffering from a certain anxiety of influence (isn't there something of a Waverley in Huck Finn? he asks); Robert Crawford, *Devolving English Literature*, 2nd edn (Edinburgh: Edinburgh University Press, 2000), 215.

43. For example in H. J. Eckenrode, 'Sir Walter Scott and the South', *North American Review* 206, October (1917); Wolfgang Schivelbusch, *Die Kultur der Niederlage: Der amerikanische Süden 1865, Frankreich 1871, Deutschland 1918* (Frankfurt am Main: Fischer Taschenbuch Verlag, 2003), 65–70.

44. See Rigney, 'Plenitude, Scarcity'.

45. Michel Foucault, 'What is an Author?' (1969), in *Textual Strategies: Perspectives in Post-Structuralist Criticism*, ed. Josué V. Harari (Ithaca, NY: Cornell University Press, 1979).

46. Twain, *The Unabridged Mark Twain*, II: 423.

47. Grace Warren Landrum, 'Notes on the Reading Matter of the Old South', *American Literature* 3, March (1931); Emily B. Todd, 'Walter Scott and the Nineteenth-Century American Literary Marketplace: Antebellum Richmond Readers and the Collected Editions of the Waverley Novels', *Papers of the Bibliographical Society of America* 93 (1999). Scott's widespread appeal also crossed the gender divide: Ronald J. Zboray, *A Fictive People: Antebellum Economic Development and the American Reading Public* (Oxford: Oxford University Press, 1993), 164, 169.

48. Osterweis echoed Twain in arguing that people in the South had stuck to Scott while Northerners had moved on to new styles of writing, including Dickens. *Mary Chesnut's Civil War* gives ample evidence, however, of an interest in Dickens; Osterweis, *Romanticism and Nationalism, passim*.

49. Richard Ivanhoe Cooke gave an address at William and Mary College, on 15 May 1847, on the anniversary of the political independence of Virginia; see Landrum, 'Sir Walter Scott and His Literary Rivals in the Old South', 262. Ivanhoe Talley (1850–8) was son of Jameson Madison Talley; Library of Virginia: Virginia Historical Inventory (http://www.lva.lib.va.us).

50. Louis Marshall Fielding built his home Ivanhoe in Fauquier Co., VA, sometime between 1840 and 1860; Library of Virginia: Virginia Historical Inventory (http://www.lva.lib.va.us). The records of the plantation names are spread over various sources: Georgia (http://www.ga.nrcs.usda.gov); South Carolina (http://south-carolina-plantations.com); Louisiana (http://files. usgwarchives.org/la/stmary/vitals/medical/coroner.txt); Mississippi (http:// www.covingtonhistory.co.uk/Mississippi.html). For the names of towns, see http://www.usps.com.

51. John Graves, *Goodbye to a River: A Narrative* (New York: Random House, 1960), 127. My thanks to Sylvia Jones for this reference.
52. There are only very generalized references to Scott names in George R. Stewart, *Names on the Land: A Historical Account of Placenaming in the United States*, revised and enlarged; 1st edn 1945 (Boston: Houghton Mifflin, 1958), 250, 270. A brief survey of Scott names worldwide is given in Stuart Kelly, *Scott-Land: The Man Who Invented a Nation* (Edinburgh: Polygon, 2010), 72–4.
53. 'Ivanhoe, Texas', *Texas State Historical Association* [online], available at: http://www.tshaonline.org/handbook/online/articles/II/hli13.html.
54. 'Survey of Civil War Ships', *National Underwater and Marine Agency* [online], http://www.numa.net/expeditions/survey_of_civil_war_ships.html.
55. See n.53 above.
56. Allen Tate, *The Fathers* (Denver: Alan Swallow, 1960), 32. Ivanhoe also figures in the depiction of a dysfunctional family in Alfred Hitchcock's *Shadow of a Doubt* (1943); Barry Keith Grant, *Shadows of Doubt: Negotiations of Masculinity in American Genre Films* (Detroit: Wayne State University Press, 2011), 3.
57. Harper Lee, *To Kill a Mockingbird* (London: Arrow Books, 2006 [1960]), 118. In light of this, it came as no surprise that the recent film *The Curious Case of Benjamin Button* (2008; dir. David Fincher), set in New Orleans, includes a brief shot of the young protagonist reading *Ivanhoe*.
58. Charles W. Chesnutt, *The House behind the Cedars* (London: X Press, 1998 [1900]), 28. I am very grateful to Ann Rowland for having drawn my attention to this case.
59. Ibid. 87. Eric J. Sundquist provides background to the novel in racial discourses, but curiously does not mention the Scott intertext: Eric J. Sundquist, *To Wake the Nations: Race in the Making of American Literature* (Cambridge, MA: Harvard University Press, 1993), 394–400.
60. Discussions of Rebecca seem to have only come up later and concentrated, on sometimes flimsy evidence and with a tendency to tunnel vision, on the purported real-life model for Scott's character in the person of Rebecca Gratz, an acquaintance of Washington Irving; see Dianne Ashton, *Rebecca Gratz: Women and Judaism in Antebellum America* (Detroit: Wayne State University Press, 1997); Joseph Jacobs, 'The Original of Scott's Rebecca', *Publications of the American Jewish Historical Society* 22 (1914); Judith Mindy Lewin, 'Legends of Rebecca: *Ivanhoe*, Dynamic Identification, and the Portraits of Rebecca Gratz', *Nashim; A Journal of Jewish Women's Studies & Gender Issues* 10 (2005).
61. Michael Rothberg, *Multidirectional Memory: Remembering the Holocaust in the Age of Decolonization* (Stanford, CA: Stanford University Press, 2009).
62. Franklin Burroughs, 'Lost Causes and Gallantry: Johnny Reb and the Shadow of Sir Walter', *American Scholar* 72 (2003).
63. David W. Blight, *Race and Reunion: The Civil War in American Memory* (Cambridge, MA: Belknap Press, 2001). More generally on the public

remembrance of the Civil War, see William A. Blair, *Cities of the Dead: Contesting the Memory of the Civil War in the South, 1865–1914* (Chapel Hill: University of North Carolina Press, 2004); Drew Gilpin Faust, *The Republic of Suffering: Death and the American Civil War* (New York: Knopf, 2008); Nina Silber, *The Romance of Reunion: Northerners and the South, 1865–1900* (Chapel Hill: University of North Carolina Press, 1993).

64. Blight, *Race and Reunion*, 185.

65. Thomas Dixon, *The Clansman: An Historical Romance of the Ku Klux Klan* (Gretna: Pelican, 2005 [1905]), [preface]. On the influence of Scott on W. D. Griffith's narrative strategies of national history, see James K. Chandler, 'The Historical Novel Goes to Hollywood: Scott, Griffith, and Film Epic Today', in Gene Ruoff (ed.), *The Romantics and Us: Essays on Modern Literature and Culture* (New Brunswick, NJ: Rutgers University Press, 1990).

66. The origin of the fiery cross in Scott's poem is noted in Wyn Craig Wade, *The Fiery Cross: The Ku Klux Klan in America* (New York: Oxford University Press, 1998 [1987]), 146.

CHAPTER 5

1. Walter Scott, *Waverley; or, 'Tis Sixty Years Since*, ed. Claire Lamont (Oxford: Clarendon Press, 1981), 76. The symbolic dimensions of this liminal space are discussed in Joep Leerssen, 'Over de ontologische status en de tekstuele situering van imagotypen: Exotisme en voetnoten in Walter Scotts "Waverley" ', in E. Eweg (ed.), *Deugdelijk vermaak: Opstellen over literatuur en filosofie in de negentiende eeuw* (Amsterdam: Huis aan de Drie Grachten, 1987).

2. On framing and its importance to display, see Barbara Kirshenblatt-Gimblett, *Destination Culture: Tourism, Museums, and Heritage* (Berkeley: University of California Press, 1998), esp. 1–3.

3. On the stratification of memories in cityscapes, see M. Christine Boyer, *The City of Collective Memory: Its Historical Imagery and Architectural Entertainments* (Cambridge, MA: MIT Press, 1994).

4. The many companions to Scott's landscapes include *The Book of Waverley Gems: In a Series of Engraved Illustrations of Incidents and Scenery in Sir Walter Scott's Novels* (London: Henry G. Bohn, 1846); Society of Painters, *Landscape Illustrations of the Waverley Novels, with Descriptions of the Views* (London: Charles Tilt, 1831); *The Land of Scott: A Series of Landscape Illustrations, Illustrative of Real Scenes, described in the Novels and Tales, of the Author of Waverley; From Drawings by the Most Distinguished Artists* (London: David Bogne, 1848); *Notices and Anecdotes Illustrative of the Incidents, Characters, and Scenery described in the Novels and Romances of Sir Walter Scott, Bart.; With a Complete Glossary of all his Works* (Paris: Baudry's European Library, 1833); [Robert Forsyth], *The Waverley Anecdotes: Illustrative of the Incidents, Characters and Scenery described in the Novels and Romances of Walter Scott, Bart.* (London: J. Cochrane and J. McCrone, 1833); John MacCulloch, *The Highlands and Western Isles of Scotland, containing Descriptions of their Scenery and*

Antiquities, with an Account of the Political History and Ancient Manners, and of the Origin, Language, Agriculture, Economy, Music, Present Condition of the People; Founded on a Series of Annual Journeys Between the Years 1811 and 1821, and Forming an Universal Guide to that Country, in Letters to Sir Walter Scott, Bart. (London: Longman, 1824); M. C. Pelle, *Landscape-historical Illustrations of the Waverley Novels/Nouvelles illustrations anglaises des romans de Sir Walter Scott, Bart.* (London/Paris: Fisher, 1840); James Skene, *A Series of Sketches of the Existing Localities Alluded to in the Waverley Novels, Etched from Original Drawings* (Edinburgh: Cadell, 1829); H. I. & A. Stevens, *Scott and Scotland; or, Historical and Romantic Illustrations of Scottish Story* [*sic*] (London: H. I. & A. Stevens, n.d.).

5. George Newenham Wright et al., *Landscape-Historical Illustrations of Scotland and the Waverley Novels; from Drawings by J.M.W. Turner, Professor R.A. etc.*, 2 vols (London: Fisher, Sons and Co., 1836–8), 8. Turner had a long association with Scott as illustrator of his poetry; see Gerald Finley, *Landscapes of Memory: Turner as Illustrator of Scott* (London: Scolar Press, 1980).

6. The most extensive and influential account of the geopolitics of romantic fiction, including that of Scott, is given in Katie Trumpener, *Bardic Nationalism: The Romantic Novel and the British Empire* (Princeton, NJ: Princeton University Press, 1997). See further, Leith Davis et al. (eds), *Scotland and the Borders of Romanticism* (Cambridge: Cambridge University Press, 2004); Penny Fielding, *Scotland and the Fictions of Geography: North Britain, 1760–1830* (Cambridge: Cambridge University Press, 2008); Saree Makdisi, *Romantic Imperialism: Universal Empire and the Culture of Modernity* (Cambridge: Cambridge University Press, 1998). On Scott's role in imagining a unified geography, see also Ian Duncan, *Scott's Shadow: The Novel in Romantic Edinburgh* (Princeton, NJ: Princeton University Press, 2007), 96–115.

7. The movements of Edward Waverley are mapped in Franco Moretti, *Atlas of the European Novel 1800–1900* (London: Verso, 1998), 39–41. While Moretti confines himself to *Waverley* and *Rob Roy*, his highlighting of the protagonists' movements is echoed by other critics. On the perpetual mobility of Scott's characters, see Ian Duncan, *Modern Romance and Transformations of the Novel: The Gothic, Scott, Dickens* (Cambridge: Cambridge University Press, 1992). On the general context of Scott's imaginative mappings of Scotland, with his fixation on roads and borders, see Fielding, *Scotland and the Fictions of Geography*, esp. 79, 100. On the Highlands as an imagined space, see Kenneth McNeil, *Scotland, Britain, Empire: Writing the Highlands, 1760–1860* (Columbus: Ohio University Press, 2007); Peter Womack, *Improvement and Romance: Constructing the Myth of the Highlands* (Houndmills: Macmillan, 1989). On Scott's work as a response to modernization, see Andrew Lincoln, *Walter Scott and Modernity* (Edinburgh: Edinburgh University Press, 2007).

8. Ina Ferris, *The Romantic National Tale and the Question of Ireland* (Cambridge: Cambridge University Press, 2002); Ina Ferris, 'Writing on the Border: The National Tale, Female Writing, and the Public Sphere', in Tilottama Rajan

et al. (eds), *Romanticism, History, and the Possibilities of Genre: Re-forming Literature 1789–1837* (Cambridge: Cambridge University Press, 1998).

9. M. M. Bakhtin, 'Discourse in the Novel', in Michael Holquist (ed.), *The Dialogic Imagination* (Austin: University of Texas Press, 1981).

10. Joep Leerssen, 'Fiction Poetics and Cultural Stereotype: Local Colour in Scott, Morgan, and Maturin', *Modern Language Review* 86 (1991). See also Leerssen's article on 'Centre/Periphery' in Manfred Beller and Joep Leerssen (eds), *Imagology: The Cultural Construction and Literary Representation of National Characters* (Amsterdam: Rodopi, 2007), 278–81.

11. On temporal heterogeneity within modernity, see Reinhart Koselleck, *Futures Past: On the Semantics of Historical Time*, trans. Keith Tribe (Cambridge, MA: MIT Press, 1985 [1979]). The temporal complexities of Scott's writings have also been discussed in an illuminating way in Richard Maxwell, *The Historical Novel in Europe, 1650–1950* (Cambridge: Cambridge University Press, 2009), 59–111.

12. The idea that fiction generates a sense of contemporaneity within the nation is drawn from Jonathan Culler, 'Anderson and the Novel', *Diacritics* 29 (1999).

13. I use the term 'spatial turn' following the assertion made by Fredric Jameson among others that in contemporary cultural theory the category of space predominates over that of time; Fredric Jameson, *Postmodernism, or, The Cultural Logic of Late Capitalism* (London: Verso, 1991), 154–80. The literature on the cultural construction of space has become vast; for a survey see Sigrid Weigel, 'Zum "topographical turn": Kartographie, Topographie und Raumkonzepte in den Kulturwissenschaften', *Kulturpoetik* 2 (2002). Jonathan Boyarin notes how long it took for cultural theorists to abandon the radical separation of time and space promoted by Kant, but gives evidence of a shift in perspective from the early 1980s on: see Jonathan Boyarin (ed.), *Remapping Memory: The Politics of TimeSpace* (Minneapolis: University of Minnesota Press, 1994), esp. 1–37.

14. Trumpener, *Bardic Nationalism*, 291.

15. David Lowenthal, *The Past is a Foreign Country* (Cambridge: Cambridge University Press, 1985). In making a general link between historicism and travel I am drawing on Peter Fritzsche, *Stranded in the Present: Modern Time and the Melancholy of History* (Cambridge, MA: Harvard University Press, 2004), 55–91.

16. As Frances Yates showed in her pioneering work, mnemonic practices from classical antiquity to the Renaissance were based on spatial models; Frances A. Yates, *The Art of Memory* (Chicago: Chicago University Press, 1966). The importance of space to information retrieval is borne out in modern psychology; see Daniel L. Schacter, *Searching for Memory: The Brain, the Mind, and the Past* (New York: Basic, 1996), 47–8.

17. Ann Rigney, 'Plenitude, Scarcity and the Circulation of Cultural Memory', *Journal of European Studies* 35 (2005). On 'chronic differentiation', see

Jeffrey K. Olick, *The Politics of Regret: On Collective Memory and Historical Responsibility* (London: Routledge, 2007), 188–92.

18. Maurice Halbwachs, *La mémoire collective* (Paris: Albin Michel, 1997 [1950]), 236, 235 (translation AR). Halbwach's fascination with the spatialization of memory found its most elaborate expression in his study of memory in Palestine: Maurice Halbwachs, *La topographie légendaire des Evangiles en Terre Sainte: Etude de mémoire collective* (Paris: Presses universitaires de France, 1941).

19. Similar examples can be found going back to antiquity: when Cicero and Piso visited the ruins of the Academy in Athens, for example, their excitement at literally following in the footsteps of their Greek masters by treading 'historic ground' was stimulated in advance by their reading; Cicero, *De finibus bonorum et malorum*, trans. H. Rackham (London: Loeb Classical Library, 1967), v: 1–2. The phrase 'historic ground' is in v: 5.

20. Aleida Assmann, *Erinnerungsräume: Formen und Wandlungen des kulturellen Gedächtnisses* (München: C. H. Beck, 1999), 298–339.

21. Stevens, *Scott and Scotland*, v–vi.

22. Stuart Kelly, *Scott-Land: The Man Who Invented a Nation* (Edinburgh: Polygon, 2010).

23. Michel Foucault, 'Des espaces autres' [1967], *Architecture, Mouvement, Continuité* 5 (1984).

24. Nicola J. Watson (ed.), *Literary Tourism and Nineteenth-Century Culture* (London: Palgrave Macmillan, 2009); Nicola J. Watson, *The Literary Tourist* (London: Palgrave Macmillan, 2006). See also Alastair Durie, '"Scotland is Scott-land": Scott and the Development of Tourism', in Murray Pittock (ed.), *The European Reception of Sir Walter Scott* (London: Continuum, 2007). On the role of illustrations in clinching the connection between location and history, see Richard Hill, *Picturing Scotland through the Waverley Novels: Walter Scott and the Origins of the Victorian Illustrated Novel* (London: Ashgate, 2010), 161. According to Watson, Scott himself colluded with the development of a tourist guide to Melrose; Watson, *The Literary Tourist*, 94.

25. Watson, *The Literary Tourist*, 150–63.

26. Edgar Johnson, *Sir Walter Scott: The Great Unknown*, 2 vols (London: Hamilton, 1970), I: 335.

27. Watson, *The Literary Tourist*, 158.

28. Thomas Cook, quoted in Piers Brendon, *Thomas Cook: 150 Years of Popular Tourism* (London: Secker and Warburg, 1991), 38. On Scott's influence on organized tourism, see also John R. Gold and Margaret M. Gold, *Imagining Scotland: Tradition, Representation and Promotion in Scottish Tourism since 1750* (London: Scolar Press, 1995), Chap. 4. On the transition from independent travel to packaged tourism, see James Buzard, *The Beaten Track: European Tourism, Literature, and the Ways to Culture, 1800–1918* (Oxford: Clarendon Press, 1993); John Urry, *The Tourist Gaze*, 2nd edn (London: Sage, 2002). A basic account of tourism to Lake Katrine in particular is given in Watson, *The Literary Tourist*, 150–63. *Rob Roy* along with *The Lady of the*

Lake helped stimulate tourism to the area around Lake Katrine; see Ian Duncan's introduction to Walter Scott, *Rob Roy* (Oxford: Oxford University Press, 1998 [1817]), vii.

29. Brendon, *Thomas Cook*, 49.

30. For a more detailed account of Victoria's relationship to Scotland, see Alex Tyrell, 'The Queen's "Little Trip": The Royal Visit to Scotland in 1842', *The Scottish Historical Review* 82 (2003). As Tyrell points out, some of the organizers of the Eglinton tournament in 1839 (see Chapter 4) were also involved in stage-managing the Queen's first visit to Scotland. Part of the interior of Buckingham Palace was decorated with Scott frescoes: Richard D. Altick, *Paintings from Books: Art and Literature in Britain 1760–1900* (Columbus: Ohio State University Press, 1985), 429.

31. On Turner's engravings of Scott, see Finley, *Landscapes of Memory*. On McCulloch's *Loch Katrine*, see John Glendening, *The High Road: Romantic Tourism, Scotland, and Literature, 1720–1820* (London: Macmillan, 1997), 234–6. The 'white strand', which was regularly visualized from the same perspective as Scott's original description in *The Lady of the Lake*, was also the subject of early photographs by George Washington Wilson; Helen Groth, *Victorian Photography and Literary Nostalgia* (Oxford: Oxford University Press, 2003), 92.

32. David Duff (ed.), *Queen Victoria's Highland Journals* (Exeter: Webb and Bower, 1980), 147–8.

33. George Eyre-Todd, *To the Homes and Haunts of Scott and Burns by the Caledonian Railway* (Glasgow: McCorquodale, *c.*1911). Watson (ed.), *Literary Tourism* offers an array of case-studies illustrating the general development of tourism relating to writers.

34. Watson, *The Literary Tourist*, 150.

35. Eric Armstrong et al., *Waverley: Birth of a Legend* (n.p.: Paddle Steamer Preservation Society, 1987), 36.

36. *SS-Sir Walter Scott on Loch Katrine* (Norwich: Jarrold, *c.*1994). By now the steamship *Sir Walter Scott*, originally designed to carry tourists to admire the sites of *The Lady of the Lake* and *Rob Roy*, has itself become a prime tourist destination. So much so that the SS *Sir Walter Scott* won a Steam Heritage Award in 1989, chosen by enthusiasts of locomotion with little if any interest in matters literary. The title *Sir Walter Scott on Lake Katrine* thus refers in the first instance to this famous ship and only indirectly to the 'author of Waverley'.

37. The battlefield of Flodden, celebrated in *Marmion*, was already in Scott's lifetime the location of a pub carrying his name; see, Johnson, *Sir Walter Scott*, I: 399.

38. Urry, *The Tourist Gaze*.

39. *The Scott Banquet, August 9, 1871* (Glasgow: James Maclehose, publisher to the University, 1872), 65.

40. Walter Scott, *Chronicles of the Canongate*, ed. Claire Lamont (London: Penguin, 2003), 38.

41. Trumpener, *Bardic Nationalism*, 291.
42. For a history of the house and its ownership, see Iain G. Brown (ed.), *Abbotsford and Sir Walter Scott: The Image and the Influence* (Edinburgh: Society of Antiquaries of Scotland, 2003).
43. Virginia Woolf, 'Gas at Abbotsford', in *Collected Essays*, 4 vols (London: Hogarth Press, 1966), I: 134–9.
44. On the resonance of the study, see Thomas Dibdin, *A Bibliographical, Antiquarian, and Picturesque Tour in the Northern Counties of England, and in Scotland*, 2 vols (London: Printed for the Author by C. Richards, 1838), II: 1012. Quoted in Watson, *The Literary Tourist*, 103.
45. Kelly, *Scott-Land*, 128, 132. Kelly devotes three evocative chapters to Abbotsford (pp. 127–41). The reference to the uncanny is in the chapter entitled 'Haunted House' (p. 136).
46. Watson, *The Literary Tourist*, 105.
47. Neo-gothic architecture in United States has been described as a by-product of Scott's influence; Kerry Dean Carso, 'Diagnosing the "Sir Walter Disease"': American Architecture in the Age of Romantic Literature', *Mosaic* 35(4) (2002). The bi-level 'Sir Walter Scott' design for a prefabricated house advertised by Forest Homes, Pennsylvania, and used as the basis of Mike Bouchet's installation at the Venice Biennale in 2009 can be seen as a distant echo of Scott's fabrication of Abbotsford; http://www.foresthomes.com/americanvalues/sirwalterscott.asp (April 2011).
48. Harald Hendrix, 'Writers' Houses as Media of Expression and Remembrance: From Self-Fashioning to Cultural Memory', in Harald Hendrix (ed.), *Writers' Houses and the Making of Memory* (New York: Routledge, 2008).
49. On the construction and design of Abbotsford, see John Frew, 'Scott, Abbotsford and the Antiquaries', in Brown (ed.), *Abbotsford and Sir Walter Scott*, 37–48. On Abbotsford as a prototype for the 'romantic interior' see Clive Wainright, *The Romantic Interior: The British Collector at Home, 1750–1850* (New Haven, CT: Yale University Press, 1989), 147–207.
50. Hugh Trevor-Roper, 'The Invention of Tradition: The Highland Tradition of Scotland', in Eric Hobsbawm et al. (eds), *The Invention of Tradition* (Cambridge: Cambridge University Press, 1983).
51. This point about the many references to Scott's written work in the objects displayed is indebted to Watson, *The Literary Tourist*, 99.
52. The contrast between Bryon's Newstead Abbey and Abbotsford was first drawn in Washington Irving, *Abbotsford, and Newstead Abbey* (London: John Murray, 1835). It is the subject, too, of Stephen Bann's pioneering analysis of the semiotics of both buildings: 'Byron and Scott' in Stephen Bann, *The Clothing of Clio: A Study of the Representation of History in Nineteenth-Century Britain and France* (Cambridge: Cambridge University Press, 1984), 93–111.
53. Julie Lawson, 'Rushkin on Scott's Abbotsford', in Brown (ed.), *Abbotsford and Sir Walter Scott*, 165.

54. [J. McVickar], 'Abbotsford', *Dublin Weekly Journal: A Repository of Music, Literature, and Entertaining Knowledge* 22, 30 March (1833). The relationship between the demolition of the Tolbooth, the building of Abbotsford, and the writing of the novel is discussed in David Hewitt and Alison Lumsden (eds), *The Heart of Mid-Lothian*, Edinburgh Edition of the Waverley Novels (Edinburgh: Edinburgh University Press, 2004), 474–5.

55. I use the notion of a 'display' building here on a par with the notion of 'display' text developed in M. Louise Pratt, *Toward a Speech Act Theory of Literary Discourse* (Bloomington: Indiana University Press, 1977), 132 f.

56. On the early development of the rhetoric of museum display, see Bann, *The Clothing of Clio*, 77–92.

57. A more detailed account of the collection can be found in Hugh Cheape et al., 'Sir Walter Scott, the Abbotsford Collection and the National Museums of Scotland', in Brown (ed.), *Abbotsford and Sir Walter Scott*, 49–89. For more details on Scott's eclectic collection and their provenance, see Wainright, *The Romantic Interior*, 179–207. While his collection did indeed contain some objects from the colonies (including horns from South Africa, Malaysian krises, Inca relics), usually gifts, the relative importance attributed to them by Trumpener as a 'repository of empire' seems exaggerated; Trumpener, *Bardic Nationalism*, 243.

58. For a catalogue of the Library in Abbotsford, see J. G. Cochrane, *Catalogue of the Library at Abbotsford* (Edinburgh: Constable, 1838).

59. An excellent account of the many aspects of the building of Abbotsford is provided in Iain G. Brown, 'Scott, Literature and Abbotsford', in Brown (ed.), *Abbotsford and Sir Walter Scott*, 4–36. Also highly informative regarding the different phases of the building and the composition of the interior: Wainright, *The Romantic Interior*, 147–207. Wainright includes on p. 158 a very early photograph of the house made W. H. Fox Talbot in 1845, originally published as part of the collection *Sun Pictures in Scotland* (1845). The phrase 'The *Waverley* in stone' is quoted on p. 5. A more hagiographic account, which nevertheless gives a good overview of the contents of the house, is offered in W. S. Crockett, *Abbotsford* (London: A&C Black, 1905).

60. On the emergence of historical fiction from Scott's engagement with antiquarianism, see also Ann Rigney, *Imperfect Histories: The Elusive Past and the Legacy of Romantic Historicism* (Ithaca, NY: Cornell University Press, 2001), 124–30.

61. Letters 14–15 March, 27 March, 14 November 1822; quoted in Brown (ed.), *Abbotsford and Sir Walter Scott*, 18.

62. A work left unfinished at Scott's death and recently published for the first time, see Walter Scott, *Reliquiae Trotcosienses, or the Gabions of the Late Jonathan Oldbuck Esq. of Monkbarns*, ed. Gerard Carruthers and Alison Lumden (Edinburgh: Edinburgh University Press, 2004). A manuscript counterpart relating to the design of the landscaped gardens at Abbotsford,

in which Scott was also intimately involved, is called *Sylva Abbotsfordiensis*; available through the Faculty of Advocates, Edinburgh.

63. Duncan, *Modern Romance*, 152.

64. The link between the financial burden of Abbotsford and Scott's prodigious literary output has been made, for example, in Brown (ed.), *Abbotsford and Sir Walter Scott*, 16–17.

65. See Jeanne Cannizzo, '"He was a Gentleman even to his Dogs": Portraits of Scott and his Canine Companions', ibid. 115–35.

66. Irving, *Abbotsford, and Newstead Abbey*.

67. Crockett, *Abbotsford*, 44.

68. Johnson, *Sir Walter Scott*, II: 1249. This is also recalled in Brown (ed.), *Abbotsford and Sir Walter Scott*, xiii.

69. *Abbotsford: 12 Photos for your Album* (Dundee: Valentine, *c.*1900). Visualizations were supplemented on occasion by dramatic portrayals of 'the author of Waverley' c.q. 'the laird of Abbotsford'; these included a funerary masque set in Abbotsford called the *Vision of the Bard*, written in 1832 by S. Knowles, and a radio play by W. E. Gunn dealing with his financial difficulties called *Scott's Folly* (broadcast 21 September 1935). The name 'Abbotsford' was also disseminated through souvenir objects and publishing spin-offs like the *Abbotsford Series of the Scottish Poets*, ed. J. E. Todd (1891–) and the *Abbotsford Song Book: A Collection of Songs for Two Voices* (1901).

70. Richard Maxwell, 'Walter Scott, Historical Fiction, and the Genesis of the Victorian Illustrated Book', in Richard Maxwell (ed.), *The Victorian Illustrated Book* (Charlottesville: University Press of Virginia, 2002), 35–7. This article includes many illustrations to Scott's novels based on objects at Abbotsford.

71. Black's 1872 edition of the poetical works was bound in wood allegedly grown at Abbotsford; Groth, *Victorian Photography*, 101.

72. Disappointed comments by William Howitt, Nathaniel Hawthorne, and Theodor Fontane among others are cited in Kelly, *Scott-Land*, 133–6; Watson, *The Literary Tourist*, 103–5. Hawthorne's visit is also recounted in Erin Hazard, 'The Author's House: Abbotsford and Wayside', in Watson (ed.), *Literary Tourism*, 68–9.

73. There are so many Abbotsford streets that it is difficult to do an exhaustive search, but initial findings suggest that, as far as Great Britain is concerned, there is a high concentration in Scottish cities while examples also occur in major cities in England (Manchester, Birmingham, Blackburn, among others). While Scott street names generally date from the period between 1870 and 1910, there are some later exceptions, most notably Edinburgh where Scott names were given to a housing estate in Inch as late as 1950 (see further Chapter 7).

74. See, for example, the cities of Abbotsford in Wisconsin (USA) and British Columbia (Canada); the suburbs of Abbotsford in Melbourne (Australia) and Dunedin (N. Zealand); the Abbotsford streets in Johannesburg (South

Africa), Winnipeg (Canada), Hamilton (New Zealand), Leederville (Western Australia), and, in the United States, Boston and Larimer County (Colorado).

75. Sara Jeannette Duncan, 'The Hesitation of Miss Anderson', *The Pool in the Desert* (1903), 99–161 (p. 105); quoted in Trumpener, *Bardic Nationalism*, 243–4.

76. Shakespeare, Scott, and Columbus were later joined by Robert Burns in 1880 and by the American poet Fitzgreene Halleck (1790–1867), the latter illustrating the principle that monumentalization is no guarantee of lasting literary fame.

77. William Cullen Bryant, *Address on the Unveiling of the Statue of Sir Walter Scott in Central Park, November 4, 1872* (New York: G. P. Putnam's Sons, 1873).

78. Walter Scott, *The Journal of Sir Walter Scott*, ed. W. E. K. Anderson (Edinburgh: Canongate, 1998), 13, 15.

79. Durie, '"Scotland is Scott-land"'; Alastair Durie, 'Tourism in Victorian Scotland: The Case of Abbotsford', *Scottish Economic and Social History* 12 (1992), 43. For an early example of a 'guide to' Abbotsford, see J. H. Lizars and James Morton, *Abbotsford: The Seat of Sir Walter Scott, Bart.* (Edinburgh: Lizars, 1832).

80. In the early 1990s the annual number of visitors was between 70,000 and 80,000; Durie, 'Tourism in Victorian Scotland'. The recent figure of 31,000 for 2004 put forward by Stuart Kelly is considerably smaller: Kelly, *Scott-Land*, 138. That the power of Abbotsford as a memory site has been eroded became very evident to the present writer on a trip to Edinburgh in January 2005: requests for directions to Abbotsford drew blank looks from the local staff members at an Edinburgh hotel, one of whom surmised, in an effort to be helpful: 'Abbotsford, isn't that the new centre for genetics research?' *Sic transit gloria mundi.*

81. The following account of the development of Abbotsford as tourist site is based on the detailed accounts given in Crockett, *Abbotsford*; Durie, 'Tourism in Victorian Scotland'. My thanks to the staff at Abbotsford for giving me access to the visitors' books.

82. This pattern of visits by 'secondary' royalty continued into the twentieth century; the scrapbooks of newspaper cuttings in the Corson collection in Edinburgh University Library reveal a steady flow of such visitors throughout the century; my thanks to Paul Barnaby for permission to consult these scrapbooks. This tradition has been continued down to the present day: the current Abbotsford website mentions a recent 'Royal Visit', referring to a visit by the Princess Royal rather than by the Queen herself: http://www.scottsabbotsford.co.uk/ (accessed 3 January 2010).

83. For the general background to the rise of organized tourism in Scotland, see Brendon, *Thomas Cook*; Buzard, *The Beaten Track*; Glendening, *The High Road*.

84. See further Roger Siviter, *Waverley: Portrait of a Famous Route* (Southampton: Kingfisher Railway Productions, 1988).

85. Crockett, *Abbotsford*. Also quoted in Trumpener, *Bardic Nationalism*, 243. Durie put the percentage of visitors from the United States in the 1870s at between 25 and 33%; Durie, 'Tourism in Victorian Scotland', 49–50.

86. Ibid. 50–1. The visit by General Bradley is recorded in a newspaper clipping from 9 October 1947 (Corson collection).

87. Benedict Anderson, 'Exodus', *Critical Inquiry* 20 (1994).

88. On the ships called *Walter Scott*, see above Chapter 4, n.38.

89. 'The Scott Centenary (*From the Times*)', *Edinburgh Evening Courant* (11 August 1871).

90. Thomas Mellon, *Thomas Mellon and His Times*, ed. Mary Louise Briscoe (Pittsburgh: University of Pittsburgh Press, 1994). I am grateful to Dr. Brian Lambkin, Director of the Centre for Migration Studies at the Ulster-American Folk Park, for drawing my attention to this autobiographical account.

91. Ibid. 316.

92. Ibid.

93. For a more elaborate version of this argument, see Ann Rigney, 'Embodied Communities: Commemorating Robert Burns, 1859', *Representations*, 115 (2011). On the relationship and rivalry between Burns and Scott within the Scottish diaspora, see Mary Ellen Brown, *Burns and Tradition* (London: Macmillan, 1984). The development of Burns' cottage as a pilgrimage destination is well described in Karyn Wilson-Costa, 'The Land of Burns: Between Myth and Heritage', in Watson (ed.), *Literary Tourism*, 37–48.

94. Mellon, *Thomas Mellon and His Times*, 238.

95. Ibid.

96. Ibid. 330. Mellon's spontaneous reaction was in line with the cult of writers' graves that was also part of literary tourism in the nineteenth century; Samantha Matthews, *Poetical Remains: Poets' Graves, Bodies, and Books in the Nineteenth Century* (Oxford: Oxford University Press, 2004).

97. Mellon, *Thomas Mellon and his Times*, 335.

98. Ibid. 325–6.

CHAPTER 6

1. I am particularly grateful to Paul Barnaby for his help as curator of the Corson collection at the Edinburgh University Library in the preparation of this chapter.

2. A detailed account of the building and the design of the monument is given in James Colston, *History of the Scott Monument, Edinburgh; To which is prefixed a biographical sketch of Sir Walter Scott, Bart.* (Edinburgh: Printed for the Magistrates and Town Council, and Sold at the Monument, 1881). Charles Dickens once referred to it as 'the spire of a Gothic church taken off and stuck in the ground', quoted in Andrew Lownie, *The Literary Companion to*

Edinburgh (London: Methuen, 2000), 78. Another commentator in 1840 referred to it as the 'full-sized portrait of a dwarf', in Hugh Miller, *Leading Articles on Various Subjects*, ed. John Davidson, 4th edn (Edinburgh: William P. Nimmo, 1872), 115.

3. Scholars have had little to say on the monument, with the exception of Ian Duncan, who has commented briefly on its design and its profiling of a pantheon of characters; Ian Duncan, *Modern Romance and Transformations of the Novel: The Gothic, Scott, Dickens* (Cambridge: Cambridge University Press, 1992), 177–8.

4. A drive to relativize Scott's importance and highlight the writers he over-shadowed is behind the design of books as different as Ian Duncan, *Scott's Shadow: The Novel in Romantic Edinburgh* (Princeton, NJ: Princeton University Press, 2007); Douglas S. Mack, *Scottish Fiction and the British Empire* (Edinburgh: Edinburgh University Press, 2006); and Katie Trumpener, *Bardic Nationalism: The Romantic Novel and the British Empire* (Princeton, NJ: Princeton University Press, 1997).

5. Trumpener, *Bardic Nationalism*, 291. Also Mack, *Scottish Fiction and the British Empire*, 11.

6. M. Christine Boyer, *The City of Collective Memory: Its Historical Imagery and Architectural Entertainments* (Cambridge, MA: MIT Press, 1994); Dolores Hayden, *The Power of Place: Urban Landscapes as Public History* (Cambridge, MA: MIT Press, 1995).

7. Reinhart Koselleck, 'Kriegerdenkmale als Identitätsstiftungen der Überleben-den', in Odo Marquard et al. (eds), *Identität* (München: Wilhelm Fink, 1979).

8. 'Jede Gruppe, die sich als solche konsolidieren will, ist bestrebt, sich Orte zu schaffen und zu sichern, die nicht nur Schauplätze ihrer Interaktionsformen abgeben, sondern Symbole ihrer Identität und Anhaltspunkte ihrer Erinn-erung. Das Gedächtnis braucht Orte, tendiert zur Verräumlichung' (trans. AR). Jan Assmann, *Das kulturelle Gedächtnis: Schrift, Erinnerung und poli-tische Identität in frühen Hochkulturen* (München: C. H. Beck, 1997 [1992]), 39.

9. For a vivid account of Scott's pre-eminence in Edinburgh at the beginning of the nineteenth century, the man to emulate and the man to beat, see esp. Duncan, *Scott's Shadow*.

10. Pierre Nora (ed.), *Les lieux de mémoire*, 3 vols (Paris: Gallimard, 1997 [1984–92]).

11. Benedict Anderson, *Imagined Communities: Reflections on the Origins and Spread of Nationalism* (London: Verso, 1991 [1983]).

12. Benedict Anderson, 'Exodus', *Critical Inquiry* 40 (1994).

13. On the trans-European emergence of national pantheons, see Joep Leerssen, *National Thought in Europe: A Cultural History* (Amsterdam: Amsterdam University Press, 2006). See also his database on comparative nationalisms at www.romanticnationalism.net.

14. On the representative value of individuals and their role in visualizing the nation, see also Ann Rigney, *The Rhetoric of Historical Representation: Three Narrative Histories of the French Revolution* (Cambridge: Cambridge University Press, 1990), 137–70. More recently, a similar point has been made regarding iconic photographs and their affective role in public culture in Robert Hariman and John Louis Lucaites, *No Caption Needed: Iconic Photographs, Public Culture, and Liberal Democracy* (Chicago: University of Chicago Press, 2007).

15. J. G. Lockhart, *The Life of Sir Walter Scott, Bart.; New Popular Edition* (London: A&C Black, 1893 [1837–8]), 256–7. See also Edgar Johnson, *Sir Walter Scott: The Great Unknown*, 2 vols (London: Hamilton, 1970), I: 436–9.

16. Johnson, *Sir Walter Scott*, I: 455–8. A graphic account of the formal admission of his authorship in 1827 is given in Lockhart, *The Life of Sir Walter Scott, Bart.*, 652–3.

17. David Brewer, *The Afterlife of Character, 1726–1825* (Philadelphia: University of Pennsylvania Press, 2005), 189–206.

18. See above Chapter 2, n.75 for references to Scott's identity in the theatre.

19. That Scott was not only a consummate story-teller but also a supremely self-conscious narrator has been highlighted by a number of commentators; see esp. Ina Ferris, 'Melancholy, Memory, and the "Narrative Situation" of History in Post-Enlightenment Scotland', in Leith Davis et al. (eds), *Scotland and the Borders of Romanticism* (Cambridge: Cambridge University Press, 2004); Jerome McGann, 'Walter Scott's Romantic Postmodernity', in Davis et al. (eds), *Scotland and the Borders of Romanticism*; Fiona Robertson, *Legitimate Histories: Scott, Gothic, and the Authorities of Fiction* (Oxford: Clarendon Press, 1994).

20. While long dismissed, the 'late' Scott is now becoming the object of renewed critical scrutiny; see, for example, Caroline McCracken-Flesher, 'Prediction of Things Past: Scott and the Triumph of the Author's Antiquity', *Anglistik* 23 (2012).

21. Jane Millgate, *Scott's Last Edition: A Study in Publishing History* (Edinburgh: Edinburgh University Press, 1987).

22. Quoted in Judith Wilt, *Secret Leaves: the Novels of Walter Scott* (Chicago: University of Chicago Press, 1985), 1.

23. On Scott's impact as a public figure in Edinburgh see esp. Duncan, *Scott's Shadow*.

24. The link between Scott and 'health' was made most forcibly by Carlyle, who did not mean it as a compliment but rather as a symptom of a lack of real complexity and passion (he also compared Scott to a warm bath). See further James Frederick Rogers, 'The Healthiest of Men', *Scientific Monthly* 5, July (1917). In a remarkable set of articles written in 1832, Harriet Martineau portrayed Scott in an alternative way as having succeeded in becoming 'cheerful' despite his own experience of physical pain rather than because of natural good health: Harriet Martineau, 'The Achievements of the Genius of

Scott', and 'Characteristics of the Genius of Scott', *Tait's Edinburgh Magazine*
9 (1832).

25. Scott's autobiographical sketch written in 1808 later comprised the first
    chapter of Lockhart's biography and begins by remarking on the current
    fascination with the private lives of public men; Lockhart, *The Life of Sir
    Walter Scott, Bart.*, 1–18.

26. Scott, quoted ibid. 749, repeated in *Tribute to Walter Scott on the One
    Hundredth Anniversary of his Birthday by the Massachusetts Historical Society;
    August 15, 1871* (Boston: Privately Printed from the Proceedings of the
    Society, 1872), 4.

27. On the proliferation of Scott portraits, see Richard D. Altick, *Paintings from
    Books: Art and Literature in Britain 1760–1900* (Columbus: Ohio State
    University Press, 1985), 163.

28. This comment on Scott's eccentric position vis-à-vis the Romantic cult of the
    celebrity draws on Ghislaine McDayter, *Byromania and the Birth of Celebrity
    Culture* (Albany: State University of New York Press, 2009); Tom Mole,
    Byron's Romantic Celebrity: Industrial Culture and the Hermeneutic of Intimacy
    (Basingstoke: Palgrave Macmillan, 2007); Tom Mole (ed.), *Romanticism and
    Celebrity Culture, 1750–1850* (Cambridge: Cambridge University Press,
    2009); Clara Tuite, 'Tainted Love and Romantic Literary Celebrity', *English
    Literary History* 74 (2007).

29. The framing of Scott's journal by Lockhart is discussed in McCracken-
    Flesher, 'Production of Things Past'.

30. Duncan, *Modern Romance*, 182.

31. Lockhart's biography has also been translated into Japanese, as recently as
    2001; with thanks to Yoriko Kobayashi-Sato for this information.

32. Duncan, *Modern Romance*, 186–7.

33. Samuel Smiles, *Self-Help*, ed. Peter W. Sinnema (Oxford: Oxford University
    Press, 2008 [1859]), 99–100. For similar Victorian portraits of Scott as a
    hard-working man with regular habits, see John Dennis, 'A Talk about Sir
    Walter Scott for Young Readers', in Donald McCleod d.d. (ed.), *Good Words*
    (London: Isbister, 1890); Charles Pebody, 'The Scott Centenary: Sir Walter
    at His Desk', *Gentleman's Magazine* 7 (1871), 307. Dennis also recom-
    mended to his young public the 'healthy, out-of-door freshness' of Scott's
    verse (p. 762) as if it were the equivalent of patent medicine. Scott also fed
    into the idea of the Victorian 'gentleman', the middle-class version of the
    medieval knight: Alice Chandler, *A Dream of Order: The Medieval Ideal in
    Nineteenth-Century English Literature* (London: Routledge & Kegan Paul,
    1971); Marc Girouard, *The Return to Camelot: Chivalry and the English
    Gentleman* (New Haven, CT: Yale University Press, 1981).

34. Anon., '[Death of Walter Scott]', *The Athenaeum*, 29 September (1832).

35. Anon., 'Funeral of Sir Walter Scott', *The Scotsman*, 29 September (1832).

36. Clipping 37 in the Corson Collection, Edinburgh University Library.

37. Explanation given by Lockhart, who quoted from the physician's report rather than from the newspaper: Lockhart, *The Life of Sir Walter Scott, Bart.*, 753–4.
38. *Edinburgh Evening Courant*, 27 September (1832).
39. Thomas Carlyle, *Critical and Miscellaneous Essays*, 7 vols (London: Chapman and Hall, 1872), VI: 56.
40. Extensive accounts of the funeral were given in Anon., 'Funeral of Sir Walter Scott', *Scotsman*, 29 September (1832); [Thomas Dick Lauder], 'Funeral of Sir Walter Scott: by an eyewitness', *Tait's Edinburgh Magazine, and Literary Miscellany*, November (1832). See also Lockhart, *The Life of Sir Walter Scott, Bart.*, 753–4.
41. C. S. M. Lockhart, *The Centenary Memorial of Sir Walter Scott, Bart.* (London: Virtue, 1871), 104–5.
42. Anon., '[Death of Sir Walter Scott]', *Morning Chronicle*, 29 September (1832).
43. Revd J. McVickar, *Tribute to the Memory of Sir Walter Scott, Baronet* (New York: George P. Scott, 1833), 42. This tribute was first presented to a public meeting in New York held in November 1832 to honour Scott, and subsequently published by subscription.
44. *Edinburgh Evening Courant*, 27 September (1832).
45. 'Mort de Sir Walter Scott' (27 September 1832); C. A. Sainte-Beuve, *Premiers lundis*, Nouvelle édition (Paris: Calmann Lévy, 1894), 115.
46. *Edinburgh Evening Courant*, 24 September (1832).
47. 'Sir Walter Scott', *Morning Courier* and *New York Enquirer*, 12 November (1832); quoted in Sainte-Beuve, *Premiers lundis*, 115; Jane Weiss, 'Sir Walter Scott and Company: New York's Literary Culture in 1830', http://triton.oldwestbury.edu/weissj/domestic/sirwalter.html (2002).
48. 'Sir Walter Scott', *Fraser's Magazine*, October (1832).
49. McVickar, *Tribute to the Memory of Sir Walter Scott, Baronet*.
50. Anon., *Cursory Observations on the Death of Sir Walter Scott, Addressed Chiefly to the Inhabitants of Edinburgh* (Edinburgh: Stillies & Bros, 1832).
51. On the portraits, see Altick, *Paintings from Books*, 185. The Corson Collection at Edinburgh University Library holds many poems written in praise of Scott or his works, including at least ten commemorative poems. The tomb at Dryburgh, later visited by Thomas Mellon among others, was frequently included in illustrations to later editions; see Helen Groth, *Victorian Photography and Literary Nostalgia* (Oxford: Oxford University Press, 2003), 85. It also figured prominently in George Washington Wilson, *Sir Walter Scott and His Country: A Reading, Descriptive of a Series of Lantern Slides* (Aberdeen: G. W. W. Registered; printed by John Avery, 1889).
52. James Sheridan Knowles, *The Vision of the Bard* (New York: James Kennaday, 1832). The order of scenes given in this version printed in New York differs from the lengthy account given in the London *Times* on 30 October

1832; quoted in H. Philip Bolton, *Scott Dramatized* (London: Mansell, 1992), 494–5.

53. On the background to Burns' monument and Edinburgh's Acropolis on Calton Hill, see Duncan, *Scott's Shadow*, 9.

54. *Edinburgh Evening Courant*, 6 October (1832). Other phrases used include the 'desire to perpetuate his memory in some lasting memorial'; 'to erect a memorial in Edinburgh that would be worthy of the name of Sir Walter Scott'.

55. On private reading pleasures, see for example Anon., 'Death of Sir Walter Scott', *New Monthly Magazine*, 1 July (1832). An interesting variation on this concept of a repository of private memory was to be found in the private 'tower of memory' erected by Sir William Smith-Merriott on his estate in Kent in 1858, containing illustrations to Scott's works and a copy of the Chantrey bust; H. G. L. King, 'A Tower of Memory', *Walter Scott Quarterly* 1 (1927).

56. See the report of these discussions in *Edinburgh Evening Courant*, 6 October (1832).

57. The embezzlement is mentioned in Lockhart, *The Life of Sir Walter Scott, Bart.*, 761.

58. *Cursory Observations on the Death of Sir Walter Scott.*

59. The Irish poet Moore was one of those who supported the idea of investing in Abbotsford rather than in a monument: Thomas Moore, *Memoirs, Journal and Correspondence of Thomas Moore*, ed. Lord John Russell, 8 vols (London: Longman, 1854), VI: 294.

60. A detailed account of the controversy about the design is given in Gerald Finley, *Landscapes of Memory: Turner as Illustrator of Scott* (London: Scolar Press, 1980), 232–8. For more details of the often cantankerous discussions about the design, see also the reports included in the *Scott Monument*, item A434, Bernard C. Lloyd Sir Walter Scott Collection, Aberdeen University Library. With thanks to Alison Lumsden.

61. My account of the inauguration of the monument is based on Colston, *History of the Scott Monument, Edinburgh.*

62. For a list of dignitaries see ibid. 80. The inauguration in 1840 also included the last representatives of the almost defunct Edinburgh City Guard; Ina Ferris, '"On the Borders of Oblivion": Scott's Historical Novel and the Modern Time of the Remnant', *Modern Language Quarterly* 70 (2009), 473–94 (p. 475).

63. This confirms Ian Duncan's depiction of Edinburgh culture in the decades after Scot as being oriented towards the formation of an 'imperial British culture'. Duncan, *Scott's Shadow*, 11.

64. *Edinburgh Evening Courant*, 6 October (1832).

65. Colston, *History of the Scott Monument, Edinburgh*, 173.

66. The appearance of the Freemasons was described by one spectator as a 'spectre of the past strangely resuscitated'; Miller, *Leading Articles on Various Subjects*, 112.

67. Koselleck, 'Kriegerdenkmale als Identitätsstiftungen der Überlebenden'.

68. Eviatar Zerubavel, *Time Maps: Collective Memory and the Social Shape of the Past* (Chicago: University of Chicago Press, 2003).

69. The phrase 'homage of the whole enlightened world' was used in a commemorative speech in Glasgow, reported in the *Edinburgh Evening Courant*, 27 September (1832). References to the importance of Scott for tourism can be found, for example, in Anon., *Cursory Observations on the Death of Sir Walter Scott*.

70. David Cannadine, 'The Context, Performance and Meaning of Ritual: The British Monarchy and the "Invention of Tradition", c. 1820–1977', in Eric Hobsbawm et al. (eds), *The Invention of Tradition* (Cambridge: Cambridge University Press, 1992 [1983]); David Cannadine, 'The Transformation of Civic Ritual in Modern Britain: The Colchester Oyster Feast', *Past and Present*, 94 (1982); Simon Gunn, *The Public Culture of the Victorian Middle Class: Ritual and Authority in the English Industrial City 1840–1914* (Manchester: Manchester University Press, 2000).

71. Cannadine, 'The Transformation of Civic Ritual in Modern Britain'. For the later period, see David Glassberg, *American Historical Pageantry: The Uses of Tradition in the Early Twentieth Century* (Chapel Hill: University of North Carolina Press, 1990).

72. For a valuable survey see Roland Quinault, 'The Cult of the Centenary, c.1784–1914', *Historical Research* 71 (1998). See also Peter Burke, *Circa 1808: Restructuring Knowledges / Um 1808: Neuordnung der Wissensarten* (Munich: Deutscher Kunstverlag, 2008), 44.

73. The importance of anniversaries in secular societies is discussed in Eviatar Zerubavel, 'Calendars and History: A Comparative Study of the Social Organization of National Memory', in Jeffrey K. Olick (ed.), *States of Memory: Continuities, Conflicts, and Transformations in National Retrospection* (Durham, NC: Duke University Press, 2003); Eviatar Zerubavel, *Hidden Rhythms: Schedules and Calendars in Social Life* (Berkeley: California University Press, 1985 [1981]); Zerubavel, *Time Maps*.

74. For discussions of particular festivals, see Mona Ozouf, *La fête révolutionnaire, 1789–1799* (Paris: Gallimard, 1976); Dieter Düding et al. (eds), *Öffentliche Festkultur: Politische Feste in Deutschland von der Aufklärung bis zum Ersten Weltkrieg* (Hamburg: Rowohlt, 1988); Meike Hölscher, 'Performances, Souvenirs, and Music: The Diamond Jubilee of Queen Victoria 1897', in Astrid Erll and Ann Rigney (eds), *Mediation, Remediation, and the Dynamics of Cultural Memory* (Berlin: de Gruyter, 2009); Patrick Joyce, *Visions of the People: Industrial England and the Question of Class 1848–1914* (Cambridge: Cambridge University Press, 1991), 183–5; Sabine Wieber, 'Staging the Past: Allotria's "Festzug Karl V" and German National Identity', *Rethinking History* 10 (2006).

75. For examples of festivals devoted to artists see *Michelangelo nell'Ottocento. Il centenario del 1875, catalogo mostra Firenze, Casa Buonarroti, 14 giugno—7 novembre 1994* (Milano: Charta, 1994); Celia Applegate, *Bach in*

Berlin: Nation and Culture in Mendelssohn's Revival of the St. Matthew Passion (Ithaca, NY: Cornell University Press, 2005); Monica Berté, *'Intendami chi puù': Il sogni di Petrarca nazionale nelle ricorrenze dall'unità d'Italia ad oggi. Luoghi, tempi e forme di un culto* (Roma: Edizioni dell'Altana, 2004); Michael Dobson, *The Making of the National Poet: Shakespeare, Adaptation and Authorship, 1660–1769* (Oxford: Clarendon Press, 1992); Jean-Marie Goulemot and Eric Walter, 'Les centenaires de Voltaire et de Rousseau: Les deux lampions des Lumières', in Pierre Nora (ed.), *Les lieux de mémoire*, 3 vols (Paris: Gallimard, 1997), I: 351–82; Marcus C. Levitt, *Russian Literary Politics and the Pushkin Celebration of 1880* (Ithaca, NY: Cornell University Press, 1989); Maria McHale, 'Moore's Centenary: Music and Politics in Dublin, 1879', *Proceedings of the Royal Irish Academy* 109 (2009); S. Schoenbaum, *Shakespeare's Lives* (Oxford: Clarendon Press, 1970), 1154–61. In France the funerals of writers were also major events: Avner Ben-Amos, *Funerals, Politics, and Memory in Modern France 1789–1996* (Oxford: Oxford University Press, 2000). Of particular interest because of its transnational perspective, see Jenny Graham, *Inventing Van Eyck: The Remaking of an Artist for the Modern Age* (Oxford: Berg, 2007).

76. See, for example, the poem by Ida White containing the immortal lines: 'What is a hundred or a thousand years? | An urn wherein to shrine his name, | Whose wit our laughter wakes, his pathos, tears, | While time is conquered, won is fame.' [Ida L. White], *Lady Blanche and Other Poems* (London: Hamilton, Adams, & Co., 1875). According to one commentator, 'We should think, if it were possible for a saint to swear, that undesirable result would be produced when Scott discovered that in honour of his hundredth birthday his name had been made to rhyme with "what"'; anon., 'The Scott Centenary Festival', *Saturday Review*, 19 August (1871): 245.

77. A concert was held in Melbourne, and banquets in Dunedin and Hobart (Tasmania); for brief announcements see *Sydney Morning Herald* (24 August 1871), *The Mercury Hobart Tasman* (18 August 1871), *North Otago Times* (18 July 1871), and, for a fuller report, *Otago Witness* (31 August 1899). For the events in Toronto and Boston, see below; for New York, see *The New York Times*, 13 August 1871; for Montreal, see *Montreal Daily Star*, 16 August 1871; for Halifax, where certain tensions arose between the residents of Scottish descent and those who were not, see Cameron Pulsifer, 'A Highland Regiment in Halifax: The 78th Highland Regiment of Foot and the Scottish National/Cultural Factor in Nova Scotia's Capital, 1869–71', in Marjory Harper et al. (eds), *Myth, Migration and the Making of Memory: Scotia and Nova Scotia c.1700–1990* (Halifax: Fernwood, 1999).

78. Lockhart, *The Centenary Memorial of Sir Walter Scott, Bart.*

79. [J.H.], 'The Scott Centenary Celebration', *The Leisure Hour: A Family Journal of Instruction and Recreation*, 1 July (1871), 404.

80. For an extensive analysis of the Burns' celebrations see Ann Rigney, 'Embodied Communities: Commemorating Robert Burns, 1859', *Representations*, 115 (2011). My analysis is based primarily on James Ballantine (ed.),

Chronicle of the Hundredth Birthday of Robert Burns (Edinburgh: A. Fullerton & Co., 1859). For an excellent study of the political dimensions of an earlier Burns' festival in 1844 that attracted enormous crowds to Ayrshire, see Alex Tyrell, 'Paternalism, Public Memory and National Identity in Early Victorian Scotland: The Robert Burns Festival at Ayr in 1844', *History: A Quarterly Magazine and Review for the Teacher, the Student and the Expert* 90 (2005).

81. By coincidence the demonstrations turned into a show of support for Garibaldi and against his imminent extradition; see Richard Foulkes, *The Shakespeare Tercentenary of 1864* (London: Society for Theatre Research, 1984). The Schiller celebrations had also led to widespread disturbances fed by differing opinions on the way forward towards a united Germany: Rainer Noltenius, 'Schiller als Führer und Heiland: Das Schillerfest 1859 als nationaler Traum von der Geburt des zweiten deutschen Kaiserreichs', in Dieter Düding et al. (eds), *Öffentliche Festkultur: Politische Feste in Deutschland von der Aufklärung bis zum Ersten Weltkrieg* (Hamburg: Rowohlt, 1988).

82. Richard D. Altick, *The English Common Reader: A Social History of the Mass Reading Public, 1800–1900* (Chicago: University of Chicago Press, 1957), 2, 217.

83. The *Edinburgh Evening Courant* noted on 10 August 1871 regarding the celebrations at Leith that the 'working classes sympathized with those who in a special manner showed their respect for the memory of Walter Scott, yet in many instances were prevented from abandoning their ordinary labour' because of having had no extra holiday granted them. My main source for this event are the extensive reports in the *Courant* on 10 August and in the days following (11–16 August) when reports came in from other venues.

84. Edwin Muir, 'Scott and Tradition', *Modern Scot*, Summer (1932), 120.

85. T. H. S. Escott, 'Concerning the Centenary of Scott', *Belgravia, a London Magazine* 5 (1871).

86. The parallel with the Dante celebrations is drawn explicitly in *The Scott Exhibition MDCCCLXXI. Catalogue of the Exhibition held at Edinburgh, in July and August 1871, On Occasion of the Commemoration of the Centenary of the Birth of Sir Walter Scott* (Edinburgh, 1872). In Italy there had been important celebrations of Tasso (1857), Dante (1965), Machiavelli (1869), Petrarch (1875), Boccaccio (1875), and Michelangelo (1875). With thanks to Harald Hendrix for this information.

87. 'On a series of steeds of dilapidated appearance there rode, in straggling procession, some two hundred members of a second-rate circus troupe, who were supposed to represent different characters of Scott's novels. There was Cedric the Saxon, and there, in quaint juxtaposition, an individual designed to preserve to posterity Heer van Dousterswivel. Meg Merilees rode side by side with Bailie Nicol Jarvie, and Effie Deans was accompanied by Rob Roy. The act of homage to the creations of the novelist was touching, but it was not without a strong soupcon of the ludicrous'; Escott, 'Concerning the Centenary of Scott'. Similar sentiments, probably also

originating with Escott, were repeated in comic mode in Anon., 'How We Celebrated Scott', *London Society, An Illustrated Magazine of Light and Amusing Literature for the Hours of Relaxation* 20 (1871).

88. Lockhart, *The Centenary Memorial of Sir Walter Scott, Bart.*, 143.

89. Gladstone had already demonstrated his admiration for Scott with a speech on the monument given in 1868 and published in the *Chester Courant*; reproduced in Colston, *History of the Scott Monument, Edinburgh*.

90. Toasts later became staples of the annual dinners of the Edinburgh Sir Walter Scott club, established 1894 and inspired by the tradition of Burns' suppers and the drinking to the 'Immortal memory'; James A. Mackay, *The Burns Federation 1885–1985* (Kilmarnock: Burns Federation, 1985).

91. See also Nicholas G. Zekulin, 'Turgenev in Scotland, 1871', *Slavonic and East European Review* 54 (1975).

92. The programme for the laying of the foundation stone was printed in *The New York Times*, 13 August (1871).

93. Anon., 'Walter Scott: A Centenary Tribute', *London Quarterly Review* 38, April and July (1872), 56. According to this report, delegations from Boston, Philadelphia, Albany, and Scranton were also present at the event. The centenary of 1871 seems to have also stimulated the naming of streets in new middle-class suburbs, for example in Newton, MA, after Scott's characters and works.

94. *Edinburgh Evening Courant*, 21 August (1871).

95. Peter Burke, 'Co-Memorations: Performing the Past', in Karin Tilmans et al. (eds), *Performing the Past: Memory, History, and Identity in Modern Europe* (Amsterdam: Amsterdam University Press, 2010).

96. I owe my observation of this detail to Guy Beiner's account of how participation in mass meetings in nineteenth-century Ireland was mediated by newspapers; Guy Beiner, *Remembering the Year of the French: Irish Folk History and Social Memory* (Madison: University of Wisconsin Press, 2007).

97. Quoted in *Edinburgh Evening Courant*, 11 August (1871).

98. *The Scott Banquet, August 9, 1871* (Glasgow: James Maclehose, publisher to the University, 1872), 63. On Balmoralism, see Alex Tyrell, 'The Queen's "Little Trip": The Royal Visit to Scotland in 1842', *The Scottish Historical Review* 1(213) (2003).

99. See Ian Duncan's introduction to Walter Scott, *Rob Roy* (Oxford: Oxford University Press, 1998 [1817]), vii–viii.

100. Anon., *The Scott Banquet, August 9, 1871*, 15, 21, 24.

101. Pebody, 'The Scott Centenary', 292.

102. Anon., 'A Century of Great Poets, from 1750 Downwards: no. 11.— Walter Scott', *Blackwood's Edinburgh Magazine* 110 (1871), 230.

103. On Scott's imaginative collusion with the Highland clearances see Saree Makdisi, *Romantic Imperialism: Universal Empire and the Culture of Modernity* (Cambridge: Cambridge University Press, 1998); Charlotte Sussman, 'The Emptiness at *The Heart of Midlothian*: Nation, Narration, and Population', *Eighteenth-Century Fiction* 15 (2002).

104. Henry Milton (ed.), *Speeches and Addresses of the Right Honourable Frederick Temple Hamilton, Earl of Dufferin* (London: John Murray, 1882), 137.

105. Peter Fritzsche, *Stranded in the Present: Modern Time and the Melancholy of History* (Cambridge, MA: Harvard University Press, 2004).

106. 'Before a writer can be held entitled to a centenary festival he must have fulfilled two main conditions. First, he must have enlisted the interest and touched the sympathies of men irrespective of nationality; and, secondly, he must not the less be national—the exponent of what is characteristic in the thoughts and cherished sentiments of his countrymen': [J.H.] 'The Scott Centenary Celebration', 405.

107. The huge impact of Scott in France and its resonance there with native traditions is set out in Richard Maxwell, *The Historical Novel in Europe, 1650–1950* (Cambridge: Cambridge University Press, 2009), 113–29.

108. This praise for Scottish engineers also fitted into a pattern; Christine MacLeod, *Heroes of Invention: Technology, Liberalism and British Identity, 1750–1914* (Cambridge: Cambridge University Press, 2007).

109. Anon., 'The Scott Centenary', *Edinburgh Evening Courant*, 10 August (1871), 7. The fact that both Grant and Davis visited Abbotsford is further evidence that Scott's constituency crossed the North–South divide; see Chapter 4 above.

110. The presence of Turgenev and Beets at the centenary banquet testifies to Scott's continental success, our knowledge of which has been greatly enhanced by Murray Pittock (ed.), *The Reception of Sir Walter Scott in Europe* (London: Continuum, 2007). See also Pittock's analysis of Scott within a multinational framework: *Scottish and Irish Romanticism* (Oxford: Oxford University Press, 2008). The European dimension of Scott's reception was nevertheless overshadowed in 1871 by his significance within the Anglophone world.

111. William Hazlitt, *The Spirit of the Age* (Oxford: Woodstock Books, 1989), 139.

112. [J.H.], 'The Scott Centenary Celebration', 408.

113. Robert J. C. Young, *The Idea of English Ethnicity* (Oxford: Blackwell, 2008).

114. Robert Crawford, *Devolving British Literature* (Edinburgh: Edinburgh University Press, 2000), 15. On Scott's European character, see ibid. 315. Regarding Scott's defence of Scottish distinctiveness within the union with England, see also: David Hewitt, 'Scott, Sir Walter (1771–1832)', in *Dictionary of National Biography* (Oxford: Oxford University Press, 2004).

115. Leith Davis, *Acts of Union: Scotland and the Literary Negotiation of the British Nation 1707–1830* (Stanford, CA: Stanford University Press, 1998), 1–2.

116. A renewed and forward-looking Scottish reading was offered recently in Caroline McCracken-Flesher, *Possible Scotlands: Walter Scott and the Story of Tomorrow* (Oxford: Oxford University Press, 2005). Symptomatic of this Scotto-centring is Andrew Lincoln's interesting approach to *Ivanhoe* within a broader British framework, seen as a response to Edmund Burke's inter-

pretation of the French Revolution; his reading re-introduces a Scottish subtext by suggesting that the Jews are implicitly avatars of the modern Scots; Andrew Lincoln, *Walter Scott and Modernity* (Edinburgh: Edinburgh University Press, 2007), 70.

117. *Edinburgh Evening Courant,* 16 August (1871).

118. Ibid.

119. *Edinburgh Evening Courant,* 6 October (1832); Martineau, 'The Achievements of the Genius of Scott', 446.

120. Colston, *History of the Scott Monument, Edinburgh,* 83.

121. *The Scott Banquet, August 9, 1871,* 62.

122. Priya Joshi, 'Culture and Consumption: Fiction, The Reading Public, and the British Novel in Colonial India', *Book History* 1 (1998); Priya Joshi, *In Another Country: Colonialism, Culture, and the English Novel in India* (New York: Columbia University Press, 2002). Joshi suggests that Scott's poetry remained more influential than his novels; certainly the poem 'Lochinvar' made a striking reappearance as a relic of colonial times in Arundhati Roy, *The God of Small Things* (New York: Harper, 2004 [1997]).

123. *Edinburgh Evening Courant,* 10 August (1871). Officials in Calcutta are known to have re-enacted the story of *Kenilworth* in 1840; Trumpener, *Bardic Nationalism,* 248–9; Gauri Viswanathan, *Masks of Conquest: Literary Study and British Rule in India* (New York: Columbia University Press, 1989), 248–9.

124. Anon., 'The Scott Centenary'.

125. This comparison is based on Stephen Greenblatt's account of the significance of Shakespeare and the Bible within the context of Central African explorations; see 'Martial Law in the Land of Cockaigne', in Stephen Greenblatt, *Shakespearean Negotiations: The Circulation of Social Energy in Renaissance England* (Oxford: Clarendon Press, 1988), 129–63.

126. D. Wilson, 'Address Delivered at the Toronto Celebration of the Scott Centenary, 1871', *Canadian Journal of Science, Literature, and History* 13 (1872), 343. The value of Scott's poetry was linked in the *Saturday Review* to its role in evoking scenery for those of Scottish descent living in other parts of Great Britain, the colonies, and the USA; Anon., 'The Scott Centenary Festival', 246.

127. Wilson, 'Address Delivered at the Toronto Celebration of the Scott Centenary, 1871', 343. For the comparison between Scott and Columbus, see 345. More information on Wilson, ethnologist, archaeologist, and university administrator, can be found at http://www.biographi.ca.

128. Ibid. 341.

129. Duncan Bell, *The Idea of Greater Britain: Empire and the Future of World Order, 1860–1900* (Princeton, NJ: Princeton University Press, 2007), 74–91.

130. For more on the Burns' celebrations in the United States, see Rigney, 'Embodied Communities: Commemorating Robert Burns, 1859'. The importance of Shakespeare to American self-images is discussed, without

attention to the tercentenary when the statue in Central Park was erected, in Michael D. Bristol, *Shakespeare's America, America's Shakespeare* (London: Routledge, 1990); Kim C. Sturgess, *Shakespeare and the American Nation* (Cambridge: Cambridge University Press, 2004).

131. *Tribute to Walter Scott on the One Hundredth Anniversary of his Birthday by the Massachusetts Historical Society*, 2.

132. The idea that the appreciation of Scott was mitigated by an inveterate Toryism that made him uncongenial to Modern America was echoed in Anon., 'The Scott Centenary in Edinburgh', *Harper's New Monthly Magazine* 44 (1872), and Anon., 'Editor's Easy Chair', *Harper's New Monthly Magazine* 43 (1871). According to the latter: 'Sir Walter Scott presiding at a meeting to protest against the Reform bill, or gravely asking to keep as an heir-loom the glass from which the vulgar libertine, George the Fourth, had drunk his toddy, is not a cheerful spectacle or thought' (p. 777).

133. McVickar, *Tribute to the Memory of Sir Walter Scott, Baronet*.

134. Glasgow telegram, *Edinburgh Evening Courant*, 10 August (1871).

135. John Hay, *Speech of John Hay at the Unveiling of the Bust of Sir Walter Scott in Westminster Abbey; May 21, 1897* (London: John Lane, 1897), 11, 13, 8.

136. The point that literature is a binding element within empire is also made very briefly in Simon Gikandi, *Maps of Englishness: Writing Identity in the Culture of Colonialism* (New York: Columbia University Press, 1996), xix–xx.

137. Trumpener, *Bardic Nationalism*, 246.

138. A strong endorsement of Lukács' basic point is given in Richard Waswo, 'Scott and the Really Great Tradition', in Harry E. Shaw (ed.), *Critical Essays on Sir Walter Scott: The Waverley Novels* (New York: K. Hall, 1996). On 'Modernity's Other Worlds', see Duncan, *Scott's Shadow*, 96–115.

CHAPTER 7

1. *The Scott Banquet, August 9, 1871* (Glasgow: James Maclehose, publisher to the University, 1872), 14.

2. Harriet Martineau, 'The Achievements of the Genius of Scott', *Tait's Edinburgh Magazine* 9 (1832), 446.

3. Anon., 'Death of Sir Walter Scott', *New Monthly Magazine* 1 July (1832).

4. Anon., '[Death of Sir Walter Scott]', *Morning Chronicle*, 29 September (1832).

5. W. B. O. Peabody; quoted in John O. Hayden (ed.), *Scott: The Critical Heritage* (London: Routledge & Kegan Paul, 1970), 336.

6. Thomas Carlyle, *Critical and Miscellaneous Essays*, 7 vols (London: Chapman and Hall, 1872), VI: 32.

7. Ibid. 71.

8. John Henry Raleigh, 'What Scott Meant to the Victorians', in Harry E. Shaw (ed.), *Critical Essays on Sir Walter Scott: The Waverley Novels* (New York: G. K. Hall, 1996), 47.

9. Jeffrey K. Olick, *The Politics of Regret: On Collective Memory and Historical Responsibility* (London: Routledge, 2007), 115–18.

10. Andreas Huyssen, *After the Great Divide: Modernism, Mass Culture, Postmodernism* (Bloomington: Indiana University Press, 1986). In the case of Scott, tensions were compounded by the disparity perceived between commercial success and claims to artistic greatness, bearing out the distinction between symbolic and financial capital theorized in Pierre Bourdieu, 'Le marché des biens symboliques', *L'année sociologique* 22 (1971).

11. See Introduction, n.8.

12. Deidre Lynch (ed.), *Janeites: Austen's Disciples and Devotees* (Princeton, NJ: Princeton University Press, 2000), 3–24.

13. These different trajectories are outlined on the basis of numbers of editions and critical reception in Annika Bautz, *The Reception of Jane Austen and Walter Scott: A Comparative Longitudinal Study* (London: Continuum, 2007).

14. Lynch (ed.), *Janeites*, 9.

15. Lionel Trilling, *Beyond Culture: Essays on Literature and Learning* (Harmondsworth, Middlesex: Penguin, 1966 [1963]), 44. Also referred to in Lynch (ed.), *Janeites*, 5.

16. Sigrid Weigel, 'Generation, Genealogie, Geschlecht: Zur Geschichte des Generationenkonzepts und seiner wissenschaftlichen Konzeptualisierung seit dem Ende des 18. Jahrhunderts', in Lutz Musner and Gotthard Wunberg (eds), *Kulturwissenschaften: Forschung—Praxis—Positionen* (Wien: WUV, 2002). For a generational approach, see also Marianne Hirsch, *Family Frames: Photography, Narrative, and Postmemory* (Cambridge, MA: Harvard University Press, 1997).

17. Even though it dealt with more remote ages, *Ivanhoe* too invoked a familial model in addressing those who were not disposed to think 'that his own ancestors led a very different life from himself'; Walter Scott, *Ivanhoe*, ed. Ian Duncan (Oxford: Oxford University Press, 1996 [1819]), 16.

18. Anon., 'How We Celebrated Scott', *London Society, An Illustrated Magazine of Light and Amusing Literature for the Hours of Relaxation* 20 (1871); Anon., 'The Scott Centenary Festival', *Saturday Review*, 19 August (1871).

19. Quoted in Anon., 'The Scott Centenary', *Edinburgh Evening Courant*, 11 August (1871). Anon., 'How We Celebrated Scott'.

20. Charles Pebody, 'The Scott Centenary: Sir Walter at his Desk', *Gentleman's Magazine* 17 (1871): 316. Anon., 'Editor's Easy Chair', 776.

21. Walter Bagehot, 'The Waverley Novels', in Shaw (ed.), *Critical Essays on Sir Walter Scott*.

22. Ibid. 33. For associations between Scott and 'health', see Chapter 6, n.24.

23. Anon., 'The Scott Centenary Festival', 246.

24. Ralph Waldo Emerson, *Miscellanies* (Boston: Houghton, Mifflin, 1904). Henry James, as quoted in Richard Waswo, 'Scott and the Really Great Tradition', in Shaw (ed.), *Critical Essays on Sir Walter Scott*, 73. Other associations between Scott and boyhood are to be found in Stanley Baldwin,

This Torch of Freedom: Speeches and Addresses (London: Hodder and Stoughton, 1935); George Brandes, *Main Currents in Nineteenth Century Literature* (London: William Heinemann, 1906), 127; Mowbray Morris, 'Sir Walter Scott (A Lecture at Eton)', *Macmillan's Magazine*, 356 (June) (1889); Leslie Stephen, 'Sir Walter Scott', in *Hours in a Library* (London: Smith, Elder, 1907 [1871]), 158; Hugh Walpole, 'Sir Walter Scott: A Centenary Estimate', *English Review* 55 (1932); Wilfrid Ward, 'The Centenary of Waverley', *Dublin Review* 155 (1914).

25. See Chapter 6 above; also Richard D. Altick, *The English Common Reader: A Social History of the Mass Reading Public, 1800–1900* (Chicago: University of Chicago Press, 1957), 121.

26. This presentation of *Ivanhoe* as a juvenile work coincided with the emergence of the category of adolescence accompanied by a discourse about boyhood 'health' and healthy reading for boys. See John Neubauer, *The Fin-de-Siècle Culture of Adolescence* (New Haven: Yale University Press, 1992). The close link between the historical novel and juvenile literature is discussed in more detail in Richard Maxwell, *The Historical Novel in Europe, 1650–1950* (Cambridge: Cambridge University Press, 2009), 233–73. See also above Chapter 3, n.4.

27. Altick, *The English Common Reader*, 160, 82.

28. Stephen, 'Sir Walter Scott'.

29. Virginia Woolf, '*The Antiquary*', in *Collected Essays*, 4 vols (London: Hogarth Press, 1966), I: 139–43.

30. Coleridge admitted to enjoying the Waverley novels as a form of light entertainment; Samuel Taylor Coleridge, *Collected Letters of Samuel Taylor Coleridge*, 6 vols (Oxford: Oxford University Press, 1959–71), V: 33. Even as Scott's critical prestige declined, he continued to elicit warm admiration on the part of private readers. Ruskin wrote of his 'love of Scott', associated him with 'pure delight', and wrote glowingly of his literary qualities; John Ruskin, *Praeterita: The Autobiography of John Ruskin* (Oxford: Oxford University Press, 1978 [1885–9]), 226, 323, 510–15. Karl Marx read out the Waverley novels to his children; Maxwell, *The Historical Novel in Europe, 1650–1950*, 63. Scott's influence played through, albeit often unacknowledged as infra dig, in the Victorian novel; Judith Wilt, *Secret Leaves: The Novels of Walter Scott* (Chicago: University of Chicago Press, 1985).

31. *Scotsman*, 22 September (1932). A ceremony at the Sorbonne was attended by the French President and conducted in the presence of a draped portrait of Scott [Clipping 219, Corson Collection].

32. On the perceived educational value of civic parades at this period, see David Glassberg, *American Historical Pageantry: The Uses of Tradition in the Early Twentieth Century* (Chapel Hill: University of North Carolina Press, 1990). For a theoretical model for the movement of memory between civil society and official culture, see Aleida Assmann, 'Vier Formen des Gedächtnisses', *Erwägen, Wissen, Ethik* 13 (2002).

33. The 1971 celebrations took place at the interface between the official and the academic spheres, rather than in the wider public space. It was centred on an exhibition on Scott's life, work, and the monument curated by the National Library of Scotland together with the Court of Session and the Faculty of Advocates, and on an academic conference (16–21 August). The latter opened with a reception held in Edinburgh Castle under the auspices of the Minister of State at the Scottish Office, in lieu of the civic banquet held on the earlier occasions (similarly, the exhibition had been opened by the Duchess of Gloucester rather than by the higher ranking Prince of Wales in attendance in 1932).

34. William St Clair, *The Reading Nation in the Romantic Period* (Cambridge: Cambridge University Press, 2004).

35. The fear that 'modern thrillers' had replaced Scott was expressed, for example, in the annual toast at the Edinburgh Sir Walter Scott club in 1936.

36. Chris Anderson, *The Long Tail: How Endless Choice is Creating Unlimited Demand* (London: Random House, 2006).

37. Walpole, 'Sir Walter Scott: A Centenary Estimate', 350. In the years surrounding the 1932 centenary various Scott-related statues were still being put up, but these were to honour minor characters in his novels or, as in 1935, Thomas Kemp, the architect of the Scott monument.

38. The divorce between official celebrations and actual neglect of Scott's work was the butt of some light verse; W. Hodgson Burnet, 'Scott-Great Scot', *Saturday Review of Politics* 17 September (1932).

39. See for example, Anon., 'Sir Walter Scott and the Scotsman's Heritage', *Modern Scot*, Spring (1932); John Buchan, 'The Scott that Remains', *Listener*, 21 September (1932); John Buchan, *Sir Walter Scott* (London: Cassell, 1932); Burnet, 'Scott-Great Scot'; Abbé Ernest Dimnet, 'Sir Walter Scott in France', *Listener*, 21 September (1932); W. Macneile Dixon, 'Our Debt to Scott To-Day', *Queen's Quarterly: A Canadian Review*, November (1932); W. Forbes Gray (ed.), *Scott in Sunshine and Shadow: The Tribute of His Friends* (London: Methuen, 1931); H. J. C. Grierson, *Sir Walter Scott 1832–1932* (New York: Columbia University Press, 1933); H. J. C. Grierson (ed.), *Sir Walter Scott To-day: Some Retrospective Essays and Studies* (London: Constable, 1932); 'A Century of Scott', *Listener*, 21 September (1932); Agnes Mure Mackenzie, 'Letters and Appreciations', *Listener*, 21 September (1932); W. Macneile Dixon, 'Our Debt to Scott To-Day', *Queen's Quarterly: A Canadian Review*, November (1932); *The Romance of Scott: His Home, his Work, his Country. Sir Walter Scott Centenary 1832–1932* (Edinburgh: Travel Press, 1932); Thomas Seccombe et al., *Scott Centenary Articles* (London: Oxford University Press, 1932); *Sir Walter Scott Centenary 1932; Portfolio of Etchings* (Edinburgh: R. S. Forrest, 1932).

40. G. Lewis May, 'Do We Read Sir Walter Scott? Some Reflections on the Centenary of Quentin Durward', *Cassells Weekly* 25 (1923). 'Why Apologise for Sir Walter Scott?' (1951) was the heading on a letter to the editors, *Radio Times* (9 November 1951); 'The Neglect of Scott's Novels is Deplorable' was

a headline in the *News Chronicle* (1 January 1953); 'Immortal Memory? Is Sir Walter Scott Forgotten?' appeared in the *Border Telegraph* (14 August 1956). A more recent variation on the same theme: R. D. Kernohan, ' "Will Ye No' Come Back Again?" Whatever Happened to Sir Walter Scott?', *Contemporary Review* 262 (1993). Exceptionally the *Spectator* (20 June 1952) wrote that 'Those were the days... Thank God they have passed.'

41. Anon., 'Sir Walter Scott and the Scotsman's Heritage', 64, 65.

42. The list of Scott-eulogizing statesmen included Gladstone (1868), Stanley Baldwin (1930), and Ramsay MacDonald (1932) along with the public figures present at the various commemorative ceremonies and, as of 1894, at the annual toasts to Scott's memory given at the Edinburgh Walter Scott Society. Gladstone's speech was reproduced in James Colston, *History of the Scott Monument, Edinburgh; To which is prefixed a biographical sketch of Sir Walter Scott, Bart.* (Edinburgh: Printed for the Magistrates and Town Council, 1881). A letter from Ramsay Macdonald was included in *The Romance of Scott*, 8. Baldwin's toast on the occasion of the annual Sir Walter Scott club dinner in 1930 was reproduced in Baldwin, *This Torch of Freedom: Speeches and Addresses*.

43. Donald Carswell, 'Why Scott is Neglected', *Modern Scot*, Summer (1932), 111–12.

44. A. T. Cunninghame, 'Scott in 1932', ibid.

45. Later judgements were milder; see Edwin Muir, 'Walter Scott (1771–1832)', in Bonamy Dobrée (ed.), *From Anne to Victoria: Essays by Various Hands* (London: Cassell, 1937).

46. Carlyle, *Critical and Miscellaneous Essays*; William Hazlitt, 'Sir Walter Scott', in *The Spirit of the Age* (Oxford: Woodstock Books, 1989 [1825]).

47. A 'curious inner emptiness' was the phrase used by Rebecca West, 'The Dualism of Scott', *Modern Scot*, Summer (1932), 122. The idea that his popularity was incompatible with greatness was echoed in Cunninghame, 'Scott in 1932', 118.

48. *Irish Times,* 9 November (1909).

49. *Punch,* 8 December (1954); a toast at the annual meeting of the Edinburgh Walter Scott Society in 1950 claimed that the Waverley novels are no longer read by the present generation. On 30 January 1953, the *Radio Times* announced a radio version in the following terms: 'Scott is virtually unread today, at least in England. Perhaps the radio version of the *Heart of Midlothian* will tempt some bold spirit to open up the book [...] He may even be driven to re-read the whole of the *Waverley* novels.'

50. Walter Raleigh, *The English Novel: Being a Short Sketch of its History from the Earliest Times to the Appearance of Waverley* (New York: C. Scribner, 1894). On the development of academic English studies, see D. J. Palmer, *The Rise of English Studies: An Account of the Study of English Language and Literature from its Origins to the Making of the Oxford English School* (London: Oxford University Press, 1965). Although written with reference to the United States, see also on the changing relations between scholarship and criticism

at this period: Gerald Graff, *Professing Literature: An Institutional History* (Chicago: University of Chicago Press, 1987).

51. The 1932 centenary thus saw the appearance of a scholarly edition of Scott's correspondence by Herbert Grierson, professor of English at Edinburgh University; H. J. C. Grierson (ed.), *The Letters of Sir Walter Scott,* 12 vols (London: Constable, 1932–7).

52. E. M. Forster, *Aspects of the Novel* (Harmondsworth: Penguin, 1962 [1927]), 39.

53. F. R. Leavis, *The Great Tradition: George Eliot, Henry James, Joseph Conrad* (Harmondsworth, Middlesex: Penguin, 1962 [1948]), 14.

54. Ibid. 10.

55. *Scotsman,* 24 April (1950). The council's eclectic argument was that Edinburgh 'has not paid enough tribute to Sir Walter Scott in this way, seeing that he is recognised as probably the very greatest salesman in Scotland. It would give the children in that area some interest in the Scott books and cause them to ask questions. It would also widen the international link with people in other parts of the world.'

EPILOGUE

1. Sir Walter Scott, *Old Mortality,* ed. Angus Calder (Harmondsworth: Penguin, 1975 [1816]), 64. In supplementary material he added to the magnum opus edition in 1830, Scott gave extensive background information about Robert Paterson, describing how he himself had seen him once in a graveyard; ibid. 485–94.

2. Ibid. 68.

3. On the background in eighteenth-century reflections on memory, see Catherine Jones, *Literary Memory: Scott's Waverley Novels and the Psychology of Narrative* (London: Associated University Presses, 2003), 18–23.

4. For more on this controversy, see Chapter 1, n.33 above.

5. Walter Scott, *The Tale of Old Mortality,* ed. David Hewitt, Douglas Mack, vol. 4 [b], (Edinburgh: Edinburgh University Press, 1993 [1816]).

6. Paul Connerton, *How Modernity Forgets* (Cambridge: Cambridge University Press, 2009), 88.

7. For varieties of forgetting see Adrian Forty and Susanne Küchler (eds), *The Art of Forgetting* (Oxford: Berg, 1999); Harald Weinrich, *Lethe: Kunst und Kritik des Vergessens* (München: C. H. Beck, 1997); Paul Connerton, 'Seven Types of Forgetting', *Memory Studies* 1 (2008); Anselm Haverkamp and Renate Lachmann (eds), *Memoria: Vergessen und Erinnern* (München: Wilhelm Fink, 1993); Luisa Passerini, 'Memories between Silence and Oblivion', in Katherine Hodgkin et al. (eds), *Memory, History, Nation: Contested Pasts* (London: Routledge, 2003); Paul Ricoeur, *La mémoire, l'histoire, l'oubli* (Paris: Seuil, 2000). On inertia, see esp. Jeffrey K. Olick and Joyce Robbins, 'Social Memory Studies: From "Collective Memory" to the Historical Sociology of Mnemonic Practices', *Annual Review of Sociology* 24 (1998).

8. 'Funes the Memorious' (1942) in Jorge Luis Borges, *Labyrinths*, trans. James E. Irby (London: Penguin, 2000). Nietzsche's warning on the dangers of becoming swamped by historical knowledge were formulated in his 'untimely meditation' *Vom Nutzen und Nachteil der Historie für das Leben*; Friedrich Nietzsche, *The Advantage and Disadvantage of History for Life*, trans. Peter Preuss (Indianapolis: Hackett, 1980 [1874]).

9. Ernest Renan, 'Qu'est-ce qu'une nation?' [1882], in *Oeuvres complètes d'Ernest Renan*, ed. Henriëtte Psichari (Paris: Calmann-Lévy, 1947–61). On mourning as key to twentieth-century memory cultures, see for example, Jay M. Winter, *Sites of Memory, Sites of Mourning: The Great War in European Cultural History* (Cambridge: Cambridge University Press, 1995). The preoccupation with traumatic memory (the literature is enormous) has itself been seen as an ongoing symptom of the effect of World War II; Gabrielle M. Spiegel, *The Past as Text: The Theory and Practice of Medieval Historiography* (Baltimore, MD: Johns Hopkins University Press, 1997), 34–43.

10. For more instances of Scott's resonance in contemporary culture, see also Sam Baker, 'Teaching the Waverley Novels: An Intertextual Approach', in Evan Gottlieb and Ian Duncan (eds), *Approaches to Teaching Scott's Waverley Novels* (New York: Modern Language Association of America, 2009).

11. The contrast between 'working' and 'archival' memory is taken from Aleida Assmann, *Erinnerungsräume: Formen und Wandlungen des kulturellen Gedächtnisses* (München: C. H. Beck, 1999), 130–45.

12. 'Aphasia' as a variation on forgetting involves a radical disconnect between observable phenomena and their meaning; Ann Stoler, 'Colonial Aphasia: Race and Disabled Histories in France', *Public Culture* 23 (2011).

13. Where nineteenth-century critics regularly stressed Scott's Scottishness, recent works have highlighted instead his cosmopolitanism and European-mindedness; see Robert Crawford, 'Walter Scott and European Union', *Studies in Romanticism* 40 (2001).

14. Gottlieb and Duncan (eds), *Approaches to Teaching Scott's Waverley Novels*, *passim*.

15. Pierre Nora, 'Entre mémoire et histoire: la problématique des lieux', in Pierre Nora (ed.), *Les lieux de mémoire*, 3 vols (Paris: Gallimard, 1997), I: xvii–xiii.

References

Abbotsford: 12 Photos for your Album (Dundee: Valentine, *c.*1900).

Allen, William. *Illustrations of the Novels and Tales of the Author of Waverley* (London: Archibald Constable, 1823).

Anon. 'A Century of Great Poets, from 1750 Downwards: no. 11.—Walter Scott'. *Blackwood's Edinburgh Magazine* 110 (1871), 229–56.

——'Death of Sir Walter Scott'. *New Monthly Magazine*, 1 July (1832), 300–4.

——'[Death of Sir Walter Scott]'. *Morning Chronicle*, 29 September (1832), 3.

——'[Death of Walter Scott]'. *Athenaeum*, 29 September (1832).

——'The Difference of Race between the Northern and Southern People'. *Southern Literary Messenger: A Magazine Devoted to Literature, Science and Art* 30, June (1860), 401–9.

——'Editor's Easy Chair'. *Harper's New Monthly Magazine* 43, June/November (1871), 776–8.

——'Funeral of Sir Walter Scott'. *Scotsman*, 29 September (1832), 3.

——'How We Celebrated Scott'. *London Society, An Illustrated Magazine of Light and Amusing Literature for the Hours of Relaxation* 20 (1871), 275–80.

——'Ivanhoe, and The Monastery'. *British Review, and London Critical Journal* 15 (1820), 393–454.

——'Ivanhoe, by the author of Waverley, Etc.', *Edinburgh Magazine, and Literary Miscellany, Being a New Series of The Scots Magazine* 85, January (1820), 7–16.

——'Ivanhoe, a Romance'. *Blackwood's Edinburgh Magazine* 31 (1819): 262–72.

——'Ivanhoe: A Romance'. *New Monthly Magazine and Universal Register* January–June (1820), 73–82.

——'Ivanhoe: A Romance'. *Literary Gazette; and Journal of Belles Lettres, Arts, Sciences, etc. for the Year 1819*, 25 December (1819), 817–23.

——'Ivanhoe: A Romance, by the Author of Waverley'. *Ladies Monthly Museum; or, Polite Repository of Amusement and Instruction; being an assemblage of whatever can tend to please the fancy, interest the mind, or exalt the character of the British Fair* 11 (1820), 97–101.

——'Ivanhoe: a Romance. By the Author of "Waverley"'. *Monthly Review; or Literary Journal, Enlarged* 91, January–April (1820), 71–89.

——'Ivanhoe: A Romance. By the Author of "Waverley"'. *Western Review and Miscellaneous Magazine*, May (1820): 204–24.

——'Ivanhoe: A Romance. By the Author of "Waverly" [*sic*]'. *Literary Chronicle and Weekly Review* 33, January (1820): 1–4, 21–4.

——'Ivanhoe: A Romance. By the Author of Waverly [*sic*]'. *London Magazine* 1, January–June (1820), 79–84.

——'"Ivanhoe": The Imperial Film Company's Great Production'. *The Bioscope*, 24 July (1913), 27–34.

Anon. 'On the History of Fictitious Writing in Scotland; With Remarks on the Tale entitled "The Heart of Mid-Lothian"'. *Edinburgh Magazine and Literary Miscellany*, August (1818): 107–17.

——'Producing 'Ivanhoe' at Chepstow'. *The Bioscope*, 13 July (1913), 8–11.

——'The Scott Centenary'. *Edinburgh Evening Courant*, 10–11 August (1871).

——'The Scott Centenary Celebration'. *Leisure Hour: A Family Journal of Instruction and Recreation* 1018, 1 July (1871), 405–8.

——'The Scott Centenary Festival'. *Saturday Review*, 19 August (1871), 245–6.

——'The Scott Centenary in Edinburgh'. *Harper's New Monthly Magazine* 44 (1872) 321–49.

——'Sir Walter Scott'. *Fraser's Magazine*, October (1832), 176–83.

——'Sir Walter Scott and the Scotsman's Heritage'. *Modern Scot*, Spring (1932), 63–6.

——'Review of *Tales of My Landlord. Second Series*'. *New Monthly Magazine and Universal Register* 10, July–December (1818), 250.

——'Review of *Tales of My Landlord. Second Series*'. *British Critic* 10, July–December (1818), 246–60.

——'*Tales of My Landlord, Second Series*'. *Blackwood's Edinburgh Magazine*, August (1818): 564–74.

——'*Tales of My Landlord, Second Series*'. *London Literary Gazette, and Journal of Belles Lettres, Arts, Sciences, etc.* 81, August (1818): 497–500.

——'Walter Scott: A Centenary Tribute'. *London Quarterly Review* 38, April–July (1872), 35–59.

Alexander, J. H., and David Hewitt (eds), *Scott and his Influence: The Papers of the Aberdeen Scott Conference, 1982* (Aberdeen: Assn for Scottish Lit. Studies, 1983).

Altick, Richard D. *The English Common Reader: A Social History of the Mass Reading Public, 1800–1900* (Chicago: University of Chicago Press, 1957).

——*Paintings from Books: Art and Literature in Britain 1760–1900* (Columbus: Ohio State University Press, 1985).

Anderson, Benedict. 'Exodus'. *Critical Inquiry* 20 (1994), 314–27.

——*Imagined Communities: Reflections on the Origins and Spread of Nationalism* (London: Verso, 1991 [1983]).

Anderson, Chris. *The Long Tail: How Endless Choice is Creating Unlimited Demand* (London: Random House, 2006).

Anstruther, Ian. *The Knight and the Umbrella: An Account of the Eglinton Tournament 1839* (London: Geoffrey Bles, 1963).

Appadurai, Arjun. *Modernity at Large: Cultural Dimensions of Globalization* (Minneapolis: University of Minnesota Press, 1996).

——(ed.). *The Social Life of Things: Commodities in Cultural Perspective* (Cambridge: Cambridge University Press, 1986).

Applegate, Celia. *Bach in Berlin: Nation and Culture in Mendelssohn's Revival of the St. Matthew Passion* (Ithaca, NY: Cornell University Press, 2005).

Ariès, Philippe. *L'homme devant la mort*, 2 vols (Paris: Seuil, 1977).

Armstrong, Eric, Leslie Brown, Joe McKendrick, and Clem Robb. *Waverley: Birth of a Legend* (n.p.: Paddle Steamer Preservation Society, 1987).

Ashton, Dianne. *Rebecca Gratz: Women and Judaism in Antebellum America* (Detroit: Wayne State University Press, 1997).

Assmann, Aleida. *Erinnerungsräume: Formen und Wandlungen des kulturellen Gedächtnisses* (München: C. H. Beck, 1999).

——'Vier Formen des Gedächtnisses'. *Erwägen, Wissen, Ethik* 13 (2002), 183–90.

Assmann, Jan. 'Collective Memory and Cultural Identity', trans. John Czaplicka. *New German Critique* 65 (1995), 125–33.

——*Das kulturelle Gedächtnis: Schrift, Erinnerung und politische Identität in frühen Hochkulturen* (München: C. H. Beck, 1997 [1992]).

Atwood, Margaret. *Alias Grace* (Toronto: McClelland & Stewart, 1996).

Austen, Jane. *The Novels*, ed. R. W. Chapman, 5 vols (London: Oxford University Press, 1923).

Bagehot, Walter. 'The Waverley Novels' (1858), in Harry E. Shaw (ed.), *Critical Essays on Sir Walter Scott: The Waverley Novels* (New York: G. K. Hall, 1996), 21–46.

Baker, Sam. 'Teaching the Waverley Novels: An Intertextual Approach', in Evan Gottlieb and Ian Duncan (eds), *Approaches to Teaching Scott's Waverley Novels* (New York: Modern Language Association of America, 2009), 59–66.

Bakhtin, M. M. 'Discourse in the Novel', in *The Dialogic Imagination*, ed. Michael Holquist (Austin: University of Texas Press, 1981), 259–422.

Baldwin, Stanley. *This Torch of Freedom: Speeches and Addresses* (London: Hodder and Stoughton, 1935).

Ballantine, James (ed.), *Chronicle of the Hundredth Birthday of Robert Burns* (Edinburgh: Fullerton, 1859).

Bann, Stephen. *The Clothing of Clio: A Study of the Representation of History in Nineteenth-Century Britain and France* (Cambridge: Cambridge University Press, 1984).

——ed. *Romanticism and the Rise of History* (Twayne: University of Nebraska Press, 1995).

Barber, Edwin A. 'Printed Textiles'. *Bulletin of the Pennsylvania Museum* 9 (1911), 28–33.

Barham, Richard Harris. *Personal Reminiscences by Barham, Harness, and Hodder*, ed. Richard Henry Stoddard (New York: Scribner, Armstrong, 1875).

Barthes, Roland. 'La mort de l'auteur' (1968), in *Le bruissement de la langue* (Paris: Seuil, 1984), 61–7.

Basu, Laura. *Remembering an Iron Outlaw: The Cultural Memory of Ned Kelly and the Development of Australian Identities*, unpublished PhD thesis, Utrecht University, 2010.

Bautz, Annika. *The Reception of Jane Austen and Walter Scott: A Comparative Longitudinal Study* (London: Continuum, 2007).

Beazley, Samuel. *Ivanhoe: or, The Knight Templar: Adapted from the Novel of that Name; First Performed the 2nd of March, 1820 at the Theatre Royal, Covent Garden* (London: W. Smith, 1820).

Beiner, Guy. *Remembering the Year of the French: Irish Folk History and Social Memory* (Madison: University of Wisconsin Press, 2007).

Bell, Barbara. 'The Nineteenth Century', in *A History of the Scottish Theatre*, ed. Bill Findley (Edinburgh: Polygon, 1998), 137–206.

——'The Performance of Victorian Medievalism', in *Beyond Arthurian Romances: The Reach of Victorian Medievalism*, ed. Lorretta M. Holloway and Jennifer A. Palmgren (London: Palgrave Macmillan, 2005), 191–216.

——'Sir Walter Scott and the National Drama', in *Scott in Carnival*, ed. J. H. Alexander and David Hewitt (Aberdeen: Association for Scottish Literary Studies, 1993), 459–77.

Bell, Duncan. *The Idea of Greater Britain: Empire and the Future of World Order, 1860–1900* (Princeton, NJ: Princeton University Press, 2007).

Beller, Manfred, and Joep Leerssen (eds). *Imagology: The Cultural Construction and Literary Representation of National Characters* (Amsterdam: Rodopi, 2007).

Ben-Amos, Avner. *Funerals, Politics, and Memory in Modern France 1789–1996* (Oxford: Oxford University Press, 2000).

Bennett, Joseph. *Jeanie Deans: An Opera in Four Acts and Seven Tableaux; Written and Composed Expressly for The Royal Carl Rosa Opera Company. Words by Joseph Bennett. Music by Hamish MacCunn* (London: Phipps and Connor, 1894).

Berté, Monica. *'Intendami chi può': Il sogni di Petrarca nazionale nelle ricorrenze dall'unità d'Italia ad oggi. Luoghi, tempi e forme di un culto* (Roma: Edizioni dell'Altana, 2004).

Billig, Michael. *Banal Nationalism* (London: Sage, 1995).

Bithell, Caroline. 'The Past in Music: Introduction'. *Ethnomusicology Forum* 15 (2006), 3–16.

Blackwood, Graham, Bill Smith, and David Speed (eds). *The Hearts Quiz Book* (Edinburgh: Mainstream Publishing, 1987).

Blair, William A. *Cities of the Dead: Contesting the Memory of the Civil War in the South, 1865–1914* (Chapel Hill: University of North Carolina Press, 2004).

Blight, David W. *Race and Reunion: The Civil War in American Memory* (Cambridge, MA: Belknap Press, 2001).

Bolter, J. David, and Richard Grusin. *Remediation: Understanding New Media* (Cambridge, MA: MIT Press, 2000).

Bolton, H. Philip. *Scott Dramatized*, Novels on Stage 2 (London: Mansell, 1992).

The Book of Waverley Gems: In a Series of Engraved Illustrations of Incidents and Scenery in Sir Walter Scott's Novels (London: Henry G. Bohn, 1846).

Borges, Jorge Luis. *Labyrinths*, trans. James E. Irby (London: Penguin, 2000).

Boucicault, Dion. *Jeanie Deans or The Heart of Midlothian; A Drama in Three Acts.* ms.; Harvard Theatre Collection [act 1 only], *c.*1863.

Bourdieu, Pierre. 'Le marché des biens symboliques'. *L'année sociologique* 22 (1971), 49–126.

Boyarin, Jonathan (ed.). *Remapping Memory: The Politics of TimeSpace* (Minneapolis: University of Minnesota Press, 1994).

Boyer, M. Christine. *The City of Collective Memory: Its Historical Imagery and Architectural Entertainments* (Cambridge, MA: MIT Press, 1994).

Boym, Svetlana. *The Future of Nostalgia* (New York: Basic Books, 2001).

Brandes, George. *Main Currents in Nineteenth Century Literature* (London: William Heinemann, 1906).

Brendon, Piers. *Thomas Cook: 150 Years of Popular Tourism* (London: Secker and Warburg, 1991).

Brewer, David. *The Afterlife of Character, 1726–1825* (Philadelphia: University of Pennsylvania Press, 2005).

Bristol, Michael D. *Shakespeare's America, America's Shakespeare* (London: Routledge, 1990).

Brockliss, Laurence, and David Eastwood (eds). *A Union of Multiple Identities: The British Isles, c.1750–c.1850* (Manchester: Manchester University Press, 1997).

Bromley, Fred. *Companion to the Trial of Effie Deans* (Philadelphia: J. Hedenberg, c.1850).

Brooks, Peter. *The Melodramatic Imagination: Balzac, Henry James, Melodrama, and the Mode of Excess* (New York: Columbia University Press, 1985).

Brough, Robert, and William Brough. *The Last Edition of Ivanhoe, with All the Newest Improvements; an Extravaganza in Two Acts, as Performed at the Theatre Royal, Hay-Market* (London: Webster, n.d. [1850]).

Brown, Iain G. (ed.). *Abbotsford and Sir Walter Scott: The Image and the Influence* (Edinburgh: Society of Antiquaries of Scotland, 2003).

Brown, Mary Ellen. *Burns and Tradition* (London: Macmillan, 1984).

Bryant, William Cullen. *Address on the Unveiling of the Statue of Sir Walter Scott in Central Park, November 4, 1872* (New York: G. P. Putnam's Sons, 1873).

Buchan, John. 'The Scott that Remains'. *Listener*, 21 September (1932), 407–10.

——*Sir Walter Scott* (London: Cassell, 1932).

Bunn, Alfred. *Ivanhoe: or, The Jew of York; a New Grand Chivalric Play in Three Acts* (Birmingham: Beilby and Knotts, 1820).

Burke, Peter. *Circa 1808: Restructuring Knowledges / Um 1808: Neuordnung der Wissensarten* (Munich: Deutscher Kunstverlag, 2008).

——'Co-Memorations: Performing the Past', in Karin Tilmans, Frank van Vree and Jay Winter (eds), *Performing the Past: Memory, History, and Identity in Modern Europe* (Amsterdam: Amsterdam University Press, 2010), 105–18.

——'History as Social Memory', in Thomas Butler (ed.), *Memory, History, Culture, and the Mind* (Oxford: Blackwell, 1989), 97–113.

——'Performing History: The Importance of Occasions'. *Rethinking History* 9(1) (2005), 35–52.

Burnet, W. Hodgson. 'Scott-Great Scot'. *Saturday Review of Politics*, 17 September (1932), 289.

Burroughs, Franklin. 'Lost Causes and Gallantry: Johnny Reb and the Shadow of Sir Walter'. *American Scholar* 72 (2003), 73–92.

Busnel, François. 'Entretien avec Jacques Le Goff'. *Lire. fr*, May 2005.

Buzard, James. *The Beaten Track: European Tourism, Literature, and the Ways to Culture, 1800–1918* (Oxford: Clarendon Press, 1993).

Byron, Henry J. *Ivanhoe in Accordance with the Spirit of the Times; an Extravaganza* (London: Samuel French, n.d. [1858]).

Cairns, Francis. 'Orality, Writing, and Reoralisation: Some Departures and Arrivals in Homer and Apollonius Rhodius', in H. L. C. Tristram (ed.), *New Methods in the Research of Epic (Neue Methoden der Epenforschung)* (Tübingen: Narr, 1998), 63–84.

Calcraft, John William. *Ivanhoe, or the Jewess* (Leith: A. Allardice, n.d.).

Calinescu, Matei. *Rereading* (New Haven, CT: Yale University Press, 1993).

Cannadine, David. 'The Context, Performance and Meaning of Ritual: The British Monarchy and the "Invention of Tradition", c. 1820–1977', in Eric Hobsbawm and Terence Ranger (eds), *The Invention of Tradition* (Cambridge: Cambridge University Press, 1992 [1983]), 101–64.

——'The Transformation of Civic Ritual in Modern Britain: The Colchester Oyster Feast'. *Past and Present* 94 (1982), 107–30.

Carlyle, Thomas. *Critical and Miscellaneous Essays*, 7 vols (London: Chapman and Hall, 1872).

Carruthers, Mary. *The Book of Memory: A Study of Memory in Medieval Culture* (Cambridge: Cambridge University Press, 1990).

Carso, Kerry Dean. 'Diagnosing the "Sir Walter Disease": American Architecture in the Age of Romantic Literature'. *Mosaic* 35 (2002), 122–43.

Carswell, Donald. 'Why Scott is Neglected'. *Modern Scot*, Summer (1932), 111–13.

Caruth, Cathy. *Unclaimed Experience: Trauma, Narrative, and History* (Baltimore, MD: Johns Hopkins University Press, 1996).

Certeau, Michel de. *The Practice of Everyday Life*, trans. Steven Rendall (Berkeley: University of California Press, 1988 [1980]).

Chandler, Alice. *A Dream of Order: The Medieval Ideal in Nineteenth-Century English Literature* (London: Routledge & Kegan Paul, 1971).

Chandler, James. *England in 1819: The Politics of Literary Culture and the Case of Romantic Historicism* (Chicago: University of Chicago Press, 1998).

——'The Historical Novel Goes to Hollywood: Scott, Griffith, and Film Epic Today', in Gene Ruoff (ed.), *The Romantics and Us: Essays on Modern Literature and Culture* (New Brunswick, NJ: Rutgers University Press, 1990), 237–73.

Cheape, Hugh, Trevor Cowie, and Colin Wallace. 'Sir Walter Scott, The Abbotsford Collection and the National Museums of Scotland', in Iain G. Brown (ed.), *Abbotsford and Sir Walter Scott: The Image and the Influence* (Edinburgh: Society of Antiquaries of Scotland, 2003), 49–89.

Chesnutt, Charles W. *The House behind the Cedars* (London: X Press, 1998 [1900]).

Chibnall, Marjorie. *The Debate on the Norman Conquest* (Manchester: Manchester University Press, 1999).

Cicero. *De finibus bonorum et malorum*, trans. H. Rackham (London: Loeb Classical Library, 1967).

Clayton, Jay. 'The Alphabet of Suffering: Effie Deans, Tess Durbeyfield, Martha Ray, and Hetty Sorrel', in Jay Clayton and Eric Rothstein (eds), *Influence and Intertextuality in Literary History* (Madison: University of Wisconsin Press, 1991), 37–60.

Cochrane, J. G. *Catalogue of the Library at Abbotsford* (Edinburgh: Constable, 1838).

Coleridge, Samuel Taylor. *Collected Letters of Samuel Taylor Coleridge*, 6 vols (Oxford: Oxford University Press, 1959–71).

Colley, Linda. *Britons: Forging the Nation 1707–1837* (New Haven, CT: Yale University Press, 1992).

Colston, James. *History of the Scott Monument, Edinburgh; To which is prefixed a biographical sketch of Sir Walter Scott, Bart.* (Edinburgh: Printed for the Magistrates and Town Council, 1881).

Connerton, Paul. *How Modernity Forgets* (Cambridge: Cambridge University Press, 2009).

—— *How Societies Remember* (Cambridge: Cambridge University Press, 1989).

—— 'Seven Types of Forgetting'. *Memory Studies* 1 (2008), 59–71.

Cooper, Fox. *Ivanhoe: A Historical Drama in Three Acts, Dramatised from Sir Walter Scott's Novel* (London: John Dicks, n.d. [c.1859]).

Cox, Philip. *Reading Adaptations: Novels and Verse Narratives on the Stage, 1790–1840* (Manchester: Manchester University Press, 2000).

Crawford, Robert. *Devolving British Literature*, 2nd edn (Edinburgh: Edinburgh University Press, 2000 [1992]).

—— 'Walter Scott and European Union'. *Studies in Romanticism* 40 (2001), 137–52.

Criminal Trials, Illustrative of the Tale Entitled 'The Heart of Midlothian,' Published from the Original Record: with a Prefatory Notice, Including Some Particulars of the Life of Captain Porteous (Edinburgh: Archibald Constable, 1818).

Crockett, W. S. *Abbotsford* (London: A&C Black, 1905).

—— *The Scott Country*, 5th edn (London: A&C Black, 1920 [1905]).

—— *The Scott Originals: An Account of Notables and Worthies; The Originals of Characters in the Waverley Novels* (London: T. N. Foulis, 1912).

Crooks, Esther J., and Ruth W. Crooks. *The Ring Tournament in the United States* (Richmond, VA: Garrett and Massie, 1936).

Culler, Jonathan. 'Anderson and the Novel'. *Diacritics* 29 (1999), 20–39.

Cunninghame, A. T. 'Scott in 1932'. *Modern Scot*, Summer (1932), 114–18.

Cursory Observations on the Death of Sir Walter Scott, Addressed Chiefly to the Inhabitants of Edinburgh (Edinburgh: Stillies & Bros, 1832).

Dailey, Jeff S. *Sir Arthur Sullivan's Grand Opera* Ivanhoe *and its Theatrical and Musical Precursors* (Lampeter: Edwin Mellon Press, 2008).

Davis, Leith. *Acts of Union: Scotland and the Literary Negotiation of the British Nation 1707–1830* (Stanford, CA: Stanford University Press, 1998).

Davis, Leith, Ian Duncan, and Janet Sorensen (eds). *Scotland and the Borders of Romanticism* (Cambridge: Cambridge University Press, 2004).

Davis, Thomas. *Literary and Historical Essays* (Dublin: James Duffy, 1846).

Davis, Tracy C., and Peter Holland (eds). *The Performing Century: Nineteenth-Century Theatre's History* (London: Palgrave Macmillan, 2007).

deGategno, Paul. *Ivanhoe: The Mask of Chivalry* (New York: Twayne, 1994).

Dekker, George. *The American Historical Romance* (Cambridge: Cambridge University Press, 1987).

Dennett, Daniel C. *Darwin's Dangerous Idea: Evolution and the Meanings of Life* (New York: Simon and Schuster, 1995).

Dennis, John. 'A Talk about Sir Walter Scott for Young Readers', in *Good Words*, ed. Donald McCleod d.d. (London: Isbister, 1890), 756–63.

Deschamps, Emile. *Ivanhoe. Opéra en trois actes imité de l'anglais par MM [E.Deschamps et G. de Wailly]* (n.p.: n.p. [*c.*1826]).

Dibdin, James C. *The Annals of the Edinburgh Stage; With an Account of the Rise and Progress of Dramatic Writing in Scotland* (Edinburgh: Richard Cameron, 1888).

Dibdin, Thomas. *A Bibliographical, Antiquarian, and Picturesque Tour in the Northern Counties of England, and in Scotland.* 2 vols (London: Printed for the Author by C. Richards, 1838).

—— *The Heart of Midlothian: A Romantic National Drama; Founded on the Popular Tale of the Same Name* (Edinburgh: James L. Huie, 1823).

—— *Ivanhoe: or, The Jew's Daughter; A Romantic Melo–Drama; in Three Acts.* (New York: Samuel French, n.d. [1820]).

Dimnet, Abbé Ernest. 'Sir Walter Scott in France'. *Listener*, 21 September (1932), 410–12.

Dixon, Thomas. *The Clansman: An Historical Romance of the Ku Klux Klan* (Gretna: Pelican, 1905 [2005]).

Dixon, W. Macneile. 'Our Debt to Scott To-Day'. *Queen's Quarterly: A Canadian Review* November (1932), 382–592.

Dobson, Michael. *The Making of the National Poet: Shakespeare, Adaptation and Authorship, 1660–1769* (Oxford: Clarendon Press, 1992).

Düding, Dieter, Peter Friedemann, and Paul Münch (eds). *Öffentliche Festkultur: Politische Feste in Deutschland von der Aufklärung bis zum Ersten Weltkrieg* (Hamburg: Rowohlt, 1988).

Duff, David (ed.). *Queen Victoria's Highland Journals* (Exeter: Webb and Bower, 1980).

Duncan, Ian. *Modern Romance and Transformations of the Novel: The Gothic, Scott, Dickens* (Cambridge: Cambridge University Press, 1992).

—— 'Primitive Inventions: *Rob Roy*, Nation, and World System'. *Eighteenth-Century Fiction* 15 (2002), 81–102.

—— *Scott's Shadow: The Novel in Romantic Edinburgh* (Princeton, NJ: Princeton University Press, 2007).

Durie, Alastair. '"Scotland is Scott-land": Scott and the Development of Tourism', in Murray Pittock (ed.), *The European Reception of Sir Walter Scott* (London: Continuum, 2007), 313–22.

Durie, Alastair. 'Tourism in Victorian Scotland: The Case of Abbotsford'. *Scottish Economic and Social History* 12 (1992), 42–54.

Eckenrode, H. J. 'Sir Walter Scott and the South'. *North American Review* 206, October (1917), 595–603.

Eco, Umberto. 'From Internet to Gutenberg'. Lecture presented to the Italian Academy of Advanced Studies in America, 12 November 1996. Available at http://www.umbertoeco.com/en/from–internet–to–gutenberg–1996.html

Elias, Amy J. *Sublime Desire: History and Post-1960s Fiction* (Baltimore, MD: Johns Hopkins University Press, 2002).

Ellis, John. 'The Literary Adaptation: An Introduction'. *Screen* 23 (1982), 3–5.

Emerson, Ralph Waldo. *Miscellanies* (Boston: Houghton, Mifflin, 1904).

Erll, Astrid. *Gedächtnisromane: Literatur über den Ersten Weltkrieg als Medium englischer und deutscher Erinnerungskulturen in den 1920er Jahren* (Trier: WVT, 2003).

——*Kollektives Gedächtnis und Erinnerungskulturen* (Stuttgart: Metzler, 2005).

——*Prämediation – Remediation: Der indische Aufstand in imperialen und post-kolonialen Medienkulturen (1857 bis zur Gegenwart)* (Trier: WVT, 2007).

——and Ansgar Nünning (eds). *Cultural Memory Studies: An International and Interdisciplinary Handbook* (Berlin: de Gruyter, 2008).

Escott, T. H. S. 'Concerning the Centenary of Scott'. *Belgravia, a London Magazine* 5 (1871), 382–8.

Eyre-Todd, George. *To the Homes and Haunts of Scott and Burns by the Caledonian Railway* (Glasgow: McCorquodale, c.1911).

Faust, Drew Gilpin. *The Republic of Suffering: Death and the American Civil War* (New York: Knopf, 2008).

Felman, Shoshana, and Dori Laub. *Testimony: Crises of Witnessing in Literature, Psychoanalysis, and History* (London: Routledge, 1992).

Ferris, Ina. *The Achievement of Literary Authority: Gender, History, and the Waverley Novels* (Ithaca, NY: Cornell University Press, 1991).

——'"On the Borders of Oblivion": Scott's Historical Novel and the Modern Time of the Remnant'. *Modern Language Quarterly* 70 (2009), 473–94.

——*The Romantic National Tale and the Question of Ireland* (Cambridge: Cambridge University Press, 2002).

——'Writing on the Border: the National Tale, Female Writing, and the Public Sphere', in Tilottama Rajan and Julia M. Wright (eds), *Romanticism, History, and the Possibilities of Genre: Re-forming Literature 1789–1837* (Cambridge: Cambridge University Press, 1998), 86–106.

Fielding, Penny. *Scotland and the Fictions of Geography: North Britain, 1760–1830* (Cambridge: Cambridge University Press, 2008).

——*Writing and Orality: Nationality, Culture, and Nineteenth-Century Scottish Fiction* (Oxford: Oxford University Press, 1996).

Finley, Gerald. *Landscapes of Memory: Turner as Illustrator of Scott* (London: Scolar Press, 1980).

Fishwick, Marshall. 'F.F.V.'s'. *American Quarterly* 11 (1959), 147–56.

Flower, Eliza. *Musical Illustrations of the Waverley Novels, etc.* (London: Jos. Alfred Novello, *c*.1831).

Font, Lourdes M. 'Five Scenes from a Romance: The Identification of a Nineteenth-Century Printed Cotton'. *Metropolitan Museum Journal* 22 (1987), 115–32.

Ford, Richard. *Dramatisations of Scott's Novels: A Catalogue* (Oxford: Oxford Bibliographical Society, 1979).

Forster, E. M. *Aspects of the Novel* (Harmondsworth: Penguin, 1962 [1927]).

[Forsyth, Robert]. *The Waverley Anecdotes: Illustrative of the Incidents, Characters and Scenery described in the Novels and Romances of Walter Scott, Bart.* (London: J. Cochrane & J. McCrone, 1833).

Forty, Adrian, and Susanne Küchler (eds). *The Art of Forgetting* (Oxford: Berg, 1999).

Foster, Gaines M. *Ghosts of the Confederacy: Defeat, the Lost Cause, and the Emergence of the New South, 1865 to 1913* (New York: Oxford University Press, 1987).

Foucault, Michel. 'Des espaces autres' (1967). *Architecture, Mouvement, Continuité* 5 (1984), 46–9.

——*L'archéologie du savoir* (Paris: Gallimard, 1969).

——'What is an Author?' (1969), in Josué V. Harari (ed.), *Textual Strategies: Perspectives in Post-Structuralist Criticism* (Ithaca, NY: Cornell University Press, 1979), 141–160.

Foulkes, Richard. *The Shakespeare Tercentenary of 1864* (London: The Society for Theatre Research, 1984).

Franzen, Jonathan. *The Corrections* (New York: Farrar, Straus and Giroux, 2001).

Fritzsche, Peter. *Stranded in the Present: Modern Time and the Melancholy of History* (Cambridge, MA: Harvard University Press, 2004).

Fuhrman, Christina. 'Scott Repatriated?: *La dame blanche* Crosses the Channel'. *Praxis Series*, Special issue, ed. Gillen D'Arcy Wood (2005), available at http://www.rc.umd.edu/praxis/opera/index.html.

Garside, Peter D. 'Walter Scott and the "Common" Novel, 1808–1819'. *Cardiff Corvey: Reading the Romantic Text* 3 (1999): available at http://www.cardiff.ac.uk/encap/journals/corvey/articles/cc03_n02.html.

Geary, Patrick J. *The Myth of Nations: The Medieval Origins of Europe* (Princeton, NJ: Princeton University Press, 2003).

——*Phantoms of Remembrance: Memory and Oblivion at the End of the First Millennium* (Princeton, NJ: Princeton University Press, 1994).

Genette, Gerard. *Palimpsestes: La littérature au second degré* (Paris: Seuil, 1982).

Geser, Hans. '"Yours Virtually Forever": Death Memorials and Remembrance Sites in WWW'. *Sociology in Switzerland: Online Publications* (1998), available at http://socio.ch/intcom/t_hgeser07.htm.

Giddings, Robert. 'Scott and Opera', in Alan Bold (eds), *Sir Walter Scott: The Long Forgotten Melody* (London: Vision, 1983), 194–218.

Gikandi, Simon. *Maps of Englishness: Writing Identity in the Culture of Colonialism* (New York: Columbia University Press, 1996).

Girouard, Marc. *The Return to Camelot: Chivalry and the English Gentleman* (New Haven, CT: Yale University Press, 1981).

Gladwell, Malcolm. *The Tipping Point: How Little Things Can Make a Big Difference* (New York: Little, Brown, 2000).

Glassberg, David. *American Historical Pageantry: The Uses of Tradition in the Early Twentieth Century* (Chapel Hill: University of North Carolina Press, 1990).

Glendening, John. *The High Road: Romantic Tourism, Scotland, and Literature, 1720–1820* (London: Macmillan, 1997).

Gold, John R., and Margaret M. Gold. *Imagining Scotland: Tradition, Representation and Promotion in Scottish Tourism since 1750* (London: Scolar Press, 1995).

Gordon, Catherine. *British Paintings of Subjects from the English Novel: 1740–1870* (New York: Garland, 1988).

Gottlieb, Evan. *Feeling British: Sympathy and National Identity in Scottish and English Writing, 1707–1832* (Lewisburg, PA: Bucknell University Press, 2007).

——and Ian Duncan (eds). *Approaches to Teaching Scott's Waverley Novels* (New York: Modern Language Association of America, 2009).

Goulemot, Jean-Marie, and Eric Walter. 'Les centenaires de Voltaire et de Rousseau: Les deux lampions des Lumières', in Pierre Nora (ed.), *Les lieux de mémoire*, 3 vols (Paris: Gallimard, 1997), I: 351–82.

Graff, Gerald. *Professing Literature: An Institutional History* (Chicago: University of Chicago Press, 1987).

Graham, Jenny. *Inventing Van Eyck: The Remaking of an Artist for the Modern Age* (Oxford: Berg, 2007).

Grant, Barry Keith, *Shadows of Doubt: Negotiations of Masculinity in American Genre Films* (Detroit: Wayne State University Press, 2011).

Graves, John. *Goodbye to a River: A Narrative* (New York: Random House, 1960).

Gray, W. Forbes (ed.). *Scott in Sunshine and Shadow: The Tribute of His Friends* (London: Methuen, 1931).

Greenblatt, Stephen. *Shakespearean Negotiations: The Circulation of Social Energy in Renaissance England* (Oxford: Clarendon Press, 1988).

Grierson, H.J.C. (ed.). *Sir Walter Scott To-day: Some Retrospective Essays and Studies* (London: Constable, 1932).

——(ed.). *The Letters of Sir Walter Scott*, 12 vols (London: Constable, 1932–7).

——*Sir Walter Scott 1832–1932* (New York: Columbia University Press, 1933).

Groth, Helen. *Victorian Photography and Literary Nostalgia* (Oxford: Oxford University Press, 2003).

Grusin, Richard. *Premediation: Affect and Mediality after 9/11* (London: Palgrave Macmillan, 2010).

——'Premediation'. *Criticism* 46 (2004), 17–39.

Gumbrecht, Hans Ulrich. *The Powers of Philology: Dynamics of Textual Scholarship* (Urbana: University of Illinois Press, 2003).

Gunn, Simon. *The Public Culture of the Victorian Middle Class: Ritual and Authority in the English Industrial City 1840–1914* (Manchester: Manchester University Press, 2000).

Halbwachs, Maurice. *La mémoire collective* (Paris: Albin Michel, 1997 [1950]).

——*La topographie légendaire des Evangiles en Terre Sainte: Etude de mémoire collective* (Paris: Presses universitaires de France, 1941).

——*Les cadres sociaux de la mémoire* (Paris: Albin Michel, 1994 [1925]).

Hariman, Robert, and John Louis Lucaites. *No Caption Needed: Iconic Photographs, Public Culture, and Liberal Democracy* (Chicago: University of Chicago Press, 2007).

Hartman, Geoffrey H. 'Public Memory and its Discontents', in Marshall Brown (ed.), *The Uses of Literary History* (Durham, NC: Duke University Press, 1995), 73–9.

Haverkamp, Anselm, and Renate Lachmann (eds). *Memoria: Vergessen und Erinnern* (München: Wilhelm Fink, 1993).

Hay, John. *Speech of John Hay at the Unveiling: of the Bust of Sir Walter Scott in Westminster Abbey; May 21, 1897* (London: John Lane, 1897).

Hayden, Dolores. *The Power of Place: Urban Landscapes as Public History* (Cambridge, MA: MIT Press, 1995).

Hayden, John O. (ed.). *Scott: The Critical Heritage* (London: Routledge & Kegan Paul, 1970).

Hazard, Erin. 'The Author's House: Abbotsford and Wayside', in Nicola Watson (ed.), *Literary Tourism and Nineteenth-Century Culture* (London: Palgrave Macmillan, 2009), 63–72.

Hazlitt, William. 'Sir Walter Scott', in *The Spirit of the Age* (Oxford: Woodstock Books, 1989 [1825]), 131–56.

Heart of Midlothian Football Club (n.p.: Tempus, 1998).

Heart of Midlothian; or the Lily of St. Leonard, A Caledonian Tale of Great Interest, on which is founded the Piece of that Name, Performed with Unbounded Applause at the Different Theatres (London: Printed for the Company of Booksellers, 1822).

Heber, Reginald. *Narrative of a Journey Through the Upper Provinces of India, from Calcutta to Bombay, 1824–1825 (with notes upon Ceylon)*, ed. Amelia Heber (London: John Murray, 1828).

Hendrix, Harald. 'Writers' Houses as Media of Expression and Remembrance: From Self-Fashioning to Cultural Memory', in Harald Hendrix (ed.), *Writers' Houses and the Making of Memory* (New York: Routledge, 2008), 1–11.

Hewitt, David. 'Scott, Sir Walter (1771–1832)', in *Dictionary of National Biography* (Oxford: Oxford University Press, 2004).

Hill, Richard. *Picturing Scotland through the Waverley Novels: Walter Scott and the Origins of the Victorian Illustrated Novel* (London: Ashgate, 2010).

Hirsch, Marianne. *Family Frames: Photography, Narrative, and Postmemory* (Cambridge, MA: Harvard University Press, 1997).

Hodgkin, Katherine, and Susannah Radstone (eds). *Memory, History, Nation: Contested Pasts* (London: Transaction, 2003).

Hofmeyr, Isabel. *The Portable Bunyan: A Transnational History of* The Pilgrim's Progress (Princeton, NJ: Princeton University Press, 2004).

Hölscher, Meike. 'Performances, Souvenirs, and Music: The Diamond Jubilee of Queen Victoria 1897', in Astrid Erll and Ann Rigney (eds), *Mediation, Remediation, and the Dynamics of Cultural Memory* (Berlin: de Gruyter, 2009), 173–86.

Hugo, Victor. *Les misérables*, 4 vols (Paris: Nelson, n.d. [1862]).

Hutcheon, Linda. *A Poetics of Postmodernism: History, Theory, Fiction* (London: Routledge, 1988).

——*A Theory of Adaptation* (London: Routledge, 2006).

——*A Theory of Parody: The Teachings of Twentieth-Century Art Forms* (New York: Methuen, 1985).

——and Mario J. Valdés. 'Irony, Nostalgia, and the Postmodern: A Dialogue'. *Poligrafías* 3 (1998–2000), 29–54.

Hutton, Patrick H. *History as an Art of Memory* (Hanover, NH: University Press of New England, 1993).

Huyssen, Andreas. *After the Great Divide: Modernism, Mass Culture, Postmodernism* (Bloomington: Indiana University Press, 1986).

——'Present Pasts: Media, Politics, Amnesia'. *Public Culture* 12 (2000), 21–38.

——*Present Pasts: Urban Palimpsests and the Politics of Memory*, (Stanford, CA: Stanford University Press, 2003).

Ivanhoe; Or, the Knight Templar, and the Jew's Daughter. An Ancient Tale of English Chivalry: From the Celebrated Romance of 'Ivanhoe' by the Author of 'Tales of my Landlord' etc. (London: J. Bailey, 1821).

Irving, Washington. *Abbotsford, and Newstead Abbey* (London: John Murray, 1835).

[J.H.]. 'The Scott Centenary Celebration'. *The Leisure Hour: A Family Journal of Instruction and Recreation*, 1 July (1871), 405–8.

Jacobs, Joseph. 'The Original of Scott's Rebecca'. *Publications of the American Jewish Historical Society* 22 (1914), 53–60.

Jakobson, Roman. 'Closing Statement: Linguistics and Poetics', in Thomas A. Sebeok (ed.), *Style in Language* (Cambridge, MA: MIT Press, 1960), 350–77.

——and Petr Bogatyrev. 'On the Boundary between the Studies of Folklore and Literature', in Ladislaw Matejka and Krystyna Pomorska (eds), *Readings in Russian Poetics: Formalist and Structuralist Views* (Cambridge, MA: MIT Press, 1971), 91–3.

Jameson, Fredric. *Postmodernism, or, The Cultural Logic of Late Capitalism* (London: Verso, 1991).

[Jeffrey, Francis]. 'Novels, by the Author of Waverley'. *Edinburgh Review* 65, January (1820), 1–54.

Jenkins, Henry. *Convergence Culture: Where Old and New Media Collide* (New York: New York University Press, 2006).

Johnson, Edgar. *Sir Walter Scott: The Great Unknown*, 2 vols (London: Hamilton, 1970).

Johnson, Guion Griffis. *Ante-Bellum North Carolina: A Social History* [electronic edn] (Chapel Hill: University of North Carolina Press, 1937).

Jolles, André. *Einfache Formen: Legende, Sage, Mythe, Rätsel, Spruch, Kasus, Memorabile, Märchen, Witz* (Halle: M. Niemeyer, 1930).

Jones, Catherine. *Literary Memory: Scott's Waverley Novels and the Psychology of Narrative* (London: Associated University Presses, 2003).

Joshi, Priya. 'Culture and Consumption: Fiction, the Reading Public, and the British Novel in Colonial India'. *Book History* 1 (1998), 196–220.

—— *In Another Country: Colonialism, Culture, and the English Novel in India* (New York: Columbia University Press, 2002).

Joyce, Patrick. *Visions of the People: Industrial England and the Question of Class, 1848–1914* (Cambridge: Cambridge University Press, 1991).

Junior, Allan. *Sir Walter Scott: A Centenary Momento in Scene and Story* (London: Valentine and Sons, 1932).

Kellner, Hans. 'Narrativity in History: Post-Structuralism and Since'. *History and Theory* 26 (1987), 1–29.

Kelly, Stuart. *Scott-Land: The Man Who Invented a Nation* (Edinburgh: Polygon, 2010).

Kernohan, R. D. ' "Will Ye No' Come Back Again?" Whatever Happened to Sir Walter Scott?', *Contemporary Review* 262 (1993), 261–5.

Kerr, James. 'Scott's Fable of Regeneration: *The Heart of Midlothian*'. *English Literary History* 53 (1986), 801–20.

Keymer, Thomas, and Peter Sabor (eds). *The Pamela Controversy: Criticisms and Adaptations of Samuel Richardson's Pamela, 1740–1750*, 6 vols (London: Pickering and Chatto, 2001).

Kidd, Colin. 'Sentiment, Race and Revival: Scottish Identities in the Aftermath of Enlightenment', in Laurence Brockliss and David Eastwood (eds), *A Union of Multiple Identities: The British Isles, c.1750–c.1850* (Manchester: Manchester University Press, 1999), 110–26.

King, H. G. L. 'A Tower of Memory'. *Walter Scott Quarterly* 1 (1927), 145–6.

Kirshenblatt-Gimblett, Barbara. *Destination Culture: Tourism, Museums, and Heritage* (Berkeley: University of California Press, 1998).

Knight, Stephen. *Robin Hood: A Mythic Biography* (Ithaca, NY: Cornell University Press, 2003).

—— (ed.). *Robin Hood: An Anthology of Scholarship and Criticism* (Cambridge: D. S. Brewer, 1999).

Knowles, James Sheridan. *The Vision of the Bard* (New York: James Kennaday, 1832).

Koselleck, Reinhart. *Futures Past: On the Semantics of Historical Time*, trans. Keith Tribe (Cambridge, MA: MIT Press, 1985 [1979]).

——'Kriegerdenkmale als Identitätsstiftungen der Überlebenden', in Odo Marquard and Karlheinz Stierle (eds), *Identität* (München: Wilhelm Fink, 1979), 255–76.

Lacy, M. Rophino. *The Maid of Judah; or, The Knights Templar; A Serious Opera in Three Acts* (London: Davidson [1833]).

Lacy, Thomas Hailes. *The Heart of Mid-Lothian; or, the Sisters of St. Leonard's: A Drama, (with unregistered effects) in Three Acts.* (London: Thomas Hailes Lacy, n.d. [*c*.1863]).

The Land of Scott: A Series of Landscape Illustrations, Illustrative of Real Scenes, described in the Novels and Tales, of the, Author of Waverley; From Drawings by the Most Distinguished Artists (London: David Bogne, 1848).

Landrum, Grace Warren. 'Notes on the Reading Matter of the Old South'. *American Literature* 3, March (1931), 60–71.

——'Sir Walter Scott and his Literary Rivals in the Old South'. *American Literature* 2 (1930), 256–76.

Landsberg, Alison. *Prosthetic Memory: The Transformation of American Remembrance in the Age of Mass Culture* (New York: Columbia University Press, 2004).

Langer, Lawrence L. *The Holocaust and the Literary Imagination* (New Haven, CT: Yale University Press, 1985).

Lanoire, Maurice. 'Walter Scott'. *La revue de Paris* 39, September-October (1932), 393–410.

Lascelles, Mary. *The Story-teller Retrieves the Past: Historical Fiction and Fictitious History in the Art of Scott, Stevenson, Kipling, and Some Others* (Oxford: Clarendon Press, 1980).

[Lauder, Thomas Dick]. 'Funeral of Sir Walter Scott: By an Eyewitness'. *Tait's Edinburgh Magazine, and Literary Miscellany*, November (1832), 196–202.

Lawson, Julie. 'Rushkin on Scott's Abbotsford', in Iain G. Brown (ed.), *Abbotsford and Sir Walter Scott: The Image and the Influence* (Edinburgh: Society of Antiquaries, 2003), 161–8.

Leask, Nigel. *Curiosity and the Aesthetics of Travel Writing, 1770–1840* (Oxford: Oxford University Press, 2002).

Leavis, F. R. *The Great Tradition: George Eliot, Henry James, Joseph Conrad* (Harmondsworth, Middlesex: Penguin, 1962 [1948]).

Lee, Harper. *To Kill a Mockingbird* (London: Arrow Books, 2006 [1960]).

Leerssen, Joep. 'Fiction Poetics and Cultural Stereotype: Local Colour in Scott, Morgan, and Maturin'. *Modern Language Review* 86 (1991), 273–84.

——*National Thought in Europe: A Cultural History* (Amsterdam: Amsterdam University Press, 2006).

——'Nationalism and the Cultivation of Culture'. *Nations and Nationalism* 12 (2006), 559–78.

——'Over de ontologische status en de tekstuele situering van imagotypen: Exotisme en voetnoten in Walter Scotts «Waverley»', in E. Eweg (ed.), *Deugdelijk vermaak: Opstellen over literatuur en filosofie in de negentiende eeuw* (Amsterdam: Huis aan de Drie Grachten, 1987), 125–35.

Leerssen, Joep. 'The Rhetoric of National Character: A Programmatic Survey'. *Poetics Today* 21(2) (2000), 265–90.

Levitt, Marcus C. *Russian Literary Politics and the Pushkin Celebration of 1880* (Ithaca, NY: Cornell University Press, 1989).

Lewin, Judith Mindy. 'Legends of Rebecca: *Ivanhoe*, Dynamic Identification, and the Portraits of Rebecca Gratz'. *Nashim; A Journal of Jewish Women's Studies and Gender Issues* 10 (2005), 178–212.

Lincoln, Andrew. *Walter Scott and Modernity* (Edinburgh: Edinburgh University Press, 2007).

Listener. 'A Century of Scott'. *Listener*, 21 September (1932), 400.

Lizars, J. H., and James Morton. *Abbotsford: The Seat of Sir Walter Scott, Bart.* (Edinburgh: Lizars, 1832).

Lockhart, C. S. M. *The Centenary Memorial of Sir Walter Scott, Bart.* (London: Virtue, 1871).

Lockhart, J. G. *The Life of Sir Walter Scott, Bart.; New Popular Edition* (London: A&C Black, 1893 (1837–8)).

Lotman, Juri. *The Structure of the Artistic Text*, trans. Ronald Vroon (Ann Arbor: University of Michigan, 1977 [1970]).

—— *Universe of the Mind: A Semiotic Theory of Culture*, trans. Ann Shukman (London: I. B. Tauris, 1990).

Lowenthal, David. *The Past is a Foreign Country* (Cambridge: Cambridge University Press, 1985).

Lownie, Andrew. *The Literary Companion to Edinburgh* (London: Methuen, 2000).

Lukács, Georg. *The Historical Novel*, trans. Hannah and Stanley Mitchell (Harmondsworth: Penguin, 1962 [1936–7]).

Lynch, Deidre (ed.). *Janeites: Austen's Disciples and Devotees* (Princeton, NJ: Princeton University Press, 2000).

Macaulay, Thomas Babington. *Critical, Historical and Miscellaneous Essays*, 3 vols (New York: A. L. Burt, n.d.).

McCracken-Flesher, Caroline. *Possible Scotlands: Walter Scott and the Story of Tomorrow* (Oxford: Oxford University Press, 2005).

—— 'Narrating the (Gendered) Nation in Walter Scott's *The Heart of Midlothian*'. *Nineteenth-Century Contexts* 24 (2002), 291–316.

—— 'Prediction of Things Past: Scott and the Triumph of the Author's Antiquity'. *Anglistik* 23 (2012), 41–50.

McCrorie, Ian. *Clyde Pleasure Steamers: An Illustrated History* (Greenock: Orr, Pollock, 1986).

MacCulloch, John. *The Highlands and Western Isles of Scotland, containing Descriptions of their Scenery and Antiquities [...] Founded on a Series of Annual Journeys Between the Years 1811 and 1821, and Forming an Universal Guide to that Country, in Letters to Sir Walter Scott, Bart.* (London: Longman, 1824).

McDayter, Ghislaine. *Byromania and the Birth of Celebrity Culture* (Albany: State University of New York Press, 2009).

McDiarmid, John. *Sketches from Nature* (Edinburgh: Oliver Boyd, 1830).

McGann, Jerome. 'Ivanhoe: Education in a New Key'. Available at http://www.rc.umd.edu/pedagogies/commons/innovations/IVANHOE.html

——'Like Leaving the Nile: IVANHOE, a User's Manual'. *Literature Compass* 2 (2005), 1–26.

——*The Point is to Change It: Poetry and Criticism in the Continuing Present* (Tuscaloosa: University of Alabama Press, 2007).

——*The Scholar's Art: Literary Studies in a Managed World* (Chicago: University of Chicago Press, 2006).

——'Walter Scott's Romantic Postmodernity', in Leith Davis, Ian Duncan, and Janet Sorensen (eds), *Scotland and the Borders of Romanticism* (Cambridge: Cambridge University Press, 2004), 113–29.

MacHaffie, Fraser G. *Jeanie Deans 1931–1967: An Illustrated Biography* (Coatbridge: Jeanie Deans, 1977).

——*Waverley: The Story of the Last Seagoing Paddle-Steamer in the World*, 4th edn (Glasgow: Waverley Excursions, 1982).

McHale, Maria. 'Moore's Centenary: Music and Politics in Dublin, 1879'. *Proceedings of the Royal Irish Academy* 109 (2009), 387–408.

Mack, Douglas S. *Scottish Fiction and the British Empire* (Edinburgh: Edinburgh University Press, 2006).

Mackay, James A. *The Burns Federation 1885–1985* (Kilmarnock: The Burns Federation, 1985).

Mackenzie, Agnes Mure. 'Letters and Appreciations'. *Listener*, 21 September (1932), 414.

McLaren, Moray. 'Scott and Scotland'. *Listener*, 21 September (1932), 412–13.

MacLeod, Christine. *Heroes of Invention: Technology, Liberalism and British Identity, 1750–1914* (Cambridge: Cambridge University Press, 2007).

McNeil, Kenneth. *Scotland, Britain, Empire: Writing the Highlands, 1760–1860* (Columbus: Ohio University Press, 2007).

Macneile Dixon, W. 'Our Debt to Scott To-Day'. *Queen's Quarterly: A Canadian Review*, November (1932): 581–92.

McVickar, Revd J. *Tribute to the Memory of Sir Walter Scott, Baronet* (New York: George P. Scott, 1833).

[——]. 'Abbotsford'. *Dublin Weekly Journal: A Repository of Music, Literature, and Entertaining Knowledge* 22, 30 March (1833), 169–74.

Makdisi, Saree. *Romantic Imperialism: Universal Empire and the Culture of Modernity* (Cambridge: Cambridge University Press, 1998).

Manning, Susan. 'Did Mark Twain Bring down the Temple on Scott's Shoulders', in Janet Beer and Bridget Bennett (eds), *Special Relationship: Anglo-American Affinities and Antagonisms, 1854–1936* (Manchester: Manchester University Press, 2002), 8–27.

Marini, G. M., and Ottone Nicolaj. *Il Templario: melodramma in tre atti di G.M. Marini, musica del maestro Ottone Nicolaj, da rappresentarsi al regio teatro alla Scala, il Carnevale 1866* (Milano: Franceso Lucca, 1866 [1840]).

Marschner, Heinrich. *The Templar and the Jewess / Der Templer und die Jüdin* (New York: Metropolitan Opera House, n.d.).

Martineau, Harriet. 'The Achievements of the Genius of Scott'. *Tait's Edinburgh Magazine* 9 (1832), 445–60.

——'Characteristics of the Genius of Scott'. *Tait's Edinburgh Magazine* 9 (1832), 301–14.

Matthews, Samantha. *Poetical Remains: Poets' Graves, Bodies, and Books in the Nineteenth Century* (Oxford: Oxford University Press, 2004).

Maxwell, Richard. *The Historical Novel in Europe, 1650–1950* (Cambridge: Cambridge University Press, 2009).

——'Walter Scott, Historical Fiction, and the Genesis of the Victorian Illustrated Book', in Richard Maxwell (ed.), *The Victorian Illustrated Book* (Charlottesville: University Press of Virginia, 2002), 1–51.

May, G. Lewis. 'Do We Read Sir Walter Scott? Some Reflections on the Centenary of Quentin Durward'. *Cassells Weekly* 25 (1923), 782.

Maza, Sarah. *Private Lives and Public Affairs: The Causes Célèbres of Prerevolutionary France* (Berkeley: University of California Press, 1993).

Meisel, Martin. *Realizations: Narrative, Pictorial, and Theatrical Arts in Nineteenth-Century England* (Princeton, NJ: Princeton University Press, 1983).

Mellon, Thomas. *Thomas Mellon and his Times*, ed. Mary Louise Briscoe (Pittsburgh: University of Pittsburgh Press, 1994).

Meyer-Spacks, Patricia. *Gossip* (Chicago: University of Chicago Press, 1985).

——'Private and Social Reading'. *Ideas* 5 (1998). Available at http:// nationalhumanitiescenter.org/ideasv52/spacks.htm.

Michaud, Philippe-Alain. *Aby Warburg and the Image in Motion*, trans. Sophie Hawkes (New York: Zone Books, 2004 (1998)).

Michelangelo nell'Ottocento. Il centenario del 1875, catalogo mostra Firenze, Casa Buonarroti, 14 giugno–7 novembre 1994 (Milano: Charta, 1994).

Miller, Hugh. *Leading Articles on Various Subjects*, edited by his Son-in-Law the Revd John Davidson, 4th edn (Edinburgh: William P. Nimmo, 1872).

Millgate, Jane. *Scott's Last Edition: A Study in Publishing History* (Edinburgh: Edinburgh University Press, 1987).

Milton, Henry (ed.). *Speeches and Addresses of the Right Honourable Frederick Temple Hamilton, Earl of Dufferin* (London: John Murray, 1882).

Mitchell, C. Bradford (ed.). *Merchant Steam Vessels of the United States 1790–1868* (Staten Island, NY: Steamship Historical Society of America, 1975).

Mitchell, Jerome. *More Scott Operas: Further Analysis of Operas Based on the Works of Sir Walter Scott* (Lanham: University Press of America, 1996).

——*The Walter Scott Operas: An Analysis of Operas Based on the Works of Sir Walter Scott* (Tuscaloosa: University of Alabama Press, 1977).

Mole, Tom. *Byron's Romantic Celebrity: Industrial Culture and the Hermeneutic of Intimacy* (Basingstoke: Palgrave Macmillan, 2007).

Mole, Tom. (ed.). *Romanticism and Celebrity Culture, 1750–1850* (Cambridge: Cambridge University Press, 2009).

Moncrieff, William Thomas. *Ivanhoe! or, The Jewess; A Chivalric Play, in Three Acts; Founded on the Popular Romance of "Ivanhoe"* (London: John Lowndes, 1820).

Moody, Jane. *Illegitimate Theatre in London 1770–1840* (Cambridge: Cambridge University Press, 2000).

—— and Daniel O'Quinn (eds). *The Cambridge Companion to British Theatre, 1730–1830* (Cambridge: Cambridge University Press, 2007).

Moore, Thomas. *Memoirs, Journal and Correspondence of Thomas Moore*, ed. Lord John Russell, 8 vols (London: Longman, 1854).

Moretti, Franco. *Atlas of the European Novel 1800–1900* (London: Verso, 1998).

Morris, Mowbray. 'Sir Walter Scott (A Lecture at Eton)'. *Macmillan's Magazine* 356 (1889), 151–60.

Muir, Edwin. 'Scott and Tradition'. *Modern Scot*, Summer (1932), 118–20.

—— 'Walter Scott (1771–1832)', in Bonamy Dobrée (ed.), *From Anne to Victoria: Essays by Various Hands* (London: Cassell, 1937), 528–45.

[Murray, William Henry]. *Ivanhoe, The Waverley Dramas, from the Novels of Sir Walter Scott, Bart.* (London: George Routledge, 1845 [1824]).

Natter, Wolfgang. *Literature at War, 1914–1940: Representing the "Time of Greatness" in Germany* (New Haven, CT: Yale University Press, 1999).

Neubauer, John. *The Fin-de-Siècle Culture of Adolescence* (New Haven, CT: Yale University Press, 1992).

Nicoll, Allardyce. *A History of English Drama 1660–1900*, 4 vols (Cambridge: Cambridge University Press, 1955).

Nietzsche, Friedrich. *The Advantage and Disadvantage of History for Life*, trans. Peter Preuss (Indianapolis, IN: Hackett, 1980 [1874]).

Nikolopoulou, Anastasia. 'Historical Disruptions: The Walter Scott Melodramas', in Michael Hays and Anastasia Nikolopoulou (eds), *Melodrama: The Cultural Emergence of a Genre* (New York: St. Martin's, 1996), 121–43.

Nock, O. S. *Great Locomotives of the L.N.E.R.* (Wellingborough: Patrick Stephens, 1988).

Noltenius, Rainer. 'Schiller als Führer und Heiland: Das Schillerfest 1859 als nationaler Traum von der Geburt des zweiten deutschen Kaiserreichs', in Dieter Düding, Peter Friedemann, and Paul Münch (eds), *Öffentliche Festkultur: Politische Feste in Deutschland von der Aufklärung bis zum Ersten Weltkrieg* (Hamburg: Rowohlt, 1988), 237–58.

Nora, Pierre (ed.). *Les lieux de mémoire*, 3 vols (Paris: Gallimard, 1997 [1984–92]).

Notices and Anecdotes Illustrative of the Incidents, Characters, and Scenery described in the Novels and Romances of Sir Walter Scott, Bart.; With a Complete Glossary of all his Works (Paris: Baudry's European Library, 1833).

O'Brien, Michael. *Rethinking the South: Essays in Intellectual History* (Baltimore, MD: Johns Hopkins University Press, 1988).

Olick, Jeffrey K. *The Politics of Regret: On Collective Memory and Historical Responsibility* (London: Routledge, 2007).

Olick, Jeffrey K. (ed.). *States of Memory: Continuities, Conflicts, and Transformations in National Retrospection* (Durham, NC: Duke University Press, 2003).

——and Joyce Robbins. 'Social Memory Studies: From "Collective Memory" to the Historical Sociology of Mnemonic Practices'. *Annual Review of Sociology* 24 (1998), 105–40.

——, Vered Vinitzky-Seroussi, and Daniel Levy (eds). *The Collective Memory Reader* (New York: Oxford University Press, 2011).

Osterweis, Rollin G. *Romanticism and Nationalism in the Old South* (New Haven, CT: Yale University Press, 1949).

Ozouf, Mona. *La fête révolutionnaire, 1789–1799* (Paris: Gallimard, 1976).

Palmer, D. J. *The Rise of English Studies: An Account of the Study of English Language and Literature from its Origins to the Making of the Oxford English School* (London: Oxford University Press, 1965).

Passerini, Luisa. 'Memories between Silence and Oblivion', in Katherine Hodgkin and Susannah Radstone (eds), *Memory, History, Nation: Contested Pasts* (London: Routledge, 2003), 238–54.

Pebody, Charles. 'The Scott Centenary: Sir Walter at His Desk'. *Gentleman's Magazine* 7 (1871), 292–316.

Pelle, M. C. *Landscape-historical Illustrations of the Waverley Novels/Nouvelles illustrations anglaises des romans de Sir Walter Scott, Bart.* (London: Fisher, 1840).

Pitt, George Dibdin. *The Whistler!: The Fate of the Lily of St. Leonard's, a Melo Drama, in Three Acts* (London: J. Duncombe [1833]).

Pittock, Murray (ed.). *The Reception of Sir Walter Scott in Europe* (London: Continuum, 2007).

——*Scottish and Irish Romanticism* (Oxford: Oxford University Press, 2008).

—— *The Invention of Scotland: The Stuart Myth and the Scottish Identity, 1638 to the Present* (London: Routledge, 1991).

—— *The Myth of the Jacobite Clans: The Jacobite Army in 1745*, 2nd edn (Edinburgh: Edinburgh University Press, 2009).

Pocock, Isaac. *Rob Roy MacGregor; or, Auld Lang Syne! A Musical Drama, in Three Acts, founded on the Popular Novel of Rob Roy* (London: John Miller, 1818).

Pratt, M. Louise. *Toward a Speech Act Theory of Literary Discourse* (Bloomington: Indiana University Press, 1977).

Prebble, John. *The King's Jaunt: George IV in Scotland, August 1822; 'One and Twenty Daft Days'* (Edinburgh: Birlinn, 1988).

Pulsifer, Cameron. 'A Highland Regiment in Halifax: The 78th Highland Regiment of Foot and the Scottish National/Cultural Factor in Nova Scotia's Capital, 1869–71', in Marjory Harper and Michael Vance (eds), *Myth, Migration and the Making of Memory: Scotia and Nova Scotia c.1700–1990* (Halifax: Fernwood, 1999), 141–56.

Quinault, Roland. 'The Cult of the Centenary, c.1784–1914'. *Historical Research* 71 (1998), 303–23.

Radstone, Susannah, and Kate Hodgkin (eds). *Contested Pasts: The Politics of Memory* (London: Routledge, 2003).

—— and Bill Schwarz (eds). *Memory: Histories, Theories, Debates* (New York: Fordham University Press, 2010).

Ragussis, Michael. 'The Birth of a Nation in Victorian Culture: The Spanish Inquisition, the Converted Daughter, and the "Secret Race"'. *Critical Inquiry* 20 (1994), 477–508.

—— *Theatrical Nation: Jews and Other Outlandish Englishmen in Georgian Britain* (Philadelphia: University of Pennsylvania Press, 2010).

—— 'Writing Nationalist History: England, the Conversion of the Jews, and *Ivanhoe*'. *English Literary History* 60 (1993), 181–215.

Raleigh, John Henry. 'What Scott Meant to the Victorians', in Harry E. Shaw (ed.), *Critical Essays on Sir Walter Scott: The Waverley Novels* (New York: G. K. Hall, 1996), 47–69.

Raleigh, Walter. *The English Novel: Being a Short Sketch of its History from the Earliest Times to the Appearance of Waverley* (New York: C. Scribner, 1894).

Renan, Ernest. 'Qu'est–ce qu'une nation?' (1882), in Henriëtte Psichari (ed.), *Oeuvres complètes d'Ernest Renan* (Paris: Calmann-Lévy, 1947–61), 886–907.

Richardson, Thomas Miles. *The Death of Captain Porteous in the Porteous Riots in Edinburgh in 1736* (London: Fisher, 1836).

Ricoeur, Paul. *La mémoire, l'histoire, l'oubli* (Paris: Seuil, 2000).

—— *Temps et récit*, 3 vols (Paris: Seuil, 1983–5).

Rigney, Ann. 'All This Happened More or Less: What a Novelist Made of the Bombing of Dresden'. *History and Theory* 48 (2009), 5–24.

—— 'The Concept of Narrative in Historical Theory', in Nancy Partner and Sarah Foote (eds), *The Sage Handbook of Historical Theory* (New York: Sage, 2013).

—— 'Divided Pasts: A Premature Memorial and the Dynamics of Collective Remembrance'. *Memory Studies* 1 (2007), 89–97.

—— 'The Dynamics of Remembrance: Texts between Monumentality and Morphing', in Astrid Erll and Ansgar Nünning (eds), *Cultural Memory Studies: An International and Interdisciplinary Handbook* (Berlin: De Gruyter, 2008), 345–53.

—— 'Embodied Communities: Commemorating Robert Burns, 1859'. *Representations* 115 (2011), 71–101.

—— 'Fiction as a Mediator in National Remembrance', in Stefan Berger, Linas Eriksonas, and Andrew Mycock (eds), *Narrating the Nation: The Representation of National Narratives in Different Genres* (Oxford: Berghahn Books, 2009), 79–96.

—— *Imperfect Histories: The Elusive Past and the Legacy of Romantic Historicism* (Ithaca, NY: Cornell University Press, 2001).

—— 'Plenitude, Scarcity and the Circulation of Cultural Memory'. *Journal of European Studies* 35 (2005), 209–26.

—— *The Rhetoric of Historical Representation: Three Narrative Histories of the French Revolution* (Cambridge: Cambridge University Press, 1990).

Roach, Lewis. 'The Story of Ivanhoe: Sir Walter Scott's Great Story as Picturized in the Universal Film; Pictures Storyized by Lewis Roach'. *Photoplay Magazine* 4 (1913), 27–34.

Robertson, Fiona. *Legitimate Histories: Scott, Gothic, and the Authorities of Fiction* (Oxford: Clarendon Press, 1994).

Rogers, James Frederick. 'The Healthiest of Men'. *Scientific Monthly* 5 (July) (1917), 50–6.

The Romance of Scott: His Home, his Work, his Country (Edinburgh: Travel Press, 1932).

Rothberg, Michael. *Multidirectional Memory: Remembering the Holocaust in the Age of Decolonization* (Stanford, CA: Stanford University Press, 2009).

Roughead, William (ed.). *Trial of Captain Porteous* (Glasgow: William Hodge, 1909).

Roy, Arundhati. *The God of Small Things* (New York: Harper, 2004 (1997)).

Ruskin, John. *Praeterita: The Autobiography of John Ruskin* (Oxford: Oxford University Press, 1978 [1885–9]).

Sainte-Beuve, C. A. *Premiers lundis*, Nouvelle édition (Paris: Calmann Lévy, 1894).

Salaman, Redcliffe N. *The History and Social Influence of the Potato* (Cambridge: Cambridge University Press, 1985 [1949]).

Samuels, Maurice. *The Spectacular Past: Popular History and the Novel in Nineteenth-Century France* (Ithaca, NY: Cornell University Press, 2004).

Sanders, Julie. *Adaptation and Appropriation* (London: Routledge, 2006).

Saussure, Ferdinand de. *Cours de linguistique générale* (Paris: Payot, 1995 [1916]).

Schacter, Daniel L. *Searching for Memory: The Brain, the Mind, and the Past* (New York: Basic, 1996).

Schiller, Friedrich. 'Die Schaubühne als eine moralische Anstalt betrachtet' (1784). Available at http://gutenberg.spiegel.de/buch/3328/1.

Schivelbusch, Wolfgang. *Die Kultur der Niederlage: Der amerikanische Süden 1865, Frankreich 1871, Deutschland 1918* (Frankfurt am Main: Fischer, 2003).

Schoenbaum, S. *Shakespeare's Lives* (Oxford: Clarendon Press, 1970).

The Scott Banquet, August 9, 1871 (Glasgow: James Maclehose, publisher to the University, 1872).

The Scott Exhibition MDCCCLXXI. Catalogue of the Exhibition held at Edinburgh, in July and August 1871, On Occasion of the Commemoration of the Centenary of the Birth of Sir Walter Scott (Edinburgh: n.p., 1872).

Scott, Walter. *Chronicles of the Canongate*, ed. Claire Lamont (London: Penguin, 2003 [1827]).

—— *The Heart of Midlothian*, ed. Claire Lamont (Oxford: Oxford University Press, 1982 [1818]).

—— *The Heart of Mid-Lothian*, ed. David Hewitt and Alison Lumsden (Edinburgh: Edinburgh University Press, 2004 [1818]).

—— *Ivanhoe*, ed. Ian Duncan (Oxford: Oxford University Press, 1996 [1819]).

—— *The Journal of Sir Walter Scott*, ed. W. E. K. Anderson (Edinburgh: Canongate, 1998).

—— *The Lady of the Lake* (Milton Keynes: Dodo Press, n.d. [1810]).

—— *Old Mortality*, ed. Angus Calder (Harmondsworth: Penguin, 1975 [1816]).

—— *Reliquiae Trotcosienses, or the Gabions of the Late Jonathan Oldbuck Esq. of Monkbarns*, ed. Gerard Carruthers and Alison Lumsden (Edinburgh: Edinburgh University Press, 2004).

—— *Rob Roy*, ed. Ian Duncan (Oxford: Oxford University Press, 1998 [1817]).

—— *Rob Roy*, ed. David Hewitt (Edinburgh: Edinburgh University Press, 2008 [1817]).

—— *The Talisman* (Milton Keynes: Dodo Press, n.d. [1825]).

—— *The Tale of Old Mortality*, ed. David Hewitt and Douglas Mack, (Edinburgh: Edinburgh University Press, 1993 [1816]).

—— *Waverley; or, 'Tis Sixty Years Since*, ed. Claire Lamont (Oxford: Clarendon Press, 1981 [1814]).

[——]. *Aymé Verd: of De opstand der Hugenooten in de 16e eeuw. Onuitgegeven roman van Sir Walter Scott naar de derde Fransche uitgave*, 2 vols (Gorinchem: A. Van der Mast, 1843).

[——]. *Moredun. Een verhaal van omstreeks 1210 door Sir Walter Scott. Voorafgegaan door eene inleiding behelzende de geschiedenis van het handschrift. Uit het Engelsch vertaald door J.B. Rietstap*, 2 vols (Rotterdam: H. Nigh, 1855).

Sebald, W. G. *Vertigo*, trans. Michael Hulse (London: Harvill, 1999 [1990]).

Seccombe, Thomas, et al. *Scott Centenary Articles* (London: Oxford University Press, 1932).

Shaw, Philip. *Waterloo and the Romantic Imagination* (London: Palgrave Macmillan, 2002).

Shope, Bradley. 'Masquerading Sophistication: Fancy Dress Balls of Britain's Raj'. *Journal of Imperial and Commonwealth History* 39 (2011), 375–92.

Silber, Nina. *The Romance of Reunion: Northerners and the South, 1865–1900* (Chapel Hill: University of North Carolina Press, 1993).

Simmons, Clare A. *Reversing the Conquest: History and Myth in Nineteenth-Century British Literature* (New Brunswick, NJ: Rutgers University Press, 1990).

Sir Walter Scott Centenary 1932; Portfolio of Etchings (Edinburgh: R. S. Forrest, 1932).

Siviter, Roger. *Waverley: Portrait of a Famous Route* (Southampton: Kingfisher Railway Productions, 1988).

Skene, James. *A Series of Sketches of the Existing Localities Alluded to in the Waverley Novels, Etched from Original Drawings* (Edinburgh: Cadell, 1829).

Smiles, Samuel. *Self-Help*, ed. Peter W. Sinnema (Oxford: Oxford University Press, 2008 [1859]).

Soane, George. *The Hebrew: a Drama* (London: J. Lowndes, 1820).

—— *Rob Roy, the Gregarach; A Romantic Drama, in Three Acts; as Performed at the Theatre Royal, Drury Lane* (London: Richard White, 1818).

Society of Painters. *Landscape Illustrations of the Waverley Novels, with Descriptions of the Views* (London: Charles Tilt, 1831).

Solterer, Helen. *Medieval Roles for Modern Times: Theater and the Battle for the French Republic* (University Park: Pennsylvania State Press, 2010).

Solterer, Helen. 'The Waking of Medieval Theatricality, Paris 1935–1995'. *New Literary History* 27 (1996), 257–90.

Sorensen, Janet. '*Rob Roy*: The Other Eighteenth Century?', in Robert Mayer (ed.), *Eighteenth-Century Fiction on Screen* (Cambridge: Cambridge University Press, 2002), 192–210.

Spiegel, Gabrielle M. *The Past as Text: The Theory and Practice of Medieval Historiography* (Baltimore, MD: Johns Hopkins University Press, 1997).

SS–Sir Walter Scott on Loch Katrine (Norwich: Jarrold, *c*.1994).

St Clair, William. *The Reading Nation in the Romantic Period* (Cambridge: Cambridge University Press, 2004).

Stephen, Leslie. 'Sir Walter Scott', in *Hours in a Library* (London: Smith, Elder, 1907 [1871]), 186–229.

Stephens, John Russell. *The Censorship of English Drama 1824–1901* (Cambridge: Cambridge University Press, 1980).

—— *The Profession of the Playwright: British Theatre 1800–1900* (Cambridge: Cambridge University Press, 1992).

Stevens, H. I., and A. Stevens. *Scott and Scotland; or, Historical and Romantic Illustrations of Scottish Story* [*sic*] (London: H. I. & A. Stevens, n.d.).

Stewart, D. *The Heart of Midlothian; or, The Affecting History of Jeanie and Effie Deans; Abridged from the Original* (Newcastle upon Tyne: Mackenzie and Dent, 1833).

Stewart, George R. *Names on the Land: A Historical Account of Placenaming in the United States* (Boston: Houghton Mifflin, 1958).

Stoler, Ann. 'Colonial Aphasia: Race and Disabled Histories in France'. *Public Culture* 23 (2011), 121–56.

Stoneman, Patsy. *Brontë Transformations: The Cultural Dissemination of Jane Eyre and Wuthering Heights* (London: Prentice Hall, 1996).

Stubbs, Jonathan. 'Hollywood's Middle Ages: The Development of *Knights of the Round Table* and *Ivanhoe*, 1935–53'. *Exemplaria* 21 (2009), 398–417.

Sturgess, Kim C. *Shakespeare and the American Nation* (Cambridge: Cambridge University Press, 2004).

Sturgis, Julian. *Ivanhoe: A Romantic Opera; Adapted from Sir Walter Scott's Novel; words by Julian Sturgis; music by Arthur Sullivan* (London: Chappell, 1891).

Sundquist, Eric J. *To Wake the Nations: Race in the Making of American Literature* (Cambridge, MA: Harvard University Press, 1993).

Sussman, Charlotte. 'The Emptiness at *The Heart of Midlothian*: Nation, Narration, and Population'. *Eighteenth-Century Fiction* 15 (2002), 103–26.

Symonds, Deborah A. *Weep not for Me: Women, Ballads, and Infanticide in Early Modern Scotland* (University Park: Pennsylvania State University Press, 1997).

Tambling, Jeremy. 'Scott's "Heyday" in Opera', in Murray Pittock (ed.), *The Reception of Sir Walter Scott in Europe* (London: Continuum, 2006), 284–92.

Tate, Allen. *The Fathers* (Denver: Alan Swallow, 1960).

Taylor, Diana. *The Archive and the Repertoire: Performing Cultural Memory in the Americas* (Durham, NC: Duke University Press, 2003).

Taylor, William R. *Cavalier and Yankee: The Old South and American National Character* (Cambridge, MA: Harvard University Press, 1979).

Terdiman, Richard. *Present Past: Modernity and the Memory Crisis* (Ithaca, NY: Cornell University Press, 1993).

Terry, Daniel. *The Heart of Mid-lothian, a Musical Drama, in Three Acts; First Produced at the Theatre Royal, Covent Garden, Saturday, 17th April, 1819* (London: William Stockdale, 1819).

Thackeray, William Makepeace. 'Rebecca and Rowena: A Romance upon Romance by Mr. Michael Angelo Titmarsh' (1850), in *A Shabby Genteel Story; Novels by Eminent Hands; Rebecca and Rowena; The Rose and the Ring* (Moscow: Raduga, 1985).

Thierry, Augustin. *Dix ans d'études historiques* (Brussels: J. P. Meline, 1835).

Todd, Emily B. 'Establishing Routes for Fiction in the United States'. *Book History* 12 (2009), 100–28.

——'Walter Scott and the Nineteenth-Century American Literary Marketplace: Antebellum Richmond Readers and the Collected Editions of the Waverley Novels'. *Papers of the Bibliographical Society of America* 93 (1999), 495–517.

Tournament at Ashby-de-la-Zouche; As described by Sir Walter Scott, in the popular novel of "Ivanhoe," containing the best account of the Ancient and Chivalrous feat of Arms in our Language, and admirably Illustrative of the approaching Tournament at Eglington [*sic*] *Castle* (n.p.: n.p., [1839]).

Trevor-Roper, Hugh. 'The Invention of Tradition: The Highland Tradition of Scotland', in Eric Hobsbawm and Terence Ranger (eds), *The Invention of Tradition* (Cambridge: Cambridge University Press, 1983), 15–41.

Tribute to Walter Scott on the One Hundredth Anniversary of his Birthday by the Massachusetts Historical Society; August 15, 1871 (Boston: Privately Printed from the Proceedings of the Society, 1872).

Trumpener, Katie. *Bardic Nationalism: The Romantic Novel and the British Empire* (Princeton, NJ: Princeton University Press, 1997).

Tuite, Clara. 'Tainted Love and Romantic Literary Celebrity'. *English Literary History* 74 (2007), 59–88.

Twain, Mark. *The Unabridged Mark Twain*, vol. 2, ed. Lawrence Teacher (Philadelphia: Running Press, 1979).

Tynjanov, Juri. 'On Literary Evolution', in Ladislaw Matejka and Krystyna Pomorska (eds), *Readings in Russian Poetics: Formalist and Structuralist Views* (Cambridge, MA: MIT Press, 1978 [1927]), 66–77.

Tyrell, Alex. 'Paternalism, Public Memory and National Identity in Early Victorian Scotland: The Robert Burns Festival at Ayr in 1844'. *History: A Quarterly Magazine and Review for the Teacher, the Student and the Expert* 90 (2005), 42–61.

——'The Queen's "Little Trip": The Royal Visit to Scotland in 1842'. *Scottish Historical Review* 82 (2003), 47–73.

Uricchio, William, 'Television's First Seventy-Five Years: The Interpretive Flexibility of a Medium in Transition', in Robert Kolker (ed.), *The Oxford*

Handbook of Film and Media Studies (Oxford: Oxford University Press, 2008), 286–305.

Uricchio, William and Roberta E. Pearson. *Reframing Culture: The Case of the Vitagraph Quality Films* (Princeton, NJ: Princeton University Press, 1993).

Urry, John. *The Tourist Gaze*, 2nd edn (London: Sage, 2002).

Valman, Nadia. *The Jewess in Nineteenth-Century British Literary Culture* (Cambridge: Cambridge University Press, 2007).

Viswanathan, Gauri. *Masks of Conquest: Literary Study and British Rule in India* (New York: Columbia University Press, 1989).

Vonnegut, Kurt, Jr. *Slaughterhouse-Five: or The Children's Crusade, A Duty-Dance with Death* (St. Albans, Herts: Panther, 1972 [1969]).

Voskuil, Lynn M. 'Feeling Public: Sensation Theater, Commodity Culture, and the Victorian Public Sphere'. *Victorian Studies* 44 (2002), 245–74.

Wade, Wyn Craig. *The Fiery Cross: The Ku Klux Klan in America* (New York: Oxford University Press, 1998 [1987]).

Wainright, Clive. *The Romantic Interior: The British Collector at Home, 1750–1850* (New Haven, CT: Yale University Press, 1989).

Walpole, Hugh. 'Sir Walter Scott: A Centenary Estimate'. *English Review* 55 (1932), 350–9.

Warburg, Aby. *Der Bilderatlas Mnemosyne*, ed. Martin Warnke (Berlin: Akademie Verlag, 2000 [1924–9]).

Ward, Wilfrid. 'The Centenary of Waverley'. *Dublin Review* 155 (1914), 281–305.

Waswo, Richard. 'Scott and the Really Great Tradition', in Harry E. Shaw (ed.), *Critical Essays on Sir Walter Scott: The Waverley Novels* (New York: G. K. Hall, 1996), 70–80.

Watson, Nicola J. *The Literary Tourist* (London: Palgrave Macmillan, 2006).

—— 'Scott's Afterlives', in Fiona Robertson (ed.), *The Edinburgh Companion to Sir Walter Scott* (Edinburgh: Edinburgh University Press, 2012).

—— (ed.). *Literary Tourism and Nineteenth-Century Culture* (London: Palgrave Macmillan, 2009).

Watson, Ritchie Devon. ' "The Difference of Race": Antebellum Race Mythology and the Development of Southern Nationalism'. *Southern Literary Journal* 35, Fall (2002), 1–13.

—— *Normans and Saxons: Southern Race Mythology and the Intellectual History of the American Civil War* (Baton Rouge: Louisiana State University, 2008).

The Waverley Gallery of the Principal Female Characters in Sir Walter Scott's Romances. From original paintings by eminent artists. Engraved under the superintendence of C. Heath (London: Tilt and Bogue, 1841).

Wedgwood, Julia. 'Sir Walter Scott and the Romantic Reaction'. *Contemporary Review* 33, August/November (1878), 514–39.

Weigel, Sigrid. 'Generation, Genealogie, Geschlecht: Zur Geschichte des Generationenkonzepts und seiner wissenschaftlichen Konzeptualisierung seit dem Ende des 18. Jahrhunderts', in Lutz Musner and Gotthard Wunberg (eds), *Kulturwissenschaften: Forschung-Praxis-Positionen* (Wien: WUV, 2002), 161–90.

—— 'Zum "topographical turn": Kartographie, Topographie und Raumkonzepte in den Kulturwissenschaften'. *Kulturpoetik* 2 (2002), 151–65.

Weinrich, Harald. *Lethe: Kunst und Kritik des Vergessens* (München: C. H. Beck, 1997).

Weinstein, Mark. 'The Millennial Scott Popularity Poll'. *Scott Newsletter* 35 (1999), 24.

Weiss, Jane. 'Sir Walter Scott and Company: New York's Literary Culture in 1830' (2002). http://triton.oldwestbury.edu/weissj/domestic/sirwalter.html.

West, Rebecca. 'The Dualism of Scott'. *Modern Scot*, Summer (1932), 121–3.

White, Hayden. 'The Value of Narrativity in the Representation of Reality' (1981), in *The Content of the Form: Narrative Discourse and Historical Representation* (Baltimore, MD: Johns Hopkins University Press, 1987), 1–25.

White, Henry Adelbert. *Sir Walter Scott's Novels on the Stage* (New Haven, CT: Yale University Press, 1927).

[White, Ida L.]. *Lady Blanche and Other Poems* (London: Hamilton, Adams, 1875).

Wieber, Sabine. 'Staging the Past: Allotria's "Festzug Karl V" and German National Identity'. *Rethinking History* 10 (2006), 523–51.

Wilde, Oscar. *Oscar Wilde: Plays, Prose and Poems* (London: Macdonald, 1982).

Wilmot, Martha. *More Letters from Martha Wilmot: Impressions of Vienna, 1819–1829*, ed. the Marchioness of Londonderry and H. M. Hyde (London: Macmillan, 1935).

Wilson, D. 'Address Delivered at the Toronto Celebration of the Scott Centenary, 1871'. *Canadian Journal of Science, Literature, and History: Conducted by the Editing Committee of the Canadian Institute* 13 (1872), 341–51.

Wilson, George Washington. *Sir Walter Scott and his Country: A Reading, Descriptive of a Series of Lantern Slides* (Aberdeen: G. W. W. Registered; printed by John Avery, 1889).

Wilson-Costa, Karyn. 'The Land of Burns: Between Myth and Heritage', in Nicola J. Watson (ed.), *Literary Tourism and Nineteenth-Century Culture* (London: Palgrave Macmillan, 2009), 37–48.

Wilt, Judith. *Secret Leaves: The Novels of Walter Scott* (Chicago: University of Chicago Press, 1985).

Wimmer, Andreas, and Nina Glick Schiller. 'Methodological Nationalism and Beyond: Nation-State Building, Migration and the Social Sciences'. *Global Networks* 2 (2002), 301–34.

Winter, Jay M. *Sites of Memory, Sites of Mourning: The Great War in European Cultural History* (Cambridge: Cambridge University Press, 1995).

Womack, Peter. *Improvement and Romance: Constructing the Myth of the Highlands* (Houndmills: Macmillan, 1989).

Woodward, C. Vann. *Mary Chesnut's Civil War* (New Haven, CT: Yale University Press, 1981).

Woolf, Virginia. *Collected Essays*, 4 vols (London: Hogarth Press, 1966).

Woolf, Virginia. *To the Lighthouse* (London: Penguin, 1989 [1927]).

Worrall, David. *The Politics of Romantic Theatricality, 1787–1832* (London: Palgrave, 2007).

——*Theatric Revolution: Drama, Censorship and Romantic Period Subcultures 1773–1832* (Oxford: Oxford University Press, 2006).

Wright, Beth. 'Walter Scott et la gravure française: A propos de la collection des estampes 'scottesques' conservée au Département des estampes, Paris'. *Nouvelles de l'estampe* 93 (1987), 6–18.

——*Painting and History during the French Restoration: Abandoned by the Past* (Cambridge: Cambridge University Press, 1997).

——'"Seeing with the Painter's Eye": Sir Walter Scott's Challenge to Nineteenth-Century Art', in Murray Pittock (ed.), *The Reception of Sir Walter Scott in Europe* (London: Continuum, 2006), 293–312.

——and Paul Joannides. 'Les romans historiques de Sir Walter Scott et la peinture française, 1822–63'. *Bulletin de la société de l'histoire de l'art français* (1983), 95–115.

Wright, George Newenham, et al. *Landscape–Historical Illustrations of Scotland and the Waverley Novels; from Drawings by J.M.W. Turner, Professor R.A. etc.*, 2 vols (London: Fisher, Sons, 1836–8).

Yates, Frances A. *The Art of Memory* (Chicago: University of Chicago Press, 1966).

Yonge, Charlotte. *A Book of Golden Deeds of All Times and All Lands, Gathered and Narrated by the Author of the "Heir of Radcliffe"* (London: Macmillan, 1864).

Young, Robert J. C. *The Idea of English Ethnicity* (Oxford: Blackwell, 2008).

Zboray, Ronald J. *A Fictive People: Antebellum Economic Development and the American Reading Public* (Oxford: Oxford University Press, 1993).

Zekulin, Nicholas G. 'Turgenev in Scotland, 1871'. *Slavonic and East European Review* 54 (1975), 355–70.

Zerubavel, Eviatar. 'Calendars and History: A Comparative Study of the Social Organization of National Memory', in Jeffrey K. Olick (ed.), *States of Memory: Continuities, Conflicts, and Transformations in National Retrospection* (Durham, NC: Duke University Press, 2003), 315–37.

——*Hidden Rhythms: Schedules and Calendars in Social Life* (Berkeley: California University Press, 1985 [1981]).

——*Time Maps: Collective Memory and the Social Shape of the Past* (Chicago: University of Chicago Press, 2003).

Index